INTRODUCTION TO PROGRAMMING AND COMPUTER SCIENCE

The main concern of this book is with using procedure-oriented languages on digital computers. In addition, it introduces the student to a wide range of ideas and concepts in computer science. The approach is one of emphasizing the process between human and computer. To this end, four languages—Fortran, Algol, PL/I, and Cobol —are discussed with the structure and corresponding features of each compared. The book is, however, not a manual for any of these languages and should be used with one of the many available books in a specific computer language, such as the same author's FORTRAN IV PROGRAMMING—A CONCISE EXPOSITION published together with this book. Although there are numerous examples in all the languages, there are more in Fortran and fewer in Cobol than in the others.

There are discussions of a variety of topics in computer science other than the strictly language topics, including numbers and number systems; Polish notation and the compilation of arithmetic expressions; recursion; Boolean algebra and logical design; hardware characteristics of input, output, and auxiliary memory devices; and, briefly, operating systems and time-sharing.

A section at the end presents a number of problems at elementary, intermediate, and advanced levels suitable for computer projects that enable students to develop an intuitive understanding of algorithms. Problems are presented after each chapter, and hints and answers at the end to almost all problems.

INTRODUCTION
TO PROGRAMMING
AND COMPUTER SCIENCE

McGRAW-HILL COMPUTER SCIENCE SERIES

RICHARD W. HAMMING
Bell Telephone Laboratories

EDWARD A. FEIGENBAUM
Stanford University

INTRODUCTION TO PROGRAMMING AND COMPUTER SCIENCE

Anthony Ralston

Chairman, Department of Computer Science
State University of New York at Buffalo

McGraw-Hill Book Company

New York, St. Louis, San Francisco, Düsseldorf, Johannesburg,
Kuala Lumpur, London, Mexico, Montreal, New Delhi,
Panama, Rio de Janeiro, Singapore, Sydney, Toronto

**INTRODUCTION TO PROGRAMMING
AND COMPUTER SCIENCE**

Library of Congress Catalog Card Number 78-136182

07-051161-6

1 2 3 4 5 6 7 8 9 0 M A M M 7 9 8 7 6 5 4 3 2 1

This book was set in Journal Roman by Creative Book Services, division of McGregor & Werner, Incorporated, and printed on permanent paper and bound by The Maple Press Company. The designer was Creative Book Services. The editor was Richard F. Dojny. Loretta Palma supervised production.

To ELIZABETH

*May she grow up to
read this with some
of the pleasure with
which I dedicate it*

contents

* May be omitted without a loss of continuity.
† May be omitted if required by a lack of time.

preface

You must talk to the media, not to the programmer. To talk to the programmer is like complaining to a hot dog vendor at a ballpark about how badly your favorite team is playing.

Marshall McLuhan

This book is concerned with talking to computers. It has been used by me and some of my colleagues at other universities in recent years as a text for a one-semester first course in computing. One of my basic premises in teaching such a course, which I hope is reflected in this book, is that it is time—past time, really—for the first course in computer science to be taught at an intellectual level similar to that of first university courses in other disciplines. This creates some special problems in computer science. Not only will a first course be taken by undergraduates majoring in an increasingly wide spectrum of disciplines, but, for the foreseeable future, also by undergraduates at all levels from, say, freshmen in the sciences to seniors in the arts and humanities. This book is not aimed specifically at any segment or level of the undergraduate population: it is my position that much the same first course in computing should be given to all undergraduate students, except, perhaps, for an honors-type course for concentrators in computer science. This is not to say that precisely the same subject matter is best for both the mathematics major and the English major, but that the differences are not so great that they cannot be accommodated by one book or in a single class. It is also not to say that courses in the social implications of computers are not good ones for many liberal arts majors, at least. They can be. But such courses are perhaps made better if the students have previously learned enough about computers qua computers to grasp fully these implications.

Almost all colleges and universities now offer an introductory course in computing or computer science. This course is taught from many points of view and with varying aims, which is as it should be at this stage of computer science education. Among these aims the following are easily distinguishable:

1. To teach only a particular computer language.
2. To teach the student what a computer algorithm is, while teaching some computer language to be used as the tool by which to convey the algorithm to the computer.
3. To introduce the student to the concept of communication with a computer by emphasizing the comparison between structures designed to do similar tasks in various languages, while again emphasizing the teaching of one language in depth and getting the idea of an algorithm across intuitively as a by-product of using the computer language or languages.

The first approach is only too reminiscent of the courses in the use of the slide rule which were formerly given to engineers. Although a student in a first course in computing should *at least* learn to use a computer via some language, a course which teaches no more than this is almost devoid of intellectual value and it is doubtful if it is worthy of college credit.

The latter two approaches both have their proponents and certainly both are defensible. Courses embodying either approach typically include an introduction to a variety of other topics in computer science. My own feeling is that, except perhaps for those who will become professional computer scientists, an ability to communicate and an understanding of the mechanism of communication should be the aim of this first course. Most students in the course will never be more than users, however sophisticated, for whom formal notions of an algorithm are mostly irrelevant since constant use will give them a sound intuitive notion of an algorithm.

This book, therefore, concentrates on computer languages, their major components, and how these components are implemented in some languages. No attempt is made to teach any specific language. I assume that any course using this book as a text will, in addition, use my *Fortran IV Programming—A Concise Exposition,* if Fortran is the language the students will actually use, or one of the many good books on the other three languages discussed here (Algol, PL/I, and Cobol). I should note my belief that whatever supplementary book is used, it should be used much more as a reference than directly as a text to lecture from. I firmly believe that the purpose of the lectures for this course (or, indeed, for any course) should not be to dot all the *i*'s or cross all the *t*'s, but rather to explain subleties and interrelations. One result of any college education should be an ability to study and learn the prosaic details of a subject on one's own; much of the study of any computer language falls in this domain.

In one sense this book is a text in comparative linguistics. Of the four languages considered, one, Cobol, is treated quite cursorily because my orientation is certainly more toward scientific data processing than business data processing. In addition, despite the very large current investment in Cobol programs in the United States, it seems likely that the basic cumbersomeness and limitations of this language will gradually cause it to be replaced by another language, perhaps PL/I. Aspects of Algol and PL/I are treated in substantially more detail than for Cobol but in illustrations and examples Fortran is used somewhat more than Algol or PL/I. This reflects not only the fact that it is the language I know best but also the fact that Fortran is now and, for the near future at least, will continue to be the most widely used language at American universities.

The four languages discussed in this book are all examples of higher level languages and, more specifically, of procedure-oriented languages. Because there are still proponents of the point of view that lower level languages, that is, machine and assembly languages, should be taught before higher level languages, it is appropriate to say a few words on this matter here. Indeed, in the early days of digital computers, it made a lot of sense to teach machine language to all users of computers just as it behooved all drivers of the first automobiles to know something about internal combustion engines. But, just as most of us now learn to drive without knowing very much about automobile engines, neither is there any reason to learn machine or assembly language—which implies learning some specifics about the computer—before learning a higher level language. In fact, in order to "drive" (i.e., to use effectively) a computer, the vast majority of all users will never need to know more than a higher level language. Of course, as it is useful to a driver to know how to check the water level in the radiator, so is it useful to the higher level language computer user to know certain basic facts about the structure and organization of computers; these are discussed in this book. Machine and assembly language is best left to a second or later course in computer science.

Given that a student should begin with higher level languages, why not be content with considering only one language? After all, most of us learn to talk only a single natural language initially. The most obvious answer to this is, since we learn our natural language intuitively as regards speaking, reading, and grammar, and then use these intuitive (and partly taught) concepts when we study a foreign language, there is just no valid analogy between learning natural and computer languages. From my point of view a better answer is obtained by analogy with children who grow up bilingually. Such children seem to go through a stage of confusion during which they cannot distinguish in their own speech between the two languages but, at a fairly early age, this confusion disappears and their language skills are usually markedly superior to monolingual children. I have no doubts, both from intuition and experience, that teaching students about more than one language simultaneously introduces an element of confusion and makes the course more difficult. But I do believe the result is a better, deeper understanding of computer languages and their structure, the most important by-product of which is an increased ability to learn other computer languages.

In addition to the computer-language aspects of this book, there is a liberal sprinkling of other topics which I believe will give students a broader view of what computer science is really about. Among these are discussions of computer arithmetic, compiling of arithmetic expressions, and logic, which I would expect the individual instructor to take or leave depending upon his own predilections. I do feel strongly that discussion of these or related topics in a first course on computers adds substantially to the intellectual value of the course and gives the beginning student a better basis on which to accept or reject computer science as a possible career.

One of the most difficult problems I had in writing this book was to try and produce something which could reasonably be followed in a linear fashion in a course. The conflict is a familiar one to all instructors of beginning computer courses. On the one hand, for motivational reasons, there is much to be said for getting the student on the computer (i.e., giving him some kind of problem to solve using the computer) as early as possible and to have him continue to use the computer throughout the course. This usually involves introducing certain concepts early in the course in a cursory or oversimplified fashion and then only really explaining them later on. On the other hand, writing a book does not lend itself to Ping-Ponging back and forth between topics. Some order in a written presentation is, I believe, necessary and desirable, and this involves a fair amount of introductory material before getting to those topics directly involved with using the computer. This can—and has, in some recent books—lead to devoting the first half of the book to nonlanguage topics.

I have partly solved this problem by restricting the introductory material considerably, omitting, in particular, almost all discussion of computer applications on the assumption that students are more and more aware of these and that, anyhow, individual instructors can handle this better than it can be done in print. But there is still enough introductory material so that it takes two or three weeks to get into the computer-language aspects themselves. In order not to have to wait a few weeks to get the students on a computer, at the first meeting of the course I give each student a deck of cards consisting of a source program and necessary data for a simple calculation (e.g., solution of quadratic equations, a compound interest calculation). The source program is written to be as nearly self-explanatory as possible to someone with no computer background whatsoever. Each source deck contains some syntactic or logical error such that the error message or incorrect output should enable the complete novice to correct the program. In the first lecture the students are taught which control cards are necessary to complete the deck; later they keypunch these cards, run the program, and rerun it until the error is corrected.

But it is still not possible to give the students their first *real* computer project as early as I would like (no later than the beginning of the third week) and still follow the text as written. My solution to this problem is embodied in the aforementioned *Fortran IV Programming—A Concise Exposition,* which begins with a section covering enough basic aspects of the Fortran language to enable students to be given meaningful computer projects early in the semester. I use this section for a few lectures in the second and third week of the semester and then return to this book. When the appropriate part of this text is reached in normal progression, I then fill in the interestices left by the earlier brief exposure. By no later than the middle of the semester—say at about Chapter 6—I am able to integrate directly with the text the introduction of language structures necessary for problems.

One of the acknowledged difficulties of teaching the first course in computer science is the problem of how to handle input and output. Not only are the language structures for input and output the most difficult parts of most languages, but they are surely the most tedious. I am thoroughly convinced that the beginning student should use one of the "free-format" or related types of input-output facilities which, while not officially part of all procedure-oriented languages, are available at almost all installations. Formatted output should not be introduced until nearly the end of the course. Moreover, when it is introduced, it should not be with stultifying detail. This is the prime reason why the discussion of formatted input and output in Chapter 10 is quite brief.

One alternative to free-format input and output is an automatic grading system, types of which are in use at a number of universities, in which all input and output is done by the system for the student. Such systems have various merits but they do tend to give students an unrealistic impression of how computing really gets done and, in particular, the student using such a system often gets no experience in developing the very important skill of generating good test data.

NOTES FOR INSTRUCTORS

Starred sections (*) in the Contents can be omitted without loss of continuity. Most of these contain topics outside the main theme of computer language, but it would seem to me to be unwise to omit all such sections. Daggered sections (†) contain material I consider of direct importance to users of procedure-oriented languages but, nevertheless, these can be omitted if lack of time necessitates some compromises. The following comments may also be useful in planning a course.

Chapter 1 contains introductory material meant to be read rather than lectured from; most instructors will probably wish to give their own introductory lecture or two. Chapter 6 is another likely candidate for reading without lecturing since most of it should be partially familiar to students by the time it is reached in normal sequence through the book. Finally, Chapter 11, intended mainly as a bridge to later courses, can be assigned for reading if insufficient time remains to discuss it in lectures. This chapter is a purposely sketchy introduction to operating systems and time sharing. One reason for this sketchiness is the diversity of computing milieus which exist for students taking a first course in computers. Another is that, by the time the end of the course is reached, many students will have developed a feeling for the topics in this chapter from their experience in the course and because many instructors will slip information on the topics discussed in Chapter 11 into their lectures as the course progresses.

Although little or no mathematical background is required for a course from this book, some instructors will wish to omit those sections which emphasize mathematics. These include Sections 3.1.1 through 3.1.5 and Section 5.1 which emphasize arithmetic concepts, Section 5.3 on compilation of arithmetic expressions, which emphasizes Polish notation, and Sections 9.1 and 9.2 on Boolean algebra and logical design.

One departure from the more usual order of introduction of topics is the relatively late (Chapter 8) discussion of language structures for iteration. There is no intention in this to downgrade the importance of repetitive calculation using different sets of data. No idea is more important for the beginning student and, indeed, this idea is introduced much earlier than Chapter 8. Rather, my attitude concerns the importance of distinguishing between language structures which really extend the capabilities of the language and those which merely provide added convenience to the users. Usually, there is too little stress placed on this point. Language structures for iteration are a particularly obvious case of an addition of convenience (an important convenience, of course), but not of capability. If one takes the point of view that the order of introduction of topics should facilitate the assignment of computer projects involving algorithms of increasing complexity, then postponing the introduction of iteration structures until relatively late is easily defensible.

To conclude these notes, I offer two outlines of courses including topics and a suggested number of lectures, one for a basic course emphasizing only language and another for a more sophisticated course. As an alternative to the latter, a full year, in-depth course could be taught from this book.

Basic Course		**More Advanced Course**	
Chapter or Section	*Number of Lectures*	*Chapter or Section*	*Number of Lectures*
1	3	1	2
2	4	2	3
3.2, 3.2.1	1	3.1	3
4.1	3	3.2	2
4.3	2	4.1, 4.2, 4.3	3
4.4, 4.4.1, 4.4.2	2	4.4	2
5.2	3	5.1	1
5.4, 5.5	4	5.2	2
6	3	5.3	2
7.1, 7.2	2	5.4, 5.5	3
7.3	4	6	2
7.4.1, 7.5	1	7.1, 7.2	1
8.1, 8.2	4	7.3	2
9.3	2	7.4, 7.5	1
10.2, 10.3	2	8.1, 8.2	3
	40	8.3	1
		9.1, 9.2	3
		9.3	1
		10.1	2
		10.2, 10.3	2
		11	2
			43

The remaining periods might be used for examinations and topics of the instructor's choice.

ACKNOWLEDGMENTS

The variety of topics and number of computer languages discussed in this book mean that I am more than usually indebted to those of my colleagues who have read all or part of the manuscript of this book and have helped me avoid numerous errors. (Those that remain are, of course, all my own responsibility.)

In particular I must thank Alan Perlis, Robert Rosin, Phyllis Fox, Erich Schmitt, Gilbert Berglass, Albert Allan, Joel Herbsman, Richard Eckhouse, and William Fredson-Cole. In addition, I must thank two years of students at the State University of New York at Buffalo who suffered through various versions of the manuscript of this book and found errors in it and made comments on it. Finally, I must thank—although mere thanks are not really enough—the legion involved in typing the manuscript, particularly, Rita Keller, Deborah Finn, Joyce Staskiewicz, Lynn Fagyas, Linda Janos, and my wife.

Anthony Ralston

conventions, notation, and abbreviations

CONVENTIONS

One of the problems in a book largely concerned with computer programming is the conventions to be used in printing programs and, particularly, program fragments in the text itself. This is especially true when, as here, more than one programming language is being discussed. The conventions we have used, hopefully consistently applied, are as follows:

> *Fortran and Cobol*—Upper case used throughout, not only in programs, but also when naming statements in text (e.g., "An EQUIVALENCE statement is . . . .").

> *Algol*—The publication language using boldface keywords is used throughout in programs and text, except that semicolons after statements are omitted in the text (e.g., "The Algol statement A := B[6] := C[I,J] is an example of . . . .").

> *PL/I*—The 60-character set is used in all programs and text; as with Algol, semicolons are omitted after statements in text.

NOTATION

Syntactical Notation

This notation, which is introduced on page 34, is as follows:

$<--->$ to be read as "The structure (whatever is contained in the brackets) of the language"

::=	to be read as "is defined to be"
		to be read as "or"
[n]	these brackets placed over the symbol ::= with an integer n inside them indicate that n is the maximum number of symbols allowed in the definition which follows ::=

The quantity in $<--->$ will always be upper case letters. For the sake of informality we shall sometimes replace the $<--->$ with lower case italics (e.g., $<$LETTER$> \rightarrow letter$).

General Notation

Symbol or Example	*Meaning*	*First used on page*
(Problem 14)	References to problems at the end of each chapter	40
$\begin{Bmatrix} vn \\ (<\text{LIST}>) \end{Bmatrix}$	Choice in syntax—quantities in braces, one of which must be chosen	199
[*label*]	Optionality in syntax—quantity in brackets which may be omitted	319
L(A)	Location of quantity in computer memory—L followed by name of quantity in parentheses	169
$(101.100)_2$	Base of number system—subscript following parenthesized number	68
$\sum_{i=1}^{n}$	Summation—Greek sigma with limits of summation above and below	70
	Logical symbols:	
$\wedge$ or $\cdot$	And	357
$\vee$ or $+$	Or	357
$\neg$ or $-$ (overbar)	Not	357
$\equiv$	Equivalence	375
$\supset$	Implication	375
	Flow chart symbols:	
$\boxed{A \rightarrow B}$	Function box	36
$\overset{\frown}{\underset{\smile}{\text{Is I = 10?}}}$	Decision box	37
④	Remote connector	37

ABBREVIATIONS

In the panels which consider language structures in various computer languages, a number of abbreviations are used for conciseness. These are always explained on the panel itself but, since abbreviations are also used occasionally in the text, we give a complete list here:

ae—arithmetic expression

ar—argument

de—designational expression

exp—expression

fn—format number

id—identifier

int—integer

ip—increment part

iv—integer variable

le—logical expression

lv—logical variable

pint—positive integer

pn—procedure name

re—relational expression

ro—relational operator

sl—statement label

slv—statement label variable

st—statement (executable)

sv—scalar variable

td—type declaration

un—unit number

var—variable

1

introduction

Computer science is concerned with information *in much the same sense that physics is concerned with energy; it is devoted to the* representation, storage, manipulation *and* presentation *of information. . . . As physics uses energy transforming devices, computer science uses information transforming devices.*

An Undergraduate Program in Computer Science—Preliminary Recommendations, *Communications of the Association for Computing Machinery,* vol. 8, pp. 543-552 (1965).

1.1   WHAT IS COMPUTER SCIENCE?

To *define* any scholarly discipline is a formidable task. Consider, for example, trying to define "mathematics" in such a way as to be understandable to the novice. The quotation above, however, provides a good starting point for a definition of computer science; indeed, many prefer the name *information science.* Still, information is no more uniquely the province of computer science than energy is of physics. The unique aspect of computer science is the computer, "computer" being a convenient shorthand (which, as we shall indicate later in this section, is somewhat misleading) for "general-purpose automatic electronic digital computer." Each of these modifying words needs some explanation:

> general-purpose—in the sense that the computers of interest to us are capable of a wide variety of calculations, as opposed to *special-purpose* computers such as a telephone switching system, a missile guidance computer, or a cash register.
>
> automatic—once started, the computer can continue in operation with no outside intervention.

electronic—all modern computers are composed of electronic circuitry, but this is not basic in principle; early computers were largely electromechanical; the material in this book depends not one whit upon the physical components of the computer.

digital—because the computers with which we shall be concerned *count*, or more importantly, deal with *discrete* quantities as opposed to analog computers which compute by measuring; common examples of the latter are the slide rule and the thermostat.

Computer science is not alone among the sciences in its dependence upon a particular machine or device; astronomy comes immediately to mind. But just as astronomers often engage in theoretical studies which do not require a telescope, research in computer science does not necessarily involve computers directly. One such area of computer science is *automata theory* (see below). Another is the study of the *structure and properties of programming languages*, an area very close to the major concern of this book.

Many students will come to a first course in computer science already familiar with desk calculators. Let us emphasize that while the desk calculator is a direct ancestor of the computer, it is a mistake to consider a digital computer to be nothing more than a "fast desk calculator." The evolution from the desk calculator to the digital computer has produced not just quantitative differences but a new species. A digital computer is a fast desk calculator in the same sense that a man is a monkey; he may be, but he is a lot more too.

One reason for the misconceptions with which students often come to computer science is the name "digital computer" itself. This name arose naturally enough. Early applications of computers were focused on their computational capabilities, that is, on their ability to manipulate digits. For example, one of the great spurs to the development of computers at the end of the Second World War was their use in calculating ballistic tables for various types of guns. Even today a great deal of the use of computers is concerned with their ability to perform numerical calculations very rapidly. But computers are much more than digit or number manipulators. A more appropriate name than digital computer for the machine we are concerned with would be *symbol manipulator*; that is, a digital computer manipulates, in a variety of ways, entities which are *symbolic representations of something else*. Using the terminology which begins this chapter, these symbols contain *information* about the entities they represent.

The idea of symbol manipulation is basic to an understanding of computer science. But what does it really mean? Let us begin by pointing out that, in both desk calculators and computers, electromechanical devices (in some desk calculators) or electronic or magnetic devices (in other desk calculators and virtually all computers) are used to represent the "symbols" upon which the device operates.

In desk calculators, these symbols represent numbers and only numbers; it is pointless to think of these symbols as representing chess pieces or mathematical symbols or letters in the Russian alphabet because they cannot be manipulated (i.e., "used") as such. Desk calculators essentially perform only the operations of arithmetic. But with digital computers (we shall continue to use the term "digital computer" to conform to normal usage despite the greater aptness of "symbol manipulator") it is meaningful to consider these internal symbols as representing chess pieces or mathematical symbols or letters in the Russian alphabet or indeed any *other entity* (even a conceptual or abstract one) that you please. This is because a digital computer can manipulate these symbols with great enough generality so that it is possible to program a digital computer to play chess (although not very well as yet), to prove mathematical theorems (but not very sophisticated ones as yet), to translate Russian to English (quite poorly, however), to compose music (not quite like Mozart!), and to do a great variety of other *nonnumerical* tasks.

The rather negative tone of the parenthetical remarks above should not be interpreted to imply that computers are actually poor at nonnumerical symbol manipulation and therefore this aspect of computers is not so important as suggested previously. In the two decades since the start of the so-called computer revolution, great strides have been made in this area. In fact, it may not be too long before nonnumeric applications of computers are more important than numeric applications. Some nonnumeric areas among the many where computers are now very successful are:

> simulation—in which the operation of a system (e.g., a telephone switching system, a manned space capsule, the manufacturing-inventory-distribution structure of a corporation) is *simulated* on a computer in order to determine how it will operate in practice under varying conditions.
>
> algebraic manipulation—in which very complex algebraic expressions are manipulated and simplified *as* algebraic expressions (rather than evaluating them for various values of the variables); such techniques can also be applied to expressions in the calculus.
>
> language translation—although not very successful in the translation of one natural language into another (e.g., Russian to English), computers have been extremely successful in translating one *computer* language into another; indeed, much of the material in this book depends upon this ability.
>
> business data processing—really a mixture of numerical and nonnumerical processing; this involves payroll, accounting, and related applications in which manipulation of alphabetic as well as numerical data is very important. This area by itself accounts for a substantial portion of all computer usage.

The applications, both present and potential, of computers as nonnumeric symbol manipulators are reason enough in themselves to emphasize the symbol-manipulation point of view. Another reason, however, is that this point of view suggests an analogy with human thought processes. The human brain may also be accurately considered to be a symbol manipulator. That the physical mechanism for the representation of symbols are the electrochemical impulses associated with neural activity is irrelevant in this context. The important fact is that these impulses are representations of external symbols analogous to the representation of external symbols by the electronic or magnetic devices inside a digital computer. One difference between computers and brains is that the representation inside computers is organized so that the symbols can be easily interpreted as numbers, which particularly facilitates numerical computation. There is no reason to believe that the organization inside our brain is specifically biased toward the performance of a specific type of symbol manipulation.

It must be emphasized that the previous paragraph is not meant to be an argument that computers are in fact "electronic brains." The differences between computers and brains are much more profound than their similarities. We shall return to this in the next section. Our purpose in indicating that both computers and brains are symbol manipulators is to impress upon the reader the versatility and power of the digital computer in relation to any of its ancestors.

Just as the general symbol-manipulating capabilities of the human brain distinguish it both quantitatively and qualitatively from the brains of lower organisms, so are digital computers different from desk calculators and all other calculating devices. For the reader to have an intuitive grasp of the profundity of the difference between computers and desk calculators on the one hand, and between computers and brains on the other, is to place him in the proper setting for a study of computer science.

Viewed in the above light, we arrive then at a description of computer science as being concerned with the study of general symbol-manipulating machines, with communication between man and machine, which is largely the subject of this book, and with the application of these machines. Like any other *science*, computer science is chiefly concerned with underlying principles and basic knowledge. A list of the major subdisciplines of computer science includes:

artificial intelligence—which is concerned with means by which computers may perform tasks (e.g., theorem proving, game playing, recognition of visual and other patterns) which would be characterized as "intelligent" if performed by human beings.

automata theory—the study of machines or devices which accept a certain set of *inputs* such that the *outputs* or, at least, the probabilities of the outputs are determined by the inputs; thus automata theory embraces the abstract study of computers and their capabilities.

logical design—which treats that stage in the design of computers between the original conception and the actual design of the electronic circuits themselves; it derives its name from its intensive use of the techniques of mathematical logic (see Chapter 9).

information storage and retrieval—involves the study of efficient methods for storing large quantities of data in a computer and methods of searching for and retrieving this data.

numerical mathematics—is concerned with techniques for solving mathematical problems on digital computers.

programming languages—the study of the design and properties of languages by which humans communicate with computers.

programming systems—closely related to programming languages; this area is concerned with the development and structure of complex programs which facilitate man-machine communication.

We shall be concerned here mainly with introducing the reader to the area of programming languages but in so doing we shall touch on various of the other disciplines listed above.

1.2   WHY STUDY COMPUTER SCIENCE?

Many students embark upon their study of computer science because of the glamor—almost the mystique—which surrounds it. If one purpose of a first course in computer science is to dispel the mystery, an equally important purpose is to replace it with a solid basis of interest in the study of computer science. Here we shall consider briefly the reasons which should serve as motivation for both the scientist and humanist to study computer science.

A. Computer science as a science.   Most people would agree that some knowledge of the basic sciences—mathematics, physics, chemistry, biology—is necessary for any educated man. To this list of sciences about which no educated person should be totally ignorant, computer science must now be added. In this sense, the study of computer science is in the best traditions of liberal education.

B. Vocational aspects of computer science.   With the possible exception of mathematics, no other science is as likely to be so practically useful to the student as computer science. Computer science itself provides a rapidly increasing number and variety of professional careers. Engineers and physical scientists find a knowledge of computers essential; so, increasingly often, do social scientists. Few jobs in business can avoid the impact of computers. The applications of computers in medicine and the health sciences (e.g., analysis of laboratory data such as cardiograms, "automatic" diagnosis) are rapidly increasing. Lawyers are beginning to make use of computers for information retrieval purposes such as looking for precedents. Computers are being used to compile concordances, to study imagery in poetry, and to do stylistic analyses of literary works. It seems certain that at some time in their lifetimes a knowledge of computer science will be of practical value to all of today's college students.

C. The sociological impact of computer science.   The immediate sociological aspect of the so-called computer revolution is in the area of automation and technological unemployment. And while this is a serious problem—automation has replaced substantial numbers of workers and society does have an obligation to meet and solve this problem—it is probably true that its effect has been exaggerated and that, in the long run, like the Industrial Revolution before it, the computer revolution will produce more jobs than it will make obsolete. What should be emphasized about the computer revolution is that its impact on society is just beginning to be felt. R. W. Hamming has pointed out that in the first seven decades of the twentieth century the speed of transportation has increased two orders of magnitude from the 5 mph horse and buggy to the 50 mph automobile to the 500 mph jet airplane and that this has made a profound difference in the way we live. By contrast, in the past two decades the speed of computation has increased more than *seven* orders of magnitude from the man using a desk calculator (about 1 thousand operations per day) to the fastest digital computers (about 1 million operations per second) and we may expect equally profound changes as a result of this. Airline reservation systems, government use of computers for tax collection, the proposed national data bank, computers for the guidance of space capsules, and their use in science, business, and industry merely suggest how computers will affect our lives in the future. The use and misuse of large data banks, particularly by government, raises enormous issues of public policy. Computer-assisted instruction may change the educational process more significantly than any innovation since the printed page. At the risk of hyperbole, we may predict that no other technological advance of this century will affect our lives more profoundly than the digital computer.

D. The philosophical impact of computers.   If, as we said in the previous section, the differences between computers and brains are much greater than their similarities, does it follow that computers should have no effect on such philosophical questions as the *mind-brain problem* and determinism and free will? In fact, the contrary is true because the thrust of computer development raises serious philosophical questions, not so much in relation to what computers *are* today but as to what they may *become*. We shall relegate such questions as "Can computers think?" or "Are computers intelligent?" to the realm of semantics, although we may safely predict that to answer these questions negatively will require increasingly narrow definitions of thinking and intelligence. It makes more sense to look at both thinking and intelligence as continuums and to ask how far into these continuums computers can proceed. Is there "no reason why we will not be able to duplicate in hardware the very powerful processes of association of which the human brain is capable, once we understand the particular processes that are involved"[†]? If so, does this imply that machines can display *emotions* or have *intuition* or be creative? Indeed, can we talk of *consciousness* in machines or should we perhaps look at consciousness as being a passive property of human beings which acts as "a kind of window through which we can observe a small part of the workings of the brain without interfering with the orderly activity of the machinery we are watching"[††]? Is there a mind-brain dichotomy or not? Is man a machine? What of free will and determinism? How, if at all, does the statistical nature of the laws of physics affect these questions?

We raise these questions not with the intent of answering them, which is generally not yet possible, nor even of discussing them, for this cannot be done meaningfully until the reader has delved much further into the nature of computers. Our purpose is merely to impress upon the reader that these are serious questions, that the advent of computers has, philosophically speaking, reopened some of these questions and thrown new light on others, and finally, that the philosophical significance of these questions provides a worthy motivation for the study of computer science.

1.3 A BRIEF HISTORY OF DIGITAL COMPUTERS

The rapidity of the development of digital computers in the last twenty years is a startling example of what can happen when scientific knowledge and technological capacity are both ripe and when the needs of society provide a spur to both. But this development, like all advances in science, has a long history

---

[†] P. Armer, Intelligent Machines, in *The Evolving Society*, Alice Mary Hilton, ed., Institute of Cybercultural Research, New York, 1966.

[††] Dean E. Wooldridge, *The Machinery of the Brain*, McGraw-Hill Book Company, Inc., 1963, p. 219.

behind it, a history of new ideas and small advances and one very remarkable man who was far ahead of his time.

The first *digital-computing instrument* was the abacus, developed originally in the Orient and introduced into Europe in the early Middle Ages. But if, as in Section 1.1, we insist that a *digital computer* exhibit a certain degree of automatism about it, then for the first digital computer, we can go back no further than 1642 when the great French mathematician Blaise Pascal, then only 19, built an elementary mechanical calculating device to help his father, the customs officer at Rouen. Later in the seventeenth century, Leibniz extended Pascal's machine, which could only perform addition and subtraction, to multiplication and division. The work of Pascal and Leibniz illustrates the first great idea in the history of automatic digital computation: the recognition that the operations of arithmetic can be mechanized.

The next great idea in the development of digital computers had to wait for the early nineteenth century and the remarkable man mentioned above, an Englishman named Charles Babbage. Babbage was a mathematician with a very strong practical bent which, since he lived in the early days of the Industrial Revolution, led him to write extensively about the advantages of machinery for mass production. In 1812, he conceived the idea of adapting the techniques of mass-production machinery to the calculation of mathematical tables. Heretofore all such tables—of which logarithms were the most notable—had been calculated by hand and were full of errors. Babbage recognized that not only would a machine be more efficient for such calculations, but it would also be much more accurate.

Babbage's first machine in 1822 was a working model of what he called a Difference Engine, whose specific purpose was to facilitate the calculation of tables. On the basis of this model, he was able to obtain support from the British government for a much expanded version of the Difference Engine. But, by 1842 the Difference Engine was still incomplete and government support was withdrawn. However, a version of this engine was used for calculating insurance tables.

Meanwhile in 1833, during a period when he was not working on the Difference Engine, Babbage conceived the idea on which his fame rests. It almost appears that Babbage, frustrated by the technological difficulties in implementing the Difference Engine, decided to free his mind of practical problems. He spent much of the remaining thirty-eight years of his life attempting to implement this new idea, a machine he called the Analytical Engine. Although he made detailed drawings of the machine and built some parts of it, the technology of the mid-nineteenth century prevented him from realizing his dreams.

The Analytical Engine was conceived as a general-purpose calculator, as opposed to the special-purpose nature of the Difference Engine. In plan, it was indeed a general-purpose automatic digital computer as defined in Section 1.1. Parenthetically, we note that Babbage's use of "Analytical" instead of the current usage of "digital" was particularly prescient in its implications. He even realized that such a machine would be capable not only of numerical computations but also of performing such tasks as playing chess.

The great idea embodied in the Analytical Engine was the recognition that computers could be "programmed"; that is, that machines could be built which would perform long sequences of arithmetic and decision operations without human intervention. By contrast, all machines until Babbage's time, like present-day desk calculators, performed only one arithmetic operation at a time. Babbage's proposal was to feed the instructions and the data to the computer on punched cards which had recently been invented by Jacquard for controlling his weaving looms. These were the forerunner of the cards we know as IBM cards, invented by Dr. Herman Hollerith in the late nineteenth century.

The distance by which Babbage was ahead of his time is clearly indicated by the fact that, despite advances in the design and quality of desk calculators and other mechanical calculators, it was not until 1939-44, when the Harvard Mark I calculator was built by Professor Howard Aiken, that a computer embodying the principles of Babbage's Analytical Engine was finally built. The Mark I consisted almost entirely of electromechanical relays and rotary switches. Whereas Babbage had wished to use cards for input (as most computers do today), the instructions for the Mark I were fed on punched paper tape. The speed of the Mark I was about 200 operations per minute. It did yeoman service in World War II computing ballistic tables and after the war computing mathematical tables.

Another electromechanical computer development at about the same time which deserves mention is the building of the Bell Relay Computers at the Bell Telephone Laboratories by a group led by G. R. Stibitz and including E. G. Andrews. One of these computers was used in the first demonstration of remote computing in 1940 when, from a teletypewriter at Dartmouth College, data was sent by telephone lines to New York, a calculation was performed, and the results printed out at Dartmouth.

The first electronic computer was the ENIAC (for Electronic Numerical Integrator and Calculator), built by Drs. J. P. Eckert and J. W. Mauchly at the Moore School of Electrical Engineering at the University of Pennsylvania. Completed in 1946, it contained almost 20,000 vacuum tubes. Data input and output were on punched cards, but instructions for each task required the wiring of a manual plugboard. The great contribution of ENIAC, which was built for the Ballistic Research Laboratory of the Aberdeen (Maryland) Proving Grounds, was its demonstration that electronic components made computing speeds possible vastly in excess of any previously obtained. ENIAC could, for example, perform about 300 multiplications per second and was over one hundred times faster than the Mark I.

With the development of ENIAC and the demand for high speed computing during and after World War II, the stage was set for the explosive development of digital computers over the last twenty years. All that was required was the spark provided by the third of the great ideas in the history of digital computers. Much of the credit for this idea must go to John Von Neumann of the Institute for Advanced Study who served as a consultant to the Moore School. But some of the credit is also due Eckert and Mauchly and Von Neumann's coworkers at IAS, notably H. H. Goldstine and A. W. Burks. Briefly, this idea was that the instructions to inform the computer of the calculation to be performed should be *stored* in the memory of the computer. This *stored program* concept is so important that without it most of the calculations now performed by digital computers would be impossible. Storing the instructions in the memory has two vital advantages:

1. The instructions may be fed to and interpreted by the computer at electronic speeds in contrast to the far slower speeds at which paper tape or cards can be input. ENIAC used wired plugboards for its instruction because it would have been wasted effort to have a machine which could multiply two numbers in 3 milliseconds (3/1000 of a second) if it took 1 second for the computer to read and interpret the card containing the instruction to multiply the numbers.

2. More importantly, by putting the instructions in the same memory as the data (i.e., by coding the instructions into numerical form), *it becomes possible to treat instructions as data. The computer may then modify its own program* by operating on instructions as if they were numbers. In particular, this makes it possible to *jump* from one portion of a program to another unconditionally or conditional on the status of something in the computer (e.g., the sign of a number). The importance of the stored program cannot be grasped fully until the student has gone more deeply into computer science.[†] Suffice it to say here that this concept accounts for much of the power and versatility of digital computers.

By the late 1940s science and technology had both progressed to the point where it was possible to design and build the first modern digital computers. Naturally enough, work on such a computer, the EDVAC (for Electronic Discrete Variable Automatic Computer), was begun at the Moore School in 1946. It was not completed until 1952. At about the same time a group under Von Neumann at the Institute for Advanced Study began to build the IAS

[†] Because it has proved to be undesirable to physically modify the program, all modern computers provide hardware which effectively allows instruction modification without permanently changing the program as written.

computer. This, too, was not completed until 1952. (It may now be seen at the Smithsonian Institution.) In the meantime, the first modern digital computer, the EDSAC (for Electronic Delay Storage Automatic Calculator), was completed at Cambridge University in 1949 by a team headed by M. V. Wilkes. In the EDSAC, which was about as fast as ENIAC, the memory consisted of an acoustic delay line in which sound pulses circulated in mercury tanks. Soon after, most memories were constructed using electrostatic storage tubes, which quickly gave way to the magnetic cores and other magnetic memory devices in use today.

The EDSAC was then the first electronic general-purpose stored program digital computer. In 1951, the first commercial digital computer, the UNIVAC 1, built by Eckert and Mauchly for Remington-Rand, was delivered to the Bureau of the Census. It is interesting to note that a leading authority estimated that about eight UNIVAC 1's could perform all the computing required in the United States. However, on January 1, 1970, more than 40,000 computers were installed in the country. Their total capacity is substantially greater than that of 40,000 UNIVAC 1's.

The development of digital computers from the EDSAC and UNIVAC 1 to the present day has involved many refinements and improvements in hardware components and computer organization, and in sophistication and speed. However, the stored program principle has remained basically unchanged. From the few hundred multiplications per second of the early electronic computers, we have come now to computers capable of more than 1 million multiplications per second, an increase of an order of magnitude every four or five years. Despite the fact that the speeds of arithmetic units of computers are now approaching the limit of the speed of light, parallel organization, in which arithmetic units are concatenated, means that the ultimate speed of digital computers is not yet in sight.

Digital computers are generally said to have gone through three generations in the past two decades. The first was characterized by vacuum tube circuitry, the second by solid state (i.e., transistor and diode) circuitry, and the third or present generation by an increasing dependence on integrated circuitry. The hardware developments which characterize these three generations have made possible and economical the very high speeds and large memory capacities of present day computers. But developments in hardware alone could not have produced the impact which computers are making on society today. Parallel developments in techniques for exploiting the power of the hardware were also necessary. Among these other developments, a primary place must be given to the creation of methods to facilitate communication between man and machine. The unifying theme of this book is a consideration of how this man-machine interaction is achieved.

1.4   WHAT DO COMPUTERS DO?

Charles Babbage was a notably unsuccessful expositor of his ideas about digital computers. But he was fortunate in arousing interest in his work in Ada Augusta, Countess of Lovelace, the only daughter of Lord Byron. Her annotated English translation of a French description of the Analytical Engine is still unequalled as an account of the Analytical Engine. At one point she wrote, "The Analytical Engine has no pretensions whatever to originate anything. It can do whatever we know how to order it to perform."

It is as true of digital computers today as it was of the Analytical Engine that they only do what they are told to do. This fact is often used to counter the argument that computers think or that they display some of the attributes of intelligence. Is not a machine which only does what it is told no more than a robot, and therefore, unthinking and unintelligent? This argument, however, misses an important point which we shall now elucidate.

When we say that a computer only does what it is told we mean, using the language of automata theory, that given the inputs to the computer and its initial "state" (i.e., essentially the initial contents of its memory), its future behavior is in theory completely predictable. It does not mean that there is necessarily any practical way to predict this behavior. In particular, it does not mean that the computer is a mere extension of the person who programmed it (i.e., who provided it with its instructions). For example, it does not follow that, given a chess position, the person who programmed a computer to play chess can predict what move the machine will make. In a similar context, there is now a computer program which plays checkers substantially better than the man who wrote the program. As another example, it is not true that the programmer of a computer to prove theorems in symbolic logic can predict whether or not the machine will be able to prove a given theorem.

Computer programs have been written to perform stylistic analysis of literary works. But the writer of such a program could not predict what output the program would produce for a given text. Many computer programs have a life of their own in the sense that they are so complex that even the person who writes the program cannot predict the logical path the computer will follow in a given case, to say nothing of predicting with any accuracy the results that will be produced. Thus, while the computer may be predictable *in theory*, in practice it is not.

It may be argued that the previous statement is a quibble. The significant thing, it might be said, is not what the practical limitations are in predicting the behavior of our computer robot. Even admitting that the computer is a very clever robot indeed, the key fact is that it *is* a robot; it *is* deterministic. To answer, if not to rebut this argument, it is necessary to take the mechanist side of the old mechanist-vitalist controversy. What evidence is there that *we* are not *programmed*, that our genetic inheritance together with our experience and environment do not *in theory* mean that our actions are predictable? Most human beings have an instinctive distaste for this argument. We believe in free will; the idea that man is a machine is abhorrent. As in Section 1.2, we raise these questions not to take sides, not to discuss them at any length, but merely to convey the idea that the questions *are* serious and cannot be lightly dismissed. Our conclusion then is that the fact that current digital computers are deterministic[†] does not in itself tell us very much about what they can and cannot do. To perceive this we must take another approach.

Our approach to the question of what computers can do will be on a much more pragmatic level than the discussion above, although we shall again draw an analogy to human thought processes. In Section 1.1 we presented the idea that a digital computer is a symbol manipulator capable of manipulating symbols with extensive generality. But how much generality? Rather than answer this question, let us put it another way by asking what problems these symbol manipulators can solve. In this context we look at a computer as a *problem solver*. Given instructions and data, our aim is always to have the computer solve a problem. We mean to use "problem solving" in a very general sense, so general that we may also look at our brain as being a problem-solver whether the problem is the sum of 2 and 2, how to put one foot after another in walking, or how to verbalize an emotion such as love. Thus, we may say that the answer, not to what computers can do but to what they actually do, is that they solve problems. What problems? All we can say now is, if the problems are not as varied as those solved by the human brain, at least they possess a far greater variety than the reader probably now imagines.

We have arrived then at an operational definition of a digital computer as a machine which *solves problems* by *manipulating symbols*. We have indicated by implication and example (Section 1.2) the wide range of problems which can be solved on digital computers. The thrust of our argument thus far has been to present the digital computer as an *abstract machine*, that is, one capable of dealing with and manipulating symbols which, when organized, represent concepts and abstractions. Our purpose in presenting the argument this way has been to give the reader the proper perspective prior to studying the concrete topics which are discussed in the remainder of this book.

[†] An example of a machine which is theoretically nondeterministic is Rosenblatt's Perceptron, which is a simulated neural network. However, nondeterministic or probabilistic machines have as yet found no significant application.

As the first of these topics, let us try to answer the question of what computers can do on a very specific level, by considering the manipulations which digital computers can apply to the symbols with which they deal. These fall into four categories:

1. Arithmetic operations—with the symbols interpreted as numbers, the four arithmetic operations can be executed.
2. Memory manipulation operations—at the heart of the symbol manipulating abilities of a computer, these enable the computer to examine, analyze, transfer from one part to another, and split apart in various ways the data and instructions stored in its memory.
3. Decision operations—which enable the computer to choose one of various courses of action based on some condition internal to the computer.
4. Input-output operations—these are the mechanisms by which the computer communicates with the outside world.

In addition, most computers can perform a variety of other operations, normally including some logical operations (cf. Chapter 9).

Before concluding this section let us consider briefly the matter of errors in digital computers. If it is true that computers do only what they are told, then does it follow that they always do what they are told? In actual fact, of course not. Computers, like other machines and humans, make errors. These errors are of different types and are worth categorizing.

Computer errors can be either *detected* or *undetected*. A human analogy to the former category is the case where we write a 7 instead of a 6 but this is detected by our eyes. Computers similarly can often detect that a number has an incorrect value. And sometimes the computer is able to correct the error. When it cannot, typically the user is informed so that he may take appropriate action. Now this is quite acceptable in most cases, even, for example, when the computer is controlling a chemical plant, as long as there is human backup in the system. But there are cases of detectable but uncorrectable computer failures for which human backup is no substitute. A case in point is the ground-based computer system which guides a manned space capsule into orbit. In such cases it is necessary to have a second computer serve as a backup to the first.

Obviously, an undetected error is potentially much more serious. Still, if we use "undetected" only in the sense that the computer does not detect its *own* errors, then, as long as something external to the computer—a human being, perhaps—can detect the error, the argument is essentially the same as above. But errors which are undetected both internally and externally can surely be disastrous. Consider the calculations involved in the design of a supersonic aircraft. Errors in such a calculation could lead to tragedy on the initial test flight or—what is worse—the design error might only appear after the aircraft had been in service for some time.

Fortunately, most computer applications are such that an error undetected at the time it is made will either be automatically corrected by the computer later in the application or will be detected at the end of the application because of physical or logical checks that can be applied to the results. But clearly, when human or substantial economic interests are involved, it is worth considerable effort—perhaps even a duplication of the work—to avoid undetected errors.

However, in case the reader is now conditioned to look askance at computer results, it should be emphasized that modern digital computers are so accurate that undetected errors are virtually unheard of. Thus, only in rare cases does the user of a digital computer worry lest the computer give him false results. It might further be noted that digital computers have grown consistently more error-free since the days of the EDSAC and UNIVAC 1. Solid state circuitry, which is much more reliable than the vacuum tube circuits previously used, has been largely responsible for this.

1.5 COMMUNICATION WITH COMPUTERS: COMPUTER LANGUAGES AND NATURAL LANGUAGES

Applicants for positions on university faculties or in industrial laboratories are usually asked about their proficiency in foreign languages. It is not unusual for this query to be given the answer, "French, German, Fortran, and Algol," the latter two being computer languages which we shall discuss later. Such an answer is not flippancy; computer languages are foreign languages in a quite precise sense. Learning to use a digital computer is, more than anything else, learning to communicate with the computer by using one of these "foreign" languages.

This is not meant to imply that computer languages are like natural languages (e.g., French, German, English) in any specific sense. Rather, it is meant to denote that computer languages can be described structurally with concepts similar to those used to describe natural languages; for example, to learn a computer language it is necessary to learn a *vocabulary* and a *grammar*.

In some important respects the computer languages to be considered in this book are different from natural languages. Three such differences are worthy of mention here:

1. Ambiguity.   Consider the English sentence

He saw the man in the park with the telescope.

Did the man have the telescope? Or did the park have the telescope? Or did *He* use the telescope to see the man in the park? The sentence is ambiguous and, except perhaps in a larger context (e.g., other sentences in the paragraph), the ambiguity cannot be resolved.

Most of us would agree that, while ambiguity surely exists in natural languages, it is usually an undesirable feature of them, although, at times, all of us use the ambiguity of language to conceal our thoughts from others. Indeed, it might be argued that ambiguity is one of the prices we pay for the richness of expression possible in natural languages.

The designers of computer languages always aim at nonambiguity, although, to achieve a convenient syntax, they often accept local ambiguities which are resolved in a larger context. Despite these efforts, the syntactic definition of computer languages may be ambiguous. Nevertheless, in their implementation on computers these languages are completely unambiguous. If the logical equivalent of the sentence, "He saw the man in the park with the telescope" were written in a computer language, the computer would *always* select one and always the same one of the interpretations mentioned above. As an example of this idea which is directly applicable to computer communication, consider the expression

$$A \div B \times C$$

In normal arithmetic usage this is ambiguous. Does it mean C times the quantity A divided by B? Or does it mean A divided by the quantity B times C? However, when this expression is communicated to a computer as part of a "sentence" in a computer language, there is no ambiguity. This expression will always be interpreted in the same way. Which way doesn't matter, as long as it's always the same way. (In fact, the former interpretation is the one always used in computer languages.)

Although implementations of computer languages are not ambiguous, the reader should not think that nonambiguity is a necessary part of any computer language implementation. In natural languages we can tolerate ambiguity because it can be resolved in the dialogue between the two users of the language. Until recently human-computer communication has not been of the dialogue form except in a very restricted sense. In particular, it has not been generally possible for the computer to immediately "query" its user about ambiguities in the program communicated to it. But such dialogue or *conversation* is becoming increasingly prevalent and possible. One result of this will surely be that richer computer languages will be developed in which ambiguity at the sentence level will be possible.

2. Context freeness.

He put the book on the table.

He used a table of logarithms.

The two meanings of "table" in these two sentences depend upon the *context* of table, that is, upon the neighboring words. Indeed, in some cases in natural languages, the meaning of a word or phrase can only be determined by considering neighboring sentences or even paragraphs. By contrast, the computer languages with which we shall deal are all *context-free* or nearly so. Most words or symbols in these languages always have the same meaning. A few words in some of these languages are context-dependent, but even then the context depends on the very near neighbors of the word. This is clearly a great convenience for the computer when it must determine the meaning of a word. We remark, however, that almost context-freeness is not a necessary property of computer languages, merely a convenient one. As the sophistication of computer languages increases, there will surely be a role for increasingly context-sensitive languages.

3. Semantic interpretation.

We consider here not a structural feature of computer languages but a pragmatic aspect of learning these languages. When a student of French learns that the French word for "house" is *maison*, he has no doubt about what *maison* will connote to a Frenchman. This is an example of a significant feature of all natural languages; they are used for communication with other human beings. Thus, learning the language is enough; there is (presumably) no need to study the anatomy or physiology of Frenchmen in order to speak their language to them. But to be able to converse with a computer, learning a computer language is not enough; it is also necessary to know something about the "anatomy" of a computer. It is a basic premise of this book that, while computers can be used by people who have very little understanding of their anatomy, to use them properly and profitably, some knowledge of their structure (logical, not electronic) is necessary. And the deeper this knowledge is, the more value will the user obtain from the computer and the more insight he will have into the kinds of problems to solve on computers.

The plan of this book is, therefore, to introduce the student to computer languages, their structure, how they are used to communicate with computers and, in parallel, to present enough information about digital computers themselves to provide the insight required to allow effective use of digital computers.

BIBLIOGRAPHIC NOTES

For the reader whose interest in the machine-brain question has been whetted we suggest the books by Von Neumann (1958), Wooldridge (1963), and Taube (1963). The first is virtually a last testament by the first great computer scientist of the electronic computer era, the second is an excellent account of the mechanist point of view, while the last is an attack, sometimes marred by overstatement and questionable reasoning, on the proponents of computer-brain analogies. After some actual experience using computers, the reader might also try Feigenbaum and Feldman (1963), which is the best available collection of articles on the field of artificial intelligence. The idea of thinking as a continuum is from the chapter by Armer in this book.

A good history of computer science has yet to be written. There is, however, some excellent historical material, particularly on Charles Babbage, in Bowden (1964). Alt (1958), Bernstein (1966), and Booth and Booth (1956) also contain some useful historical material. Rosen (1969) is an excellent historical survey of the last quarter century.

Bibliography

Alt, F.L. (1958): *Electronic Digital Computers*, Academic Press, New York.

Bernstein, J. (1966): *The Analytical Engine*, Vintage Books, New York.

Booth, A.D., and K.H.V. Booth (1956): *Automatic Digital Calculators*, Butterworths Scientific Publications, London.

Bowden, B.V., ed. (1964): *Faster Than Thought*, Pitman Publishing Corporation, London.

Feigenbaum, E.A., and J. Feldman, eds. (1963): *Computers and Thought*, McGraw-Hill Book Company, Inc., New York.

Rosen, S. (1969): Electronic Computers, A Historical Survey, *Computer Surveys*, vol. 1, pp. 7-36.

Taube, M. (1963): *Computers and Common Sense*, McGraw-Hill Book Company, Inc., New York.

Von Neumann, J. (1958): *The Computer and the Brain*, Yale University Press, New Haven, Connecticut.

Wooldridge, D.E. (1963): *The Machinery of the Brain*, McGraw-Hill Book Company, Inc., New York.

2

computers and computer languages—
basic concepts

I conceive you may use any language you choose to indulge in without impropriety.

W. S. Gilbert in *Iolanthe*

The first among languages is that which possesses the largest number of excellent works.

Voltaire (Letters)

2.1   THE PROBLEM OF COMMUNICATION

To communicate with a foreigner, whether he be Frenchman or Martian, there are just three possible approaches:

1. Learn a language he knows
2. Have him learn one that you know
3. Both learn an intermediate language that neither of you know

In dealing with other human beings, one of the first two approaches is virtually always used. To implement the third possibility, various universal languages such as Esperanto have been proposed, but their use is minimal. Occasionally, of course, two people with different native languages converse in a third language.

In dealing with digital computers only the first and third choices are open to us today. At the present state of our knowledge it is not feasible to have a

19

computer "learn" English or any other natural language.[†] By analogy with the case of communication between humans, the reader might guess that the most likely mode of communication with a computer would be by learning its language. This language, called *machine language*, consists of the operations which are built into the electronic circuitry of the computer and which were briefly outlined in Section 1.4. Indeed, in the early days of electronic computers all students learned to use computers by learning machine language first. But today this is almost never done because it is more effective and pedagogically sound to use the third approach above as we shall in this book. The study of machine language is best left for a later course in computer science.

The reason it is preferable to introduce students to computer science by teaching them an intermediate rather than machine language is that such languages make the problem solving process much easier for the user. They enable the student to start solving problems almost immediately after the start of his first course in computer science. Machine languages are not only more difficult to learn, they are also much more difficult to "speak," that is, to use. And most of the problems which almost all users will ever wish to solve can be solved using some intermediate language. Only the professional computer scientist and the very sophisticated user of computers need have more than a cursory knowledge of machine language.

The intermediate language approach consists of having the computer learn a language other than that built into its circuitry. Section 2.3.1 considers how this is accomplished. It should be clear that the intermediate language approach is not really one approach but an infinity, corresponding to the various "distances" which the intermediate language is from the other two. There are today a large class of intermediate languages which have been developed to facilitate man-machine communication. As a class, these languages are often called *problem-oriented*[††] because each was developed to have particular application to a certain category of problems. A more useful name for the class of languages which form the main subject matter of this book is *procedure-oriented* because these languages are particularly oriented toward describing procedures (or recipes) for solving problems. We shall refer to these as *P-O languages.*

[†]Whether or not this *can* be done is closely connected to the problem of whether or not it is possible to perform translations by computer (i.e., purely mechanical translations) from one natural language to another which are of equivalent quality to those produced by human translators. The accomplishments of mechanical translation to date have been quite disappointing. See *Languages and Machines: Computers in Translation and Linguistics,* National Academy of Sciences Publication 1416 (1966).

[††]*Problem-oriented* is sometimes used to refer to languages oriented toward a very particular set of problems, e.g., structural problems in civil engineering, rather than to a general class of problems, e.g., scientific calculations, as we use the term above.

From among the class of P-O languages there are four which are much more widely known and/or used than any others and form the main subject matter of this book. They are Fortran, Algol, PL/I, and Cobol. These are, respectively, acronyms for FORmula TRANslation language, ALGOrithmic Language, Programming Language I, and COmmon Business Oriented Language. The first two belong to a subset of P-O languages called *algebraic languages*. They were developed specifically to simplify man-machine communication for problems which emphasize the numerical computations so common in the solution of scientific problems such as space calculations, high energy physics problems and statistical calculations. Cobol, in contrast, as its name implies, has particular application to problems which arise in business such as payroll, accounting, and record keeping in general. PL/I, the most recently developed of these languages, is an attempt to combine into one language the main features of the other three. The rationale behind trying to obtain one language for both scientific and business problems—which superficially may seem so different—is an increasing recognition of the data processing nature of many scientific problems. Indeed, whereas the terms scientific computing and business data processing formerly were used to emphasize the differences between them, we now more commonly use the terms scientific data processing and business data processing.

Fortran, developed in 1954, was the first of these languages and is today the language used by the vast majority of all scientific programmers. Similarly, Cobol, first used in 1959, is used by almost all business programmers. Algol, first developed in 1958, was substantially revised in 1960 and again in 1962. It is used for instruction at some universities in the United States[†] and by a substantial number of scientific programmers in Europe. Outside its use in universities, Algol has never achieved significant popularity in the United States, but it is everywhere preeminent as the language for publication of computer programs. PL/I was first proposed in 1964 and has only quite recently become available for use on some computers. How widely it will be used is still moot. It is by far the richest of the four languages. By this we mean that a much greater variety and a more sophisticated class of problems can be solved with PL/I than with any of the other three languages. The discussion of PL/I in this book will at best only suggest the power of this language.

It is a basic premise of this book that the student will be using it in conjunction with a manual or other book from which he is learning one of the previously mentioned four languages. Our object here is not to teach the details of any of these languages but, rather, to consider the common and contrasting aspects of

---

[†]Another algebraic language used at a few universities in the United States is Mad, for Michigan (University) Algorithm Decoder.

all of them in an attempt to elucidate the rationale behind their various features. Various topics in computer science closely related to the use of these languages are considered. We shall, therefore, at times oversimplify the description of a feature of a particular language in order to avoid unnecessary complications.

A concept which is often difficult for the beginning student to grasp—particularly if he is given problems to solve on a computer before he learns anything more than the use of a language—is what is meant when we say a computer learns an intermediate language such as one of the four discussed above. One of the purposes of Section 2.3 is to elucidate just this point. Here let us merely mention that, in terms of actual hardware, the computer only "understands" what we have previously called machine language. The only way then that it can understand some other language is via a translation process which converts the intermediate language into machine language. We note this here to indicate a second major reason for the use of P-O intermediate languages. Using such intermediate languages, we are able to achieve a measure of *compatibility* between computers with different machine languages and, therefore among their users. Thus, if one writes a program in Fortran for one computer, this program can, usually with only minor modifications, be run on another computer if both (as is the case with most computers) can translate Fortran to their respective machine languages.

2.2   THE FUNCTIONAL PARTS OF A DIGITAL COMPUTER

Most books about digital computers contain a diagram similar to Figure 2.1. Not too many years ago such a diagram was a quite accurate description of the major logical parts of a digital computer. However, the increase in complexity of computer organization makes it at best a substantial simplification of the truth today. Nevertheless, this diagram represents a good place from which to commence consideration of the organization of a digital computer.

The names of the units in Figure 2.1 are almost self-explanatory:

> *Control unit*—consists of a large quantity of electronic circuitry which directs all the activities of the computer, determines the sequence in which instructions will be executed, interprets the instructions, fetches the data from and stores the results in memory and sees to it that the instructions are executed.
>
> *Arithmetic unit*—this piece of electronic circuitry can perform the four arithmetic operations on data sent to it from the memory unit; the operation which is performed is determined by the signal sent from the control unit; this unit and the control unit together are called the *central processing unit* (CPU).

Memory—that part of the computer in which are stored the instructions to be executed and the data on which the operations are to be performed.

Input—accepts information, both instructions and data, and stores it in the memory.

Output—receives results from the memory and presents them to the user.

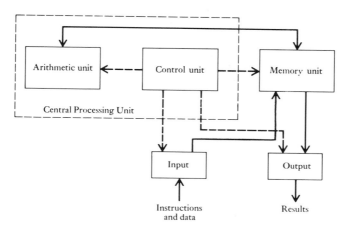

Figure 2.1 The five basic functional parts of a digital computer. The solid lines represent paths of information flow and the dashed lines show control-signal paths.

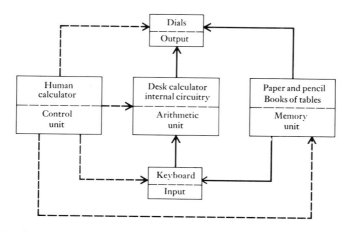

Figure 2.2 Desk calculator system.

It is instructive to compare the *automatic* computing system of Figure 2.1 with the *semiautomatic* desk calculator system of Figure 2.2. The same five parts are present. The basic difference in the two systems is the replacement of the control unit by the human controller in Figure 2.2 who provides the data and instructions one by one through the keyboard and records the output from the dials. A comparison of the two diagrams indicates clearly how, in going from the desk calculator to the digital computer system, we gain the electronic speeds of the latter in return for losing the flexible control of the former. It is one of the main challenges of digital computation to show that the flexibility and versatility of human control can practically be duplicated for many problems.

There is one other difference between Figures 2.1 and 2.2 which deserves mention. This is the direct path between the memory and processing unit in the digital computer system, opposed to the necessity of all data going through the input unit from the memory of the desk calculator system. The direct access of the digital computer system to its memory is, of course, necessary for the automatic operation of the system.

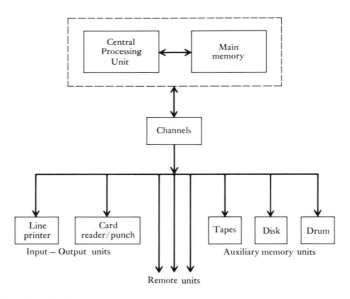

Figure 2.3   Organization of a modern computer system.

Figure 2.3 is an attempt to rectify the logical simplicity of Figure 2.1. It presents a realistic picture of the organization of current large digital computing systems. The central processing unit (CPU) and main memory boxes are the equivalent of the three boxes at the top of Figure 2.1. The *channels* are communication links between the CPU and input and output units and between the CPU and the auxiliary memory units which do not appear in Figure 2.1. These channels are more than just wire or cable connections between units. They perform such functions as determining the availability of auxiliary memory and input-output units, discovering the form of the input or output data, and doing certain error-checking functions. They can, indeed, be considered to be small special-purpose computers themselves. In fact, in some computing systems the purely communication parts of the channels are connected at the CPU end, to one or more digital computers with smaller capability than the CPU. When the channels are sufficiently powerful, they enable communication directly between the main memory and auxiliary memories and input-output units as implied in Figure 2.3. The ability to bypass the CPU when transferring data to and from main memory has the result of enabling the CPU to spend a greater percentage of its time performing actual computation.

As indicated in Figure 2.3, the input and output units may consist of a variety of devices. Those shown in Figure 2.3 are:

> *Line printer* (Figure 2.4)—available in speeds up to 1200 lines per minute each line consisting of up to 120 or, in some cases, 132 or 144 character positions per line.
>
> *Card reader* (Figure 2.5)—up to 1200 cards per minute; all card input, irrespective of the manufacturer of the computer, uses IBM cards. The *code* (i.e., combinations of holes punched) shown in Figure 2.6 is called the *Hollerith code* (cf. Section 1.3). For a discussion of the characters shown, see Section 2.5.
>
> *Card punch* (Figure 2.5)—up to 300 cards per minute.

In addition, other input-output devices used on some computers are:

> *Paper tape readers and punches*—used generally only on relatively small computing systems.
>
> *Optical page readers*—just beginning to be used extensively.

Digital computers which are designed to monitor and control real-time operations such as factory production or laboratory experiments can also accept data directly from the devices that are being controlled.

The auxiliary memory devices shown in Figure 2.3 enable the computer to "access" a variety of storage devices with different properties. The three properties of greatest interest determine

> How much can be stored?
>
> What is the cost per item stored?
>
> How fast can a given item be found (accessed) by the CPU and transmitted from one part of the computer to another?

All three of these questions should be answered relative to the main memory which is almost always magnetic cores, sometimes augmented by small amounts

Figure 2.4　　IBM 1403 line printer. *(Courtesy of IBM Corp.)*

of some other (e.g., magnetic thin film) ultra-high-speed memory. Magnetic core memory has relatively limited storage capacity (less than 5 million digits on even the largest systems), is very expensive, and has very fast access (0.5 to 1 μs)[†] on large systems. The major types of auxiliary storage, three of which are shown in Figure 2.3, are:

Magnetic drum—next to magnetic core, has fastest access and is most expensive; typical storage capacity: 5 million digits.

Magnetic disk—fast access, less expensive than drum, high volume capacity: up to one-quarter billion digits.

Data cell—low speed access and low cost; largest volume storage device: up to one-half billion digits.

Magnetic tapes—lowest cost and slowest access; medium volume capacity on a single reel of tape: about 10 million digits, but unlimited number of reels may be stored at computing center.

In addition, some computing systems provide auxiliary magnetic core

[†]Magnetic core memory is called a *random access* device because any element in it can be accessed directly without scanning over other parts of the memory (cf. Section 10.1.2) μs=microsecond=1/1,000,000 of a second.

Figure 2.5   IBM 2540 card reader-punch. *(Courtesy of IBM Corp.)*

memories of larger capacity, slower speed access, and less cost than the main memory, as an intermediate device between main core memory and drum memory.

Of the four storage devices listed above, the first three are so-called on-line devices in that the CPU has access at all times to any of the data stored on any of them.[†] On the other hand, the CPU has access to a reel of magnetic tape only if that reel is mounted on a tape unit. Even then, the relatively long time it takes to position the tape where it is desired to read or record data makes the access time for magnetic tape greater, on the average, than for disk storage. Tape storage is, therefore, used more and more mainly for long-term storage of seldom-used data and for backup (i.e., duplication of storage) of other memory devices.

In Chapter 10 we shall discuss in some detail the organization and properties of the memory devices introduced in this section.

One last feature of Figure 2.3 which we should mention here is the lines designated *remote units.* We shall, in Chapter 11, discuss remote computing in some detail. All that is necessary for the reader to understand at this point is

---

[†]This is a bit misleading for some magnetic disk devices; see Section 10. 1.2.2.

that it is possible to use modern large digital computing systems from remote locations at which the equipment may be anything from a typewriter-like terminal to a smaller digital computer, and where the connection to the central computer location is on-line (i.e., a direct, physical connection), usually by communication over telephone lines.

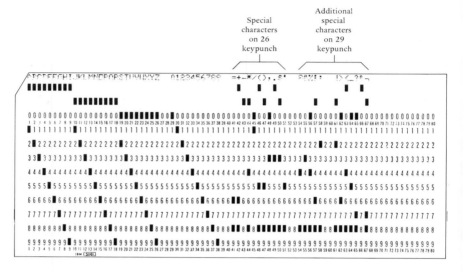

Figure 2.6 IBM card and 26 and 29 keypunch characters. All card codes shown are 29 keypunch codes; some of the 26 keypunch special characters have different codes (see Section 3.1.4).

2.3   COMPUTER LANGUAGES: TERMINOLOGY AND NOTATION

The reader may still feel that, despite the emphasis on language in Chapter 1 and Section 2.1, learning to use a computer is very different from learning a foreign language. Let us admit that there is a lot of truth in this. Nevertheless, in this section we shall, hopefully, by introducing some terminology and notation, convince the reader that the language analogy is meant very seriously indeed.

From high school English the reader is undoubtedly familiar with the terms grammar and syntax. But can he define them or, more significantly, state the difference between them? Should he run to a dictionary, he would be unlikely to help himself much for these terms are both confused and confusing in their usage with respect to natural languages. In recent years, linguists, of whom perhaps the best known is Noam Chomsky, have, in attempts to formalize concepts in language, used the terms grammar and syntax in quite distinct ways. Attempts at formalizing natural language concepts have not met with great success as yet. However, the formalism developed has proved very useful in describing computer languages which, because of their precise structure and lack of ambiguity, lend themselves to formal treatment. In this section we shall relate to computer languages a number of terms which the reader knows in a natural language context using some of the formalism referred to above. Our discussion will, however, be quite informal and heuristic.

Just as the positive integers are assumed to be given and to serve as the starting point for the formal development of mathematics,[†] so the starting point of the development of a language is its *alphabet.* We shall, in the next section, define the alphabets of the four P-O languages introduced in Section 1.2. Here we need only note that the alphabet is the set of characters from which all entities in the language are constructed. Although we normally think of the English alphabet as consisting of the 26 letters from A to Z, it is more correct to add to these characters the other symbols which are necessary in English such as the *space* between words, the *period* which ends a sentence, and the other necessary *punctuation marks.*

In its use by the computer linguist[††] a *grammar G* is an alphabet and a set of rules called *productions* for producing constructs from the alphabet which together are said to generate a language *L(G)*.

Example 2.1

Consider a grammer whose alphabet consists of the two characters a and b and the productions

$$S \rightarrow a$$
$$S \rightarrow b$$
$$S \rightarrow Sa$$
$$S \rightarrow bS$$

the first two of which are to be read, "a and b are constructs of the language" and the last two are to be read, "If S is a construct of the language, then so is S followed by a or preceded by b." What are the set of entities which make up this language?

[†]As the mathematician Leopold Kronecker said, "God created the natural numbers; everything else is man's handiwork."

[††]We warn the reader that our definition of grammar is a simplification of the usual one in computer linguistics.

The answer is any sequence of the form

   $bbb...bbaa...aaa$

that is, any number (including zero) of b's followed by any number (including zero) of a's.

We have used the symbol S in the example above because, instead of construct, we shall often use the term *string*. From our usage above it appears to follow that we should define a string to be *any sequence of characters from the alphabet of a grammar* which can be generated by its productions. Actually, we define string to be the italicized portion of the above sentence so that we may speak of strings which *belong* to a language (i.e., can be generated by the productions of its grammar) and those which do not (e.g., *aba* in Example 2.1).

Now we come to *syntax* and, while our definition of syntax may seem strange, it does in fact relate directly to the normal usage of syntax in English. The syntax of a language $L(G)$ is defined to be *the set of rules for determining whether or not a given string from the alphabet of G is in L(G)*, that is, whether or not the string could have been generated by the productions of G.

Example 2.2

What is the syntax of the grammar of Example 2.1?

The answer to this question is most simply given in terms of a *flow chart* (see Figure 2.7). We shall in Section 2.4 consider the construction and use of flow charts; here we shall rely on the almost self-explanatory nature of Figure 2.7 which assumes that at START we are given a string S from the alphabet of G. The flow chart is quickly explained:

> *Boxes 1-3:* Starting with the first character of S the string is searched for leading b's. If at any point there are no characters remaining in S, the string consists of a sequence of b's only, which is a legal string. Note that the *null string*, that is, the string with no characters at all, belongs to L. It is conventional to let the null string belong to every language.
> *Boxes 4-6:* Then a's are searched for. If at any time after the first a has been found a b is found, the string is illegal. Otherwise, the answer to the question in box 4 will be YES at some point, and S is legal.

This flow chart, then, *implicitly* embodies the syntax of the grammar of Example 2.1.

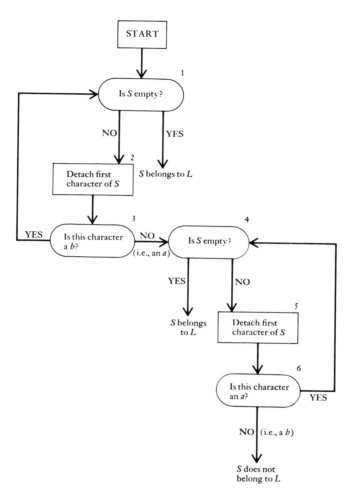

Figure 2.7   Flow chart for Example 2.2.

When we use the word syntax in connection with natural language, we are usually asking whether or not a sentence in the language has been properly constructed. This is just the point of view we have taken here for the formal language L.

From the above the reader has probably grasped our different uses of grammar and syntax. As we have used them, grammar refers to the *generation* of a language and syntax is concerned with the *recognition* of legal strings in the language. There is, therefore, a complementary relation between the productions of a grammar and the rules of syntax. Indeed, these terms are often used inter-changeably by computer scientists. For convenience in the remainder of this book, we shall use syntax when discussing both the rules by which strings are generated and the rules by which they are checked for legality.

We come next to *semantics.* Whereas syntax is concerned with correct con-struction, semantics is concerned with *meaning.* For example, in English the sentence

The fast table looked at the noisy chair.

is syntactically correct but semantically meaningless. In natural languages a significant part of semantics is intuitive; we *know* what meaning is intended by a sentence quite aside from the dictionary definition of the words. But with computer languages there must not only be explicit meaning for each syntacti-cally correct string, but the user must learn enough about the computer to understand what this meaning will be. This reenforces the statement made in Section 1.5 that, in studying computer languages, we must also learn something of the anatomy of the computer. The need to elucidate the semantics of various syntactic entities will, therefore, cause us to carefully consider various aspects of computer anatomy in the chapters that follow.

2.3.1   The Translation Process

Syntax, semantics, alphabets—we will be discussing computer languages using the terminology of natural languages. In fact, we are going to discuss these languages in terms of words, phrases, and sentences. Before doing so, however, we are at an opportune place to consider in more detail the process by which the P-O com-puter languages we shall be discussing are translated into the machine language of the computer.

First, some terminology. Two of the terms any novice must learn are *program* and *code,* and their other forms, *programmer* and *coder.* There is, however, substantial confusion over when to use program(mer) and when to use code(r). In some applications, particularly in business data processing, a programmer is someone who does the overall planning of the application. This might involve flow charting the application. The coder is the person who takes this macro-scopic description of the project and reduces it to a microscopic description, that is, a set of explicit instructions called a code which the computer executes. In scientific computing circles, more often than not, the words are used inter-changeably. Here we shall adopt the latter position but in order to avoid con-fusion we shall rarely use code or coder at all. A program, then, *is a set of instructions in any computer language for the performance* of some symbol manipulation (e.g., computation) on a digital computer. A programmer is the person who writes a program.

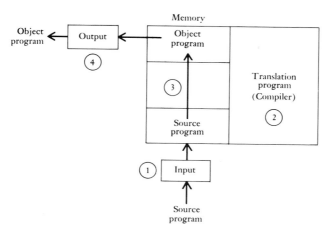

Figure 2.8   The translation process. Numbers on figure refer to discussion on this page.

Now a computer can *execute* programs, that is, actually perform computations, only for programs written in machine language. Therefore, when a program is written in a nonmachine language, such as a P-O language, the following steps, which are indicated schematically in Figure 2.8, must be performed before the program can be executed:

1. The program written in the P-O or *source* language, which is called the *source program,* must be entered into the memory of the computer through some input device. Typically, this input device is a card reader with the program having been previously punched on cards. In some cases the input device may be a typewriter-like terminal on which the program is typed directly into the computer.

2. Already in the memory is the translation program which in the case of P-O languages is called a *compiler.* This machine-language program, already written (by someone other than the user), *uses the source program as data.*

3. At *compile time,* the compiler translates the source program into the machine-language equivalent of the source program. This program, which constitutes the *output* of the compiler, is called the *object program,* with machine language being the *object language.*

4. Then at *execution time,* the object program, since it is a machine-language program, may be executed to produce the results desired by the user. Or it may be punched out on cards or stored in auxiliary memory (usually disk) where it can be used at some later time to generate results for the user.

It is important that it be clearly understood that the process described above is language translation in the usual, noncomputer meaning of that term. The object program is an exact copy of the source program in the operational sense that, when executed, it will produce precisely the results specified by the source program. Language translation of the type discussed here can be and is applied to a variety of situations where one computer language is to be translated into another. The language to be translated is always called the source language and the language into which it is to be translated, which is not always machine language, is called the object or target language. As noted in Section 1.1, translation of one computer language into another is an excellent example of the symbol-manipulation capabilities of a digital computer, the symbols being the string of characters which make up the source program and are manipulated into the string which comprises the object program.

2.3.2   Syntactical Notation

Languages may be learned at various levels. Often the aim is only to become proficient in reading, writing, and/or speaking the language. Sometimes special attention is paid to the structure itself because this knowledge may aid in the study of that or other related languages. Occasionally one goes even deeper into the underlying linguistics. Our approach thus far contains elements of the structural and linguistic levels. But this has been mainly to orient the reader properly. In the remainder of this book we shall concentrate on the reading and writing aspects of computer languages together with enough of the structural aspects so that the reader will be able to learn other computer languages more easily.

Our approach to the reading and writing of computer languages will be largely informal but to discuss some of the structural aspects of these languages it will occasionally be desirable to adopt a more formal approach. At the beginning of Section 2.3 we very briefly (cf. Example 2.1) introduced a notation for describing a grammar. Here we shall introduce another notation which is commonly used in the formal description of computer languages. The elements of this notation are:

$<\longrightarrow>$	to be read as "The structure (whatever is contained in the brackets) of the language"
$::=$	to be read as "is defined to be"
|	to be read as "or"
$[n]$	these brackets placed over the symbol $::=$ with an integer n inside them indicate that n is the maximum number of symbols allowed in the definition which follows the $::=$

Example 2.3

To define the letters of the English alphabet using this notation we would write

$$<LETTER> ::= A|B|C|D|E|F|G|H|I|J|K|L|M|N|O|P|Q|R|S|T|U|V|W|X|Y|Z$$

which would be read, "The *structure* LETTER *is defined to be* A *or* B *or* C *or...or* X *or* Y *or* Z."

Example 2.4

Using the above definition we can define the construct FOUR LETTER WORD as

$$<FOUR \ LETTER \ WORD> ::= <LETTER> \ <LETTER> \ <LETTER> \\ <LETTER>$$

which would be read, "The *structure* FOUR LETTER WORD *is defined to be* the *structure* LETTER followed by the *structure* LETTER followed by the *structure* LETTER followed by the *structure* LETTER." If we had previously defined THREE LETTER WORD in the obvious way, then the definition above could be given as

$$<FOUR \ LETTER \ WORD> ::= <THREE \ LETTER \ WORD> <LETTER> \\ | <LETTER> < THREE \ LETTER \ WORD>$$

We shall defer examples of the $[n]$ notation until Section 2.5.1.

The notation we have introduced here is known as BNF for *Backus Normal Form* after John Backus, one of the pioneers in the development of P-O languages, or sometimes for *Backus-Naur Form*, including Peter Naur, another early worker in this field.[†]

Although this notation is used to describe the strings in a computer language which can be generated, it is generally spoken of as a syntactical notation because computer scientists are usually more concerned with using it to determine if a given string is in the language. The connection between this notation and that of Example 2.1 is considered in Problem 8. In the remainder of this book our approach to computer languages will generally be quite informal. But, for nota-

---

[†]It has recently been pointed out that an Indian scholar, Panini, compiled a grammar of Sanskrit in the third or fourth century B.C. and used a notation nearly equivalent to that of BNF.

tional conciseness and convenience, we shall use BNF occasionally in the text
and quite regularly in the panels in which we shall compare structures in the four
P-O languages we shall discuss.[†]

2.4   ALGORITHMS AND HEURISTICS

If a program is a set of instructions to a computer to solve a given problem, this
implies that a program defines a rule, a method, or a recipe for solving the
problem. Computer scientists call such a rule an *algorithm*. It is possible—any
student who majors in computer science will soon find out how—to define the
notion of an algorithm in a rigorous mathematical fashion. In his first experience
with computers, however, the student should develop an intuitive feel for what
an algorithm is by writing programs, by learning what it means in practice to
derive a method for the solution of a problem which recognizes and anticipates
all possibilities.

One of the most convenient ways of describing an algorithm, one which we
have used already in Example 2.2 and which we shall use again many times in
this book, is by use of a *flow chart*. There is a great variety of notation used in
flow charting. Scientific programmers tend to use a simpler notation than
business programmers. Since business problems usually involve a heavy dependence on input and output, the flow chart notation sometimes used for such
problems has various techniques for distinguishing different types of input and
output (i.e., cards, printed paper, magnetic tapes, etc.). Here we shall confine
ourselves to a very simple flow chart notation which has thus far and will for the
rest of this book suffice for all our needs.

The elements of our flow chart notation are:

1. The *function* or *assertion* box. Examples:

   i) | Set I = 1 |

   ii) | A+B→C | (Set the value of C equal to the value of A+B)

   iii) | Compute $b^2 - 4ac$ |

This box asserts that the operations contained within it are executed when the
box is entered. This box may be entered from any number of other boxes but it

---

[†]Often in the panels we shall replace the notation<———> with the quantity in brackets
written in lower case italics; thus, <LETTER> would become *letter*.

has a *single exit*. The contents of the box may be formally or informally stated although the formal statement in the middle example is preferred. The arrow indicates that the value of the quantity at its head (C) is *replaced* by the value of the quantity at its tail (A+B). Sometimes the arrow notation is used in the form

$$\boxed{C \leftarrow A+B}$$

to conform more closely to the form of statements in computer languages (see Section 5.4).

2. The *test* or *decision* box.[†] Examples:

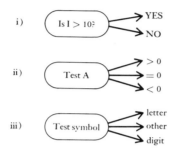

This box is used to indicate a conditional transfer of control. The box may be entered from one or more other boxes but must have more than one exit. Any self-evident mechanism for indicating the test being made is allowable.

3. The *remote connector*. Example:

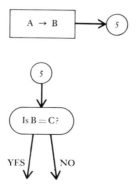

The remote connector is used when it is inconvenient or impossible to join two boxes in a flow chart directly; often this connection indicates that the two boxes are on separate pages.

[†]A diamond-shaped box is often used in preference to the oval.

In addition, all flow charts will begin with a box

$$\boxed{\text{START}}$$

and end with a box

$$\boxed{\text{STOP}}$$

Occasionally, we shall use ENTRY and EXIT instead of START and STOP.

The important thing for the reader to learn about flow charts is the desirability of drawing them even for the simplest problems. They are an invaluable aid to logical thought and the habit of drawing them is a good one. The reader may well find, as he develops expertise in computer programming, that he will outgrow the need to draw flow charts for simple problems. But he should be aware that for logically complex problems there is no substitute for them and that even the most expert programmers use them. The notation used is not really important; in any notation flow charts serve as a means for organizing thought and, therefore, for avoiding errors.

The examples which follow illustrate a number of algorithms of varying complexity and subtlety. In later chapters we shall return to discuss some of these algorithms in more detail.

Example 2.5

You are given a list of 100 numbers. Give an algorithm to find the largest number in the list.

The algorithm is as follows:

1. Compare the first two numbers; if the first is as large or larger than the second, delete the second from the list; otherwise delete the first.
2. Repeat Step 1 until only one number remains; this is the desired largest number.

Figure 2.9 is a flow chart for this very simple algorithm and contains no logical difficulties or subtleties. It does, however, as do the flow charts of Examples 2.6, 2.9, and many later ones in this book, express one of the most important ideas in computer science, namely *iteration,* or *repetitive calculation.* Many, indeed almost all problems solved on digital computers involve using the same set of instructions (or, in the present context, the same boxes in a flow chart) again and again on different data or on different intermediate results in a calculation. This idea will appear repeatedly in what follows although we shall not discuss explicit ways by which P-O languages make iteration particularly easy until Chapter 8. Suffice it to say here, if digital computers could not do repetitive calculations in a convenient fashion, they would not have assumed a place of significance in modern society.

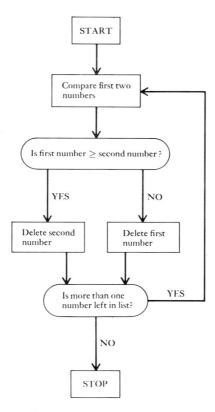

Figure 2.9   Flow chart for Example 2.5.

Example 2.6

Given a list of words or names (which might be words for a concordance or names in a payroll file), write an algorithm to alphabetize this list.

One possible algorithm is as follows:

1. Starting from the top of the list, compare the first two entries and interchange them if they are not in alphabetical order; then similarly compare the second and third entries of the list, the third and fourth, and so on.
2. Repeat the first step until no interchanges occur on a pass through the entire list.

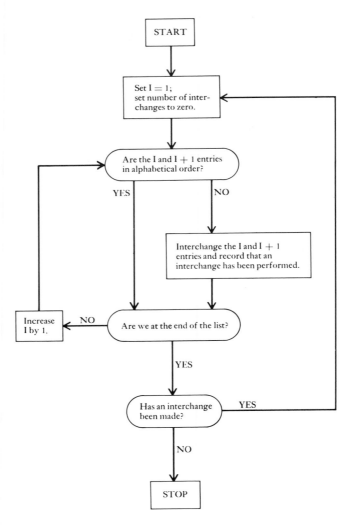

Figure 2.10   Flow chart for Example 2.6.

Figure 2.10 is a flow chart for this algorithm.

While it was easy to see that the algorithm of Example 2.5 both worked and was minimal (i.e., required the minimum amount of work), is the reader convinced that this algorithm works? If so, can it be improved upon? Are there any obvious inefficiencies? Can the reader determine the maximum number of interchanges that must be performed (Problem 14)?

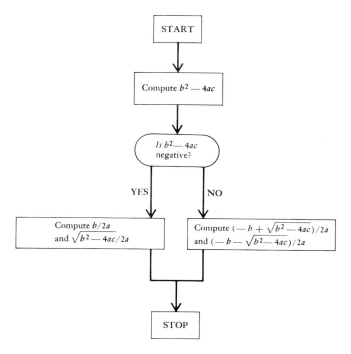

START

Compute $b^2 - 4ac$

Is $b^2 - 4ac$ negative?

YES

NO

Compute $b/2a$
and $\sqrt{b^2 - 4ac}/2a$

Compute $(-b + \sqrt{b^2 - 4ac})/2a$
and $(-b - \sqrt{b^2 - 4ac})/2a$

STOP

Figure 2.11   Flow chart for Example 2.7.

Example 2.7

Given three numbers a, b, and c which represent the coefficients of the quadratic equation

$$ax^2 + bx + c = 0 \tag{2.1}$$

find an algorithm to compute the roots of this equation.

Using the familiar quadratic formula

$$x = (-b \pm \sqrt{b^2 - 4ac})/2a$$

we get the following algorithm:

1. Compute $b^2 - 4ac$
2. If $b^2 - 4ac \geqslant 0$, compute the two roots using the $\pm$ signs in (2.1); if $b^2 - 4ac < 0$, compute the real $(b/2a)$ and imaginary $\sqrt{b^2 - 4ac}/2a$ parts of the roots.

Figure 2.11 is a flow chart for this algorithm. While this flow chart is simpler than those of the previous two examples, it is incorrect. This is because it

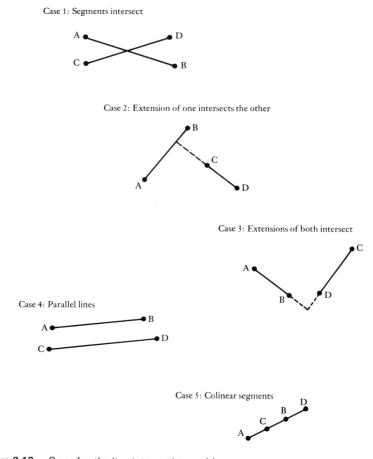

Figure 2.12   Cases for the line-intersection problem.

neglects the case in which $a = 0$ (Problem 15). Such a trivial omission is a particular example of the general rule that an algorithm for a computer must take into account all special cases which can arise in the computation.[†]

We come now to two more complicated algorithms which should give the reader something nearer the flavor of real computer problems.

[†]There is also another, more subtle error in Figure 2.11. If the roots are real and b^2 is large compared to $4ac$, then either $-b- \sqrt{b^2 - 4ac}$ (if b is negative) or $-b+ \sqrt{b^2 - 4ac}$ (if b is positive) will involve the difference of two numbers of nearly equal magnitude. The result will be one root with very few accurate digits. To avoid this problem, the root R, which involves the addition of two quantities with the same sign, should be computed as above and the other should be computed as c/Ra since the product of the two roots is c/a.

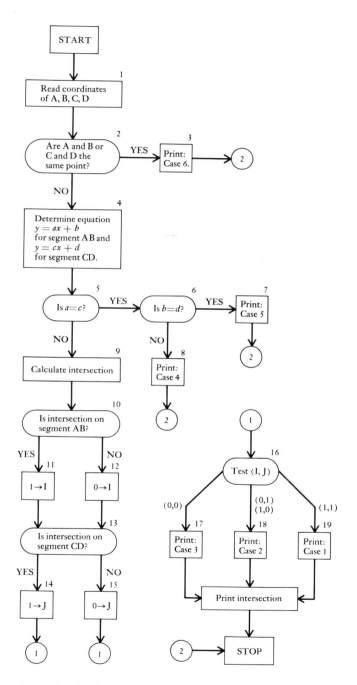

Figure 2.13 Flow chart for Example 2.8.

Example 2.8

Given the coordinates of two pairs of points in the x-y plane, each pair of which denotes the two ends of a line segment, draw a flow chart for the calculation of finding, when it exists, the intersection of the two line segments or their extensions.

Before drawing the flow chart some analysis is necessary. We can distinguish the cases shown in Figure 2.12. All other cases (Are there any?) will be called Case 6. Let us also slightly expand the problem as stated above to require that the case be identified in addition to finding the intersection.

Figure 2.13 contains the flow chart which we shall annotate box by box.

Boxes 1 and 2: Tests for one case not covered in Figure 2.12.

Box 3: In Chapter 10 we shall briefly indicate how alphabetic characters can be printed.

Box 4: We leave the mathematics here to Problem 18.

Boxes 5-8: Tests for Cases 4 and 5.

Boxes 9-15: Calculation and test for position of intersection.

Boxes 16-20: Distinguish between Cases 1, 2, and 3 and print case number and coordinates of intersection.

The instructions to read and print in this flow chart imply some means of getting data into and out of the computer. In Chapters 6 and 10 we shall consider various techniques for achieving this. The reader should study carefully and understand this flow chart.

Example 2.9

The problem of finding a knight's tour on a chessboard is an old one with a long literature. The object is, starting from any square on a chessboard, such as the square labeled (6,7) [where 6 is the vertical coordinate] in Figure 2.14, to find a sequence of 63 knight's moves[†] which results in the knight occupying each square of the board once.

There is no simple algorithm for finding a knight's tour. But it is known empirically that the following rule always works:

1. After the ith move the knight has moves i_1, i_2,...,i_n open to it. In Figure 2.14, i=3 and n=5 with the five moves enclosed in circles.

[†] A knight's move in chess is one (two) square horizontally or vertically followed by two (one) squares in the other direction (vertically or horizontally).

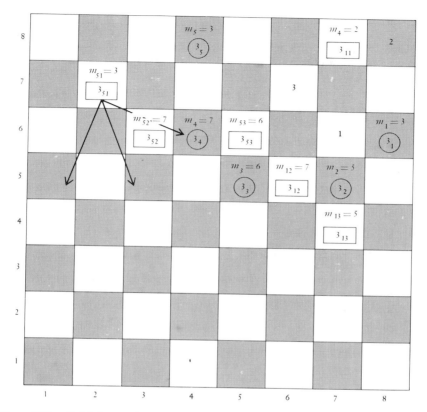

Figure 2.14   Knight's tour algorithm.

2. If move i_j is made where j lies between 1 and n, then, after the *next* move, that is the $(i+1)$st move, there will be some number m_j moves, i_{j1}, i_{j2}, ...,i_j, m_j, open. This number is shown in each box in Figure 2.14 and the actual moves are shown for $j=1$ and 5 enclosed in square boxes.

3. If some m_j has a positive value less than *all* other m_j's ($m_j=0$ of course denotes a dead end), choose move i_j as the $(i+1)$st move. The rationale behind this is that one wants to tour the corners (from which the number of possible moves will be smallest) as early as possible so as to be able to finish the tour in the relative freedom of the center of the board. In the example shown in Figure 2.14, $m_1 = m_5$ so we must go to Step 4.

4. For all equal m_j's, consider each of the possible moves i_{j1} ,...,i_{j}, m_j and count how many moves would be available at the $(i + 2)$nd stage. Call this number m_{jk}, $k=1,2,...,m_j$. These numbers are shown in Figure 2.14 in each box with a move in a square box. For the move in square (7,2), the three possible moves are shown by arrows. Note that the move into square (6,4) is a possible move because, if 3_5 is the move actually made, 3_4 would not have been made.

5. For each j find the minimum M_j of all the m_{jk}. Choose as the next move that i_j for which M_j is a minimum. If two M_j's are equal make the choice arbitrarily. In Figure 2.14, $M_1 = 2$ and $M_5 = 3$ so that the fourth move would be 3_1 in square (6,8). Note that it follows from the above that the fifth move is 3_{11} in square (8,7). (Why?)

This is not a simple problem or a simple algorithm. A flow chart to implement this algorithm is shown in Figure 2.15. The following is a box-by-box annotation of this flow chart:

> Box 1: All 64 squares of the chessboard, which is denoted by A, are set to 0. Zero represents a square that has not been occupied by the knight.
>
> Box 2: r and c are the row and column indices of the starting position.
>
> Box 3: Initial square set equal to 1; i is a counter for the number of moves; R_i and C_i store record of each move.
>
> Box 4: This box is self-explanatory but clearly implies a small program itself; in general a given box may imply a small number of statements or a large number; the programmer must choose that most convenient to himself; sometimes a box which implies a large number of statements will itself be broken into other boxes in another flow chart (see Example 7.1).
>
> Boxes 5-6: If $n=0$, no move is available and the program must print out some error message; since the algorithm presented here does in fact always work, Box 6 will never be reached *if* the program written is correct. In general, a box like Box 6 provides a useful mechanism for checking that a program works (cf. Section 6.3) as well as in programs in which the computational method is not really an algorithm and thus may fail under some conditions.
>
> Box 7: Again self-explanatory, but implying a substantial number of statements.
>
> Box 8: Step 3 of the algorithm.
>
> Boxes 9-11: Steps 4 and 5 of the algorithm, but again, a lot of programming hidden here.
>
> Box 12: Recording of move.
>
> Box 13: Test for completion of tour.
>
> Box 14: Print results.

The reader should study and understand this flow chart. He should decide if he likes it. Are there too few boxes or too many? Will it be easy to write the program statements directly from this flow chart? We shall in later chapters come back to this example to elucidate a number of points which may still be obscure.

As we said earlier, the foregoing examples were intended to give the reader an intuitive feeling for the concept of an algorithm. It has perhaps also misled him

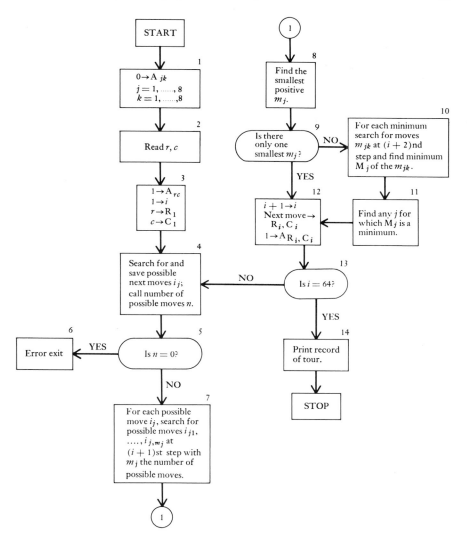

Figure 2.15 Flow chart for Example 2.9.

into thinking that any correctly written computer program is an algorithm for solving a particular problem. We dropped a hint in our discussion of the error exit in the knight's tour example that this is not so. For, if it were, we should be restricted to using computers on problems for which there is a known solution in the sense that an algorithm to solve the problem is known. But, for example, how about the entire game of chess? We can state an algorithm for playing chess (i.e., the *rules* of the game) but no algorithm is known for playing chess perfectly.[†]

What then about a computer program to play chess, that is, to make a move in response to one presented to it? In order to attempt to make the computer play well we clearly must do more than just search for a legal move according to the rules of chess. The answer to what is done in this case—or for any other problem for which no algorithm is known—is to provide the computer via the program with some feeling or guess or intuition about the problem. These are usually subsumed under the general term *heuristic*, a word we used in Section 2.1, which means "tending to discover or learn." Whereas an algorithm is a rule for the solution of a problem, a heuristic is merely a guide toward finding a solution. Examples of heuristics used in playing chess (by humans or computers) are the value of having more pieces than your opponent, the importance of early development of pieces, and the importance of control of the center of the board. A heuristic program to play chess would incorporate these ideas into its choice of what move to make.

A heuristic program then, in contrast to an algorithmic program, is one which may or may not solve the problem at hand (e.g., beat its opponent in chess) but which, even if it fails, may still provide valuable knowledge on how it can be improved to do better the next time. Beginning students in computer science are generally totally involved with problems for which algorithms exist. But, since many of the more interesting uses of computers involve applications for which no algorithm is known, an understanding of heuristics as well as algorithmics is necessary early in the education of any computer scientist.

2.5 ALPHABETS AND WORDS

We are ready now to commence consideration of the basic entities of any computer language. The most basic of these, as we indicated in Section 2.3, is its *alphabet*, which is more usually called its *character set*. Before considering the character sets of various languages we should point out that computer languages, like natural languages, often vary somewhat from place to place, that is, from use on one make of computer to another and sometimes even between two

---

[†]That such an algorithm exists, however, is certain and follows from the branch of mathematics called *game theory*. But the task of finding this algorithm is so great that there is no danger that chess will cease to be an interesting game in the foreseeable future. It has been estimated by C.E. Shannon that, if a computer could analyze one chess move each microsecond, it would take 10^{120} years to look at all possible chess games!

Figure 2.16 IBM 29 keypunch. *(Courtesy of IBM Corp.)*

models of the same computer at different installations. These various forms are naturally called *dialects.* Of the four languages we shall discuss, only Fortran has significantly different dialects. The one we shall use consistently in this book is USA Standard Fortran of the USA Standards Institute (now the American National Standards Institute). This dialect of Fortran is generally known as *Fortran IV.*

In discussing the character sets of computer languages, we must distinguish between the *implementations* of these languages on a computer and the official *definitions* of these languages. Algol in particular, as we noted in Section 2.1, is widely used as a language for publication of computer algorithms as well as for the solution of problems on computers. Its character set for publication, therefore, includes virtually all the characters one would like to be able to print. But its character-set implementation, like those of Fortran, PL/I, and Cobol, is limited by the equipment used to prepare programs for input to computers. Since that input device which accounts for the vast majority of all computer input, quite aside from the manufacturer of the computer, is the IBM keypunch (Figure 2.16), the implementation character sets of computer languages have been limited by the keyboard characters of the keypunch. Until recently, the standard keypunch was the Model 26 which contained the following 48 characters on its keyboard:

Upper case letters A through Z
Digits 0 through 9
Special characters:

	blank (space)
=	equal sign
+	plus
−	minus
*	asterisk
/	slash
(	left parenthesis
)	right parenthesis
,	comma
.	decimal point (period)
$	dollar sign
'	apostrophe (quotation mark)

The reader should note the need for a blank character. This serves the same purpose in computer languages as the space between words in natural languages. Using our BNF notation we may define

```
<LETTER> ::= A|B|C|...|X|Y|Z
<DIGIT> ::= 0|1|2|3|4|5|6|7|8|9
<FORTRAN CHARACTER> ::=
       <LETTER>|<DIGIT>| |=|+|−|*|/|(|)|,|.|$
<PL/I CHARACTER (48)> ::= <FORTRAN CHARACTER>|'
<COBOL CHARACTER> ::= <PL/I CHARACTER (48)>|;|<|>
```

Note the blank character represented by an empty space between two vertical bars. The reason for the (48) in the PL/I definition will become clear below.

Although the quotation mark is not an official part of the Fortran character set, it is included at many installations. Also, some special characters are not allowed at some installations ($ most commonly). Since the semicolon (;) and greater than (>) and less than (<) signs are not available on the 26 keypunch, these are usually not available in Cobol implementations. The > and < signs, in particular, are often replaced by the *transliterations* GT and LT. The Algol implementation character set is usually the PL/I 48-character set above, but the publication set includes all the lower case alphabetic characters as well as numerous other special characters.

Recently the 26 keypunch has been replaced at most computer installations by the 29 keypunch. This latter keypunch has a 60-character keyboard, the additional 12 special characters being:

@   "at" sign
#   number sign
%   percent symbol
;   semicolon
:   colon
¬   "not" symbol
&   "and" symbol
| "or" symbol
>   greater than
<   less than
—   break character (used as hyphen)
?   question mark

The newest of the four languages, PL/I, has recognized the advent of the 29 keypunch by defining a 60-character set also:

<PL/I CHARACTER (60)> ::=
    <PL/I CHARACTER (48)>|@|#|%|;|:|¬|&|||>|<|_|?

There is an obvious possible confusion above between the | as part of the character set and the | in our syntactic notation. This confusion is compounded by the fact that both mean "or" in somewhat different senses (see below).

All the characters above, except for letters and digits, are generally classed as *special characters*. More formally, they are often called *delimiters* because, as we shall see, they are commonly used to separate one structure of a language from another, that is, to *delimit* the beginning and end of a structure.

The various character sets defined above are summarized in Table 2.1. Throughout the remainder of this book our examples will use the following character sets:

1. Fortran—the 47-character set as defined above.

2. Cobol—the PL/I 48-character set (i.e., the Cobol character set without; or > or < with these three replaced by transliterations when necessary).

3. PL/I—the 60-character set since almost all installations using PL/I also use the 29 keypunch.

4. Algol—the *publication* language character set; the reader must realize that any actual Algol program must use transliterations of the publication characters to a keypunch character set. One such transliteration for some of the more common publication characters which need transliteration is shown in Table 2.2. A further discussion of the use of boldface type in the publication language will be found in Section 6.1.1.

Table 2.1   Character sets of Fortran, PL/I, and Cobol

Characters	Fortran	PL/I 48-char. set	PL/I 60-char. set	Cobol
A,B,C, ..., Y,Z	X	X	X	X
0,1,2, ..., 8,9	X	X	X	X
=+– */)(,.$				
blank	X	X	X	X
	Z	X	X	X
@#%:&.–?			X	
;><			X	Y

Notes:

X—indicates character is part of character set.

Y—indicates character is part of character set but not allowed at many installations.

Z—indicates character is not part of character set but often is allowed.

The semantics of the character sets discussed above are mostly obvious. But some of the special characters require some explanation.

* denotes multiplication; in computer languages multiplication is never indicated by direct juxtaposition of the two factors for a reason which will become clear later.

/ denotes division.

= does *not* always indicate equality in the usual sense; instead sometimes indicates *replacement* of the left hand side by the right hand side; see Section 5.4.

() , ; : used to separate two strings of the language much as they are used for punctuation in natural languages.

. decimal point or period.

$ @ # used as three additional alphabetic characters in the PL/I 60 character set; $ sometimes used for special control purposes in other languages.

′ used as a special string delimiter.

<> mathematical symbols denoting "less than" and "greater than," respectively.

¬ &| logical symbols denoting "not," "and," and "or" respectively; see Section 9.1.

%	used to designate special kind of language construct in PL/I.
—	used as hyphen in PL/I (— sign is used as a hyphen in Cobol).
?	keypunch character only; not used in PL/I.

In addition, certain concatenations of the special characters have a particular meaning in the various languages; we shall discuss these as we come to them.

2.5.1   Words

As in any language, the alphabets of computer languages are used to form words. These words are of two basic types: *names,* or *identifier* words, and *constant* words.

Identifiers are used to denote variable quantities, quantities which change during the course of the solution of a problem. For example, a name might represent:

i) the *distance* of a missile from its launching station

ii) the *name* of the person whose salary is being calculated in a payroll application

iii) the *position* of a chess piece on a chessboard

iv) the *word* in a concordance which is currently being worked on

v) the *disease* whose symptoms are being compared to a patient's symptoms in a medical diagnosis application

Table 2.2   Algol transliterations

Publication language	A possible 48-character set implementation
Boldface type	Word in single quotes ('——')
;	. ,
:	. .
[	(/
]	/)
<	LT
>	GT
≤	LE
≥	GE
=	EQ
≠	NE

Panel 2.1   Names

Fortran	*Algol*	*PL/I*	*Cobol*
1 to 6 alpha-numeric characters of which the first must be alphabetic	Any length sequence of alpha-numeric characters of which the first must be alphabetic	1 to 31 alphanumeric and break characters of which the first must be alphabetic	1 to 30 alphanumeric characters or hyphens as long as neither the first nor last character is a hyphen and at least one character is alphabetic

Implementation variations or restrictions

Up to 8 characters allowed in some cases	Always some maximum length restriction, often to 6 or 8 characters	Often none, but limits to as few as seven characters sometimes	Usually none

Examples

CAMEL	CAMEL	CAMEL	CAMEL
FORTY1	FORTY1	FORTYONE	FORTY–ONE
A	A	EIGHTYFOURZ	84Z
			312–7

Operationally, a name refers to a *location* or *set of locations* in the memory of a computer whose *contents* will change during the course of the solution of a problem (see Section 4.3).

The computer languages we are concerned with here define names in slightly different fashions as indicated in Panel 2.1. There are a variety of reasons for the differences in the definitions of names (and of other corresponding quantities in the four languages which we shall discuss in later chapters):

1. Historical reasons—definitions which seemed reasonable when the language was defined were shown by actual use to be capable of improvement; in some cases the techniques for constructing compilers for the language did not permit a desirable generality of definition.

2. Idiosyncrasies of original implementation—Fortran, for example, was originally implemented on a computer (IBM 704) which could conveniently store up to six characters in a group (see Section 3.1.5); hence the restriction of six characters in the length of Fortran names.

3. The class of problems at which the language is aimed—PL/I and Cobol, for example, allow long strings of characters for names in both their definitions *and* implementations to allow quantities in data processing problems to be specified without abbreviation.

Using BNF we may write, for example,

$$[6]$$
$$\text{<FORTRAN NAME>} ::= \text{<LETTER>|<FORTRAN NAME>}$$
$$\text{<LETTER>|<FORTRAN NAME><DIGIT>}$$

We note two features of this definition:

i) For the first time we have used the $[n]$ notation described in Section 2.3.2. It indicates that a Fortran name can consist of no more than six characters as stated in the preceding paragraph.

ii) The definition is *recursive,* which means that the right hand side of the definition also contains the thing being defined. In this case, the definition may be read: "A Fortran name is a letter or anything which is a Fortran name followed by a letter or anything which is a Fortran name followed by a digit (as long as the total number of characters is not more than six)." The first part of the definition embodies the restriction that the first character must be a letter.

Thus, the definition says that any string of 1 to 6 letters or digits with the first one a letter is a legal Fortran name. The concept of recursion is one of the most important in computer science, so the reader should be sure he understands the above definition; we shall discuss recursion in more detail and in a different context in Chapter 8.

Example 2.10

Which of the following are legal names in the four languages?

    A6428
    B2
    2Z4
    N-6
    Y21643
    P2Q 7
    R43228A

The first, second, and fifth are legal in all four languages. For the others:

> 2Z4 is illegal except in Cobol because the first character is a digit
>
> N-6 is illegal except in Cobol because of the hyphen
>
> P2Q 7 is illegal in PL/I and Cobol because of the space; in Fortran and Algol embedded blanks in names are ignored so that, for example, P2Q 7, P 2Q7, and P2Q7 would represent the same name; however, some implementations do have restrictions on embedded blanks
>
> R43228A is illegal in Fortran and Algol implementations which restrict the length of names to six characters

Embedded blanks are ignored not only in names but generally in Fortran and Algol.[†] Cobol and PL/I have more restrictive rules about blanks. This is discussed further in Section 6.2.1.

Constant words can be of two general kinds: *arithmetic* constants and *string* constants. The former generally conform to the reader's intuitive notion of numbers. Examples of arithmetic constants are:

i) *1* or *.5* as required in a computation
ii) *32.16* representing the acceleration due to gravity or *3.14159* representing π
iii) The *hourly wage* of a worker
iv) *Normal body temperature* (98.6°F)
v) The *number of times* a rate of interest is to be compounded in a year

Operationally, a constant name refers to a memory location whose contents will *not* change during the solution of a problem (see Section 4.1). We shall defer discussion of how arithmetic constants are stored in the memory of a computer to Section 3.2 and we shall postpone discussion of the syntax of numbers until Section 4.1.

String constants, as their name implies, are sequences of characters from the alphabet of the language, usually with little or no restriction on the allowable characters in the alphabet or on the number of characters in a string. Examples of string constants are:

i) JOHN DOE the name of an employee in a payroll
ii) 32000003010310000030010000400100, representing the 32 squares of a checkerboard position to be compared with the actual position in a game. Here 0

[†]This is true in Algol implementations which use a delimiter (e.g., a single quote) around words which appear in boldface in the publication language (e.g., **begin** becomes 'BEGIN'); if no such delimiter is used, there is usually a restriction on blanks in the publication language boldface words.

represents a blank square, 1 a white man, 2 a white king, 3 a black man, and 4 a black king with the order being from left to right and top to bottom. Therefore, the string above represents

	B		WK				
						B	
			W				B
W							
					B		
		W					
					BK		
		W					

Actually this "constant" would more likely be the *value* of a variable name which would change as the checkerboard position changed (see Section 4.3).

iii) H20, representing the chemical formula for water.

In a computer memory, a string constant would be the contents of *one or more* locations of memory whose contents do not change during the problem's solution (see also Section 3.1.5). The examples above and the reader's intuition will tell him that string constants find their main application in nonnumerical problems. We shall discuss the syntax of string constants in Section 4.2.

BIBLIOGRAPHIC NOTES

2.1   The basic references for the four languages we are referring to are American Standard Fortran (1966), USA Standard Cobol (1968), PL/I (1965), and Revised Report on the Algorithmic Language Algol 60 (1963). These are, however, quite formal presentations. There are many more readable accounts of Fortran including Dimitry and Mott (1966), Golden (1965), Ledley (1966), McCracken (1965), Organick (1966), and Stein and Munro (1966). Less formal descriptions of Algol are Andersen (1964), Baumann and Feliciano (1964), Dijkstra (1962), and McCracken (1962). Similar presentations of Cobol may be found in Ledley (1961) or McCracken (1963), and of PL/I in Pollack and

Sterling (1969) or Weinberg (1966). Sammet (1969) is the definitive general reference on all higher level languages developed up to 1968. Among the over 50 languages discussed by Sammet are substantial sections on the four languages treated in this book.

2.2   Unless and until the reader has some background in electronics he would be well advised not to delve further into the hardware design of computers. A good general reference in this area is Ledley (1960). In Chapter 9 we shall discuss further the logical design of computers and give some references for further reading then.

2.3-2.4   There are very few references on the formal structure of computer languages which are accessible to the beginning student. Two books which consider this subject are Iverson (1962) and Wegner (1968); the reader should probably not go to these books until he has read further in this one.

Bibliography

Andersen, C. (1964): *An Introduction to Algol 60,* Addison-Wesley Publishing Co., Inc., Reading, Massachusetts.

American Standard Fortran (1966): *Publication ASA X3.9* of the American Standards Association (now the American National Standards Institute), New York.

Baumann, R., and M. Feliciano (1964): *Introduction to Algol,* Prentice-Hall, Inc., Englewood Cliffs, New Jersey.

Dijkstra, E. W. (1962): *A Primer of Algol 60 Programming,* Academic Press, New York.

Dimitry, D., and T. Mott (1966): *Fortran IV Programming,* Holt, Rinehart and Winston, New York.

Golden, J. T. (1965): *Fortran IV Programming and Coding,* Prentice-Hall, Inc., Englewood Cliffs, New Jersey.

Iverson, K. E. (1962): *A Programming Language,* John Wiley & Sons, Inc., New York.

Ledley, R. S. (1960): *Digital Computer and Control Engineering,* McGraw-Hill Book Company, Inc., New York.

Ledley, R. S. (1966): *Fortran IV Programming,* McGraw-Hill Book Company, Inc., New York.

Ledley, R. S. (1962): *Programming and Utilizing Digital Computers,* McGraw-Hill Book Company, Inc., New York.

McCracken, D. D. (1962): *A Guide to Algol Programming,* John Wiley & Sons, Inc., New York.

McCracken, D. D. (1963): *A Guide to Cobol Programming,* John Wiley & Sons, Inc., New York.

McCracken, D. D. (1965): *A Guide to Fortran IV Programming*, John Wiley & Sons, Inc., New York.

Organick, E. I. (1966): *A Fortran IV Primer*, Addison-Wesley Publishing Company, Inc., Reading, Massachusetts.

PL/I: Language Specifications (1965), IBM Corporation Form C28-8201.

Pollack, S. V., and T. D. Sterling (1969): *A Guide to PL/I*, Holt, Rinehart & Winston, Inc., New York.

Revised Report on the Algorithmic Language Algol 60 (1963): *Communications of the Association for Computing Machinery*, vol. 6, pp. 1-17.

Sammet, J. E. (1969): *Programming Languages: History and Fundamentals*, Prentice-Hall Inc., Englewood Cliffs, New Jersey.

Stein, M. L., and W. D. Munro (1966): *A Fortran Introduction to Programming and Computers*, Academic Press, New York.

USA Standard Cobol (1968): *Publication USAS X3.23* of the United States of America Standards Institute (now the American National Standards Institute), New York.

Wegner, P. (1968): *Programming Languages, Information Structures, and Machine Organization*, McGraw-Hill Book Company, Inc., New York.

Weinberg, G. M. (1966): *PL/I Programming Primer*, McGraw-Hill Book Company, Inc., New York.

PROBLEMS

Section 2.3

1. What strings are generated by a language with alphabet a and b and the following productions?

$S \rightarrow aa$
$S \rightarrow bb$
$S \rightarrow aSa$
$S \rightarrow bSb$

2. What strings are generated by a language with alphabet 0,1,2,3,4,5,6,7,8,9 and . and productions

$S \rightarrow A.A$
$A \rightarrow \alpha$
$A \rightarrow A\alpha$

where α is any member of the alphabet except . and the first production is to be read "S is a string of the language if it has the form A followed by . followed by

A," and the last production is to be read "the construct (or string) A has the form A followed by a digit"?

3. a) Draw a flow chart corresponding to that of Example 2.2 for the grammar of Problem 1.

   b) Do the same for the grammar of Problem 2.

4. With computer language we *parse* strings just as we parse sentences in English. Parsing not only determines if a string belongs to a language (i.e., if its syntax is correct), but also results in a structrual description of the string by separating it into *syntactic categories* (i.e., noun phrases, etc. in English). A common parsing technique is to use a *tree structure.* Using the grammar of Example 2.1, a parse of the string *bbbaa* would look like

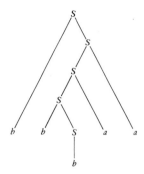

where each *node* of the tree corresponds to the left hand side of one of the productions of Example 2.1, and the node or nodes connected to it give the right hand side of this production (left to right when there are two connected nodes).

   a) Parse the string *bbaaaa* as above for the grammar of Example 2.1.

   b) Show that this grammar is ambiguous by displaying another parse for the string. (A grammar which allows more than one parse for a given string is said to be *ambiguous*).

5. Consider the grammar with alphabet *a, b,* and productions

   $S \rightarrow AB$
   $A \rightarrow a$
   $A \rightarrow AB$
   $B \rightarrow b$
   $B \rightarrow bB$

The symbols A and B are called *intermediate symbols* of the grammar.

a) What strings does this grammar generate?

b) Parse the string *abbb* as in Problem 4. How many different parses can you find? Can you state the general rule for the number of different parses for strings in this language?

Section 2.3.2

6. Rewrite the definition of FOUR LETTER WORD in Example 2.9 using the structures LETTER and TWO LETTER WORD, with the obvious definition of the latter, so that each possibility contains TWO LETTER WORD at least once.

7. For the BNF definition

$$[4]$$
$$<NONSENSE> ::= 5|4|. <NONSENSE>$$

list all possible strings for the structure NONSENSE.

8. a) Give a BNF definition of the string S of Example 2.1

b) Do the same for the strings of Problems 1, 2, and 5. You may use BNF definitions for intermediate quantities as well as S.

9. Give a BNF definition of the structure which consists of up to 5 alphabetic or numeric characters of which the first must be a digit and the last a letter.

Section 2.4

In the problems which follow, aim not at notational elegance in the boxes in the flow charts, but rather at logically correct statements in English.

10. Go to the nearest cookbook, find a reasonably complicated recipe, and draw a flow chart of the instructions. What corresponds to the inputs and outputs in the flow charts of Section 2.4? Does your flow chart have any decision boxes? Why? If the recipe consists of doing two things in parallel (e.g., making the crust and filling of a pie), have you arranged the flow chart properly from the computer point of view in the sense that function boxes (and START) have only one exit?

11. Draw a flow chart for the instructions on page 1 of the 1040 income tax form. (Assume all quantities to be inserted from later pages have already been completed.) Are these instructions an algorithm?

12. Can the following structures be part of a flow chart for a computer calculation?

a) A closed path (i.e., a sequence of arrows which come back to the point from where they started) without a decision box.

b) More than two remote connector boxes with the same number.

c) More than one STOP box.

13. Suppose you wish to have a computer play tick-tack-toe with a human opponent who communicates his moves to the computer via the input unit. Assume the human player goes first. Draw a flow chart which designates the computer's *first* move in response to the human's first move and which leaves a position in which the computer is assured of at least a draw. (Can you see that continuing this flow chart for the entire game is not easy?)

14. a) What, if any, obvious inefficiencies (i.e., parts that would lead to unnecessary manipulations) are there in the flow chart of Figure 2.10?

b) What is the maximum number of interchanges that must be performed using the algorithm of Example 2.6?

15. Correct Figure 2.11 to take into account the case $a=0$.

16. Suppose you are given two lists of alphabetic data, each in alphabetic order. Draw a flow chart for a program to *merge* these two lists into a third which will be in alphabetic order.

17. Describe the line intersection cases not shown in Figure 2.12, that is, the cases called Case 6 in Example 2.8.

18. Show how to calculate the coefficients a,b,c, and d in Box 4 of Figure 2.13 given the coordinates of points A, B, C, and D.

19. Use the algorithm described in Example 2.9 to generate by hand the first seven moves of the knight's tour whose start is shown in Figure 2.14.

20. Draw a flow chart which expands on Box 4 of Figure 2.15; that is, show in detail what has to be done to search for possible moves at a given point in the

tour while taking into account the moves that have previously been made on the tour.

21. Suppose you are given a position on a checkerboard. Draw a flow chart, the purpose of which is to indicate the next move you will make. Since it is unknown in general what the true best move in checkers is, your flow chart will be for a heuristic program. What you are really being asked to do is to decide what is important in the game of checkers and to draw a flow chart which asks reasonable questions aimed at coming up with a good move.

Section 2.5

22. For each of the four languages, indicate whether the following names are legal or illegal and why.

    a)   ABCDEF
    b)   ABC DE
    c)   R124–Z
    d)   2CEN
    e)   NC421R6

23. Write a nonrecursive BNF definition of FORTRAN NAME.

24. Write a BNF definition of COBOL NAME.

3

memory organization
and computer numbers

It is a capital mistake to theorize before one has data.

Sir Arthur Conan Doyle in *A Scandal in Bohemia*
from *The Adventures of Sherlock Holmes.*

As we mentioned in Chapter 1, the reader can write (and perhaps by this time has written) programs for a computer without knowing any detail about the logical structure and organization of computers. But it is one of the theses of this book—and if the reader has written some programs he may have realized it—that effective use of computers requires more than just a superficial feeling for the internal organization of a computer. This thesis is probably truer for scientific than for business applications, but it is relevant to both. In this chapter we shall consider those aspects of internal organization, namely the memory and how the computer manipulates numbers, which are of most importance to the P-O language user. We shall then use this discussion in the next chapter to consider some of the ways in which data can be structured inside a computer.

3.1 MEMORY ORGANIZATION

Our initial concern here is with the main memory (cf. Figure 2.3) of the computer. It is to this memory that the control unit looks for all instructions it will execute. The auxiliary memories may *store* instructions but, in order for them to be executed, they must first be transferred into the main memory.†

---

† One exception to this rule may occur in computers which have auxiliary magnetic core memories as mentioned in Section 2.2. In some of these computers, instructions can be executed directly from the auxiliary core storage.

All main computer memories have two common organizational features:

i) They are divided up into some number of subunits, each of which can store the same amount of information (e.g., the same number of digits).
ii) Each of these subunits has a number associated with it by which it can be located. This number is called an *address.*

The subunits mentioned in (i) are of one of three types, which result in three classifications of computer memory organization:

> *Digit* organization—in which each subunit has the capacity to store *one decimal digit.*
>
> *Character* organization—in which each subunit can store *one character* which may be thought of as being a member of the character set of one of the P-O languages we have been discussing; sometimes these subunits can store two decimal digits.
>
> *Word* organization—in which the contents of each subunit can be some fixed number of characters or digits; the use of "word" in this context must *not* be confused with its use in Section 2.5.1, although the contents of a memory word as used here will often be the *value* of a word as used in Section 2.5.1.

Digit organization is easily understood in terms familiar to the reader. The most common small scientific computer of the early 1960s (IBM 1620) had a memory with digit organization as indicated in Figure 3.1. Each small box in the figure has the capacity to store one decimal digit. The numbers associated with the boxes are their *addresses.* It should be understood that this diagram is purely schematic and bears no resemblance to physical implementation. Besides the 40,000 digit memory shown in the figure, this computer also could have been obtained with memories of 20,000, 60,000, 80,000, or 100,000 digits.

The reader is probably aware that most of the devices used in digital computers are *binary* devices; that is, they are always in one of two states. A transistor is either conducting or not; a magnetic core is magnetized in one of two directions; a magnetic tape is magnetized or not; many computer circuits are either on or off. How then can a computer store *decimal digits* when its internal hardware is made up of *binary* devices? Before we can answer this question and consider either character or word organization, we must first digress and introduce the binary number system and some related concepts.

We emphasize that the user of a P-O language need almost never concern himself directly with nondecimal arithmetic. The translation program (cf. Section 2.3.1) takes the user's numbers specified in decimal notation and converts them, if necessary, to the internal binary system of the computer. But, for many nonnumeric problems and even for some strictly numeric problems, it will be valuable for the user to *understand* binary numbers and some aspects of the internal binary organization of a computer even if he does not do much binary manipulation himself.

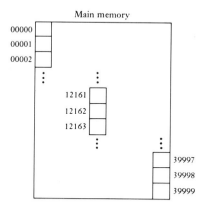

Figure 3.1 Digit-organized memory.

3.1.1 The Binary Number System

The key to understanding any number system other than the familiar decimal system is the recognition that the decimal numbers we see and write daily in *positional notation* are not true mathematical quantities but rather *symbolic representations* of true quantities. For example, 62.47 represents

$$6 \times 10^1 + 2 \times 10^0 + 4 \times 10^{-1} + 7 \times 10^{-2}$$
$$= 60 + 2 + .4 + .07$$

With this understanding the use of any *base* other than 10 becomes simple in principle if not in practice.

In the decimal system the base is 10 and there are ten symbols, 0, 1, . . . , 9. In the *binary system* the base is 2 and there are two symbols 0 and 1. Here, a number such as

1011.011

is a representation of

$$1 \times 2^3 + 0 \times 2^2 + 1 \times 2^1 + 1 \times 2^0 + 0 \times 2^{-1} + 1 \times 2^{-2} + 1 \times 2^{-3}$$

Hereafter, besides calling the 0s and 1s binary digits, we shall also use the common contraction *bits*. In the binary system the . in 1011.011 is called the *binary point.* To find the decimal equivalent of this number we perform the arithmetic indicated above to get

$$8 + 2 + 1 + .25 + .125 = 11.375$$

We shall consider below the general problem of conversion from one number system to another. But let us first consider the problem of performing arithmetic in the binary system.

The binary addition and multiplication tables are particularly simple:

Addition		
+	0	1
0	0	1
1	1	10

Multiplication		
x	0	1
0	0	0
1	0	1

Arithmetic in the binary system is precisely analogous to arithmetic in the decimal system but less familiar, particularly subtraction and division.

Example 3.1

Add 11001 to 10011.

Using the addition table we have

```
Carries      10011
             11001
            +10011
            101100
```

with the carries shown above. Each $1 + 1$ is 0 with a carry of 1 [and $1 + 1 + 1$ would be 1 with a carry of 1 (3 in decimal being 11 in binary)]. As a check on the above we may convert everything to decimal:

$$(11001)_2 = 1 \times 2^4 + 1 \times 2^3 + 1 = (25)_{10}$$
$$(10011)_2 = 1 \times 2^4 + 1 \times 2^1 + 1 = (19)_{10}$$
$$(101100)_2 = 1 \times 2^5 + 1 \times 2^3 + 1 \times 2^2 = (44)_{10}$$

The subscripts denote the base of the number system.

Example 3.2

Multiply 1101 by 1110.

Using the multiplication and the addition tables,

```
    1101
   x1110
   11010
   1101
  1101
 10110110
```

Again checking by conversion to decimal,

$(1101)_2 = (13)_{10}$
$(1110)_2 = (14)_{10}$
$(10110110)_2 = 1 \times 2^7 + 1 \times 2^5 + 1 \times 2^4 + 1 \times 2^2 + 1 \times 2$
$= (182)_{10}$

Example 3.3

Subtract 01101 from 11000.

We have

Borrowing

```
                10     1     1
          0     Ø     +0    +0    10
          X     X      0     0     0         24
        − 0     1      1     0     1        −13
        ─────────────────────────        ──────
          1     0      1     1              11
```

The difficult thing about binary subtraction is the borrowing which often must be from a number of places to the left of the one at which the subtraction is being performed.

Practice is the only short cut!

Example 3.4

Divide 11100 by 1001.

```
         11              3 1/9
1001⟌11100          9⟌28
    1001
    ────
    1010
    1001
    ────
       1
```

The reader should avoid doing binary arithmetic by conversion to decimal and back again. If he does a substantial amount of binary arithmetic, he will find it better to do it directly or to use the technique described in the next section.

3.1.2   Octal Numbers and Octal Arithmetic

The obvious disadvantage of using the binary system, besides the need to learn to do arithmetic in it, is the large number of characters it takes to write a given number. For example,

$$(1\ 418\ 372)_{10} = (1\ 01011\ 01001\ 00100\ 00100)_2$$

To overcome this disadvantage of the binary system it is convenient to take advantage of the very simple relationship between the binary and *octal* (*base 8*) system. To see this relationship we first write a number N in the binary system as

$$(N)_2 = b_n 2^n + \ldots + b_1 2 + b_0 + b_{-1} 2^{-1} + \ldots + b_{-m+1} 2^{-m+1} + b_{-m} 2^{-m}$$

$$= \sum_{i=-m}^{n} b_i 2^i \tag{3.1}$$

where each b_i is either 0 or 1.[†] Now let us assume that $n + 1$ and m are both multiples of 3, namely

$$n+1 = 3s$$
$$m = 3r \tag{3.2}$$

We can do this without any loss of generality for, if m and n in (3.1) are not multiples of 3, we just add zero leading and trailing coefficients (b_i's) until $n+1$. and m are multiples of 3. Using (3.2) we may rewrite (3.1) as

$$(N)_2 = \sum_{i=-m}^{n} b_i 2^i$$

$$= \sum_{i=-3r}^{3s-1} b_i 2^i = (b_{-3r} 2^{-3r} + b_{-3r+1} 2^{-3r+1} + b_{-3r+2} 2^{-3r+2})$$

$$+ \ldots + (b_{3s-3} 2^{3s-3} + b_{3s-2} 2^{3s-2} + b_{3s-1} 2^{3s-1})$$

$$= \sum_{j=-r}^{s-1} (b_{3j+2} 2^{3j+2} + b_{3j+1} 2^{3j+1} + b_{3j} 2^{3j}) \tag{3.3}$$

[†] The sigma notation Σ means that the quantity after the sigma sign is to be evaluated for each integral value of i between and including $-m$ and n and then the results of these evaluations are to be summed as above.

That the second line follows from the first can be seen as follows:

a) The number of terms in the first line is a multiple of 3 $(3r+3s)$—remember to count the term for $i=0$—with the powers of 2 ranging from $3s-1$ to $-3r$.

b) In the second line the number of values j takes on is $s-1+r+1=s+r$ but each term contains three coefficients and powers. Again the highest degree term is $3(s-1) + 2 = 3s-1$ and the lowest is $-3r$.

Now we rewrite (3.3) as

$$(N)_2 = \sum_{j=-r}^{s-1} (b_{3j+2} \cdot 2^2 + b_{3j+1} \cdot 2 + b_{3j}) 2^{3j}$$

$$= \sum_{j=-r}^{s-1} (b_{3j+2} \cdot 4 + b_{3j+1} \cdot 2 + b_{3j}) 8^j \qquad (3.4)$$

by factoring out the 2^{3j}. The quantity

$$c_j = b_{3j+2} \cdot 4 + b_{3j+1} \cdot 2 + b_{3j} \qquad (3.5)$$

can take on the values from 0 to 7 since each coefficient may be 0 or 1. The expression (3.5) is, therefore, a representation of a digit in the *octal* (*base 8*) system where the characters are 0,1,2,3,4,5,6,7. Thus, we may finally rewrite (3.4) as

$$(N)_8 = \sum_{j=-r}^{s-1} c_j 8^j = c_{-r} 8^{-r} + c_{-r+1} 8^{-r+1} + \dots + c_0$$

$$+ c_1 8 + \dots + c_{s-2} 8^{s-2} + c_{s-1} 8^{s-1} \qquad (3.6)$$

It follows from the development which led from (3.1) to (3.6) that, to convert a binary number to octal, it is only necessary to group the binary digits in threes starting from both sides of the binary point as in (3.5) and convert each of these to its octal equivalent. Conversely, to convert from octal to binary just take each octal digit and convert it to its binary equivalent.

Example 3.5

Convert the binary equivalent of $(1\ 418\ 372)_{10}$ to octal.

From the beginning of this section

$$(1\ 418\ 372)_{10}$$
$$= (101\ 011\ 010\ 010\ 010\ 000\ 100)_2$$
$$= (\ 5 \quad 3 \quad 2 \quad 2 \quad 2 \quad 0 \quad 4\ )_8$$

where the last line is found by dividing the binary number into triplets and writing the octal equivalent of each triplet (e.g., $(101)_2 = (5)_8$).

Example 3.6

Convert the octal number $(417.26)_8$ to binary.

In this case we expand each octal number into a binary triplet and obtain

4	1	7	·	2	6
100	001	111	·	010	110

Arithmetic in the octal system is more complex than that in the binary system but much less unwieldy because it does not involve so many digits. The octal addition and multiplication tables are:

Octal Addition

+	0	1	2	3	4	5	6	7
0	0	1	2	3	4	5	6	7
1	1	2	3	4	5	6	7	10
2	2	3	4	5	6	7	10	11
3	3	4	5	6	7	10	11	12
4	4	5	6	7	10	11	12	13
5	5	6	7	10	11	12	13	14
6	6	7	10	11	12	13	14	15
7	7	10	11	12	13	14	15	16

Octal Multiplication

x	0	1	2	3	4	5	6	7
0	0	0	0	0	0	0	0	0
1	0	1	2	3	4	5	6	7
2	0	2	4	6	10	12	14	16
3	0	3	6	11	14	17	22	25
4	0	4	10	14	20	24	30	34
5	0	5	12	17	24	31	36	43
6	0	6	14	22	30	36	44	52
7	0	7	16	25	34	43	52	61

Example 3.7

Perform the indicated calculations on the following octal numbers:

```
  632.12        7624.7         23.6
 +267.46       -5735.3        x34.2
 1121.60        1667.4         474
                              1170
                               732
                             1055.74
```

```
              13.1
      4.16 ⌐ 57.32
           41 6
           15 52
           14 52
            1 000
              416
              362
```

In the IBM 360 series of computers, *hexadecimal* (base 16) arithmetic plays an important role (see Section 3.2). As the reader should now be able to infer the conversion back and forth between binary, octal, and hexadecimal is straightforward and simple (Problem 8).

3.1.3 Conversion from One Base to Another

Converting numbers from binary to decimal is probably best done by writing the binary number as in equation (3.1) and doing the decimal arithmetic. This is best because decimal arithmetic is so easy for us. But, for converting decimal to binary and for the general problem of converting a number in one base to the equivalent number in another system, a more general technique is needed.

Suppose first we wish to convert an *integer* N expressed in a system with base (or, as it is sometimes called, *radix*) p to a system with radix q. That is, we want

$$(N)_p = \sum_{i=0}^{n} a_i p^i \rightarrow (N)_q = \sum_{i=0}^{m} b_i q^i \tag{3.7}$$

where each a_i is a known digit between 0 and $p-1$ (since the base is p) and we wish to find the b_i's where each b_i is between 0 and $q-1$.

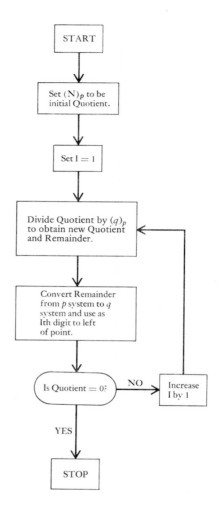

Figure 3.2   Base conversion of integers.

Now suppose we knew the b_i's. Then, with all arithmetic done in the q system, we could write

$$(N)_q/q = \sum_{i=1}^{m} b_i q^{i-1} + b_0/q \qquad\qquad (3.8)$$

Thus b_0 is the remainder if $(N)_q$ is divided by q. (If $q=10$ then we are in the decimal system and, for example, $647/10=64 + 7/10$ with $b_0 = 7$.) Therefore, if $(N)_p$ is divided by $(q)_p$ with all arithmetic done in the p system, the remainder will still be b_0 (Why?) but now b_0 will be in the p system. To proceed one step further let us divide the quotient in (3.8)—$\sum\limits_{i=1}^{m} b_i q^{i-1}$—by q again. In the q system the result is

$$(1/q) \sum_{i=1}^{m} b_i q^{i-1} = \sum_{i=2}^{m} b_i q^{i-2} + b_1/q$$

with the remainder now b_1. If the arithmetic were done in the p system the result would be $(b_1)_p$.

From the above we obtain, therefore, a general *algorithm* for converting $(N)_p$ to $(N)_q$ with all arithmetic in the p system:

Step 1: Divide $(N)_p$ by $(q)_p$. The remainder is the low order (least significant) digit of $(N)_q$ which must then be converted from the p to the q system [only if $q > p$ (Why?)].

Step 2: Repeat Step 1 until a zero quotient is obtained, using at each stage the quotient from the previous stage as dividend. The successive remainders are the successive digits of $(N)_q$ starting from the least significant end. Figure 3.2 expresses this algorithm in the flow chart form.

Example 3.8

Convert $(6753)_{10}$ to binary.

Performing all arithmetic in the decimal system, we have (with $p=10$, $q=2$, and $(q)_{10}=2$):

	Quotient	Remainder
6753/2	3376	1
3376/2	1688	0
1688/2	844	0
844/2	422	0
422/2	211	0
211/2	105	1
105/2	52	1
52/2	26	0
26/2	13	0
13/2	6	1
6/2	3	0
3/2	1	1
1/2	0	1

Therefore,

$$(6753)_{10} = (1\ 101\ 001\ 100\ 001)_2 = (15\ 141)_8$$

Example 3.9

Convert $(1\ 001\ 100)_2$ to decimal using the algorithm of this section rather than the method of Section 3.1.1.

We now perform all arithmetic in binary (with $p=2$, $q=10$, and $(q)_2 = 1010$):

	Quotient	Remainder
1001100/1010	111	$(110)_2 = (6)_{10}$
111/1010	0	$(111)_2 = (7)_{10}$

Therefore,

$$(1\ 001\ 100)_2 = (76)_{10}$$

The algorithm for converting *fractions* from one number system to another is quite analogous to the above but somewhat simpler. Let F be a fraction expressed in the p system. Then, as before, we want

$$(F)_p = \sum_{i=-n}^{-1} a_i\, p^i \quad \to \quad (F)_q = \sum_{i=-m}^{-1} b_i\, q^i \qquad (3.9)$$

If we multiply $(F)_q$ by q we obtain

$$(F)_q \cdot q = b_{-1} + \sum_{i=-m}^{-2} b_i\, q^{i+1} \qquad (3.10)$$

That is, the *integral part* of the product is b_{-1}. If we repeat this process using the remaining fractional part in (3.10) we obtain

$$\left(\sum_{i=-m}^{-2} b_i q^{i+1} \right) q = b_{-2} + \sum_{i=-m}^{-3} b_i\, q^{i+2} \qquad (3.11)$$

From this we induce the algorithm for converting $(F)_p$ to $(F)_q$ with all arithmetic done in the p system.

Step 1: Multiply $(F)_p$ by $(q)_p$. The integral part is the high order (most significant) digit of $(F)_q$ which must then be converted from the p to the q system (if $q > p$).

Step 2: Repeat Step 1 using as the multiplicand at each step the remaining fractional part from the previous step until a fractional part is zero or until as many digits as desired have been generated. The successive integral parts are the successive digits of $(F)_q$ starting from the most significant end.

Figure 3.3 contains a flow chart for this algorithm.

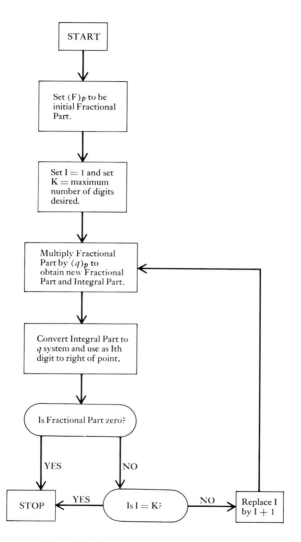

START

Set $(F)_p$ to be
initial Fractional
Part.

Set I = 1 and set
K = maximum
number of digits
desired.

Multiply Fractional
Part by $(q)_p$ to
obtain new Fractional
Part and Integral Part.

Convert Integral Part to
q system and use as Ith
digit to right of point.

Is Fractional Part zero?

YES   NO

STOP   ←—YES—   Is I = K?   —NO→   Replace I
by I + 1

Figure 3.3   Base conversion of fractions.

Example 3.10

Convert $(.31)_{10}$ to binary.

We have (with $p=10$, $q=2$, and $(q)_{10}=2$):

	Fractional Part	Integral Part
.31x2	.62	0
.62x2	.24	1
.24x2	.48	0
.48x2	.96	0
.96x2	.92	1
.92x2	.84	1

Therefore,

$$(.31)_{10} = (.010\ 011. . .)_2 = (.23. . .)_8$$

The reader should note that finite fractions in one system (i.e., fractions expressible with a finite number of digits) are generally non-terminating in other systems (i.e., as in the case of 1/3 decimal, there is no finite expansion).

Example 3.11

Convert $(.011)_2$ to decimal.

We have (with $p=2$, $q=10$, and $(q)_2 =1010$):

	Fractional Part	Integral Part
.011 x 1010	.110	$(11)_2 = (3)_{10}$
.110 x 1010	.100	$(111)_2 = (7)_{10}$
.100 x 1010	.000	$(101)_2 = (5)_{10}$

Therefore

$$(.011)_2 = (.375)_{10}$$

This is an example of the situation in which a terminating fraction in one system also terminates in the other. Since all negative powers of 2 have finite decimal expansions (Why?), all finite binary expansions have finite decimal expansions. Of course, the converse is not true.

Together the two algorithms of this section give the reader the ability to take a number in any system, separate it into integral and fractional parts and then convert it to any other system.

3.1.4 Binary–Decimal Codes

We return now to the question raised in Section 3.1 as to how a computer memory can store *digits* if the memory devices used are all *binary* devices. As the reader may have guessed, the answer to the question lies in using a number of binary devices as a logical group to represent a decimal digit. For example, the following table equates the first 10 digits in the binary and decimal systems.

Table 3.1   Binary–Decimal conversion

Binary	Decimal
0000	0
0001	1
0010	2
0011	3
0100	4
0101	5
0110	6
0111	7
1000	8
1001	9

From this table it is clear that the decimal digits 0 through 9 can each be represented by 4 binary digits. Thus by grouping four binary memory devices together we may, from a logical point of view, consider each of these groups of devices to store one decimal digit.[†] This is precisely what is done in *digit-organized memories* such as that depicted in Figure 3.1.

The correspondence between decimal digits and binary numbers in Table 3.1 is the one commonly used in digital computers with digit-organized memories. It represents a *coding* from decimal to binary and this particular coding is called *binary-coded* decimal or *BCD*. But it should be recognized that, since this coding is a purely logical matter which merely indicates the internal representation of a decimal digit by a group of binary devices, other binary-decimal codes are possible. The internal circuitry of the computer must simply be designed so that it recognizes just which decimal digit each binary group is supposed to represent and handles it accordingly.

[†] With 4 binary digits we may store 16 different combinations, so using only 10 of these represents a certain inefficiency in hardware utilization.

Other binary-decimal codes have at one time or another been used in digital computers. Two of these are:

i) *Excess -3 code* in which the correspondence is as follows:

Table 3.2   Excess–3 code

Binary	Decimal
0011	0
0100	1
0101	2
0110	3
0111	4
1000	5
1001	6
1010	7
1011	8
1100	9

In this code each decimal digit is represented by its BCD equivalent plus 3. Thus for example, 7 is represented by $(1010)_2 = (10)_{10}$. One advantage of this code is that, when the excess–3 equivalents of two decimal digits are added, their sum is 6 greater than the true sum in binary. Therefore, if the decimal sum is greater than 9, the binary sum is greater than $(15)_{10} = (1111)_2$. This means that if there should be a carry to the next higher addition stage, this will appear as a carry to a fifth binary digit.

Example 3.12

Consider the BCD and excess -3 sums of the decimal digits 4 and 6.

BCD	Excess -3
0100	0111
0110	1001
1010	10000

In the BCD case the need to carry a 1 to the next stage (suppose the 4 and 6 were part of the sum of 3$\underline{4}$ and 5$\underline{6}$) can only be determined by analyzing the four binary digits of the sum. However, in the excess–3 case, the 1 in the fifth position indicates immediately the need for a carry.

As the reader may have guessed, however, the advantage of excess–3 adduced above is offset by various disadvantages, one being that the correct excess–3 sum in the units position in the above example is not 0000 but 0011. This problem causes difficulties with all four arithmetic operations.

ii) *Biquinary code*, in which we have

Table 3.3   Biquinary code

Binary	Decimal
01 00001	0
01 00010	1
01 00100	2
01 01000	3
01 10000	4
10 00001	5
10 00010	6
10 00100	7
10 01000	8
10 10000	9

Here the first pair of binary digits indicates whether the digit is 0—4 or 5—9. The position of the 1 in the group of 5 binary digits indicates the remainder when the decimal digit is divided by 5. Although the biquinary system was used in the largest selling computer of the late 1950s (IBM 650) and allows easy *recognition* of which decimal digit is represented, its inefficient use of components (7 binary digits can express $2^7 = 128$ different combinations) and other drawbacks have resulted in its disuse.

3.1.5   Character- and Word-Organized Memories

We have indicated how digit-organized memories are in fact organized by grouping binary components together using some binary-decimal code. In Section 3.2 we shall further indicate how these digits are grouped together to represent data of various types. But first we must consider some details of character- and word-organized memories.

The organization of character-organized memories is an extension of the idea of grouping binary memory elements that we encountered in digit-organized memories. For example, in the IBM 1400 Series of computers the memory consists of some number of characters (1,400, 2,000, 4,000, 8,000, or 16,000), each of which consists of a grouping of six binary elements[†] which store characters according to the code in Table 3.4. Concerning the table:

[†] Actually there are 2 additional bits used for control and checking purposes (for a total of 8 within each character).

Table 3.4   1400 Series character codes

Character	Code						IBM 26 Keypunch card code
	B	A	8	4	2	1	
0	0	0	1	0	1	0	0
1	0	0	0	0	0	1	1
2	0	0	0	0	1	0	2
3	0	0	0	0	1	1	3
4	0	0	0	1	0	0	4
5	0	0	0	1	0	1	5
6	0	0	0	1	1	0	6
7	0	0	0	1	1	1	7
8	0	0	1	0	0	0	8
9	0	0	1	0	0	1	9
A	1	1	0	0	0	1	12−1
B	1	1	0	0	1	0	12−2
C	1	1	0	0	1	1	12−3
D	1	1	0	1	0	0	12−4
E	1	1	0	1	0	1	12−5
F	1	1	0	1	1	0	12−6
G	1	1	0	1	1	1	12−7
H	1	1	1	0	0	0	12−8
I	1	1	1	0	0	1	12−9
J	1	0	0	0	0	1	11−1
K	1	0	0	0	1	0	11−2
L	1	0	0	0	1	1	11−3
M	1	0	0	1	0	0	11−4
N	1	0	0	1	0	1	11−5
O	1	0	0	1	1	0	11−6
P	1	0	0	1	1	1	11−7
Q	1	0	1	0	0	0	11−8
R	1	0	1	0	0	1	11−9
S	0	1	0	0	1	0	0−2
T	0	1	0	0	1	1	0−3
U	0	1	0	1	0	0	0−4
V	0	1	0	1	0	1	0−5
W	0	1	0	1	1	0	0−6
X	0	1	0	1	1	1	0−7
Y	0	1	1	0	0	0	0−8

Table 3.4   1400 Series character codes (continued)

Character	Code B	A	8	4	2	1	IBM Keypunch card code
Z	0	1	1	0	0	1	0–9
blank	0	0	0	0	0	0	––––
# [=]	0	0	1	0	1	1	3–8
+	1	1	0	0	0	0	12
—	1	0	0	0	0	0	11
*	1	0	1	1	0	0	11–4–8
/	0	1	0	0	0	1	0–1
% [(]	0	1	1	1	0	0	0–4–8
¤ [)]	1	1	1	1	0	0	12–4–8
,	0	1	1	0	1	1	0–3–8
.	1	1	1	0	1	1	12–3–8
$	1	0	1	0	1	1	11–3–8
@ [']	0	0	1	1	0	0	4–8

1. The codes for the digits 1 through 9 are just the BCD codes of the previous section. The columns are headed 8,4,2,1 to indicate that these binary positions correspond to $2^3 = 8$, $2^2 = 4$, $2^1 = 2$, and $2^0 = 1$, respectively (e.g., 0101 has 1s in columns headed 4 and 1 and equals $(5)_{10}$). The code for zero has the binary equivalent of 10 since the all-zero code is reserved for the blank character. The entire code shown in Table 3.4 is often called BCD code for alphabetic and numeric (or *alphanumeric*, or sometimes, *alphameric*) characters.

2. The special characters in the table differ from those in the 48-character set of Section 2.4 by having =()' replaced by # % ¤ @. This reflects nothing more than a change in the *keyboard* characters of the 26 keypunch. That is, the keys of the 26 keypunch are labeled with some set of 48 characters. At installations where most of the use of the 26 is for punching programs in P-O languages, the 48 characters are normally those of Section 2.5. At installations where the cards are used mainly with standard tabulating equipment (sorters, collators, reproducers, accounting machines), the =()' keys are commonly labeled instead with # % ¤ @. Since 1400 series computers generally replaced tabulating installations, the internal code assumes the usage of the tabulating keyboard. We emphasize that what is punched on the card does *not* depend on the label on the key.

3. Table 3.4 also lists the IBM 26 keypunch card code. Referring back to Figure 2.6 we note that an IBM card contains 80 *columns* which may be punched in one or more of 12 *rows*, 10 corresponding to the printed digits 0 through 9 and 2 rows above the digits, the upper of which is called the 12 (or Y) row and the lower the 11 (or X) row. A comparison of Figure 2.6 and the last column of Table 3.4 shows that this column indicates which rows are punched for each of

the 48 characters. The choice of the 6-*bit* code in Table 3.4 for the alphabetic characters is thus easily seen to be that the last 4 bits are the BCD equivalent of the second punch and the first 2 are *11* for a 12 punch, *10* for an 11, and *01* for a 0 first punch (e.g., M has a code 10 0100 and is denoted by an 11 and a 4 punch). For the special characters, the code for the first two bits is the same and the code for the last four is the binary equivalent of the second punch or the *sum* of the second and third punches (e.g., * has $(1100)_2 = (12)_{10} = 4+8$ as its last four bits).

4. Six bits are required for the code since with five only 2^5 or 32 different combinations would be possible. Of the 16 ($=2^6-48$) combinations not shown in Table 3.4, some are unused and some have special meanings in 1400 series computers.

As in the digit-organized memory of Figure 3.1, each character in the 1400 series memory has an address (e.g., 0000 to 3999 for the 4,000-character memory).

In computers with character-organized memories the nonnumeric symbols can be manipulated directly since there is a definite physical representation for each character. In digit-organized memories nonnumeric symbols must first be coded using more than one memory location (e.g., the letter A might be coded into 40 in two successive digits). In digit-organized memories and in character-organized memories such as the one discussed above, *numbers* are formed by taking sequences of digits in the memory. For example, the locations 12161-12163 might contain a 3-digit number. The computer recognizes the beginning of a number by the use of an additional binary memory element associated with each digit or character. When this element stores a 1 there is said to be a *word mark* or *flag*. When the computer refers to a number, it does so by giving the *address* of the low order position (least significant digit) of the number. Thus the address plus the word mark or flag defines the number. In the example above the word mark would be at 12161 and the address of the number would be 12163. The *sign* of a number is typically indicated by some combination of the A and B bits in a character-organized memory or by the presence or absence of the flag bit in a digit-organized memory. In either case the units or addressed position of the number is used for the sign indication. Each number in these memories is said to be a *word*. Since the numbers can vary in length, computers with character- or digit-organized memories as described above are called *variable word length computers* (cf. our discussion below of word-organized memories).

The most common computer today with a character-organized memory is the IBM 360. The memory organization of this computer differs in some significant ways from that described above. Each character consists of 8 bits instead of 6.

The major reason for this is the desire to represent a character set larger than 64 including, among other additional characters, codes for the 26 lower case as well as upper case letters. Among other things, this permits more flexible and readable printed output. Since the expanded set of characters will still be no greater than $128=2^7$, 7 bits would have been sufficient but there is an additional reason for using 8 bits. This is that the 8-bit character, which is called a *byte*, can be divided into two 4-bit halves, each of which can store a BCD digit. Table 3.5 indicates for the 10 digits 0 through 9 what the contents of a byte are if

i) each digit is just an 8-bit character like any other character.

ii) the byte contains two BCD characters each representing the same digit.

EBCDIC stands for Extended Binary-Coded-Decimal Interchange Code; the reader will note that the last 4 bits of this code for digits are just the usual BCD code.

Table 3.5   Byte codes for digits

Digit	EBCDIC	Two BCD
0	1111 0000	0000 0000
1	1111 0001	0001 0001
2	1111 0010	0010 0010
3	1111 0011	0011 0011
4	1111 0100	0100 0100
5	1111 0101	0101 0101
6	1111 0110	0110 0110
7	1111 0111	0111 0111
8	1111 1000	1000 1000
9	1111 1001	1001 1001

Allowing each byte to hold two BCD digits permits decimal arithmetic to be done directly on variable length decimal numbers. This is often a convenience, particularly in business data processing problems. But the price of this convenience is loss of speed since the internal circuitry of computers can manipulate pure binary numbers more rapidly than BCD numbers. Therefore, for scientific calculations which require large amounts of arithmetic, 360 computers have a faster mode of arithmetic in which 4 contiguous bytes form a single 32-bit *word* or 8 contiguous bytes form a 64-bit *double word*.[†] We shall

---

[†] Since a double word can hold 8 characters in its 8 bytes, Fortran names on the 360 are allowed to have up to 8 characters (see Section 2.5.1 and Panel 2.1).

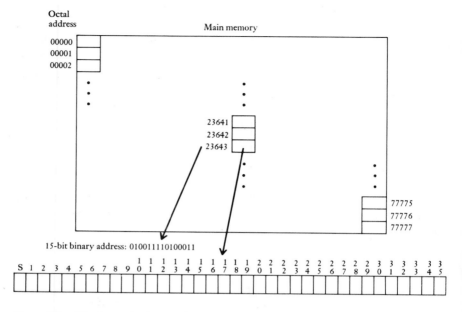

Figure 3.4   Word-organized memories.

discuss in Section 3.2 the ways in which these words are interpreted by the computer as numbers. Here we only introduce this idea as a bridge to discussing word-organized memories.

Word-organized memories are always purely binary internally. The addressable entities in the memory, which are called *words*, each have the capacity to store a fixed number of bits, most commonly 36 (IBM 7000 series) or 60 (CDC [†] 6000 series). The number of words in the memory is almost always a power of 2 because the computer uses as the address of a memory location some fixed number of bits (e.g., if 15 bits are used to represent the address, the possible addresses are 0 to $2^{15} - 1 = (32767)_{10}$ and the number of words is 2^{15}). Figure 3.4 schematically indicates word organization in the case where each word contains 36 bits and addresses are 15 bits. Addresses in the figure are given in octal for convenience. The 36 bits are labeled S for *sign* and 1 to 35 for reasons which will become clear in the next section.

Characters can also be stored in word-organized memories by dividing each word into some number of characters. For example, a 36-bit word can store six 6-bit characters and a 60-bit word can store ten 6-bit characters. Table 3.6 gives

---

[†] Control Data Corporation

the 6-bit codes for the 48-character set as used in most IBM 7000 series computers together with the corresponding 8-bit codes used in IBM 360 computers.[†] The reader will note that the last 4 bits are the same for 7000 and 360 codes except for the five characters − =+()'. The reason for this is that, on the IBM 29 keypunch (which is the one normally used at 360 installations), the codes for these five characters are not as shown in Table 3.4 but rather are, respectively, 6−8, 12−6−8, 12−5−8, 11−5−8, and 5−8. The rule stated under (3.) above in the discussion of Table 3.4 will be seen to hold for these characters on the 360.

We have thus far ignored the manner in which *instructions* rather than numbers are stored in the various memories. We note that:

1. In digit- and character-organized memories instructions are stored in a contiguous sequence of digits or characters and have a fixed length and format or, in some cases, a few fixed lengths and formats. They are addressed by the first (high order) character in the instruction.

2. In word-organized memories there is usually one instruction per word although in CDC 6000 series computers with 60-bit words the instructions are either 15 or 30 bits in length and a word, therefore, can contain 1, 2, 3, or 4 instructions.

As a final word we note that magnetic disk and drum memories and data cell and auxiliary core memories may be thought of as being organized in most computers like the main memory. Magnetic tape, however, is always organized on a digit or character basis and, if the memory is word-organized, characters must be formed into words in transfer from tape to main memory and vice versa for main memory to tape. We shall consider these matters in more detail in Chapter 10.

3.2   COMPUTER NUMBERS

From the previous section it follows naturally that a number in a computer can be either:

i) A variable number of decimal digits in a digit- or character-organized memory or

ii) A binary number consisting of some number of adjacent characters in a character-organized memory or

iii) The binary contents of a word or words in a word-organized memory.

[†] Another 8-bit code which the reader will likely encounter is the ASCII (for American Standard Code for Information Interchange) code which differs significantly from EBCDIC.

Table 3.6   7000 series and 360 series character codes

Character	7000 series code	360 series code (EBCDIC)
0	000000	1111 0000
1	000001	1111 0001
2	000010	1111 0010
3	000011	1111 0011
4	000100	1111 0100
5	000101	1111 0101
6	000110	1111 0110
7	000111	1111 0111
8	001000	1111 1000
9	001001	1111 1001
A	010001	1100 0001
B	010010	1100 0010
C	010011	1100 0011
D	010100	1100 0100
E	010101	1100 0101
F	010110	1100 0110
G	010111	1100 0111
H	011000	1100 1000
I	011001	1100 1001
J	100001	1101 0001
K	100010	1101 0010
L	100011	1101 0011
M	100100	1101 0100
N	100101	1101 0101
O	100110	1101 0110
P	100111	1101 0111
Q	101000	1101 1000
R	101001	1101 1001
S	110010	1110 0010
T	110011	1110 0011
U	110100	1110 0100
V	110101	1110 0101
W	110110	1110 0110
X	110111	1110 0111
Y	111000	1110 1000
Z	111001	1110 1001
blank	110000	0100 0000

Table 3.6 7000 series and 360 series character codes (continued)

Character	7000 series code	360 series code (EBCDIC)
=	001011	0111 1110
+	010000	0100 1110
−	100000	0110 0000
*	101100	0101 1100
/	110001	0110 0001
(	111100	0100 1101
)	011100	0101 1101
,	111011	0110 1011
.	011011	0100 1011
$	101011	0101 1011
'	001100	0111 1101

In this section we shall consider in some detail how these numbers are interpreted by the computer, that is, what the computer takes to be the *semantics* (or *meaning*) of a string of decimal or binary digits.

We mentioned in the previous section how the sign of a number was indicated, but what of the decimal point? Are all numbers in computers integers? If not, where is the binary or decimal point or how is it specified? Virtually all computers now allow and can interpret two kinds of numbers in their memories. They are *fixed-point* and *floating-point* numbers, used, respectively, for integer and real quantities. These have their analogs in P-O languages as integer and real names and integer and real constants (see Section 4.1).

A fixed-point number in a computer is one for which the computer always assumes the decimal or binary point is at the same place in all numbers. This place is either at the left-hand end of the number (all numbers considered to be less than 1 in magnitude) or at the right-hand end (all numbers treated as integers). For convenience we shall assume the latter but what we shall say is equally true in either case.

Example 3.13

What meaning is assigned by the computer to the following fixed-point numbers?

i) 483$\overline{2}$ in a digit-organized memory

ii) 100000000100000001000010000000000111 as the contents of a 36-bit word in a word-organized memory

In the first case it is assumed that the 4 is the leading digit of the number and is so marked by a flag or word mark. The bar over the 2 is the standard notation for indicating the presence of the flag or code for a minus sign. Thus, with the decimal point assumed to be at the right-hand end, this number is −4832.

In the second case, as indicated in Figure 3.4, the first bit indicates the sign. In all binary computers (i.e., computers which deal directly with binary numbers internally), 0 represents a plus sign and 1 a minus sign. This 36-bit integer is

$$-(00000\ 000100\ 000001\ 000010\ 000000\ 000111)_2 = -(67379207)_{10}$$

But all the numbers we deal with are not integers or fractions less than one. In doing arithmetic on computers there are two ways to take care of this problem. The first is that, while the computer does all its arithmetic assuming the decimal or binary point is in a fixed position, the programmer can keep track of where the point really is and can, therefore, have arithmetic performed on any kind of numbers. Such arithmetic is called *fixed-point*, that is, the decimal or binary point is fixed in the computer but the user remembers where the true one is.

Example 3.14

How would the following arithmetic operations be done in fixed-point arithmetic?

   i) Addition of $483\overline{2}$ and 2241 when the numbers are really supposed to be −48.32 and 22.41

   ii) Addition of the same two numbers when they are supposed to be −48.32 and 224.1

   iii) Multiplication of these two numbers followed by addition of 1531 when the numbers are supposed to be −48.32, 224.1, and 15.31

Answers:

   i) The computer will add these numbers as if they are −4832 and +2241, obtaining −2591. Since the right answer is −25.91, the actual location of the decimal point causes no difficulties.

   ii) If the numbers were added as they are the result would be −2591 as above, although the correct arithmetic result is +175.78. The error results because the (invisible) decimal points in the computer are not lined up

$$\downarrow$$
$$483\overline{2}$$
$$2241$$
$$\uparrow$$

when the addition is done. To overcome this problem one of the numbers must be *shifted* relative to the other. If 2241 is shifted one position in memory so that it now occupies five positions as 22410 with the word mark at the left-hand end, and if the word mark on the 4832 is moved one digit to the left to a position which we assume to hold a zero, then, addressing the two numbers by their right-hand digits, the result is the sum of

$$\begin{array}{c} \downarrow \\ 0483\overline{2} \\ 22410 \\ \uparrow \end{array}$$

with the decimal points lined up so that the result is 17578 correctly.

iii) Multiplication of two 4-digit numbers produces in general and 8-digit product ($-48.32 \times 224.1 = -10828.512$). To add 15.31 to this number we could line up the decimal points by shifting 1531 one to the left to get 15310, and then add it to 10828512 to get 10813202 which is correct. Generally, the lengths of the two operands do not have to be the same with digit-organized memories, if only the first operand is at least as long as the second.

The reader has probably concluded from this example that, in any lengthy calculation, keeping track of the decimal or binary points (a process called *scaling*) would be very tedious. Indeed, scaling is so tedious that it was the bane of the existence of all programmers in the early days of digital computers. Another difficulty with fixed-point numbers, which is barely hinted at by the example above, is the problem that arises in dealing with numbers of very disparate magnitudes. For example, in a 36-bit word binary computer (sign and 35 bits), if you wish to add a binary number whose decimal equivalent is 10^8 to another whose decimal equivalent is 10^{-4}, you cannot do it in fixed-point arithmetic because, no matter where the imaginary scaled binary point is assumed, two numbers can never differ in magnitude by more than $2^{35} \approx 3.9 \times 10^{10}$ (Problem 18). As a result of these scaling and magnitude problems, *floating-point arithmetic* was developed as the second and automatic way of handling normal decimal numbers.

A floating-point number, like a fixed-point number, is a sequence of contiguous digits or bits in the memory of the computer. But it is interpreted by the computer to have two distinct parts, one called the *exponent* part E and the other the fractional part or, by analogy with logarithmic terminology, the *mantissa* part M. The computer takes the value of the number to be

$$M \times 2^E \text{ or } M \times 10^E$$

depending upon whether the internal representation is binary or decimal, respectively.

Example 3.15

Express 46.5 as a floating-point number.

First answer (decimal computer): In a digit- or character-organized memory, although floating-point as well as fixed-point numbers have variable length, the exponent part of the floating-point number is always fixed in length, usually at 2 digits. A 10-digit floating-point representation of 46.5 with a 2-digit exponent might be

| 02 46500000 |

which would be interpreted with E = 2 and M = .465 as .465 x 10^2. Note that we have assumed the decimal point is at the *left-hand* end of the *mantissa*; this is a convention observed in almost all computers.

To represent $-.465$ x 10^2 we would add a flag as with fixed-point numbers, namely

| 02 46500000̄ |

But how would $-.465$ x 10^{-2} be represented? One possibility is

| 0̄2 46500000̄ |

in which a flag on the least significant digit of the exponent indicates it is negative. Another way of indicating negative exponents is discussed below.

From the above discussion there is no reason why 46.5 could not also be expressed as

| 03 04650000 | or | 05 00046500 |

as well as other ways (Problem 20). In most computers, however, floating-point numbers are required to be *normalized*, which means the first digit to the right of the decimal or binary point must be nonzero unless the mantissa is identically zero. Both the alternate representations of 46.5 above are called *unnormalized* numbers. Note that for a computer with 2 digits for the exponent and negative exponents denoted as above, normalized nonzero numbers in the range from

$$.99999999 \text{ x } 10^{99} \text{ to } .10000000 \text{ x } 10^{-99} = 10^{-100}$$

can be represented . (Why?)

Second answer (binary computer): Consider the case of a computer with a 36-bit word. In such a computer, part of the word is devoted to the mantissa and part to the exponent, commonly as follows for 46.5 = .7265625 x 2^6:

```
S|1        8|9                35
|0|10000110|101110100 ........... 0|
   Exponent        Mantissa
```

Here the mantissa is

$$(.101110100)_2 = (.7265625)_{10}$$

with the sign bit denoting a plus sign. Since there is no second sign bit to indicate a negative exponent, a different technique must be used than that discussed for decimal computers above. Since the exponent has 8 bits the range of numbers expressible is from 0 to

$$(11111111)_2 = (255)_{10} = (377)_8$$

Therefore, if we arbitrarily assign

$$(10000000)_2 = (128)_{10} = (200)_8$$

to correspond to a zero exponent (and, of course, design the computer circuitry to interpret it this way), then the range of exponents is from

$$-128: \quad (00000000)_2 = (0)_{10} = 128-128$$
to $\quad +127: \quad (11111111)_2 = (255)_{10} = 128+127$

This notation is called *excess—128* (cf. excess—3 in Section 3.1.4). Therefore, the exponent part of the word above

$$(10000110)_2 = (134)_{10}$$

denotes an exponent of

$$(6)_{10} = 134-128$$

and the floating-point number is

$$.7265625 \times 2^6 = 46.5$$

Assuming as above that floating-point numbers must be normalized, with an 8-bit exponent and 27-bit mantissa, nonzero numbers in the range

$$(.777777777)_8 \times 2^{(177)_8} \approx 10^{38}$$
to $\quad (.400000000)_8 \times 2^{-(200)_8} \approx 10^{-38}$

can be represented (Problem 22).

Almost all current computers have in their instruction repertoire separate instructions for doing arithmetic on floating- as well as fixed-point numbers. In performing floating-point arithmetic the computer handles the placement of the decimal or binary point automatically.

Example 3.16

Let A = $\boxed{\text{02 46500000}}$ and B = $\boxed{\text{01 93000000}}$

represent 46.5 and 9.3 as floating-point numbers in a decimal computer. What is the result of the four arithmetic operations A+B, A−B, AxB, and A÷B?

i) A+B = 55.8, which is expressed as

$\boxed{\text{02 55800000}}$

Similarly, A−B=37.2, expressed as

$\boxed{\text{02 37200000}}$

In both cases the computer notices the difference in exponents and adjusts for this internally before adding or subtracting.

ii) AxB = 432.45, which is expressed as

$\boxed{\text{03 43245000}}$

Here the mantissas are multiplied and the exponents are added; if necessary the product of the mantissas is normalized and the exponent adjusted (Problem 23).

iii) A÷B = 5.0, which is expressed as

$\boxed{\text{01 50000000}}$

The mantissas are divided, the exponents subtracted and normalization performed if necessary (Problem 23).

One additional type of floating-point number which should be mentioned is that which exists in IBM 360 computers which are base 16 (hexadecimal) machines. Here the mantissa is a 24-bit binary fraction and the exponent is a 7-bit excess−$(100)_8$ binary number. However, the number is interpreted as

$$M \times 16^{E-(64)_{10}}$$

Indeed, the mantissa should be interpreted as 6 hexadecimal, not 24 binary digits. Normalization on the 360 is not binary but rather hexadecimal normalization. Hence, a normalized floating-point number is one whose first hexadecimal digit (i.e., one of the first four binary digits) is nonzero.

Since the wide range of values expressible in floating-point numbers takes care of the magnitude problem with fixed-point arithmetic and scaling is not required at all in floating-point arithmetic, floating-point numbers are used in all but the simplest calculations on almost all computers. In scientific calculations, fixed-point arithmetic is used only when quantities are naturally integers. In business data processing calculations, however, the arithmetic performed is usually quite simple and scaling is not a problem. Therefore, fixed-point arithmetic is often used because it is somewhat faster than floating-point arithmetic.

3.2.1 Overflow and Underflow

In both fixed- and floating-point calculations the results of arithmetic operations may not be expressible in the form desired. When this happens the result is called *overflow* or *underflow*, the latter occurring only in floating-point calculations. We shall define both terms by giving specific examples.

Fixed-point overflow occurs whenever the result of the two arithmetic operations is too large in magnitude (overflow) to fit in the same amount of memory space as the operands. When variable length numbers are allowed, then the result is said to overflow if it requires more memory space than the longest operand.

Addition and subtraction: Let the following 5-digit numbers be stored in a digit-organized memory:

46231 and 68432

with the word marks at the left-hand digits. The correct sum of these two integers is 114663, but since this contains 6 digits there is an overflow. Most computers handle this by dropping the left-hand digit, storing 14663 as the sum, and giving the user some indication of the error (in P-O languages, usually a printed message).

In a 36-bit word computer let the following numbers be in two words

$$(0110.........0)_2 = (2^{34} + 2^{33})_{10}$$
$$(1011.........0)_2 = -(2^{33} + 2^{32})_{10}$$

The difference of these two numbers is

$$(2^{34} + 2^{33})_{10} + (2^{33} + 2^{32})_{10} = (2^{35} + 2^{32})_{10}$$
$$= (10010......(30 \text{ zeros}).........0)_2$$

That is, the integer *without* the sign contains 36 (not 35) bits and again there is an overflow. On some computers the 36th bit would be thrown away while on others it would replace the sign bit; in either case the user would be given an indication of the error.

Multiplication and division: For convenience let us only consider factors of equal length. All computers provide in their arithmetic units the ability to form a $2n$-bit (or digit) product from two n-bit (or digit) factors. Since the product of two integers of length n can never be more than $2n$, overflow cannot occur in fixed-point multiplication. In division of two integers, provision is always made to use a dividend of length $2n$ and a divisor of length n. Since the quotient of such a division can be of length greater than n, an overflow, called a divide overflow, can occur.

Example 3.17

Consider the division of the following two 36-bit integers

Dividend: 001100..................0
Divisor: 001000..................0

The first number is $2^{33} + 2^{32}$ and the second is 2^{33}. Before dividing the computer would first expand the dividend from 35 bits plus sign to 70 bits plus sign, so that the effective dividend would be $2^{68} + 2^{67}$. Therefore, the quotient is $2^{35} + 2^{34}$, which cannot fit in one 36-bit word with sign so that a divide overflow occurs.

Floating-point overflow occurs when the result of an arithmetic operation is a number whose exponent is larger than the largest allowable exponent. *Floating-point underflow* occurs when the exponent is smaller than the smallest allowable. Either can occur with any of the four arithmetic operations as the following examples indicate. For convenience we assume that the floating-point numbers are 10-decimal-digit numbers with 2-digit exponents having a range from -99 to $+99$ and 8-digit mantissas.

Addition and subtraction:

$$Overflow \quad \boxed{99\ 50000000} + \boxed{99\ 60000000}$$
$$.5 \times 10^{99} + .6 \times 10^{99} = 1.1 \times 10^{99} = .11 \times 10^{100}$$
$$Underflow \quad \boxed{\overline{99}\ 50000000} - \boxed{\overline{99}\ 53000000}$$
$$.5 \times 10^{-99} - .53 \times 10^{-99} = -.03 \times 10^{-99} = -.3 \times 10^{-100}$$

If all numbers are normalized this is an underflow; otherwise $-.03 \times 10^{-99}$ can be expressed as

$$\boxed{\overline{99}\ 03000000}$$

Multiplication:

Overflow $\boxed{57\ 20000000} \times \boxed{62\ 33000000}$

$(.2 \times 10^{57}) \times (.33 \times 10^{62}) = .066 \times 10^{119} = .66 \times 10^{118}$

Underflow $\boxed{5\overline{7}\ 20000000} \times \boxed{6\overline{2}\ 33000000}$

$(.2 \times 10^{-57}) \times (.33 \times 10^{-62}) = .66 \times 10^{-120}$

Division:

Overflow $\boxed{44\ 50000000} \div \boxed{6\overline{0}\ 25000000}$

$.5 \times 10^{44} \div .25 \times 10^{-60} = 2.0 \times 10^{104} = .2 \times 10^{105}$

Underflow $\boxed{6\overline{0}\ 25000000} \div \boxed{44\ 50000000}$

$.25 \times 10^{-60} \div .5 \times 10^{44} = .5 \times 10^{-104}$

On most computers the result of an operation which overflows is the largest number expressible by the machine ($\boxed{99\ 9999999}$ in the examples above) and an indication to the user. Similarly, underflow usually results in a zero result (Why is this reasonable?) and an indication to the user.

3.2.2 Negative Numbers and Complements

Implicit in the previous discussion of computer numbers has been the assumption that negative numbers are stored with a sign and an absolute value as we normally write them. This assumption is correct for the mantissas of floating-point numbers but it is not always true for fixed-point numbers, particularly binary numbers. For reasons connected with circuit economy and efficiency, fixed-point negative numbers in binary computers are often stored in *complement* form.

Complements are of two types. The *ones complement* of a binary number is the result of changing each zero to one and one to zero. The corresponding decimal concept is the *nines complement* in which each digit is replaced by its difference when subtracted from nine.

The *twos complement* of a binary number may be defined as the ones complement plus a one added in the least significant place. Correspondingly, the *tens complement* of a decimal number is the nines complement plus one added in the least significant place. Either the twos or tens complements of a number may be alternatively defined as the difference when the number is subtracted from the number 1000---0 in the appropriate number system, where the *1* is one place to the left of the most significant digit of the number being complemented. This is illustrated in the following example.

Example 3.18

Show:
  a) the ones and twos complements of 10011011, and
  b) the nines and tens complements of 684317

a) Ones complement:

  $10011011 \rightarrow 01100100$

Twos complement:

01100100	or	100000000
+1		−10011011
01100101		01100101

b) Nines complement:

  $684317 \rightarrow 315682$

Tens complement:

315682	or	1000000
+1		−684317
315683		315683

There are binary computers using each of the three possible forms of negative numbers: sign and absolute value, ones complement, and twos complement. For convenience we shall use the sign and absolute value form throughout this book.

3.2.3 Roundoff

We have pointed out that the user of a P-O language seldom, if ever, has to worry about the internal computer representation of the decimal numbers with which he deals. Indeed, many users of such languages have little or no knowledge of much of the material presented thus far in this chapter, although it is our belief that this is generally unwise. When the user of a P-O language writes a decimal number on a computer which is decimal internally, he can be sure, except for some very minor exceptions which we shall not discuss here, that the internal representation of his number will be precisely the same as its external representation on a programming form or punched card. But what, if any, pitfalls are there for the user whose external decimal numbers will be converted to binary internally?

We noted in Section 3.1.3 that, in general, finite decimal fractions do not have finite binary expansions. Thus, for example

$$(9.7)_{10} = (1001.1\ 0110\ 0110\ 0110\ 0110.\ .\ .)_2$$

Therefore, it is certain that a decimal 9.7 in a program will not appear inside a binary computer as an exact binary equivalent of 9.7. Part of the translation process discussed in Section 2.3.1 consists, on a binary computer, of converting all decimal numbers to binary numbers using an appropriate combination of the algorithms of Section 3.1.3.[†]

Example 3.19

How would $(9.7)_{10}$ be converted to a binary floating-point number in a 36-bit word computer with an 8-bit excess—$(200)_8$ exponent and a 27-bit mantissa?

Step 1: $(9)_{10}$ would be converted to $(1001)_2$. Since the mantissa must be less than 1, we must express 1001 as $.1001 \times 2^4$. Thus, the true exponent is 4 and the machine exponent is $(204)_8$.

Step 2: Since the integer part required 4 bits, there are 23 left for the fractional part of the original number. .7 would be converted to 1 0110 0110 0110 0110 0110 011. Then these *24* bits would be rounded to 23 by adding 1 in the least significant place to obtain

1 0110 0110 0110 0110 0110 10

The final result is then

0 10000100 10011 0110 0110 0110 0110 0110 10

Because of the rounding, this number differs from $(9.7)_{10}$ by no more than 1/2 in the least significant place. Thus, if the above number were converted back to decimal, the result would differ from 9.7 by no more than

$$2^{-28} * 2^4 = 2^{-24}.$$

The difference of up to 2^{-24} between the external value 9.7 and its internal representation in binary, which results, in effect, when the infinite binary expansion of 9.7 is rounded as described above, is called *roundoff error*. Occasionally, in a poor translation program the conversion from decimal to binary will be *truncated* after enough bits to fill the computer word have been generated.

[†] On IBM 360 computers decimal numbers may be converted directly to binary by a machine language instruction.

Clearly this technique leads to greater errors on the average than rounding (Problem 32). [†]

One surprising result of the error in decimal to binary conversion is that different external decimal numbers have the same internal representation even when we would not expect so. For example, even though

$$2^{27} = 134,217,728 > 10^8$$

so that there are more 27-bit binary combinations than 8-digit decimal combinations, we cannot express all 8-digit decimal numbers with unique 27-bit binary mantissas.

Consider the 10^7 numbers

$$9,000,000.0,\ 9,000,000.1\ ,...,\ 9,999,999.9$$

The integer part of these numbers when converted to binary requires 24 bits since

$$2^{23} = 8,388,608 < 9,000,000$$

Therefore, there are only 3 bits or eight combinations left for the ten fractional parts .0,.1,. . .,.9, so that there are only 8,000,000 different binary combinations to express these 10,000,000 numbers (Problem 33).

The reader might conclude that, since on decimal computers this roundoff error is not encountered, therefore binary computers are in some sense inferior arithmetic engines. That this roundoff error is unique to nondecimal computers is true, but the roundoff error incurred during the *calculation* in the computer is generally much more significant than that described above and occurs on both decimal and binary computers. For example, the sum of the two decimal floating-point numbers

$$\boxed{01\ 53264178} + \boxed{02\ 62413752}$$

is really

$$
\begin{array}{r}
5.3264178 \\
+62.413752 \\
\hline
67.7401698
\end{array}
$$

which, rounded back to 8 digits, is 67.740170. But in the computer the addition would normally be performed by first shifting

---

[†] Note that since the IBM 360 is a hexadecimal machine, a difference of 1 digit in a number on this computer is equivalent to 4 binary digits.

$$\boxed{01\ 53264178}\ \text{to}\ \boxed{02\ 05326417}$$

in the arithmetic unit (where unnormalized numbers are always allowed) and then adding

$$
\begin{array}{r}
62413752 \\
+05326417 \\
\hline
67740169
\end{array}
$$

to get a final result of

02 67740169

The error thus caused by the fixed finite word length of floating-point numbers is also usually called roundoff error, although rounding did not occur in the example above. An obvious case where rounding does occur in computation is when a $2n$ bit or digit product is rounded to length n before storage back in memory. Since errors like the above occur at all stages of a computation, they are typically much more important than the roundoff caused by the original decimal to binary conversion. The scientific programmer particularly must be aware, in any lengthy computation, that the concatenation of many roundoff errors may cause an error in his result far larger than any single roundoff. Analysis of these errors is an important branch of *numerical analysis*.

BIBLIOGRAPHIC NOTES

Many books discuss binary arithmetic, binary-decimal codes, and related topics. The most comprehensive of these is Knuth (1969); Ledley (1962), Richards (1955), and Ware (1963) also treat these areas. Binary arithmetic is important in a number of mathematical recreations, most prominently in the game of Nim; see Kraitchik (1953) and Problem 2. There is no good general reference to the topic of memory organization; the reader would do well to get the manual for the computer he is using and study the memory organization for that computer. A more complete discussion of the conversion anomaly discussed in Section 3.2.3 may be found in Goldberg (1967).

Bibliography

Goldberg, I.B. (1967): 27 Bits Are Not Enough for 8 Digit Accuracy, *Communications of the Association for Computing Machinery*, vol. 10, pp. 105-106.
Knuth, D.E. (1969): *The Art of Computer Programming*, vol 2, *Seminumerical Algorithms*, Addison-Wesley Publishing Company, Reading, Massachusetts.

Kraitchik, M. (1953): *Mathematical Recreations*, Dover Publications Inc., New York.

Ledley, R.S. (1962): *Programming and Utilizing Digital Computers*, McGraw-Hill Book Company, Inc., New York.

Richards, R.K. (1955): *Arithmetic Operations in Digital Computers*, D. Van Nostrand Company, Inc., Princeton, New Jersey.

Ware, W.H. (1963): *Digital Computer Technology and Design*, vol. 1, John Wiley & Sons, Inc., New York.

PROBLEMS

Section 3.1.1

1. Suppose you wished to explain to someone who knew only the digits 0, 1, 2, . . . , 9 how to generate the successive positive integers. Draw a flow chart for an algorithm which accepts an input any decimal integer and gives as its output that integer plus 1.

2. Perform the following binary calculations:

   a) $10110 + 01101$

   b) $10100 - 01001$

   c) 110101×1011

   d) $1011011 \div 101$

   e) $1011 + 101101 + 011001 + 101101 - 101001 - 1111$

   f) $(100110 + (1011 \times 10101)) \div ((110 \times 101) - 111)$

   g) $1011.101 + 110.1101 - 10111.1 + 11.11011$

3. The game of Nim is played using k piles of objects (coins, poker chips, or anything) each of which contains n_i objects at the start. Two players alternately play by removing any number of (but at least one) objects from any one pile. The aim of the game is to remove the last object.

   a) Consider the particular version of Nim with $k=5$ and $n_1 = 1$, $n_2 = 2$, $n_3 = 3$, $n_4 = 4$, and $n_5 = 5$. Write the numbers n_i in binary one under another.

   b) Add these numbers *ignoring* the carry from one column to the next. This sum is called *add-without-carry* or sometimes the *logical sum.*

   c) Deduce three possible moves which will result in a logical sum of 000 for the objects in the five piles.

   d) Show that at the next move the other player must produce a nonzero logical sum no matter what move he makes.

   e) From this see if you can deduce a general algorithm for winning at Nim.

4.   In an alternate form of Nim the aim is *not* to take the last object. Can you deduce an algorithm for this? (Hint: This algorithm is just like the one above until quite near the end of the game.)

Section 3.1.2

5.   Perform the following octal calculations:

   a) $6.3417 + 2.6153 - 1.6423 - 4.0717$
   b) 674253×366674
   c) $46153 \div 321$
   d) $((623.1 + 124.7) \times 3.624)/7.113$

6.   Convert each of the numbers in the previous problem to binary.

7.   The quinary system has radix 5.
   a) Write the addition and multiplication tables for quinary arithmetic.
   b) Perform the following calculations in quinary:

   i) $3214 - 2134 + 1042 - 233$
   ii) 4214×1123
   iii) $44301 \div 2213$

8.   a) Derive a relationship between hexadecimal (base 16) and binary similar to that between octal and binary.

   b) From this indicate how to carry out conversions between any pair of binary, octal, and hexadecimal numbers.

   c) Perform the following conversions

   i) $(A46.B)_{16}$ to binary and octal
   ii) $(67423.501)_8$ to binary and hexadecimal
   iii) $(11011010001.1101100011)_2$ to octal and hexadecimal
where A, B, C, D, E, and F are used as symbols for the last 6 hexadecimal digits.

Section 3.1.3

9.   Perform the following base conversions:

   a) $(249.307)_{10}$ to binary and octal
   b) $(11011.0101110)_2$ to decimal and octal
   c) $(64273.15624)_8$ to binary and decimal
   d) $(76.9473)_{10}$ to quinary and duodecimal (base 12)
   e) $(17342.21677)_8$ to quinary and duodecimal

10. Prove that all finite length quinary fractions have finite decimal expansions. Is the converse true?

Section 3.1.4

11. BCD (but not excess−3) is an example of a *weighted 4-bit code*, which means that each of the four binary places has associated with it a weight which indicates the value to be associated with a 1 bit in that position. For BCD the weights are 8, 4, 2, and 1 so that, for example, 1001 = 8 + 1 = 9, since the two 1s correspond to weights of 8 and 1.

    a) If the four weights are 7, 3, 2, and 1, write the binary equivalents of the digits 0 through 9 (e.g., 8=1001 = 7 + 1).

    b) The weights need not all be positive. Find the equivalents of the digits 0 through 9 if the weights are 7, 5, 3, and −6 (e.g., 1=1001 = 7−6).

12. Given the excess−3 numbers 1011 and 0101, what is their (a) sum, (b) difference, (c) product, and (d) quotient? Express all answers in excess−3.

13. Suppose a fifth bit called the C (for check) bit is added to all BCD codes in order to make the number of 1 bits odd (the codes are then said to have *odd parity*). Show that it will always be possible to detect any error inside a computer which causes one of the 5 bits to be changed. (See Section 10.1.2 also.)

14. The same result as in the previous problem could have been achieved with *even parity* in which the C bit would be chosen to give an even number of 1 bits. Can you think of a reason why even parity is almost never used instead of odd parity?

Section 3.1.5

15. Comparing Table 3.6 with Table 3.4 and using the note on the IBM 29 keypunch at the end of Section 3.1.5, state the relationship between the 360 series codes of Table 3.6 and IBM 29 keypunch codes.

16. Consider a digit-organized memory which uses flags to indicate the beginning of a number in the highest-order digit and a minus sign in the lowest-order digit.

    a) What is the minimum length number on such a computer? Why?

    b) Denoting flags by overbars and assuming the leftmost flag denotes the beginning and the rightmost digit is the least significant digit of a number, what is the proper interpretation of the following string of digits $2\overline{8}47\overline{6}3\overline{9}0\overline{1}10\overline{4}2\overline{0}6\overline{8}9$?

17. a) Using the code of Table 3.6, indicate how the word BINARY would be stored in the word shown in Figure 3.4.

b) What would the 36 bits generated in part a represent using the code of Table 3.4?

Section 3.2

18. Let the numbers

   A = 66.23   B = 14.45
   C = 107.1   D = 2.634

be stored as 4-digit numbers (without decimal points, of course) in a computer with a digit-organized memory with signs as flags in the least significant digit. Which of the following calculations will require scaling and why? (Assume that the multiplication of two 4-digit numbers produces an 8-digit number internally.)

   a) A + B
   b) A + B − C
   c) B x C
   d) (B x C) + D
   e) (A x B) − D

19. On a computer with a 36-bit word (35 bits plus sign), what is the ratio of the largest to the smallest fixed-point numbers which can be stored assuming the imaginary, scaled binary point may be set anywhere in the word by the programmer (i.e., put in one place to make a number large and in another to make it small)?

20. On a decimal computer with a 2-digit exponent and an 8-digit mantissa for floating-point numbers, show all the ways the number 46.5 may be stored as a floating-point number if unnormalized numbers are allowed.

21. Suppose, for floating-point numbers in a binary computer, bit number 1 was interpreted as the sign of the exponent in bits 2 through 8 with a zero being a minus exponent and a 1 a plus exponent. Would this be equivalent to excess− 128 notation? Why?

22. Express in decimal form as A x 10^B where A lies between .1 and 1.0

    a) the magnitude of the largest normalized number expressible with an 8-bit, excess−128 exponent and a 27-bit mantissa.

    b) the magnitude of the smallest nonzero number.

23. Indicate step by step how the calculation, shifting, and normalizing in the calculations of Example 3.16 would be done.

Section 3.2.1

24. On a computer with a 5-bit word (4 bits plus sign), which of the following fixed-point calculations would cause overflow?

    a) 01101 + 00110

    b) 11011 + 01001 − 01110

    c) 11010 − 01011

    d) 11001 + 10110 + 01111

Assume calculations are performed in left to right order and that negative numbers are stored as sign (1) and absolute value.

25. Give examples of floating-point overflow and underflow for all four arithmetic operations for a 36-bit word binary computer with an 8-bit excess−128 exponent and a 27-bit mantissa in which all numbers are normalized.

Section 3.2.2

26. Convert each of the negative numbers in Problem 24 to the form of a negative sign (1) and ones complement.

27. Repeat Problem 26 using twos complement.

28. a) Show that, if negative numbers are stored as sign and twos complement, the sum of any two numbers (whose true result does not overflow) is given correctly by adding the two numbers with the signs appended as the most significant bit and ignoring a carry out of the sign position (e.g., 01100 + 11000 = 00100).

    b) Show that, if ones complements are used instead, the correct result is obtained if a carry out of the sign position is added in at the least significant position, for example,

```
    01100
    10111
   100011
        1
    00100
```

(This is referred to as *end-around carry*.)

29. Prove that the two techniques of forming twos complements in Example 3.18 are equivalent.

Section 3.2.3

30. Convert the following decimal numbers to normalized binary floating-point form (8-bit, excess—128 exponent, 27-bit mantissa) with an error of no more than 1/2 in the least significant place.

  a) 46.32
  b) 6.74
  c) 15.471

31. For Example 3.19, give an estimate of the *actual* error as an integer times a negative power of 2. (Hint: Carry out the decimal to binary conversions to more than 27 places.)

32. Repeat the calculations of Problem 30 using truncation instead of rounding.

33. Using the rounding technique of Example 3.19, calculate which of the 10 million digits 9,000,000.0, 9,000,000.1, . . . , 9,999,999.9 have the same representations in (27, 8) format (27-bit mantissa, 8-bit exponent).

34. Consider the situation in which, on a 36-bit word computer, *double-precision* floating-point numbers are stored in two words each with an 8-bit, excess—128 exponent and a 27-bit mantissa where the exponent in the second word is 27 less than the first and the mantissa is the next 27 bits of the number.

  a) Convert the floating-point number of Example 3.19 to double-precision form.

  b) What are the maximum and minimum nonzero magnitudes which can be stored in double precision form? (Hint: Remember the second exponent is 27 less than the first.)

4

constants and variables—
types and structures

*All this knowledge with which vanity fills the balloon-like brains of our proud
pedants, is therefore but a huge mass of words and figures, which form in the
brain all the works by which we distinguish and recall objects.*

Julien Offray de la Mettrie in *Man a Machine* (1748)

But I cannot approve any mode of discovery unless carried on by recording data.

Francis Bacon in *Novum Organum* (1620)

In this chapter we shall consider the various types of quantities dealt with by the
programmer who uses a P-O language. Where appropriate we shall use the
material in the previous chapter on memory organization and computer
numbers. We shall therefore be picking up where we left off at the end of
Chapter 2. In Section 2.5 we considered how the variable quantities or *variables*
in a computation are *named.* Here we shall consider in more detail the various
forms that can be taken on by the variables and the constants which together
form the *data* for the computation, and how the data can be grouped together to
form different kinds of aggregates.

Data can be of two basic types, arithmetic and string, as we indicated in
Section 2.5.1. We shall consider each of these in turn.

4.1 ARITHMETIC CONSTANTS

The discussion of Section 3.2 leads to the idea that arithmetic data should be of
at least two types, fixed-point and floating-point. The scientific languages—

Panel 4.1   Fixed-point constants

	FORTRAN	ALGOL	PL/I	COBOL
	Called *integer* constants	Called *integer* constants	Called *fixed-point* constants and can be *decimal* or *binary* or *sterling*	Called *numeric literals*
Syntax	Any sequence of digits preceded optionally by a + or − sign	Any sequence of digits preceded optionally by a + or − sign	*Decimal*: Any sequence of digits with or without a decimal point and optionally preceded by a sign *Binary*: Same except digits must be 0s and 1s and must be followed by a B *Sterling*: Integer for pounds, decimal point, integer <20 for shillings, decimal number <12 for pence followed by L	Any sequence of digits preceded optionally by a + or − sign with or without a decimal point except that the final character cannot be a decimal point

Semantics

Always manipulated as an integer	Always manipulated as an integer	Decimal or binary point kept track of in all calculations by computer	Decimal point kept track of in all calculations by computer
		If constant will not fit in a single word, leading digits may be truncated and/or error message given.	

Examples

Correct

Always manipulated as an integer	Always manipulated as an integer	Decimal or binary point kept track of in all calculations by computer	Decimal point kept track of in all calculations by computer
6475	6475	6475	6475
-326	-326	-326	-326
+847	+847	+847	+847
		-413.0	-413.0
		27.	
		10010B	
		-101.11B	
		62.7.1.5L	
		(62 pounds, 7 shillings, 1 1/2 pence)	

Incorrect

Always manipulated as an integer	Always manipulated as an integer	Decimal or binary point kept track of in all calculations by computer	Decimal point kept track of in all calculations by computer
-263. (dec. pt.)	-263. (dec. pt.)	10210B (digit 2)	37. (last character cannot be .)
		62.7.12L (too many pence)	

Fortran, Algol, and PL/I—do indeed allow both types. Fortran and Algol, however, but not PL/I, restrict all fixed-point quantities to be integers. Cobol, concerned as it is with business data processing and therefore seldom with complicated calculations, allows only fixed-point numbers. In addition to fixed- and floating-point data, two other data types, double-precision and complex, are allowed in Fortran and PL/I. We shall now discuss the precise specifications of constants of each data type and following this we shall consider how names for variables of the various types are specified. For convenience, we shall assume in what follows that we are dealing with a word-oriented memory or a character-oriented memory with a word defined as a certain number of characters.

Fixed-point. The syntax and semantics for fixed-point constants are summarized in Panel 4.1. These constants are always stored in the memory in fixed-point format, one to a word. The decimal (or binary) point in PL/I and Cobol constants is *not* explicitly stored; it only serves as information to the compiler about where the true decimal point is. PL/I and Cobol allow decimal points in fixed-point constants specifically to facilitate the manipulation of financial data. This explains why PL/I also allows sterling constants. In PL/I on the IBM 360 system, decimal fixed-point constants are meant to be stored as BCD digits, 2 to a byte, while binary fixed-point constants will be stored in a word as pure binary. PL/I allows these two types of constants because this language was designed specifically with the 360 in mind. Note that although the syntax does not limit the number of digits in the constant, the memory structure of the computer forces a semantic interpretation which will truncate some digits if too many are specified.

Example 4.1

Specify the syntax of a Fortran or Algol integer constant in BNF.

<INTEGER CONSTANT> ::= <DIGIT> | – <DIGIT> | + <DIGIT> |
    <INTEGER CONSTANT> <DIGIT>

The definition is just a formal statement of the informal definition in Panel 4.1.

One thing to note in the BNF definition of the above example is the use of the symbols – and + to represent themselves. Any symbol which does not appear in brackets (<––->) in a BNF definition represents itself and is called a *literal*.

Floating-point. Panel 4.2 outlines the syntax and semantics of floating-point constants. Cobol allows no floating-point arithmetic. All the floating-point constants are stored, one to a word, in floating-point form as described in Section 3.2. Normally, decimal and binary floating-point numbers in PL/I would be stored internally as binary floating-point numbers. Thus, $6.4E1$ $(=6.4 \times 10^1 = (64)_{10})$ and $10000.E2B$ $(=(1000000)_2 = (64)_{10})$ would have identical internal representations. The E notation is necessary to denote exponentiation because no input device for a computer enables the user to specify the level (height) on a line. Thus, 10^{-14} is represented as $E-14$; the E replaces the 10 to distinguish it from the digits which make up the rest of the number. The Algol publication language specifies the use of the digits 10 before the exponent but printed in a smaller type face, level with the rest of the line; the exponent is then also level with the rest of the line and normal size (e.g., $6.4_{10}-2$).[†]

Example 4.2

In normal scientific notation what do the correct examples in Panel 4.2 represent?

$2.75E+08 = 2.75 \times 10^8$
$-.86327E-14 = -.86327 \times 10^{-14}$
$6823.1 = 6823.1$
$32E+4 = 32 \times 10^4$
$1001.1E+8B = (1001.1)_2 \times 2^8 = (9.5)_{10} \times 2^8$
$_{10}-12 = 10^{-12}$

If d represents a string of digits, the allowable forms for floating-point constants in Fortran are

$\pm.d$ $\qquad \pm d.d$ $\qquad \pm d.$
$\pm.dE\pm d$ $\qquad \pm d.dE\pm d$ $\qquad \pm d.E\pm d$ $\qquad \pm dE\pm d$

In addition, Algol allows

$_{10}\pm d$

by itself while, for decimal floating-point constants in PL/I, those in the top line above for Fortran are not allowed, while all the ones with E with or without the following $\pm d$ are allowed. If the exponent is too large or too small to fit into the floating-point format of the computer, it will be truncated on the right and/or an error message will result. If the nonexponent part exceeds some number of

---

[†]In actual usage the $_{10}$ in Algol is normally transliterated to E or sometimes, to '.

Panel 4.2 Floating-point constants

FORTRAN

Called *real* constants

i) Any sequence of digits with a decimal point; optionally preceded by a + or − sign and optionally followed by an exponent part consisting of an E followed by an optional + or − sign followed by an integer

ii) An integer constant followed by an exponent part as defined under (i)

ALGOL

Called *real* constants

Syntax

i) Any sequence of digits with a decimal point; optionally preceded by a + or − sign

ii) A 10 followed by an optional + or − followed by an integer

iii) A concatenation of the previous two in which the decimal point may be omitted

PL/I

Called *floating-point* constants; may be either *binary* or *decimal*

Decimal: Any sequence of one or more digits with an optional decimal point; optionally preceded by a sign; always followed by an E followed optionally by either a + sign (also optional) and an integer or a − sign and an integer

Binary: As above except the digits preceding the E must be 0s and 1s and the entire constant must be followed by a B

Semantics

The exponent part is interpreted as 10 to the power specified by the optionally signed integer after the E or 10.

The exponent part is interpreted as 10 (for decimal constants) or 2 (for binary constants) to the power specified by the optionally signed integer after the E.

Examples

Correct

2.75E+08	$2.75_{10}+08$	2.75E+08
-.86327E-14	$-.86327_{10}-14$	-.86327E-14
6823.1	6823.1	6823.1E
32E+4	$32_{10}+4$	32E+4
	$10-12$	1001.1E+8B

Incorrect

E-12 (exponent part by itself not allowed)

6823.1_{10} (Exponent must follow 10)

6823.1 (E must appear)

E-8 (interpreted as a variable E minus a fixed-point 8; digit must precede exponent)

Note:
Floating-point constants are not allowed in Cobol.

115

digits, the added precision will just be lost in the decimal-to-binary conversion or the number will be interpreted as double-precision (see below).

Double-precision.   Double-precision numbers are floating-point numbers which occupy two consecutive computer words, thereby containing more significant digits in the mantissa. The two words are structured in one of two ways:

i) | S | exponent | mantissa | | mantissa |

in which the mantissa in the second word is merely a continuation of the first. Thus, if a word is 32 bits and the exponent is 7, the total mantissa length is 56 bits (24 + 32). This form is characteristic of the IBM 360 series.

ii) | S | exponent | mantissa | | S | exponent | mantissa |

in which both halves have the same format as single-precision floating-point numbers. If the mantissa is n bits in length then the value of the exponent of the second half is n less than that of the first half. (Why?) The signs are the same in both halves. Thus, in a 36-bit word with 8-bit exponent the total mantissa length is 54 bits (27 + 27).

Not all computers have hardware which can do arithmetic with double-precision numbers; nevertheless, even on computers which do not, double-precision arithmetic can be simulated using appropriate machine-language programs.

Example 4.3

What is the internal representation of $(9.7)_{10}$ as a double-precision floating-point number in the second format above?

Referring to Example 3.19 we obtain:

First half: 0 10000100 10011 0110 0110 0110 0110 0110 01
Second half: 0 01101001 10 0110 0110 0110 0110 0110 0110 1

Rounding is done only at the end of the second half. The first exponent is $(204)_8$, the second is $(151)_8 = (204)_8 - (33)_8 = (132)_{10} - (27)_{10}$. (What is the maximum discrepancy between an external number and its internal double-precision representation?)

As indicated in Panel 4.3, only Fortran has an explicit syntactic designation for double-precision numbers. A double-precision number in Fortran consists of any of the floating-point formats having an exponent part, with the E replaced by a D (for double-precision exponent). Thus the allowable formats are

$$\pm.d\text{D}\pm d \quad \pm d.d\text{D}\pm d \quad \pm d.\text{D}\pm d \quad d\text{D}\pm d \quad (d-\text{string of digits})$$

In addition, some Fortran implementations assume that a string of digits with decimal point and more than some number of digits (usually 8 if there is a 27-bit mantissa or 7 if the mantissa is 24 bits) is a double-precision constant. In PL/I and some Algol implementations, numbers with decimal points and more than some number of digits are automatically converted to double (or, in PL/I, greater) precision internally.

Complex.   As indicated in Panel 4.4, Fortran allows the specification of complex constants as:

<COMPLEX CONSTANT> ::= (<FLOATING POINT CONSTANT>,
      <FLOATING POINT CONSTANT>)

that is, as an ordered pair of single-precision constants separated by a comma and enclosed in parentheses. The first constant is the real part and the second

Panel 4.3   Double-precision constants

FORTRAN	*ALGOL*	*PL/I*	*COBOL*
	Syntax		
Same as for floating-point constants with exponent parts with E replaced by D	Not explicitly allowed, but sometimes implemented implicitly with numbers containing more than some number of digits	Not explicitly defined, but precision attribute implies storage in as many consecutive words of memory as necessary up to maximum allowed in implementation	Not allowed

Examples

2.75D08
−.86327D−14
32D+4

the imaginary part. PL/I allows the specification of imaginary constants but not complex constants. However, imaginary constants can then be used in arithmetic operations to give complex values to variables (see Section 4.3) so that complex arithmetic can be effected. Algol has no explicit way to represent complex or imaginary numbers. Nevertheless, there are programming techniques by which the Algol programmer can do calculations involving complex numbers.

4.2   STRING CONSTANTS

All the arithmetic constants of the previous section consist, of course, of strings of characters. We singled out arithmetic constants as a special class for the obvious reason that so much of the application of digital computers is in numeric computation. As we stressed in Chapter 1, digital computers are specifically designed to facilitate this particular type of symbol manipulation. In this section by contrast, we shall be concerned with strings in their *nonnumeric* context. In the languages which we are considering the major use for nonnumeric strings is in business data processing problems. Therefore it will be no surprise that the purely scientific languages, Fortran and Algol, have quite primitive facilities for handling strings compared to PL/I and Cobol.

We shall take the point of view here that, whereas there were a number of different *types* of arithmetic constants—fixed-point, floating-point, etc.—there is really only one type of string constant which is generally called a *character-string* constant. There is, however, a special subclass of character-string constants, called *logical* constants, whose discussion we shall postpone to Chapter 9.

Panel 4.5 delineates the salient facts about string constants. A number of explanatory and additional comments needs to be made about these constants:

1. Some Fortran implementations allow Hollerith constants to be expressed as a string of characters in quotes as in the other languages. The quotes, which are called *delimiters* (cf. Section 2.5), obviate the necessity for counting the number of characters in the constant. A common error in Fortran is to have the integer before the H not agree with the number of characters after the H.

2. Blanks are *not* ignored in string constants; they are treated as any other character of the language; thus SILLY EXAMPLE has 13 characters.

3. In Algol, strings can only be used as parameters in procedures (see Chapter 7) which are to be manipulated eventually by procedures written in machine language. Strings in Fortran are normally used only for headings and related purposes in the results output by the program. To facilitate this, strings can be named in input and output statements and the DATA statement (see Section 6.2.3).

4. PL/I, in addition to the syntax of Panel 4.5, allows integers in parentheses before the string constant. These indicate the number of repetitions of the string in quotes. Thus (3)'BANG' means 'BANGBANGBANG' and (14)'1'B means '11111111111111'B.

5. The Cobol nonnumeric literal '16431' should not be confused with the numeric literal 16431. The former may be manipulated (moved around in memory) but cannot be used as an arithmetic operand while the latter may be an arithmetic operand.

Panel 4.4 Complex constants

FORTRAN
Called complex constants

PL/I
Called imaginary constants

Syntax

Two floating-point constants separated by a comma and enclosed in parentheses

Any decimal fixed- or floating-point constant followed by an I

Semantics

The two numbers are treated, respectively, as the real and imaginary parts of a complex number

Treated as the imaginary part of a complex number with real part 0; complex numbers with nonzero real part formed as sum of fixed- or floating-point constant and imaginary constant

Examples

(2.6, 4.5E7)
(14E3, 8.64)

87I
4.68I
2.3E5I

Note:
Complex constants are not allowed in Algol and Cobol.

4.3 VARIABLES—NAMES, TYPES, AND ATTRIBUTES

As we said in Section 2.5.1, the names we defined there specify quantities which can vary during the course of a computation. These quantities are called the *variables* of a computer program and thus the discussion of Section 2.5.1 explains how to *name* variables.

It is worth noting specifically that the memory location specified by the name holds at any particular time a particular value *which has the form of one*

Panel 4.5   Character-string constants

	FORTRAN	ALGOL	PL/I	COBOL
	Called *Hollerith* constants	Called *strings*	Called *character-string* or *bit-string* constants	Called *nonnumeric literals*
Syntax	An unsigned integer followed by H, followed by a string of one or more characters from the character set	A string of zero or more characters in the character set except ' enclosed in '____'	*Character:* A string of zero or more characters from the character set but only pairs of ' are allowed, the whole string to be enclosed in '____'. *Bit:* As above except characters must be all 0s or 1s and string must be followed by a B	A string of any characters in the language except ' enclosed in '____'
Semantics	The number before the H indicates the number of characters after the H which make up the constant; Hollerith constants can be used only in very restricted ways in Fortran	Use in Algol very restricted	Double quote in string interpreted as single quote; can be used with almost same generality as arithmetic constants	Can be manipulated with about same generality as arithmetic constants
Examples	13HSILLY EXAMPLE 7H42+ * /) (5H16431	'SILLY EXAMPLE' '42+ * /) (' '16431'	'SILLY EXAMPLE' '42+ * /) (' '16431' 'DON''T DO IT' '101001'B	'SILLY EXAMPLE' '42+ * /) (' '16431'

of the constants discussed in the previous two sections. The reader is urged to convince himself that he understands the difference between the *name* of a variable and the *value* in the computer of that variable at a given time. Now it is a fact that the values a given name assumes are always of the same *type,* that is fixed-point, floating-point, character-string, etc. (Problem 13). The question we 𝓌𝒾 .ɪ to consider first in this section is how to specify that the values of a given name are to be a given type.

It might be surmised that the type of data to which a variable name refers could be inferred by the computer when that variable is first given a value by, for example, inputting a number to the memory location assigned to a given variable name. However, the compiler, which operates on the program before any data is ever fed to it, needs to know what kind of data a variable name refers to in order to perform the translation properly. For example, if a variable name refers to a fixed-point variable, this requires on most computers different machine-language arithmetic instructions than if it refers to a floating-point variable.

A specification that a given variable name is to have values of a certain type is called a *type declaration.* The words used in such declarations are given in Panel 4.6. In Algol the type must always be declared explicitly in a form discussed below. But, in Fortran and PL/I, names not declared explicitly are given a certain type by *default* as shown in Panel 4.6. In PL/I arithmetic type is declared as to mode (REAL or COMPLEX), base (BINARY or DECIMAL), and scale (FIXED or FLOAT). This is reasonable in light of our previous discussion of PL/I constants. If no type is specified, the default option specifies all three depending on the first letter of the name; if mode, base, or scale is specified the others are automatic, independent of the first letter of the name. Neither Fortran nor Algol have declaration words for strings since string variables are allowed in neither.

The manner in which words in Panel 4.6 are actually used to declare the type of variables is indicated in Panel 4.7.[†] From the BNF definition a list is, of course, nothing more than a sequence of variable names separated by commas.

In the examples in Panel 4.7 it should be noted that

REAL I7,;A,B41

is redundant in Fortran as regards the last two variables, since the default condition would have assigned the type REAL to them in any case; the same is true in PL/I.

[†]The { } in Panel 4.7 indicate a choice is to be made from the items in the braces.

In Fortran and Algol the INTEGER specification indicates that the variable named is an integer whose value will be stored in fixed-point form. But in PL/I the FIXED specification, while it implies storage in Fixed-point form, allows the presence of a decimal point which is consistent with the definition of fixed-point constants in Panel 4.3 (Problem 2).

In PL/I we may specify the *precision* of a variable together with its type. This is particularly important with fixed-point data since, as with fixed-point constants, it is desirable to be able to specify the position of the decimal point. This

Panel 4.6   Type declaration words

FORTRAN	*ALGOL*	*PL/I*
INTEGER	integer	{ FIXED
REAL	real	{ FLOAT
DOUBLE PRECISION		{ REAL
COMPLEX		{ COMPLEX
LOGICAL	boolean	
		{ BINARY
		{ DECIMAL
		{ BIT
		{ CHARACTER

A type declaration is a string of one to three words, one each from each of the first three groups *or* one word from the last group.

Default Options

If first letter of name
I,J,K,L,M,N,
INTEGER; otherwise REAL

If no specifications and first letter of name is I,J,K,L,M,N, FIXED REAL BINARY; otherwise FLOAT REAL DECIMAL; if one or two from first three pairs specified, others are taken as DECIMAL, FLOAT and/or REAL; this over-simplifies the quite complicated PL/I situation.

is done by grouping two integers in parentheses, for example, (7,3) which indicates that the data has 7 digits, 3 after the decimal point. Therefore, if we write

DECLARE R14 FIXED (7,3);

this implies R14 can take on values with magnitudes in the range 0000.000 to 9999.999. If the precision is not specified, fixed-point variables are assumed to be integers.

The BIT or CHARACTER declarations in PL/I *must* be followed by an integer in parentheses representing the length of the string. In turn, this integer may be optionally followed by the word VARYING which indicates that the strings with this variable name may have varying length up to the maximum. Thus,

DECLARE A12 BIT (10) VARYING;

states that A12 denotes a bit string of 1 to 10 bits.

PL/I calls the type or precision of a variable *attributes.* In PL/I variables may have various other attributes besides those discussed in this section, some of

Panel 4.7   Explicit type declarations

FORTRAN	*ALGOL*	*PL/I*
td word <LIST>	*td word* <LIST>	DECLARE $\left\{ \begin{array}{c} vn \\ (<LIST>) \end{array} \right\}$ *td words*

where

<LIST> ::= *vn* \| <LIST>, *vn*

Semantics

The variable name or names on the list are assigned the type specified.

Examples

REAL I7,A,B41	real 17,A,B41;	DECLARE (I7, A, B41) REAL;
LOGICAL C1, A14		DECLARE (C1, A14) BIT;
		DECLARE R14 FLOAT BINARY;

vn—variable name
td word(s)—type declaration word(s)

which we shall consider in later sections. For scientific calculations the attributes discussed in this section are the basic ones for PL/I. For Fortran and Algol the discussion of this section has been accurate and complete.

In Cobol the type of a name is specified not by a type declaration word but rather in a PICTURE clause. This consists of the word PICTURE followed by a sequence of characters which indicate the type and size of the data item. Among the variety of options available to the Cobol programmer are:

1. A sequence of n A's represents a variable name whose values are words of length n, each position of which is one of the 26 letters (e.g., PICTURE AAAAA for 5-letter words).

2. A sequence of n X's, A's, or 9's which contains at least one X represents a variable name whose values are alphanumeric strings of length n; that is, each position (irrespective of whether it contains A, X, or 9) may be an alphabetic or numeric character or, since Cobol defines "alphanumeric" more generally than we have previously, any other character in the character set of the language, or even sometimes characters not in the character set but available in the computer (e.g., all sixty 29 keypunch characters).

3. A sequence of n 9s interspersed with a single V indicates a variable with numeric values of length n with the position of the decimal point indicated by the V (e.g., financial data of less than one million dollars would have a picture of 999999V99).

In order to facilitate editing data for output as well as for some other purposes, a variety of other *picture specifications* are also allowed in Cobol. PL/I has a picture facility similar to that in Cobol to facilitate data processing applications. This facility is embodied in the PICTURE attribute. The reader will probably have noted the somewhat primitive aspect of picture specifications; words or formulas would both be preferable ways to describe complexity.

4.4   DATA AGGREGATES

In many problems, the data are not just an unrelated set of single variables. Often there are relationships between variables which, if they could be recognized in the language, would make the programming much simpler. For this reason all the languages we have been discussing allow groupings of variables into larger constructs; these are the subject of this section.

4.4.1   Arrays

If you were analyzing the rhythmic structure of a poem in a computer you would naturally be looking at groups of words, perhaps a line or two at a time.

Rather than give each word of the group a different variable name such as WORD1, WORD2,..., WORD10, it would be convenient to be able to somehow refer to the whole group with one variable name. Indeed, if the group is of *variable* length, such a facility is essential. If you were doing a correlation analysis involving many observations of two variables, it would be useful to be able to refer to each group of observations by a single variable name or perhaps, even better, to refer to the group of pairs of observations by a single name. Situations such as the two above arise very commonly in problems for computer solution. In order to handle them conveniently, Fortran, Algol, and PL/I provide the ability to name *arrays* of numbers. Indeed, arrays are the only type of higher level data structure allowed in Fortran and Algol. Cobol also allows arrays but only in the context of a construct called a structure, which is also allowed in PL/I and which we shall discuss in Section 4.4.3.

An array may be:

a) a sequence of numbers in some linear order (i.e., there is a first number, a second number, etc., to a last number), or

b) a higher-dimensional pattern of numbers in which, for example, in two dimensions, numbers which are not on one of the edges of the array (see Figure 4.1) have four neighbors, on either side, above and below. Fortran and Cobol explicitly limit the number of dimensions an array may have to three, but many implementations allow more, often seven. Algol and PL/I do not explicitly limit the number of dimensions but implementations always limit this number, usually to seven or less.

The one-dimensional array described under (a) above is mathematically equivalent to a *vector*, while a two-dimensional array is equivalent to a *matrix*. In line with this terminology, variables which refer to a single quantity are often called *scalar variables* and those which refer to more than one quantity are called *array variables*.

If computer languages allow a single name to specify all the elements of an array, then they must provide some mechanism by which to refer to individual elements. This mechanism is the *subscript*. A subscript is the mathematician's way of denoting the position of an element in an array. The number of subscripts denotes the dimension of the array. For example, in the two-dimensional array or matrix of Figure 4.1, each *element* has two subscripts, by convention the first being the *row* subscript and the second the *column* subscript.

Since the devices used to provide input for computers do not allow any way of indicating the relative height of a character on a line, subscripts, like exponents, cannot be denoted directly as they are in Figure 4.1. In the case of exponents as parts of constants, we solved this problem with the E notation by writing, for example, E-14 instead of 10^{-14}. In the case of subscripts we denote

$$
\begin{matrix}
a_{11} & a_{12} & a_{13} & a_{14} \cdots a_{1n} \\
a_{21} & a_{22} & a_{23} & a_{24} \cdots a_{2n} \\
a_{31} & a_{32} & a_{33} & a_{34} \cdots a_{3n} \\
\cdot & \cdot & \cdot & \cdot \qquad \cdot \\
\cdot & \cdot & \cdot & \cdot \qquad \cdot \\
\cdot & \cdot & \cdot & \cdot \qquad \cdot \\
a_{m1} & a_{m2} & a_{m3} & a_{m4} \ldots a_{mn}
\end{matrix}
$$

Figure 4.1   A two-dimensional array.

them by including them in parentheses (Fortran, PL/I, and Cobol) or square brackets (Algol) as indicated in Panel 4.8. From this panel it follows that for Fortran

$$
\overset{[3]}{<\text{SUBSCRIPT LIST}>} ::= <\text{SUBSCRIPT}>|<\text{SUBSCRIPT LIST}>,
$$
$$
<\text{SUBSCRIPT}>
$$

For a particular implementation of Fortran which allows k subscripts, we would modify the above definition by replacing the [3] by [k].

At any given instant of time, the subscripts of a subscripted variable name[†] are the values of the subscripts in the subscript list. The examples in Panel 4.8 indicate that subscripts may be variables as well as constants so that, for example, the second subscript of C2(I, 1) is always 1 while the first has at any time the value of the variable I. Neither the discussion above nor Panel 4.8 indicates the allowable form of subscripts. This varies substantially among the languages as indicated in Panel 4.9. Regarding Panel 4.9, note that:

1. Fortran and Cobol subscripts are automatically integers because of the syntax; in Algol and PL/I the semantics cause the *value* of each subscript to be integral.
2. We shall discuss arithmetic expressions and their valid forms in Section 5.2.
3. Some Fortran systems relax the syntax of subscripts to allow subscripts to be arithmetic expressions or restricted classes of arithmetic expressions.
4. Since an arithmetic expression may contain subscripted variables, the Algol

---

[†]The reader should note here that we have in fact introduced a distinction between the terms "identifier" and "variable name" which we have heretofore used synonomously. *Identifier* still refers to, for example, in Fortran, a string of one to six alphameric characters headed by a letter but a *variable name* may be an identifier which refers to a scalar quantity or an array, or it may be an array identifier followed by a subscript list.

Panel 4.8   Subscripted variables

FORTRAN and PL/I	ALGOL	COBOL

Syntax

vn (<SUBSCRIPT LIST>)   vn [<SUBSCRIPT LIST>] †   vn <SPACE>
                                                       (<SUBSCRIPT
                                                       LIST>)

where a subscript list is a sequence of subscripts (see Panel 4.9) separated by commas. Fortran and Cobol limit the number of subscripts to 3, but Algol and PL/I have no restrictions on this number although implementations will restrict the number.

Semantics

The *value* of each element of the subscript list is a subscript of the variable.

Examples

A(1,2)	A[1,2]	A (1,2)
BA(I,J,K)	BA[I,J,K]	BA (I,J,K)
C2(I,1)	C2[I,1]	C2 (I,1)

vn—variable name

and PL/I syntax allows subscripts to be subscripted, etc. For example, in Algol we might have A[J[2+K]].

The difference between the allowable subscript forms in Fortran and Cobol on the one hand and Algol and PL/I on the other is an excellent example of a restriction in the former two purely for reasons of ease of implementation. It has been removed in the latter two (more recently developed languages) as more has been learned about the compilation process and the needs of P-O language users.

Example 4.4

Which of the following are invalid Fortran subscripted variable names?

    A62(4,Z6)
    B17(L2*5)
    N(6,4,9)

---

†Since square brackets are not part of the normal character set, in implementations they must be transliterated into parentheses or some combination of characters from the character set such as .(for [and). for] .

> R6Z(I+5,4+K)
> V(N5+6)
> X4(N+7.3)

Answer:

A62(4,Z6)—unless it appears in an INTEGER type declaration, Z6 is a variable of type REAL.

B17(L2*5)—the constant must *precede* the variable ($c*v$).

R6Z(I+5,4+K)—the variable must *precede* the constant (K+4, not 4+K).

X4(N+7.3)—only fixed-point constants allowed.

Before concluding this section we note that each of the variable names in Example 4.4 (A62, B17, N, R6Z, V, X4) can be used by itself to refer to the whole array in ways which we shall consider in later chapters. In addition, PL/I

Panel 4.9   Subscripts

Fortran	*ALGOL and PL/I*	*COBOL*
	Syntax	

Any expression of the form
  i) c
  ii) v
  iii) $v \pm k$ or
  iv) $c*v \pm k$
where c and k are fixed-point constants and v is a variable name of type INTEGER
	Any valid arithmetic expression	A variable name or a numeric literal

	Semantics	
The asterisk indicates multiplication	The value of the subscript is the integral part of the value of the expression	The value of the variable name or the literal must be an integer

Examples

	Algol		*PL/I*	
R(I,1,J)	R(I,1,J)		R(I,1,J)	R (I,1,J)
J(3*I,14,K−2)	J[3*I,14,K−2]		J(3*I,14,K−2)	
	P13[A+B−C*12.2,J1]		P13(A+B−C*12.2,J1)	

Panel 4.10   Allowable subscript values

FORTRAN and COBOL   _ALGOL and PL/I_

Positive integers only   Positive integers, negative integers, and zero

allows the programmer to specify at appropriate places the _cross section_ of an array. For example, C(2*) represents the second row of the array C. It is important, however, that the reader understand that because a given identifier may be used to refer an entire array, an identifier may be an array name or a scalar name _but not both_ at the same time.[†]

4.4.2   Dimensioning and Storage Allocation

When an unsubscripted variable A appears in a program the compiler knows it must assign a single memory location to this variable. But, when the subscripted variable A(I,J) appears, the compiler will not know what values I and J may take on and, therefore, it cannot know whatout some collateral information how many locations to set aside for A. In this section we shall discuss how the compiler is informed of the size of arrays and how it uses this information to allocate memory.

The number of memory locations occupied by an array is determined by the range of values its subscripts take on. For example, if A is a one-dimensional (singly subscripted) array whose subscripts in the actual computation may take on values from 1 to 10, ten memory locations are required. But suppose the only possible values of the subscript are 5 to 10. Are only six locations required? The answer to this question varies from Fortran and Cobol to Algol and PL/I. Panel 4.10 indicates that Fortran and Cobol allow only positive integers as subscripts. More than this, both assume that all subscripts have a range from 1 to some maximum value. Thus, even if the actual subscripts take on the values 5 to 10, Fortran and Cobol allocate 10 locations to the array.

The four languages have quite different mechanisms for informing the compiler of the allowable range of subscripts. "Allowable" in this context means that, if in the computation the specified range is exceeded, then typically the computation will be terminated and an error message will result or the error will not be caught and some unpredictable series of actions will occur, usually and hopefully (Why?) ending in another detectable error. Panel 4.11 indicates how

---

[†]In Algol and Pl/I it is possible to use the same variable name in different parts of the program for different purposes; see Section 6.1.2.

Panel 4.11 Dimension specifications

FORTRAN	ALGOL	PL/I	COBOL
		General mechanism	
A DIMENSION statement	As part of an **array** type declaration	As an attribute in a DECLARE statement	In an OCCURS clause in the structure definition; see Section 4.4.3
		Syntax	
DIMENSION $<$ LIST $>$	**array** $<$ LIST $>$; where $<$ LIST $>$ ::= $<$ ITEM $>$ $\|$ $<$ LIST $>$, $<$ ITEM $>$ and where each item is	DECLARE $<$ LIST $>$;	*vn* OCCURS *pint* TIMES
a variable name followed by, in parentheses, a list of elements separated by commas, one for each dimension of the array	a variable alone or a variable name followed by, in brackets, a list of elements separated by commas, one for each dimension of the array and where each element is	a variable name followed by an attribute which consists of, in parentheses, a list of elements separated by commas, one for each dimension of the array	
an unsigned positive integer.	two arithmetic expressions[†] separated by a colon.[‡]	two arithmetic expressions[†] separated by a colon[‡] or a single arithmetic expression.	

130

Each positive integer indicates the maximum value of the subscript.

The values of the expressions, *at the time the array is allocated*, are the minimum and maximum values, respectively, of each subscript for each variable to the left until the next square brackets are encountered.

The values of the expressions, *at the time the array is allocated*, are the minimum and maximum values, respectively, of each subscript; if there is only one expression the minimum value is assumed to be 1.

The integer between OCCURS and TIMES indicates the maximum value of the subscript; multiple subscripts are indicated by a sequence of OCCURS clauses; see Section 4.4.3.

Examples

DIMENSION A(10), C(10),B(6,12,9)

array A,C[1:10],
  B[1:6,1:12,1:9];
array R[−4:B+2*C];
array S[I:J,B:14,−8:12];

DECLARE A(10), C(10),
  B(6,12,9);
DECLARE S(I:J,B:14,−8:12);

A OCCURS 10 TIMES

vn—variable name
pint—positive integer

† These expressions can contain only constants in a case which we shall discuss in Chapter 6.

‡ The colon must be transliterated into some other characters in the 48-character set; it is one of the special characters in the PL/I 60-character set while for the 48-character set the defined transliteration is two decimal points (. .).

131

subscript ranges are denoted in the four languages. The Fortran and Cobol mechanisms are much the simplest, allowing only positive integers in the DIMENSION statement or OCCURS clause. (In fact, in one case Fortran allows variable names in place of positive integers in DIMENSION statements, but this occurs in a case where no actual storage is being allocated; see Chapter 7.) A full understanding of Cobol subscripts must await a reading of Section 4.4.3. In addition to the form shown in Panel 4.11, Algol allows **array** to be preceded by **real, integer,** or **boolean** (see Chapter 9). In the absence of one of these three words the array is assumed to be real. Fortran allows an alternative construction in which the variable name with its dimensions does not appear in a dimension statement but rather in a type statement (e.g., INTEGER A(10) is equivalent to DIMENSION A(10), INTEGER A).

Panel 4.11 indicates that the subscript ranges in Algol and PL/I need not be rigidly specified but can be any arithmetic expressions. In the case of the example given in Panel 4.11,

array S[I:J,B:14,-8:12] ;

the compiler knows the third subscript can take on 21 consecutive values from -8 to 12 but it has no knowledge of the upper and lower bounds of the first subscript or the lower bound of the second. How then can it know how much memory to allocate to the array S? We shall consider this question in Section 6.1.2. Here we shall discuss only the case where all subscripts are constants.

In a Fortran program every dimension statement of the form exhibited in Panel 4.11 or type statement containing dimensions results in the assignment of a number of words of memory equal to

a) the single positive integer for a one-dimensional array

b) the product of the positive integers for an array of dimension greater than one (e.g., DIMENSION B(6,12,9) results in the allocation of 6 x 12 x 9 = 648 words of memory)

If, however, the array was declared to be DOUBLE PRECISION or COMPLEX, twice the amount of storage indicated above is allocated (Why?).

In Algol and PL/I arrays, when all the subscripts are constants, we must take for each subscript the difference between the upper and lower bounds plus one (e.g., 12-(-8)+1 = 21) and then apply the rules above to determine how much storage is allocated.

Even though computer memories have gotten substantially larger in recent years, there is a Parkinson's law that says that computer programmers will write programs to fill up the available memory. Therefore, if a program involves

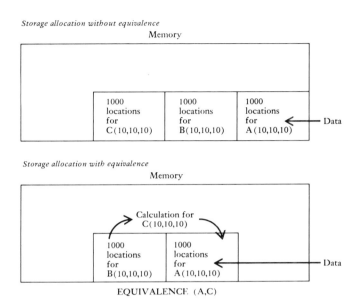

Figure 4.2   The use of the EQUIVALENCE statement.

dimensioned arrays which require allocation of many locations in memory, it is desirable to have some way of making as efficient use of memory as possible. In Fortran the mechanism for doing this is the EQUIVALENCE statement.

Suppose an array A(10,10,10) refers to some data read into memory (see Figure 4.2) which in turn is used to calculate another array B(10,10,10) which, later in the calculation, is used to generate still another array C(10,10,10). Ordinarily 1000 = 10 x 10 x 10 locations would be needed for A, B, and C. But, if by the time C is calculated, the data in A are no longer needed, it would make sense to reuse the 1000 locations allocated to A for the array C. One way of doing this would be just to rename C as A. But this may cause confusion in reading the program if A and C both have some mnemonic significance. In Fortran we accomplish this using the statement

EQUIVALENCE (A,C)

which tells the compiler to assign the same locations to A and C. Panel 4.12 gives a general description of the equivalence statement and indicates various ways in which the data can be assigned to the same locations in memory.

One part of Panel 4.12 which requires further discussion is the note with the statement EQUIVALENCE (A(2,1),B(2)) which states that A(2,1) is the second

Panel 4.12 Storage allocation

FORTRAN

Equivalence statement.

Syntax

EQUIVALENCE followed by a list of elements separated by commas, where each element of the list is a sequence of variable names, subscripted or unsubscripted, separated by commas, with the whole element enclosed in parentheses.

Semantics

All variables within each pair of parentheses occupy the same storage locations; if the variable is an array name *without* subscripts, then the element of the array with all subscripts equal to 1 is the one referenced.

Examples

i) Let A and B be dimensioned A(5,3) and B(6); then the following EQUIVALENCE statements are identical:

EQUIVALENCE (A,B)	—refers to A (1,1) and B(1).
EQUIVALENCE (A,B(1))	
EQUIVALENCE (B(1), A(1,1))	—order of the variables is irrelevant.
EQUIVALENCE (A(1,1),B)	
EQUIVALENCE (A(2,1),B(2))	—puts second element of both arrays in same location and, therefore, also the first elements.
EQUIVALENCE (A(4),B(4))	—puts fourth elements of both arrays in same location (see text).

ii) With A and B dimensioned as above and C,D,E,F unsubscribed:

EQUIVALENCE (A,B,C), (D,E,F)   —D,E, and F are assigned the same location and A(1,1), B(1), and C are assigned the same location.

iii) With A and B dimensioned as above and G dimensioned G(3,3), then

EQUIVALENCE (A,B), (A(7),G)

allows the last 9 elements of A (the seventh through the fifteenth) to be overlapped by G. Note that here, as in the first example, we may refer to the seventh element of A as A(7) even though A is a two-dimensional array.

ALGOL and PL/I

Dynamic storage allocation to be further described in Chapter 6.

COBOL

No analog of equivalence.

element of A. This assumes, of course, that the elements of the two-dimensional array A are stored in a particular fashion in sequential words of the computer memory. In fact, it is generally true in Fortran and most Algol implementations that arrays are stored by first varying the first subscript, then the second, etc.

Example 4.5

In what order are the elements of two- and three-dimensional arrays stored in Fortran and Algol (if storing is by column)?

The first element of any array in Fortran is the one with all subscripts equal to 1. Thus in Fortran the array A(5,5) would be stored in the order

A(1,1),A(2,1), . . . ,A(5,1),A(1,2),A(2,2), . . . ,A(5,2), . . . ,A(4,5),A(5,5)

In matrix terminology we call this *storing by columns.* Similarly, B(2,3,4) would be stored in the order

B(1,1,1), B(2,1,1), B(1,2,1), B(2,2,1), B(1,3,1), B(2,3,1),
    B(1,1,2), . . . ,B(2,3,2), B(1,1,3), . . . ,B(2,3,4)

The Algol array C[-3:1,2:3] would be stored in the order

C[-3,2], C[-2,2], . . . ,C[0,2], C[1,2], C[-3,3], . . . ,C[1,3]

PL/I, however, stores arrays by row rather than by column because this is the preference of most people who work with matrices. Knowledge of the order in which elements of arrays are stored in computer memories may be useful in finding errors in programs and in performing tricky kinds of storage allocation.

Other parts of Panel 4.12 requiring discussion are the EQUIVALENCE (A(4),B(4)) and EQUIVALENCE (A,B), (A(7),G) statements. In an equivalence statement an array element with more than one subscript may be replaced by one with a single subscript which corresponds to the position where the element with more than one subscript would be (Problem 22). Thus, for example, A(4) refers to the fourth element of A which, from Example 4.4, we see could have been written instead as A(4,1). Similarly, instead of A(7) we could have written A(2,2).

In Algol there is no mechanism similar to the equivalence statement in Fortran. However, Algol has in its program structure a way of allocating memory and releasing it when it is no longer needed. We shall discuss this program structure and mechanism in Section 6.1.2. Suffice it to say here that the ability to allocate and free storage as needed, which is called *dynamic storage alloca-*

tion, provides a much more flexible means of storage allocation than the essentially *static* allocation of Fortran.

PL/I has a program structure and allocates storage in a manner similar to Algol. However, in addition to the automatic dynamic storage allocation facilities of Algol, PL/I also gives the programmer more direct control over the storage allocated to a given name by allowing him to allocate and free storage for a variable with special statements in his program (see Section 6.1.2). Also, PL/I allows an analog of equivalence in Fortran through the DEFINED option in a DECLARE statement. For example, DECLARE X FIXED, Y FIXED DEFINED X; assigns Y to the same location as X.

4.4.3 Structures

Arrays provide a simple, relatively unsophisticated way of grouping related quantities into a whole. However, particularly in data processing applications, data is often naturally structured in a more complex fashion. As an example, consider a standard payroll file. The *employee names* in the file form a normal linear (one-dimensional) array. This file will also contain other information, such as the hours the employee has worked in the last pay period, both regular and overtime, the rate of pay for this employee, both regular and overtime, as well as various other data. Each of the additional pieces of data attached to each employee name could be structured as a linear array, thereby making the whole payroll file a two-dimensional array as indicated in Figure 4.3. One problem with the arrangement in Figure 4.3 is that, as an array of numbers stored in a computer, all the fine structure of the payroll file is lost. There is no indication that the second and third columns contain related quantities nor that the fourth and fifth also contain related quantities nor that each of these latter relate back to columns two and three.

As another example of the need for data structures more complex than arrays, consider the problem of playing any board-type game like checkers or chess on a computer. At any given time, when it is the computer's turn to move, there will be a certain *board position.* A typical computer program to play the game will, much like a human player, consider various possible moves that can be made, possible responses by the opponent to each of these, possible next moves by the computer, and so on down to some depth. At some point the program will apply some kind of evaluation procedure to all the sequences of moves it has considered and on the basis of this evaluation choose a move. A good computer program will not consider all possible moves or responses to these; by use of heuristics (cf. Section 2.4), obviously bad moves by either the computer or its opponent (which might be another computer or a human player) will be eliminated. At any rate, when applying the evaluation procedure, the program will in effect be considering the possible paths on a *game tree,* an

NAME(1)	HRSREG(1)	HRSOVR(1)	RATREG(1)	RATOVR(1)
NAME(2)	HRSREG(2)	HRSOVR(2)	RATREG(2)	RATOVR(2)
NAME(3)	HRSREG(3)	HRSOVR(3)	RATREG(3)	RATOVR(3)
.	.	.	.	.
.	.	.	.	.
.	.	.	.	.

Figure 4.3   Payroll file as a two-dimensional array.

example of which is shown in Figure 4.4. Each path from the top of the tree to one of the positions at the bottom must be evaluated. The heuristics are used to terminate "uninteresting paths." Our purpose here is not to consider game trees in any further detail but merely to point out that this *tree structure* cannot in any simple and efficient fashion be stored in the computer as an array.

Both PL/I and Cobol have facilities which enable programmers to store and manipulate more complicated data structures than arrays. Cobol calls these more complicated entities *files*, while PL/I just calls them *structures.*

The basic notion in both files and structures is that of the *level* of an element of data (i.e., analogous to the level of each intersection of the tree in Figure 4.4). In arrays all elements are implicitly at the same level; that is, no elements are implicitly more important than any others. In a structure (which word we shall use hereafter instead of "file") each element has a *level number* which relates it to other elements in much the same way that the paragraphs and subparagraphs of a typical outline are related.

The forms of structures in Cobol and PL/I are indicated in Panel 4.13. The Cobol Data Division will be discussed further in Chapter 6. The first example in Panel 4.13 refers to our previous payroll example and indicates the relationships of entities in the structure. This structure, like any other, can be displayed graphically as a tree as shown here.

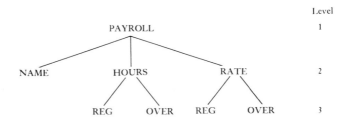

Elements of structures are named like other variables except that, when there is some possible ambiguity, *qualification* of the name is required. Thus, in the

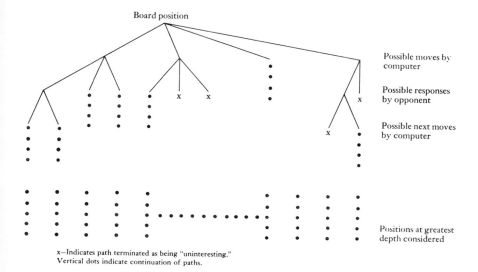

x—Indicates path terminated as being "uninteresting."
Vertical dots indicate continuation of paths.

Figure 4.4   A game tree.

example above, the whole structure may be referred to as PAYROLL, or parts of it may be referred to as HOURS or RATE. But to refer to REG or OVER is ambiguous. In PL/I we could use HOURS.REG or HOURS.OVER to distinguish these from RATE.REG and RATE.OVER. Correspondingly, in Cobol we would use REG IN HOURS or OVER IN RATE. If there were another structure in the same program with the name HOURS in it then we would qualify HOURS as PAYROLL.HOURS (PL/I) or HOURS IN PAYROLL (Cobol).

Note that the actual data resides only in the lowest *node* on any path, that is, NAME, HOURS.REG, HOURS.OVER, RATE.REG, RATE.OVER. In either Cobol or PL/I, data structures such as described above may be manipulated by designating any node of the tree, in which case *all lower nodes* are automatically included. That is, an instruction to move HOURS from one part of memory to another moves.

to the desired location. Indeed, many Cobol computations are largely involved with such manipulations of data structures.

Panel 4.13   Structures

PL/I

Called *structures*

Form

After DECLARE, a sequence, separated by commas, of variable names each preceded by a *level number*, which is a positive integer, and followed optionally by a subscript list in parentheses; the first level number must be 1, all succeeding level numbers must be 2 or greater.

COBOL

Called *files* and *records*

After preliminary information in DATA DIVISION of the program, a list of variable names one to a line preceded by a level number, which is a 2-digit positive integer between 01 and 49 (leading zeros may be omitted in some implementations) and (except on level 01) followed usually by a PICTURE clause, optionally by an OCCURS clause and a period (also in level 01); in addition to 01 through 49, level numbers 66 (used for renaming data names), 77 (used for constants), and 88 (used for specific values of a variable) may also be used. Various optional clauses may be inserted on each level.

A file contains one or more records; the name of each record appears on level 01; the level numbers subsequent to 01 indicate the hierarchy of elements in the record; the OCCURS clause indicates how many different items there are corresponding to the variable.

Semantics

The level numbers indicate the hierarchy of the elements in the structure; the name at level 1 is the name of the structure; the subscript list indicates that the item indicated is an array, all elements of which are at the indicated level.

```
DECLARE 1 PAYROLL, 2 NAME,        01 PAYROLL.
2 HOURS, 3 REG, 3 OVER,             02 NAME.
2 RATE, 3 REG, 3 OVER;              02 HOURS.
                                        03 REG.
                                        03 OVER.
                                    02 RATE.
                                        03 REG.
                                        03 OVER.
```

In both cases above the PICTURE attribute and PICTURE clause, respectively, have been omitted.

```
DECLARE 1 A, 2 B, 3 C(2,2),       01 A.
3 D, 2 E(3), 3 F, 4 G(2),           02 B.
3 H;                                    03 C OCCURS 4 TIMES.
                                        03 D.
                                    02 E OCCURS 3 TIMES.
                                        03 F.
                                            04 G OCCURS 2 TIMES.
                                        03 H.
```

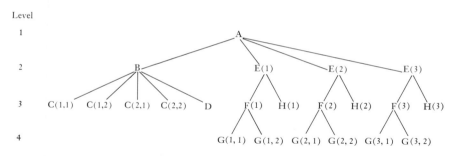

Figure 4.5   PL/I tree structure.

The second example in Panel 4.13 indicates the use of arrays within structures. The PL/I example, shown as a tree structure in Figure 4.5, indicates that on level 3, C is a 2 x 2 array, etc. We could then refer to an element of the array C as C(1,2), but if C appears as an element of another structure we could refer to C(1,2) as:

B.C(1,2) or A.B.C.(1,2)

To refer to an element of G we write G(2,1) where the first subscript refers to the higher level array E and the second to G itself. In Cobol multiple subscripts occur when a name at one level is subscripted and a name at a higher level is also subscripted. Since Cobol is limited to three subscripts, names at only three levels can have OCCURS clauses. The Cobol structure with subscripts in Panel 4.13 is not quite the same as the PL/I structure because of the C(2,2) in one and the C OCCURS 4 TIMES in the other. To simulate the double subscripting of PL/I in Cobol we could write

03 C OCCURS 2 TIMES.
    04 CBAR OCCURS 2 TIMES.

Then referring to an element in CBAR we could write

CBAR (1,2).

4.4.4   Lists and List Structures

The reader may have noticed the usefulness of "lists" in describing the syntax of some of the structures discussed in this chapter. Lists are certainly a convenient data structure in many types of nonnumeric computer applications. Although

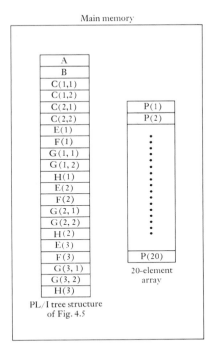

Main memory

| A |
| B |
| C(1,1) |
| C(1,2) |
| C(2,1) |
| C(2,2) |
| E(1) |
| F(1) |
| G(1, 1) |
| G(1, 2) |
| H(1) |
| E(2) |
| F(2) |
| G(2, 1) |
| G(2, 2) |
| H(2) |
| E(3) |
| F(3) |
| G(3, 1) |
| G(3, 2) |
| H(3) |

PL/I tree structure
of Fig. 4.5

| P(1) |
| P(2) |
| ⋮ |
| P(20) |

20-element
array

Figure 4.6   Storage of arrays and structures.

the structures we shall discuss in this section (lists and list structures) are not allowable data structures in any of the languages we are discussing, they are sufficiently important and interesting in computer applications to merit some discussion here. Moreover, as we shall see, there are strong resemblances between these structures and those discussed in the previous sections.

A *list* is a linear or one-dimensional array of data items. Or it may be looked upon as a one-level structure. Lists differ from one-dimensional arrays and one-level structures in the way they are stored in the main memory of the computer. Arrays and structures are always stored in contiguous memory locations as indicated in Figure 4.6 where the structure is that of Figure 4.5. By contrast, lists need not and usually are not stored contiguously. Therefore, it follows that each memory word of a list must contain two things:

i) the data item, often called the *symbol* part because lists are commonly used for nonnumeric symbol manipulation.

ii) a pointer or *link* to the next element in the list.

Sometimes list elements contain additional information; in particular, it is not

Main memory

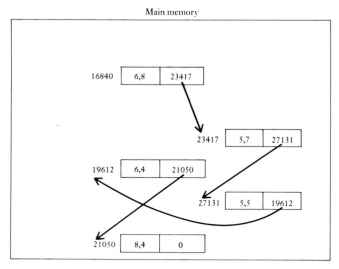

Figure 4.7   Storage of lists.

uncommon to have a pointer *back* to the previous element in the list. On a
36-bit word computer a list element might appear as

S1   2021   35

SYMBOL	LINK

with the 15-bit link being in the normal place for an address in a machine-
language instruction. As an example, a list of the moves a knight could make
after the third move in the knight's tour shown in Figure 2.14 might be stored as
shown in Figure 4.7. The symbol part consists of the row and column
coordinates of the move, separated by a comma, stored in the first 18 bits of the
word using the code of Table 3.6 (Problem 31). Bits 18, 19, and 20 of each word
would be blank. The 0 link in the word at address 21050 indicates that this word
terminates the list.

One important advantage of list storage over the arrays and structures we
have considered previously is clearly the flexibility it gives in *allocation of
storage*. To store a 100-element list, 100 contiguous locations are not needed,
but rather any 100 empty locations. Compilers and other language processors
which deal with lists always include a *list of available space* which is structured
as a list itself and contains the locations of all currently empty cells (words). The
real value of this type of facility is that it negates the need for fixing the *size* of a
structure in the source program. Since storage does not have to be allocated in
blocks there is no need for the compiler to know maximum sizes of lists when it

Main memory

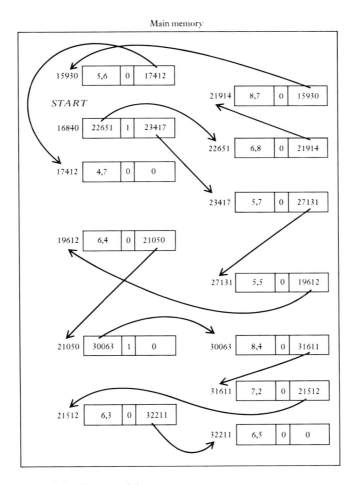

Figure 4.8   Storage of list structures.

compiles the program. This is particularly useful in various symbol-manipulating programs in which the maximum size of a structure cannot be predicted prior to the calculation. This occurs, for example, in game-playing programs in which the maximum depth as well as the number of branches in the game tree may not be known. Even if they were, it would be inefficient to set aside the maximum amount of storage which would ever be needed when, during most of the calculation, much less would be needed.[†]

[†]Programs which process lists usually contain a mechanism, picturesquely called *garbage collectors,* for returning unused words to the list of available space.

But lists, as we have discussed them thus far, will not allow the storage of a multilevel structure such as a game tree. For this we need not lists but *list structures* in which a given list may have sublists and sublists of sublists, etc. Again using the knight's tour illustrated in Figure 2.14, we illustrate a list structure in Figure 4.8 in which the main list contains the possible moves after Move 3, and Moves 1 and 5 are on sublists which also contain the moves which can be made at the next stage from each of the original moves. Figure 4.8 is best understood using the following schematic with all addresses removed:

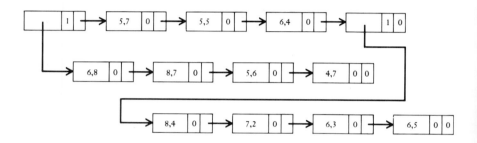

In the figure and schematic we have added a bit before the address part of the word to indicate whether the 20-bit symbol part holds a symbol (0 bit) or an address of a sublist (1 bit). Each of the two sublists contains the original move followed by all moves which can be made from it. The end of a sublist, like the end of the main list, is indicated by a 0 link.

Another significant advantage of list storage is the flexibility it allows in *editing* the lists by appending, inserting, deleting elements, etc. A number of computer languages exist whose purpose is to facilitate the manipulation of lists. Also, the PL/I language provides substantial list-processing-like facilities and there are extensions of both Fortran (called SLIP) and Algol (called Formula Algol) to permit list processing to be done in Fortran and Algol programs. However, discussion of these languages is beyond the scope of this book. On this subject the reader is referred to the Bibliography.

BIBLIOGRAPHIC NOTES

The details of the syntax of constants and variables may be found in the language references for Fortran, Algol, PL/I, and Cobol given at the end of Chapter 2, or from the descriptions of these languages in the manuals for a given computer.

Computer scientists are paying more attention to the subject of data structures because of the increasing importance of nonnumeric calculations; see Knuth (1968) and Wegner (1968). Because of the growing tendency to try to solve very large problems, storage allocation is of more and more importance. Chapter 9 of Hassitt (1967) contains some interesting material on this subject but the reader should probably go a bit further in this book before turning to that material. For further material on lists, list structures, and list-processing languages, we suggest the introductory material in Newell (1964) and Part 4 in Rosen (1967).

Bibliography

Hassitt, A. (1967): *Computer Programming and Computer Systems*, Academic Press, New York.

Knuth, D. E. (1968): *The Art of Computer Programming*, vol. 1: *Fundamental Algorithms*, Addison-Wesley Publishing Company, Reading, Mass.

Newell, A., et al. (1964): *Information Processing Language — V Manual, Second Edition*, Prentice-Hall, Inc., Englewood Cliffs, N.J.

Rosen, S., ed. (1967): *Programming Systems and Languages*, McGraw-Hill Book Company, New York.

Wegner, P. (1968): *Programming Languages, Information Structures, and Machine Organization*, McGraw-Hill Book Company, New York.

PROBLEMS

Section 4.1

1. Let integer fixed-point constants be stored as binary integers with the binary point at the right-hand end of the word. On a 36-bit-word computer how would the following be stored?

   a) 637
   b) -49
   c) 212
   d) 10110B (PL/I)

2. Any of the four languages can store integers as fixed-point numbers inside the computer. But PL/I and Cobol allow fixed-point constants which can have interior decimal points. Discuss methods which might be used to store such

constants internally in the computer, assuming that the decimal point position would be somehow retained in the memory.

3. Write BNF definitions of:
  a) numeric literals in Cobol. (Hint: Define *decimal part* and then use *this* definition in that of numeric literal.)
  b) binary fixed-point constants in PL/I.

4. On a binary computer with a 36-bit word, a 27-bit mantissa, and an 8-bit excess-128 exponent, how would the following floating-point numbers be stored?

  a) 2.5E4
  b) -3.125E-1
  c) 1011.01E13B (PL/I)

5. On a computer with the same characteristics as in Problem 4, suppose an Algol or PL/I system allowed double-precision constants and recognized that a constant was double-precision when it had more than a certain number of (nonexponent) digits specified. What minimum number of digits should indicate that a constant is double-precision on such a computer? Why?

6. Suppose a language for a computer with the characteristics of Problem 4 allowed numbers of higher than double-precision in such a way that numbers of nth precision occupied n words, in each of which the exponent was $(27)_{10}$ less than in the previous one. What is the largest n that can be considered? Why?

Section 4.2

7. Explain the reasons for the restrictions in Algol, PL/I, and Cobol on the use of ' in strings.

8. Strings are normally stored inside the computer as a sequence of characters using, for example, the code of Table 3.6. Using this code, show how the nonnumeric literal '16431' would be stored in Cobol.

9. Using the code of Table 3.6 on a 36-bit-word computer, how would the following be stored?

  a) 'SILLY EXAMPLE'
  b) '42 + *) ('
  c) (4) 'D''ONT' (PL/I)

10. Repeat Problem 9 for a computer with a byte-organized memory using the code of Table 3.6.

Section 4.3

11. From a knowledge of the 360 computer for which PL/I was originally designed, explain why PL/I has a wider variety of type declaration words and combinations of them than the other three languages.

12. Which of the following type declarations in PL/I are redundant or have redundant parts and why?

a) DECLARE (I7, A, B41) REAL;
b) DECLARE (A, J14, C30) FIXED BINARY;
c) DECLARE (D10, E, KY) FLOAT DECIMAL;

13. Explain why it is necessary that a variable name in a program must always have values of one type only.

14. From the programmer's point of view, what are the relative merits of allowing default options in variable typing as in Fortran or PL/I or requiring type declarations as in Algol?

Section 4.4.1

15. Give a BNF definition of subscript in Fortran.

16. State which of the following are illegal subscripted variable names in Fortran. Give a reason.

a) R(6, I, 7.3)
b) A(I + 4, 2 * J- 3)
c) N14(I;J)
d) P62Z(2 * K + 8, 9 + LL)
e) TUVW (1,400 * I, 1,200 * J- 10,000)

17. If the array of Figure 4.1 is named A, which elements of the array are specified by the following in PL/I?

a) A(*, 4)
b) A(6, *)

Section 4.4.2

18. a) Discuss the possible advantages of allowing subscripts to have zero and negative values as well as positive values.

   b) Would you expect the flexibility of allowing subscripts to be specified by arithmetic expressions to be very useful?

19. How many memory locations are set aside in memory by the following dimension specifications?

   a) DIMENSION B(6,4,7), C25(10,2)
   b) **array** A1, B4[-7:6, -3 * 2:8+4, 0:7], D[1:4, -8:18];
   c) DECLARE S(10, -7:6+3), T4(-5:104, -6 * (-3):25);

20. a) If A is dimensioned 10 x 15 and if A(1,1) is stored in location 6400, and successive elements of A are stored in successively higher locations, in what location are the following elements stored?
   i) A(6,9) and A(9,6) in Fortran
   ii) A(6,9) and A(9,6) in PL/I

   b) How do the answers to (a)(i) change if A is declared double-precision?

21. Consider the following situation:

   i) A 10 x 15 array A is to be read in as starting data for a calculation.
   ii) From this a 10 x 30 array B is to be calculated, after which the last 10 columns of A will no longer be needed.
   iii) From B, a 5 x 15 array C is to be calculated.
   iv) Finally, a 10 x 10 array D is to be calculated from C, after which the last 5 rows of B will no longer be needed.

   Write an EQUIVALENCE statement to make the most efficient use of memory given the above information.

22. a) Derive a relationship between the positions of an element in a Fortran array as stored in the computer and its subscripts for two-dimensional arrays. That is, find a function which relates N, the position in the array relative to the first element, and I and J, the subscripts of the element and ID and JD, the dimensions of the array.

   b) Repeat (a) for three-dimensional arrays.

   c) Repeat (a) and (b) for PL/I arrays.

23. Suppose you wished two arrays dimensioned $i \times j$ and $k \times l$, respectively, to be stored contiguously in memory. Show how an EQUIVALENCE statement might be used to accomplish this.

Section 4.4.3

24. a) Given the position

0	x	x
0	0	–
–	–	x

in a game of tick-tack-toe, draw a game tree which expresses all possible paths the rest of the game might take.

b) Write this tree as PL/I and Cobol structures.

25. Draw a tree corresponding to the Cobol structure in the second example of Panel 4.13.

26. Use PL/I or Cobol structures to show how you might organize a file consisting of the following data:

i) student's name
ii) Social Security number
iii) parents' names
iv) student's address
v) parents' addresses
vi) birthplaces of student and parents
vii) main field of study
viii) grade-point average

27. In the Cobol structure

```
01 AB.
  02 ABC.
  02 C  OCCURS 5 TIMES.
    03 D  OCCURS 4 TIMES.
      04 FCD OCCURS 3 TIMES.
    03 E14F OCCURS 6 TIMES.
      04 G.
  02 H OCCURS 3 TIMES.
```

show how to refer to the following elements:
  a) the second in FCD, corresponding to the second in C and the third in D
  b) the fourth in E14F, corresponding to the first in C
  c) the first in D, corresponding to the second in C
  d) the second in H

28. Suppose you wanted to store the structure in Figure 4.5 in Fortran some-how. Suggest means by which you might accomplish this.

Section 4.4.4

29. a) Consider the following list in memory where the first part of each word is a data item and the second part of each word is a pointer (link) to the next element in the list:

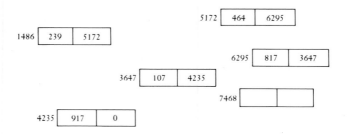

Show what would have to be inserted at location 7468 and what other changes would have to be made so that location 7468 would hold a data item 487 which would fall on the list between items 817 and 107.

  b) If 107 instead of 917 were to be made the last item in the list (i.e., 917 is to be deleted), what changes would have to be made?

30. Use the notation on p. 146 to indicate how the tree structure of Figure 4.5 would be organized as a list.

31. Indicate the contents of each of the memory words in Figure 4.7 in binary.

5

computer languages —
arithmetic and simple decision making

What would life be without arithmetic, but a scene of horrors?

Time destroys the boundless conceits of men; it confirms decision founded on reality.

Cicero in *De Natura Deorum*

Since this chapter is concerned with the means of expressing the actual calculation processes of arithmetic in programming languages, it will be of greater interest to scientific than business programmers. The facilities for arithmetic in Cobol are quite limited, as we shall see in this chapter. For scientific programmers an understanding of the material in this chapter lies at the heart of their competence. The material in the first section, in particular, which is never found in programming manuals, should be understood.

5.1 COMPUTER ARITHMETIC AND REAL ARITHMETIC

Our discussion of roundoff, overflow, and underflow in Chapter 3 illustrated some anomalies of computer arithmetic as compared to arithmetic in the real number system. In this section we shall show that the main effect of these anomalies is that the common laws of arithmetic do not hold in computer arithmetic.

The reader is surely familiar with the associative, commutative, and distributive laws of arithmetic. If a, b, and c, are real numbers, these state that:

Associative laws
Addition: $a+(b+c) = (a+b)+c$
Multiplication: $a \cdot (b \cdot c) = (a \cdot b) \cdot c$

Commutative laws
Addition: $a+b = b+a$
Multiplication: $a \cdot b = b \cdot a$

Distributive law
$a \cdot (b+c) = a \cdot b + a \cdot c$

In arithmetic as performed in a computer, only the two commutative laws hold for both fixed- and floating-point arithmetic. Indeed, even these may not hold on a computer which allows zero to have a plus or minus sign and which does not have consistent rules for setting this sign.[†] Overflow and underflow are one cause of the failure of the associative and distributive laws on computers as the following two examples indicate.

Example 5.1

On a binary computer with a 6-bit word[††] and negative numbers stored as absolute value and sign, show how overflow causes violation of the associative and distributive laws in fixed-point calculations. Let

		S12345	
a	=	111000	$(-3/4)$
b	=	010000	$(1/2)$
c	=	011000	$(3/4)$

and let us assume that when overflow occurs the carry out of position 1 replaces the sign bit. Then using normal arithmetic

		S12345	
$a+b$	=	101000	$(-1/4)$
$(a+b) + c$	=	010000	$(1/2)$

[†] On binary computers, if negative numbers are stored as absolute value and sign, then all zeros in the non-sign bits with a 0 or 1 in the sign position represents zero. If negative numbers are stored in ones complement form then all 1s represents a minus zero. If negative numbers are stored in twos complement form no minus zero is possible. (Why?)

[††] For illustrative purposes only; the extension to 36-bit or other word lengths is obvious.

correctly but

$$b+c \quad = \quad 101000 \qquad (-1/4)$$
$$a+(b+c) \quad = \quad 000000 \qquad (0)$$

since both $b+c$ and $a+(b+c)$ overflow. Also,

$$a \cdot b \quad = \quad 101100 \qquad (-3/8)$$
$$a \cdot c \quad = \quad 110010 \qquad (-9/16)$$
$$a \cdot b + a \cdot c \quad = \quad 111110 \qquad (-15/16)$$

but

$$a \cdot (b+c) \quad = \quad 000110 \qquad (3/16)$$

Therefore, both the associative law for addition and the distributive law fail.

Example 5.2

On a decimal computer with a floating-point format consisting of an 8-digit mantissa and a 2-digit signed exponent (range −99 to +99), show how overflow and underflow cause violation of the associative and distributive laws. Assume overflow results in ten 9s with the proper sign of the mantissa and underflow results in a positive zero mantissa and a zero exponent.

i) Associative law for multiplication:
Let $a = 10^{-40}$
$b = 10^{60}$
$c = 10^{60}$

Then

$$a \cdot (b \cdot c) = a \cdot \boxed{99 \ 99999999}$$
$$= \boxed{59 \ 99999999}$$

But

$$(a \cdot b) \cdot c = 10^{20} \cdot 10^{60} = \boxed{81 \ 10000000}$$

With the sign of each exponent reversed there is a similar example for underflow (Problem 1).

ii) Associative law for addition:
Let $a = 10^{-95}$
$b = 10^{-99}$
$c = -1.001 \times 10^{-99}$

Then

$$a+(b+c) = a + \boxed{00\ 00000000}$$
$$= \boxed{9\overline{4}\ 10000000}$$

But

$$(a+b)+c = \boxed{9\overline{4}\ 10001000} + c$$
$$= \boxed{9\overline{5}\ 99999990}$$

iii) Distributive law:

Let $a = 10^{-40}$
   $b = .7 \times 10^{99}$
   $c = .8 \times 10^{99}$

Then

$$a\cdot(b+c) = a\cdot\boxed{99\ 99999999}$$
$$= \boxed{59\ 99999999}$$

But

$$a\cdot b + a\cdot c = .7 \times 10^{59} + .8 \times 10^{59}$$
$$= \boxed{60\ 15000000}$$

The reader should note that in the associative law for addition illustration in Example 5.2 it was assumed that when the number

$$\boxed{94\ 09999999}$$

was normalized to

$$\boxed{95\ 99999990}$$

a zero was inserted on the right. Depending upon how arithmetic is actually performed in the arithmetic unit of the computer, it might be better to insert a 5 if the place inserted could be any digit from 0 to 9. But normally the last 9 itself would be a rounded value and, therefore, 0 is the indicated choice for the inserted digit. (Why?)

In Chapter 3 we mentioned the need for scientific users of computers to be aware of the effects of roundoff error. Indeed, the rounding of numbers is another cause of the failure of the associative and distributive laws, although we shall not illustrate this here. A related topic, which is appropriate to discuss here, is the loss of significance due to subtraction. Consider the two floating-point numbers

$$17.686371 = \boxed{02\ 17686371}$$
$$17.684137 = \boxed{02\ 17684137}$$

in each of which the 8 digits might have physical significance. But the difference of these two numbers

$$.002234 = \boxed{0\overline{2}\ 22340000}$$

only has 4 significant digits. Thus, while each factor may have been accurate to five parts in 10^9 (8-digit accuracy), the difference may be accurate to no more than one part in 10^4 because of the loss of digits in subtraction and the possible addition of the errors in the two factors (Problem 3). No one involved in scientific calculation can afford to be unaware of the perils involved in the subtraction of nearly equal quantities (or, equivalently, the addition of quantities of nearly equal magnitude and opposite sign).

The purpose of this section has not been to worry the new user of a computer about the arithmetic results he will get but rather to provide a *caveat* against plunging into lengthy computer calculations with the assumption that all is just the same as familiar arithmetic. With this section behind us we may now begin consideration of how the operations of arithmetic are specified in P-O languages.

5.2   ARITHMETIC EXPRESSIONS

To continue our analogy to the terminology of natural language, arithmetic expressions correspond to *phrases*. They are the main building blocks used to form the *sentence* or *statement* called an *assignment statement* which we shall discuss in Section 5.4.

Informally an arithmetic expression consists of *any combination of variables and constants which conforms to the ordinary laws of algebra.* Thus A+B is a valid arithmetic expression but

A + * B

is not.[†] Implicit in the above is that the combination of the variables and constants is to be achieved by using the operations of arithmetic. Our first consideration in this section is which arithmetic *operators* can be used in forming arithmetic expressions. Panel 5.1 indicates the allowable operators and their notation which, with one exception, are the same for the four languages.

Besides the operators listed in Panel 5.1, Cobol allows another means for indicating arithmetic operations which we shall consider in Section 5.4. We

---

[†]Some languages, including PL/I, allow A+−B, which is interpreted as A+(−B).

emphasize that the operators in Panel 5.1 *must* be used in all combinations of arithmetic variables. For example, to multiply A and B, A*B must be written, not just AB. The reason for this is, of course, that AB denotes the single variable name AB.

The first two operators in Panel 5.1 may be either *unary* or *binary*. That is, they may be used with one operand (unary) as

    +A

or

    −B

or with two operands (binary), as

    C + D
    R − 21.7E4

The other four operators, however, are always binary:

    A * D
    2.0/GE7
    H2 ** 3
    I÷J

Panel 5.1   Arithmetic operators

Name of Operator	Symbol
Add	+
Subtract	−
Multiply	*
Divide	/
Exponentiation	** (↑ in Algol)
Integer divide (Algol only)	÷

The integer divide operator ($\div$) in Algol is reserved for the special case where both operands are integers and is discussed in Section 5.2.1.

The inclusion of the exponentiation operator with the four usual arithmetic operators in Panel 5.1 requires some explanation. This operator has the meaning of raising to a power; thus H2**3 is equivalent to H2*H2*H2 and H2**(−2) means 1/(H2*H2). But, if the exponent (3 and −2, respectively, in the examples above) is not an integer, there is no immediate analogy with multiplication or division. In this case the evaluation must be performed using the logarithm and exponential functions. Thus to evaluate

$$A ** B$$

we take the current values of the variables A and B and form†

$$B \cdot \ln A$$

from which

$$A ** B = e^{B \cdot \ln A}$$

The necessary logarithm and exponential function calculations are done using programmed approximations to these functions. Even when the exponent is an integer or an integer variable, the computation is often performed using logarithms and exponentials because, for example, it is more efficient to compute

$$A ** 20$$

as

$$e^{20 \cdot \ln A}$$

than it is to compute it as

$$A*A*A*A*A*A*A*A*A*A*A*A*A*A*A*A*A*A*A*A$$

because the machine-language instructions for the 19 multiplications require more time than the instructions needed to calculate the logarithm and exponential. Typically, compilers use the logarithm-exponential approach if the integer exponent is greater than about 7.

But why include exponentiation as an operator at all? Why not require that all exponentiation be done by the programmer using logarithms and exponentials? If there is to be a special operator for exponentiation, why not also for sine or cosine or other common functions? The answer to this is simply that the exponentiation operator is so common that it is a great convenience for the programmer to provide a special operator for it.

---

† ln is the notation for the natural logarithm, that is, the logarithm to the base e; this function and the standard exponential function are virtually always the ones used for exponentiation on computers.

The reader should not confuse the $**$ operator ($\uparrow$ in Algol) with the D and E notation used previously. The latter can appear only in constants and always implies a power of 10 (or sometimes 2 in PL/I). The $**$ operator is used to raise any number, constant or variable, to a power. Thus, A$**$10 may not be replaced by AE10 (which would be treated as a variable name), but 2.6E8 may be replaced in an expression by 2.6$*$10.$**$8.

Where the word "variables" appears in the definition of expression at the beginning of this section, the implication is that only scalar variables—that is, unsubscripted variables or array variables with subscripts but no array variables without subscripts—are allowed. This is correct except in PL/I which also allows expressions where variables are arrays and even structures. However, we shall not discuss these features of PL/I in this book. The interested reader is referred to the main PL/I reference at the end of Chapter 2. Because of this feature of PL/I, expressions in that language, all of whose variables are scalar variables, are called *scalar expressions*. This terminology is not used or needed in the other languages. PL/I also allows expressions containing string variables but we shall not discuss them here.

5.2.1   Mode

Our heuristic definition of arithmetic expressions in the previous section barely even hints at the formal problems involved in forming such expressions. In one particular this definition is misleading for it implies that different types of variables and constants can be included in the same arithmetic expression. But in Fortran this is not true. In Fortran, as in Algol and PL/I, an arithmetic expression is said to have a certain *mode* which is determined by the "dominant" type of variable or constant in the expression. For example, an expression containing both integer and real quantities is said to have real mode. In Fortran, as we shall discuss below, variables of different types may be mixed in arithmetic expressions only in certain ways. In PL/I and Algol there are no such restrictions, but it is necessary to set up rules which determine procedure when certain types of variables are intermixed. Since all arithmetic is fixed-point in Cobol the problem of mode does not arise in this language.

Panel 5.2 considers the problem of mode in Fortran, Algol, and PL/I. The hierarchical order of the modes means that the mode of the expression is determined by the mode of the variable or constant highest in the hierarchy. Thus in Algol, if there is any real variable or constant, the whole expression is real. In Fortran double-precision and complex have equal status which results in no ambiguity since, as indicated in Table 5.1, double-precision and complex types

Panel 5.2   Mode

FORTRAN	*ALGOL*	*PL/I*

Possible modes in hierarchical order

FORTRAN	ALGOL	PL/I
Double precision- Complex Real Integer	Real Integer	⎰ Complex ⎱ Real ⎰ Floating ⎱ Fixed

Restrictions on mixing mode

FORTRAN	ALGOL	PL/I
1. Subscripts (always integer) allowed in any expression 2. Integer exponents allowed in any expression 3. Function arguments not restricted in any way (see Chapter 7) 4. See Table 5.1	None	None

Table 5.1   Fortran mixed-mode restrictions

Mode of expression	*Allowable types of variables and constants in expression*[†]			
	Integer	*Real*	*Double-Precision*	*Complex*
Integer	Yes	No	No	No
Real	No	Yes	No	No
Double-Precision	No	Yes	Yes	No
Complex	No	Yes	No	Yes

cannot be intermixed in the same expression.[††] In PL/I mode is determined separately between complex and real and floating and fixed. Thus, an expression may have mode complex, fixed or floating, or real, fixed or floating.

[†] Some Fortran compilers allow any mixture of modes, in which case all quantities in the expression are converted to the highest mode in the hierarchy in the expression. When double-precision and complex are mixed, typically the real parts of all quantities are converted to double-precision and the imaginary parts are carried as single-precision.

[††]Except for subscripts and exponents, see Panel 5.2.

The restrictions on mixing modes in arithmetic expressions in Fortran exist for purely historical reasons: the writers of early Fortran compilers wished to avoid the difficulties of implementing mixed mode. Indeed, as indicated in the footnote, many Fortran compilers now allow mixed mode with no restrictions despite the formal language restriction on it.

The previous discussion implies that if a Fortran expression contains all integer variables and constants, the result is an integer. This is also true in Algol, except that the use of the / operator always produces a real result no matter what the operands. Thus any expression in Algol which contains a / is real. Only by using the ÷ operator can an integral result be produced in division. This brings up the question in Algol (as well as the other languages) of the result of the division of two integers since, although the true result of addition, subtraction, or multiplication of two integers is integral, the true result of the division of two integers is, in general, not integral. In Algol the result of 5/2 is 2.5 in floating-point form since the use of / always results in a real result. But what about 5/2 in Fortran, Cobol, or PL/I or 5÷2 in Algol? In all except PL/I the answer is that the result is truncated by throwing any resulting fractional part away whether the result is positive or negative. Thus

$$5/2 \rightarrow 2 \text{ (Algol: } 5 \div 2 \rightarrow 2)$$

and

$$-5/2 \rightarrow -2 \text{ (Algol: } -5 \div 2 \rightarrow -2)$$

A convenient mathematical way of expressing this is that, if I and J are integer variables,

$$I/J \text{ (or } I \div J \text{ in Algol)} \rightarrow \text{sign } (I/J) [| I/J|]$$

where the sign function is + or − as in ordinary algebra and the notation [   ] specifies the *largest integer* less than or equal to the quantity inside the brackets.[†] This function is often called the *entier* function (cf. Section 7.1). Since the quantity inside the brackets is [I/J], that is, the *absolute value*[††] of I/J, this expresses formally the informal description above. The above should warn the reader that integer division should be avoided except in special cases.[†††]

The PL/I situation for integer arithmetic is quite different from Fortran and Algol. The reader will recall from Section 4.1 that data with the attribute

---

[†]Thus [2.7] = 2, but [−2.7] = −3.

[††]|x| = x if x ⩾ 0, but = −x if x < 0.

[†††]One case is the determination of whether or not one integer is a divisor of another (Problem 7).

FIXED are not restricted to be integers but can be decimal or binary numbers. Thus, when a PL/I expression has fixed mode, this means its value in the computer is stored in fixed- rather than floating-point form and need not be integral. The value of 5/2 in PL/I is, therefore, 2.5. The computer keeps track of where the decimal or binary point is in the fixed point storage of 2.5.

A similar problem to the above arises in the case of exponentiation involving integers where the exponent is negative so that the true result is not integral. Algol solves this problem by making the result real and PL/I by giving it the attribute FLOAT; Fortran truncates the result as with integer division. Raising integer factors to negative exponents should generally be avoided.

All the languages have strict rules against raising negative numbers to real powers even when the complex type is allowed. This is because the very small number of times in which this facility would be useful does not justify the difficulty in providing it. The reader should check the rules for the language he is using as well as the particular rules involving the indeterminate quantity $0**0$.

One question not touched on by the above discussion is how the conversion of numbers from one type to another is accomplished. Consider the expression

$$A+B * C-2.0 ** R$$

Suppose A and C are real variables and B and R are double-precision variables. How is the computation accomplished? The answer to this question varies among compilers and languages. Rather than pursue this matter in detail here we shall only make the general statement that conversions of type are generally made in the smallest context in which they are required. Thus:

 i) $2.0**R$ would be computed in double-precision since one operand is double-precision

 ii) $B*C$ would similarly be computed in double-precision

 iii) the remaining additions and subtractions would be done in double-precision

Only in very rare cases will the scientific programmer need to concern himself with the details of how type conversion is accomplished. A good general rule is to avoid expressions of mixed mode even when the language allows them. If variables of different type must be combined arithmetically, the preconversion of all variables to one type can be done by a technique to be described in Section 5.4.

5.2.2 Hierarchy and Parentheses

We stressed in Chapter 1 that the string of characters given to the compiler of any computer language must be unambiguous. The example of a possible ambiguity we gave in Section 1.5 was of an arithmetic expression A/B*C. In this section we consider the language rules which, in total, render any arithmetic expression unambiguous.

These rules are threefold and are generally the same in all four languages. The first is the *rule of hierarchy* which orders the operators in such a way as to indicate the order of evaluation.

Example 5.3

Using the ordinary rules of algebra, what different interpretations can be given to the following expression?

A * B ** C * D ** E

Among the possibilities are, using normal algebraic notation and lower case letters for the variables:

1. $(ab)^c d^e$
2. $ab^c d^e$
3. $((ab)^{cd})e$
4. $(ab)^{cd^e}$
5. $(ab^cd)^e$

Can the reader find any other possible interpretations? Can he guess, before reading ahead, which is the one which the compiler would choose?

The rule of hierarchy divides the operators in Panel 5.1 into various groups with subtle differences between the languages:

	Fortran	Algol	PL/I	Cobol
high	**	↑	** — (unary)	— (unary)
	— (unary)	/ * ÷	/ *	**
	/*	+ — (binary	+ —	/ *
low	+ —	and unary)		+ —

The ordering indicates that the operations with high precedence in the hierarchy are performed first. The rather subtle difference in the hierarchy of the unary minus among the four languages deserve some comments:

1. Whether the unary minus is higher or lower in the hierarchy than exponentation determines whether

—A ** B

is interpreted as

$$(-A) ** B \qquad \text{(Cobol)}$$

or

$$-(A ** B) \qquad \text{(Fortran)}$$

2. The equal precedence of the unary minus and exponentiation in PL/I is, in effect, the same as the Fortran hierarchy since the exception to the left-to-right rule (to be disussed below) means that $-A**B$ in PL/I is interpreted as $-(A**B)$.

3. Placing the unary minus below the multiplication and division operators is not different from placing it above these operators but below exponentiation (cf. Problem 9). (Why?)

The position in the hierarchy of the unary plus is, of course, immaterial. (Why?)

Example 5.4

Using the hierarchy rules above, what is the correct interpretation of $-A+B*C-D**E+F$?

Answer: $-a+bc-d^e+f$ in all four languages (with $**$ replaced by $\uparrow$ in Algol).

Using the hierarchy rules it also follows that the correct interpretation of the expression in Example 5.3 is the one numbered 2. In later chapters, when we discuss other types of operators (function, relational, logical), we shall add to the hierarchy list above.

But hierarchy rules throw no light on the correct interpretation of

$$A/B * C$$

since / and * are equal in the hierarchy. The second of the three rules mentioned above resolves this ambiguity. This rule is that, among operators of equal precedence in the hierarchy, *proceed from left to right* in attaching operands to operators. PL/I explicitly contains one exception to this rule, namely that for the exponentiation and unary minus operators, evaluation is from right to left because it is generally thought that this is algebraically more natural (Problem 8). Compilers for the other languages sometimes also implement right to left evaluation in exponentiation so that the programmer should be careful about concatenating exponentiation operators without using parentheses (see below).

The left-to-right rule means that A/B*C has the interpretation $(a/b)c$. The following example considers some other cases.

Example 5.5

What are the correct interpretations of the following:

    i) A/B/C * D
    ii) A * B ** C ** D/E

  Answers:

    i) ad/bc
    ii) $\dfrac{a(b^c)d}{e}$

if the left-to-right rule for exponentiation is used but

$$\dfrac{a(b)c^d}{e}$$

if right-to-left evaluation in exponentiation is used.

In the examples above we have freely used parentheses to increase readability and to remove any ambiguity which might otherwise exist for the reader. All of the four languages we are discussing allow parentheses to be used freely to:

i) remove visual ambiguity for the programmer. (For the compiler there is never any ambiguity.)
ii) allow contructions which the first two rules do not allow.

As an example of (i), we might write

    (A/B) * C

even though this is equivalent to A/B*C. As an example of (ii), we must write

    A/(B * C)

to indicate a/bc.

The third of our three rules for removing any ambiguity in arithmetic expressions is that *the use of parentheses overrides the first two rules*. That is, the first two rules (hierarchy and left-to-right) are applied *only* within parentheses and *never* across parentheses. Thus, in the example just above,

A/(B * C)
↑

indicates *a/bc* because the left-to-right rule cannot be applied across the parenthesis indicated by the arrow.

Example 5.6

Use parentheses as needed to write arithmetic expressions whose correct interpretation is each of the five possibilities in Example 5.3.

Answers:

1. (A * B) ** C * D ** E
2. A * B ** C * D ** E
3. ((A * B) ** (C * D)) ** E
4. (A * B) ** (C * D ** E)
5. (A * B ** C * D) ** E

In Example 5.6 we used the minimum number of parentheses possible to express the desired meaning in each case. To use the minimum number is both good and bad—good, because the fewer parentheses the less time required for compilation but, bad, because using few parentheses makes it easier to make errors. Thus, while

A * B ** C * D ** E

represents ab^cde, for visual clarity it might be well to write

A * (B ** C) * (D ** E)

On the other hand, it is perfectly correct to write

(((A * B) ** (C * D)) ** E)

instead of the third expression in Example 5.6, but the outer pair of parentheses are completely superfluous and should be omitted. One place where it is good programming practice to always use parentheses to avoid any possible ambiguity is

A ** (B ** C)

to represent $(a)^{b^c}$ and

(A ** B) ** C

to represent

$(a^b)^c$

As the above implies, the programmer should use just enough parentheses to achieve logical correctness and visual clarity.

With these rules we have an explicit, unambiguous interpretation of any arithmetic expression which, to slightly embellish the informal definition given at the start of Section 5.2, we now define as *any combination of constants, variables, operators, and parentheses conforming to the normal rules of algebra and the restrictions already noted in this section.* We consider a more formal definition using BNF in Problems 9 and 10. Some examples of arithmetic expressions in Fortran, PL/I, or Cobol are the following:

```
ALPHA ** JI+(2.0E3 * B(I))—C2
BETA (I,J+7)/(GAN * HELP)+4.0 * Q6
R7 ** S6+PQR ** 16/(HI(14) ** HI(13))
```

To obtain correct Algol expressions, replace subscript parentheses by brackets and ** by ↑ in the above.

At the beginning of Section 5.2 we gave an example of an invalid arithmetic expression containing two consecutive operators. Indeed, the official definitions of P-O languages never allow two consecutive operators in arithmetic expressions, but some compilers allow cases such as

A ** —2

when the meaning $(1/a^2)$ is perfectly clear in ordinary arithmetic.

5.3 COMPILATION OF ARITHMETIC EXPRESSIONS

We shall not discuss in depth the details of the process of compilation which "reads" the source program and translates it into an object program. This is more properly treated in an advanced course in programming. However, in this section we shall consider in some detail a very basic part of the compilation process, namely, the reading and recognition of the meaning of arithmetic expressions. Our purpose is to give the reader some insight into what happens between the time he submits a source program and receives results back, as well as to introduce the student to some material of interest to all computer scientists.

When a computer reads a card with the arithmetic expression

    A+B

punched on it, the translation process consists of:

i) assigning memory locations to A and B, if this has not already been done by an occurrence of A and/or B earlier in the program, and

ii) generating machine-language code which, on a typical computer, would consist of two instructions such as

    CLA L(A)
    ADD L(B)

where CLA is a mnemonic for *clear* (the accumulator—see Section 9.2.2) *and add,* and L(A) denotes that the *address* part of the instruction would be the *location* (L) of A assigned in (i) and similarly for L(B).

But instead of punching A+B the programmer could have punched, among other possibilities,

    (A+B)
    A+(B)
    ((A+B))

all of which should result in the same translation. The basic problem of compilation then is to have the compiler *recognize* the intent of the programmer from the symbols punched on the card. Having done this, it is comparatively simple to use the *syntax* and *semantics* of the language to produce the desired translation.

The reader must begin by understanding that, when the card with A+B or any of the other possibilities above is read by the computer, the result is some pattern of bits or digits in the memory of the computer called the *card image*. Figure 5.1 indicates this for the case of a 36-bit-word binary computer. The 6-bit codes shown are taken from Table 3.6.

Now let us suppose that the compiler proceeds with the compilation process and reaches a point at which it expects to find the first character of an arithmetic expression as the first character of the words shown in Figure 5.1. (In Section 5.4 we shall make clear how the compiler can expect to find an arithmetic expression at a given place in a program.) The compiler must then look at the succeeding characters and attempt to determine the correct interpretation of the expression. This process is called the *arithmetic scan*.

By analogy with English grammar, the process by which the arithmetic expression is examined in order to determine how the pieces fit together is called *parsing*. The basic problem of parsing arithmetic expressions is to determine what the operands are for each operator. This would be a problem of some difficulty even if no parentheses were allowed in arithmetic expressions, but with parentheses the problem is significantly more difficult and interesting. In the remainder of this section we shall consider various aspects of the parsing problem for arithmetic expressions.

But first, let us point out some simplifications we shall make in all our examples, none of which really change the parsing problem in any significant sense:

1. All variables will be a single letter and no constants will be used. This avoids the not difficult problem of recognizing variables and constants (Problem 11).
2. It will be assumed there are no spaces.
3. It will be assumed (as is the case in all computers and for all languages; cf. Section 6.2) that a special character or some other mechanism after the last character of the arithmetic expression indicates the end of the expression.

Consider now the compilation of the expression

A+B * C

When the scan reaches the + sign the compiler knows that A is the left operand, but it cannot determine the right operand (B*C) until after it reaches the end of the expression. With more complicated expressions the problem of associating operands with operators becomes correspondingly more difficult. It generally involves effectively scanning back and forth across the statement, which is time

i) A + B

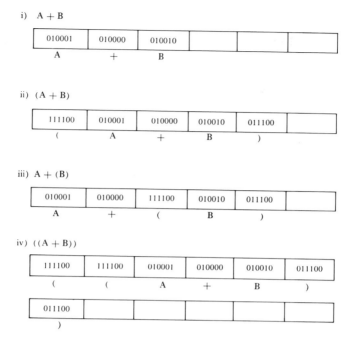

Figure 5.1   Coding of card data in memory.

consuming. Of course, one of the major objects of compilation is speed.

Parentheses complicate the problem still further, as in the expression

A+(B * C) * (D+(E+F/(G ** H)))

Here the compiler must keep track of the level of each parenthesis, search for the lowest level parenthesis or set of parentheses, compile these lowest-level quantities, and then work back up to higher levels, always keeping track of which operands go with which operators.

What would be nice, therefore, is a way of writing expressions in which:

i) operands could be easily associated with operators, and
ii) the "tyranny of parentheses" was absent.

If such a notation could be found *and* if a reasonably straightforward way could be found to convert arithmetic expressions in our usual notation to this new notation we could accomplish the compilation in a logically simple and efficient manner. Indeed, such a notation does exist and is widely used in the compilation of arithmetic expressions.

5.3.1   Polish Notation

The notation which achieves the aims discussed above is called Polish notation because of the difficulty of pronouncing the name of its originator, J. Lukasiewicz, a Polish logician. This notation removes the tyranny of parentheses by doing away with them entirely *without causing any resulting ambiguity.* At the same time it provides a straightforward way of associating operands and operators.

There are two forms of Polish notation—*Polish prefix notation* (PPN) and *Polish suffix*[†] *notation* (PSN). We shall emphasize the latter because it is the more useful in compiling arithmetic expressions. In PPN every *triad* consisting of an operator (+, −, *, /, ÷, **, or ↑) and two operands is written with the operator followed by its two operands in left-to-right order. For example, A + B becomes

   +AB

Conversely, in PSN the triad is written with the two operands preceeding the operator so that A+B is written

   AB+

Since arithmetic expressions in normal notation may be thought of as having a single *major* operator (see below for method of choice of major operator) with two operands, where each of the operands may in turn consist of a major operator and operands, etc., the definition above enables us to convert arithmetic expressions in normal notation to Polish notation. The algorithm is as follows:

1. Assign to every operator a number equal to the number of levels of parentheses surrounding it [e.g., in (A/(B+C))*D, 0 is assigned to *, 1 to /, and 2 to +].
2. Choose as major operator any one with the lowest number assigned to it such that no other operator with this number is lower in the operator hierarchy (see p. 164) or, if equal in the operator hierarchy, lies to the right of the operator chosen. This step assures that the effects of the left-to-right as well as the hierarchy rules are preserved in the Polish string.[††] For example, for A+B*C, + is

---

† Sometimes called *postfix* notation.
†† In PL/I a major operator of ** must have no other ** operators at the same parenthesis level to its *left*.

the major operator with B*C as the right operand. In A/B*C, * is the major operator with A/B the left operand.

3. The remainder of the expression forms the left and right operands of the major operator.

4. For the left and right operands repeat Steps 1 through 3 until all operators have been handled. Place each operand in relation to its operator as defined above for A+B for PPN and PSN.

For example, applying the algorithm to the expression given in Step 1, we get in PPN:

1. Major operator *, left operand A/(B+C), right operand D.
2. A/(B+C) has major operator /, left operand A, right operand B+C.
3. B+C has major operator +, left operand B, right operand C.

Assembling these in reverse order we get

B+C → +BC
A/(B+C) → /A+BC
(A/(B+C)) * D → * /A+BCD

Similarly, in PSN this expression becomes (Problem 13)

ABC+/D *

The above algorithm implies that the Polish string corresponding to a particular arithmetic expression is unique. This is not necessarily so. For example, the PSN string for A+B−C may be

ABC−+

even though the algorithm above gives

AB+C−

This is so because A+B−C may be considered to be A+(B−C) or (A+B)−C.

But the important question is not whether an arithmetic expression has a unique Polish string, but rather, whether any valid Polish string (i.e., one formed from a valid arithmetic expression) represents a *unique* arithmetic expression. For if we are somehow going to convert an arithmetic expression into PSN inside the computer and then compile it, we must be certain that the Polish string uniquely specifies the arithmetic expression from which it was derived.

To show that each Polish string does indeed represent a unique arithmetic expression we need only consider the problem of translating a Polish string back into an arithmetic expression. Consider the string

AX * B+CX * D−/

Working from right to left we proceed as follows:

Expression	Comment
/	Major operator
/ −	Start of right operand of /
/ − D	Right operand of −
/ * − D	Start of left operand of −
/ * X − D	Right operand of *
/ C * X − D	Left operand of * − completes left operand of −, right operand of /
+ / C * X − D	Start of left operand of /
+ B / C * X − D	Right operand of +
* + B / C * X − D	Start of left operand of +
* X + B / C * X − D	Right operand of *
A * X + B / C * X − D	Left operand of * − completes left operand of +, left operand of /

Without using parentheses the above is visually ambiguous. However, the construction should indicate unequivocally that the arithmetic expression obtained is

(A * X+B)/(C * X−D)   (5.1)

Although this example is not a formal proof of the uniqueness of the arithmetic expression corresponding to each Polish string, we hope the reader is convinced.†

---

† The above discussion avoids two possible problems related to the uniqueness of Polish notation. One of these—how to handle the unary minus—is discussed on p. 176. The other is the potential problem of using ** for exponentiation as well as multiplication, because in a Polish string ** can represent two multiplication operations. For example, the PSN string ABC**D** could represent (A*(B*C))**D or A*(B**C)*D. To avoid this problem inside the computer it is necessary only to replace ** for exponentiation by a single, unique *internal* character. Here we shall avoid the problem without losing any generality by omitting exponentiation from all of our examples.

Example 5.7

Convert the PPN equivalent of the string in the previous example to normal notation. Using the algorithm adduced above on the expression in (5.1), we obtain as the PPN equivalent of this string (Problem 13)

/+ * AXB— * CXD

Proceeding now from left to right we obtain

```
            /
       +   /
   *   +   /
  A *  +   /
 (A * X) + /
((A * X) + B) /
((A * X) + B) /          —
((A * X) + B) /    *     —
((A * X) + B) /  C *     —
((A * X) + B) /  (C * X) —
((A * X) + B) / ((C * X) — D)
```

Here, each time both operands for an operator were assembled, we have indicated this by parentheses.

It is an interesting property of Polish strings and, for computer compilation needs, a very useful property, that they can be translated back to normal arithmetic expressions by proceeding from right to left or left to right in either PSN or PPN.

Example 5.8

Perform the translation of the PSN string

AX * B+CX * D—/

from left to right.

Expression	*Comment*
A	
A X	
(A * X)	Since each operator is preceded by its two operands, * must be associated with A and X
(A * X) B	
((A * X) + B)	Similarly, A*X and B are the two operands which precede +
((A * X) + B) C	
((A * X) + B) C X	
((A * X) + B) (C * X)	The two operands which immediately precede * are C and X
((A * X) + B) (C * X) D	
((A * X) + B) ((C * X) − D)	
((A * X) + B) / ((C * X) − D)	

As the above example indicates, the algorithm for left-to-right translation of PSN is to associate each operator with the *two most recently assembled operands*. As we shall indicate in Section 5.3.2, this provides us with a simple method of compiling from the PSN string.

Our discussion of Polish notation thus far indicates that, not only does it avoid parentheses, but also no hierarchy rules are necessary. However, our discussion has been incomplete in one respect. We have not considered the unary plus and minus operators. For example, what is the Polish equivalent of

    −A+B

To answer this we must distinguish between the unary and binary minus operators, which we shall do by denoting the former by ~. (Since the unary + may always be ignored (Why?), it presents no problem). In PPN, −A is represented as ~A while in PSN −A becomes A~.

Example 5.9

What do the following PSN strings represent?

    i) AB ~ C+ *

    ii) AB − C+ *

Answers:

i)
```
    *
    *      +
    *      + C
    *  —   + C
    * (— B + C)
 A * (— B + C)
```

where we have converted the $\sim$ to a $-$ in the translation, but have remembered that only one operand is to be associated with it.

ii)
```
    *
    *         +
    *         + C
    *    —    + C
    *    — B  + C
    * (A — B) + C
```

which is not a valid arithmetic expression.

Without a different notation for the unary and binary minuses, ambiguity in Polish strings would be possible. For example, if we assume that the PSN string

AB—C— *

represents a valid arithmetic expression, but that the minus signs could be binary or unary, then it could represent either

(A—B) * (—C)

or

A * (— B — C)

In this section we have developed a notation which is parenthesis-free and requires no hierarchy rules. In the next section we shall indicate how we can use this notation in compiling arithmetic expressions.

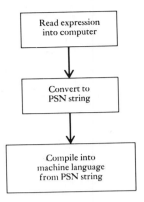

Figure 5.2   Compilation of arithmetic expressions.

5.3.2   Compiling Arithmetic Expressions

The flow chart of Figure 5.2 illustrates the method we have outlined for compiling arithmetic expressions. Our need, therefore, is for algorithms to accomplish the steps in the bottom two boxes.

The reader may think that we elucidated an algorithm for the translation of arithmetic expressions into PSN in the previous section when we indicated how this translation could be performed. However:

i) we must remember that a computer algorithm is a formally expressed set of rules to accomplish a task on a computer, and

ii) a description for pedagogical purposes of a way of accomplishing a task does not necessarily result in a good algorithm when formalized for a computer.

If the reader considers the method adduced in the previous section, he will quickly realize that the successive search for major operators involves just the scanning back and forth across the expression which we hoped we could avoid using Polish notation. The algorithm we shall present here requires first that we assign to each of the levels of the operator hierarchy on p. 164 a number reflecting the level or *binding strength* of the operator. Thus, for Fortran we have

Operator	Binding Strength
**	4
— (unary)	3
/ *	2
+ —	1

It is also convenient to give the character (a binding strength of 5. We use this in the algorithm shown in Figure 5.3 to convert normal expressions to Polish strings. This algorithm assumes the input is a normal arithmetic expression followed by a terminal symbol which we denote by ≠. Its output is the PSN string corresponding to this expression.

Some of the terminology in Figure 5.3 requires explanation. A *symbol* is any element of the PSN string. The *operator stack* is a list or string of operators

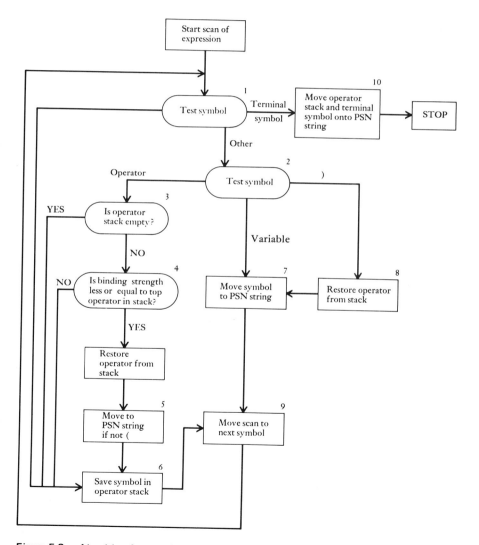

Figure 5.3 Algorithm for translation of arithmetic expressions to PSN.

organized into what is usually called a *push-down list*. Any time an operator is placed on the stack all operators previously in the stack are "pushed down" in the same way as coins in a coin holder or a plate stack in a cafeteria. When an operator is removed from the top of the stack ("restored"), the other operators "pop-up" one place.

We annotate this flow chart as follows:

> Boxes 1 and 2: Symbols divided into categories of), ≠, (, Operators, and Variables.
>
> Box 3: If empty, comparison in Box 4 cannot be made; operator automatically saved in stack.
>
> Box 4: If new operator has greater binding strength it goes on stack because this means right operand of top operator has not yet been found.
>
> Box 5: Right operand has been found if top of operator stack is not a left parenthesis.
>
> Box 6: Next operator or left parenthesis put on stack; left parentheses must be put on stack so that, for example, in A/(B*C), * gets on Polish string before /.
>
> Box 7: All variables (and constants) go directly to PSN string.
>
> Box 8: Right parenthesis always means that PSN string should be "completed" for symbols scanned since last left parenthesis.
>
> Box 9: Continues scan.
>
> Box 10: All remaining operators go to string.

This algorithm is best understood by applying it to an example. Let us consider the string

$$(A * X+B)/(C * X—D)\neq$$

The operation of the algorithm on this string is illustrated in Table 5.2. The numbers in the last column refer to the numbers on the boxes in Figure 5.3. Although we shall not discuss this further here, the reader should attempt to assure himself that the algorithm of Figure 5.3 really does work.

Example 5.10

Show how the algorithm of Figure 5.3 converts the string

$$(A—B) * (—C)$$

to a PSN string.

Symbol scanned	Operator stack (top at right)	PSN string (top at right)	Path through flow chart
(	(		1—6—9
A	(	A	1—2—7—9
—	—	A	1—2—3—4—5—6—9
B	—	AB	1—2—7—9
)		AB —	1—2—8—7—9
*	*	AB —	1—2—3—6—9
(	*(	AB —	1—6—9
—	*~	AB —	1—2—3—4—5—6—9
C	*~	AB — C	1—2—7—9
)	*	AB — C ~	1—2—8—7—9
≠		AB — C ~ * ≠	1—10

The reader should compare this result to the translation of A*(−B−C)≠ (cf. p. 177; see also Problem 17).

Table 5.2   Operation of arithmetic expression to PSN Algorithm

Symbol scanned	Operator stack (top at right)	PSN string (top at right)	Path through flow chart
(	(		1—6—9
A	(	A	1—2—7—9
*	*	A	1—2—3—4—5—6—9
X	*	AX	1—2—7—9
+	+	AX *	1—2—3—4—5—6—9
B	+	AX * B	1—2—7—9
)		AX * B +	1—2—8—7—9
/	/	AX * B +	1—2—3—6—9
(	/(	AX * B +	1—6—9
C	/(	AX * B + C	1—2—7—9
*	/*	AX * B + C	1—2—3—4—5—6—9
X	/*	AX * B + CX	1—2—7—9
—	/—	AX * B + CX *	1—2—3—4—5—6—9
D	/—	AX * B + CX * D	1—2—7—9
)	/	AX * B + CX * D —	1—2—8—7—9
≠		AX * B + CX * D — / ≠	1—10

This algorithm then, in a single pass over the string, translates it into PSN. It remains to indicate how the PSN string is used to compile the arithmetic expression into machine language. The clue to this is contained in the previous section where we indicated that, in the left-to-right translation of PSN strings to arithmetic expressions, the left and right operands for each operator are the two most recently assembled operands. The outline of the algorithm to accomplish the compilation is shown in Figure 5.4. The box in Figure 5.4 which requires some explanation is the one numbered 2. Whenever an operator is encountered in the scan, the top two items in the stack are its left and right operands. The compiler will take these two items and generate the machine language instructions necessary to perform the desired operation and then place the resulting instructions *as a single item* on the operand stack. Thus the items on the operand stack may be single variables or previously compiled instructions. As an example, we consider the PSN string in Table 5.2. In Table 5.3 we have indicated the application of the algorithm of Figure 5.4 to this string. In this table the notation ⌊____⌋ is used to set off items which are compiled machine-language instructions for the quantity above the ⌊____⌋. Thus, for example, ⌊A * X⌋ indicates that the item in the stack is a set of machine-language instructions such as

CLA	L(A)	
MPY	L(X)	(MPY—multiply)

Table 5.3   Compilation of PSN strings

Symbol scanned	Operand stack (top at right)	Path through flow chart
A	A	1—3—4
X	AX	1—3—4
*	⌊A * X⌋	1—2—3—4
B	⌊A * X⌋B	1—3—4
+	⌊(A * X) + B⌋	1—2—3—4
C	⌊(A * X) + B⌋ C	1—3—4
X	⌊(A * X) + B⌋ CX	1—3—4
*	⌊(A * X) + B⌋ ⌊C * X⌋	1—2—3—4
D	⌊(A * X) + B⌋ ⌊(C * X)⌋ D	1—3—4
—	⌊(A * X) + B⌋ ⌊(C * X) — D⌋	1—2—3—4
/	⌊((A * X) + B) / ((C * X) — D)⌋	1—2—3—4
≠		1

When the STOP box is reached, the stack contains a single item which is the compiled version of the arithmetic expression. For this example the set of instructions, somewhat simplified, might be

```
CLA    L(A)
MPY    L(X)
ADD    L(B)
STO    TEMP1    (STO—Store; TEMP1—a temporary location in memory)
CLA    L(C)
MPY    L(X)
SUB    L(D)
STO    TEMP2
CLA    TEMP1
DIV    TEMP2
```

In this section we have indicated how arithmetic expressions can be compiled with a single pass over the original expression and a single pass over the resulting PSN string. Further refinements of this procedure are possible. For example, in the translation to PSN, the compiler might recognize that certain parts of the string could be compiled immediately, such as AX* in the example above. In this way the two stages we have presented here can in effect be compressed into a single stage (Problem 19).

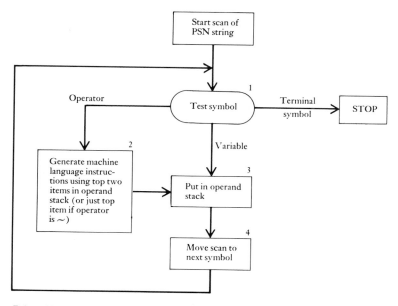

Figure 5.4   Algorithm for compilation of PSN strings.

5.4   ARITHMETIC ASSIGNMENT STATEMENTS

In natural languages the sentence is the smallest construct capable of expressing ideas and, of course, all written language is made up of concatenations of sentences. In computer languages the constructs analogous to sentences are called *statements*. All computer programs are concatenations of statements. In Fortran, statements are the largest construct defined short of the entire program. In Algol and PL/I a larger construct called a *block*, analogous to a paragraph in English, is defined. Cobol defines certain concatenations of statements as *sentences* and combinations of sentences as *paragraphs*. We shall discuss these larger constructs in Section 6.1.2.

Statements in P-O languages are of various types. Although we did not call it a statement at that time, we had an example of a statement with type declarations in Section 4.3 (see Panel 4.7) and DIMENSION and EQUIVALENCE statements in Section 4.4.2 (see Panels 4.11 and 4.12). The statements discussed in Chapter 4 were all examples of *non-executable statements*; that is, they provide information for the compiler to aid in the compilation process rather than causing any part of the desired calculation to be performed. In this section we shall begin discussion of *executable statements*, statements which cause part of the calculation or symbol manipulation to be performed. The first of these is the *arithmetic assignment statement*. In Fortran, Algol, and PL/I this is the statement which is used to accomplish all arithmetic calculations. Cobol also allows assignment statements but in addition allows another mechanism for carrying out simple calculations (see below).

Panel 5.3 describes the arithmetic assignment statements in the various languages. Note the following:

1. It is important that the reader understand that the = sign in assignment statements does not have its usual meaning but rather has the meaning of *replacement*. For this reason a better symbol would be ← but this does not exist as a keypunch character. Because = does not have its usual meaning, statements such as

    N = N+1

are possible and useful; the above has the effect of increasing the value of N by 1.

2. In Algol and PL/I evaluation of all subscripts precedes the evaluation of the expression and the replacement by its value of the previous values of the variable names. The following Algol statement indicates the need for such a rule:

    B[A+4.6,I] := A := C * D;

Panel 5.3 Arithmetic assignment statements

Syntax

FORTRAN

$\langle$ AAS $\rangle$ :: =
$\langle$ SV NAME $\rangle$ =
$\langle$ AE $\rangle$

ALGOL

$\langle$ AAS $\rangle$ :: =
$\langle$ SV NAME$_1$ $\rangle$: = $\langle$ SV
NAME$_2$ $\rangle$: = $\cdots$: =
$\langle$ SV NAME$_n$ $\rangle$: = $\langle$ AE $\rangle$;

PL/I

$\langle$ AAS $\rangle$ :: =
$\langle$ SV NAME$_1$ $\rangle$,
$\cdots$, $\langle$ SV
NAME$_n$ $\rangle$ =
$\langle$ AE $\rangle$;

COBOL

$\langle$ AAS $\rangle$ :: =
COMPUTE $\langle$ VN $\rangle$ = $\langle$ AE $\rangle$

Semantics

The value of the expression *replaces* the value of the variable name or names on the left.

Examples

FORTRAN

A = B + C
C2 (I, J + 7) =
  2.0 * D4 − ALPHA ** I
D4 = R + S ** T
D5 = R + S ** T
D6 = R + S ** T

ALGOL

A : = B + C;
C2 [I, J + 7] : =
  2.0 * D4 − ALPHA ↑ I;
D4 : = D5 : = D6 : = R + S ↑ T;

PL/I

A = B + C;
C2 (I, J + 7) =
  2.0 * D4 − ALPHA ** I;
D4, D5, D6 = R + S ** T;

COBOL

COMPUTE A = B + C

COMPUTE D4 = R + S ** T
COMPUTE D5 = R + S ** T
COMPUTE D6 = R + S ** T

AAS—arithmetic assignment statement
AE—arithmetic expression
SV—scalar variable
VN—variable name

185

Without such a rule it would be ambiguous whether the subscript A+4.6 was to be evaluated before or after the value of A was replaced by C*D.

3. The type of the variable on the left-hand side of the assignment statement need not be the same as the type of the expression on the right. When the types are different, the expression is evaluated and then the value is converted to the type of the left-hand side variable before replacement. For example, in Fortran the statement

    N = A+B * C

would cause A+B*C to be evaluated as a real (floating-point) expression which would then be *truncated* (fractional part ignored) and converted to a fixed-point value which would replace the current value of N. This process is called *fixing* the real expression. Among other things this provides a simple mechanism for converting a number of one type to another. Thus,

    A = I

converts the integer value of I to a floating-point number which replaces the value of A. This is called *floating* the integer variable.

4. In 2. above and in Panel 5.3 the reader will have noted the semicolon following each statement in Algol and PL/I but the absence of such punctuation in Fortran and Cobol. The reason for this is connected with the structure and preparation of programs in the four languages and is considered in Chapter 6.

5. Since PL/I allows arrays and structures in expressions (see Section 5.1), it also allows them on the left side of assignment statements. We shall not discuss this here.

Table 5.4   Mode conversion in Fortran

Right-side mode / Left-side mode	Integer	Real	Double-precision	Complex
Integer	---	Fix	Fix	Prohibited
Real	Float	---	Truncate DP to real	Prohibited
Double-precision	Float double-precision	Expand to DP	---	Prohibited
Complex	Prohibited	Prohibited	Prohibited	---

Note:
Table entries indicate action before assignment.

Example 5.11

Show how the type conversion above can be used to find the fractional part of a floating-point number in Fortran.

Let A be a floating-point variable. Then the following statements have the desired effect.

I = A	Integer part of A → I
B = I	Integer part converted back to floating point
C = A − B	Fractional part of A is value of C

Not all mixtures of left-hand side and right-hand side mode are allowed in Fortran. Table 5.4 indicates which are allowed and the action taken for them.[†] Algol with only real and integer modes allows all possible combinations.[††] So does PL/I, despite a large variety of modes. For example, PL/I specifies that, with a complex value on the right and a real one on the left, the result should be the *real part* of the complex number. Conversely, converting real to complex results naturally in a zero imaginary part. All other PL/I conversions, no matter how unnatural or unlikely, are defined explicitly in the language.

In Cobol, data manipulation and calculations are indicated by means of *verbs*. COMPUTE in Panel 5.3 is one such verb. In addition, Cobol provides five other verbs which can be used to effect arithmetic calculations. These are described in Panel 5.4. Anything that can be accomplished by the verbs in Panel 5.4 can also be accomplished using the COMPUTE verb. For example

    MOVE A TO B

is equivalent to

    COMPUTE B = A

In addition to the syntax described in Panels 5.3 and 5.4, instructions on whether or not to round the result and what to do in case of overflow can be added to the Cobol statements.

[†] Fortran compilers which allow mixing of mode (cf. footnote on p. 161), usually allow all conversions. For example, a right-side integer and left-side complex results in a floating-point imaginary part equal to zero and a floating-point real part equal to the right-side integer.

[††] But conversion from real to integer in Algol is not by truncation but rather by rounding; that is, .5 is added to the real number and the result is truncated.

Panel 5.4 Arithmetic verbs in Cobol

Verb	Syntax	Semantics	Examples
ADD	ADD vn_1, vn_2, ..., vn_k TO vn	$vn_1 + vn_2 + ... + vn_k$ replaces vn	ADD D, 47 TO F
	ADD vn_1, vn_2, ..., vn_k GIVING vn	$vn_1 + vn_2 + ... + vn_k$ replaces vn	ADD D, 47, F GIVING P
SUBTRACT	SUBTRACT vn_1, vn_2, ..., vn_k FROM vn	$vn - (vn_1 + vn_2 + ... + vn_k)$ replaces vn	SUBTRACT A, 2 FROM R
	SUBTRACT vn_1, vn_2, ..., vn_k FROM vn_m GIVING vn	$vn_m - (vn_1 + vn_2 + ... + vn_k)$ replaces vn	SUBTRACT A, 2 FROM 18 GIVING T4
MULTIPLY	MULTIPLY vn_1 BY vn	$vn_1 * vn$ replaces vn	MULTIPLY S BY T
	MULTIPLY vn_1 BY vn_2 GIVING vn	$vn_1 * vn_2$ replaces vn	MULTIPLY F BY 16 GIVING H
DIVIDE	DIVIDE vn_1 INTO vn	vn/vn_1 replaces vn	DIVIDE A INTO B
	DIVIDE vn_1 BY vn_2 GIVING vn	vn_1/vn_2 replaces vn	DIVIDE C BY 4 GIVING R
	DIVIDE vn_1 INTO vn_2 GIVING vn	vn_2/vn_1 replaces vn	DIVIDE 8 INTO D GIVING S
MOVE	MOVE vn_1 TO vn	vn_1 replaces vn	MOVE A TO B

vn—variable name

Notes:
1. Whenever vn appears with a subscript above, a constant may be used instead of a variable name.
2. All commas in the syntax may be replaced by spaces.
3. Under Semantics, all references refer to the *value* of the variable name.

Example 5.12

Write assignment statements in the four languages to compute the amount A that accumulates after n years when a principal P is placed at a rate of interest r compounded q times a year.

The formula is $A = P (1 + r/q)^{nq}$.

Fortran

> A(N) = P * ((1.0+R/Q) ** (N * Q))
>   (Is there a mixed mode problem here?)

Algol

> A[N] := P * ((1.0+R/Q)↑(N * Q));

PL/I

> A(N) = P * ((1.0+R/Q) ** (N * Q));

Cobol

> COMPUTE A (N) = P * ((1.0+R/Q) ** (N * Q))

Finally, we note that the use of = or := in assignment statements before the right-hand side arithmetic expressions in all four languages indicates (cf. Section 5.3) one way the compiler can know when to expect the next character to be the beginning of an arithmetic expression.

5.5 ARITHMETIC DECISION STATEMENTS

All calculations of interest on digital computers have the property that, at some point or points, a choice must be made of which of two or more possible paths the calculation is going to take next. All of the flow charts we have exhibited thus far have this property. In this section we shall indicate how such decisions can be made based on the values of arithmetic expressions. But first we must show how the normal sequential execution of statements can be interrupted unconditionally.

5.5.1   Labels

Since the normal mode in all languages is to execute statements in sequence, the ability to choose one of two or more paths implies the need for some method to specify a statement in a program which is not the next one in sequence. This is illustrated in Figure 5.5. How is the decision statement to be able to refer to a statement out of sequence as the next one to be executed? The answer to this is by means of *statement labels*. Panel 5.5 describes the approach to labels in the four languages. Only PL/I has label facilities which require more explanation than that contained in Panel 5.5. The fact that labels are called label constants in PL/I implies correctly that there are also *label variables*. A label variable is merely a variable whose values are label constants. It must appear in a DE-CLARE statement; for example,

DECLARE R LABEL;

Then an assignment statement

R = Z24R;

assigns the label constant Z24R to R. Label variables may also be subscripted as

DECLARE S(4) LABEL;

and then used subscripted to refer to one of an array of label constants [e.g., GO TO S(J)].

Panel 5.6 indicates how statement labels are associated with statements in programs. This will be discussed further in Section 6.2.1.

————
————
————

Decision statement
Next statement in sequence

————
————

Other statement to be transferred to

————
————

Figure 5.5   Decisions in programs.

Panel 5.5 Statement labels

FORTRAN	ALGOL	PL/I	COBOL
Called *labels*	Called *labels*	Called *label constants*	Called *procedure names*

Syntax

FORTRAN	ALGOL	PL/I	COBOL
A 1- to 5-digit positive integer	An unsubscripted variable name or an unsigned integer (with the latter almost never permitted in implementations)	A variable name without a subscript or with an integer subscript	A variable name, but without the restriction that one character must be alphabetic (see Panel 2.1)

Examples

FORTRAN	ALGOL	PL/I	COBOL
362	362		362
14072	14072		14072
	I7	I7	I7
	Z24R	Z24R	Z24R
		B (4)	
		N2 (−6)	

Panel 5.6 Association of statement labels with statements

FORTRAN	ALGOL	PL/I	COBOL
Punched in columns 1 to 5 of card; see Section 6.2.1	Separated from statement by colon		Punched beginning in column 8 of card; separated from first statement of paragraph by period and space; see Section 6.2.1

Examples

L1 : A : = B;   L1 : A = B;
R (3) : C = D * E;

5.5.2   Unconditional Transfer Statements

A common need in programming is to return to the beginning of a program to reexecute a sequence of statements on a new set of data or to carry out another step of an iterative process (see Chapter 8). Figure 2.10 (p. 40) illustrates this need. After the increase of the counter I by 1, control is transferred back to the beginning of the sorting loop. Transfers of the kind we are discussing here are not dependent on any condition in the computer; they are *unconditional*.

Fortran, Algol, PL/I, and Cobol have identical means of implementing unconditional transfer statements as shown in Panel 5.7. (In Cobol the statement label may be omitted if it is going to be inserted later by an ALTER statement.)

In addition to simple GO TO statements, all four languages allow more complicated versions of this statement in which the transfer is unconditional but the place in the program to which control is transferred depends upon the value of some variable. Suppose, for example, you wish to write a program to compute trigonometric functions in such a way that the one of the six functions—sine, cosine, tangent, cotangent, secant, cosecant—which is to be computed is to be denoted by an input variable I. What we wish to accomplish is shown in Figure 5.6. All four languages have statements to carry out this task. Panel 5.8 describes these; note:

1. The two Fortran statements are called, respectively, *assigned* and *computed* GO TO statements. The former must be preceded somewhere in the execution of the program by an ASSIGN statement of the form

    ASSIGN *sl* TO *iv*

which gives the integer variable (*iv*) the value of the statement label (*sl*). (The ALTER statement in Cobol mentioned above is quite similar to the Fortran ASSIGN.) In the assigned GO TO, the statement label to which control is transferred by the integer variable must be in the list of *sl*'s of the assigned GO TO. In case the *sl* is not in the list or, for a computed GO TO, if *iv* is greater than the number of *sl*'s in the list, the result is undefined and will virtually always cause trouble. Note that any time one of these GO TO statements can be used, so can the other be used. For example,

    ASSIGN 20 TO I
    GO TO I, (10,20,30,40,50,60)

is precisely equivalent to

    I = 2
    GO TO (10,20,30,40,50,60),I

For both GO TO statements the *iv* must be *unsubscripted*.

2. A designational expression (*de*) can be one of a number of things, only two of which we mention here. One is an ordinary statement label, in which case the Algol GO TO in Panel 5.8 is identical to that of Panel 5.7. The second is something called a switch designator which is a *switch identifier* (*si*) followed by a subscript expression in brackets. An *si* is an ordinary indentifier and the value of its subscript, I, refers to the Ith element in a *switch list* which is itself just a sequence of designational expressions. To accomplish in Algol the kind of transfer indicated above in Fortran, we could write

> **switch** I := L1, L2, L3, L4, L5, L6;
> **go to** I [2] ;

which would transfer control to the statement labeled L2, the second in the list. The **go to** *de* statement in Algol, therefore, includes in a single statement all and more (because of the *de*'s we have not discussed) than all the Fortran GO TO statements.

3. The PL/I GO TO *slv* statement has more flexibility than the Fortran or Algol statements in the sense that assigned lists of values of the *slv* are not necessary. To perform the transfer above we would write

> DECLARE I LABEL;
> I = L2;
> GO TO I;

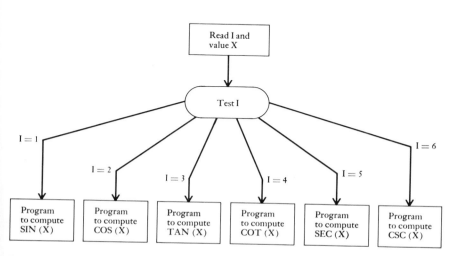

Figure 5.6   Example of a multiple switch.

4. The Cobol GO TO is essentially identical to the Fortran computed GO TO. However, if the value of the variable name is greater than the number of elements in the list, the result is defined; control passes to the next statement in sequence.

5.5.3   Conditional Statements

All four languages have transfer statements in which the statement transferred to depends upon some *condition* inside the computer. In the four languages these statements are logically all variations of

IF α THEN β ELSE γ

where α expresses the relevant condition and β and γ are statements (which in some languages may themselves be IF statements, as described later in this section) to be executed depending upon whether the condition is satisfied or not. However, the languages differ considerably in their actual implementation of conditional transfer statements.

The conditions inside the machine which are tested by IF statements are of three kinds:

1. The *sign* of an arithmetic expression (or whether it is zero)
2. The *relation* between the values of two arithmetic expressions
3. The *truth* or *falsity* of a logical expression

Panel 5.7   Simple unconditional transfer statements

FORTRAN, ALGOL, PL/I, and COBOL

Syntax

GO TO followed by a label (**go to** in Algol)

Semantics

The next statement executed is the one whose label corresponds to that following GO TO.

Examples

                    GO TO 100
                    GO TO L (PL/I) (**go to** L in Algol)
                    GO TO S (I) (PL/I only)

FORTRAN	*ALGOL*	*PL/I*	*COBOL*

Syntax

Assigned:

GO TO *iv*,   **go to** *de*;   GO TO *slv*;   GO TO <LIST>
  (< LIST >)   DEPENDING ON *vn*
    or   where

Computed:

GO TO (< LIST >),   < LIST > :: = *pn* |
  iv   < LIST > , *pn*
    where
< LIST > :: =
  sl | < LIST > , *sl*

Semantics

| *Assigned*: Next statement executed is one whose *sl* equals value of *iv* | Next statement has label equal to value of *de* | Next statement executed has label equal to value of *slv* | Next statement executed is one whose procedure name is *vn*th in list of *pn*'s |

Computed: Next statement executed is one whose label is the *iv*th in the list of labels

Examples

| GO TO I, (10, 20, 30, 40, 50, 60) GO TO (10, 20, 30, 40, 50, 60), I | **go to** TRIG [I] ; | GO TO J; | GO TO 10, 20, 30, 40, 50, 60 DEPENDING ON I |

de—designational expression
iv—integer variable
pn—procedure name
sl—statement label
slv—statement label variable

The latter we shall consider in Chapter 9. The relations mentioned above are the six usual arithmetic relations:

$<$ less than
$>$ greater than
$\leqslant$ less than or equal
$\geqslant$ greater than or equal
$=$ equal
$\neq$ not equal

Table 5.5 indicates how these six relational operators are indicated syntactically in Fortran, PL/I, and Cobol. In Algol they are indicated as above but must be transliterated in actual use.

Panel 5.9 illustrates some of the salient facts about IF statements in the four languages; note:

1. *Relational expressions* in the four languages are subclasses of larger constructs called variously logical expressions (Fortran), scalar expressions with bit string values (PL/I), and Boolean expressions (Algol). As we define it here, a relational expression has the form

$$ae_1 \; ro \; ae_2$$

where the relational operator (ro) is one of the operators in Table 5.5 and the ae's are any arithmetic expressions (which, in Fortran, must have the same mode), with the exception that in Cobol the ro may be

     IS

or

     IS NOT

(with either IS optional) when the second ae is

     POSITIVE

or

     NEGATIVE

or

     ZERO

All relational expressions are either *true* or *false*; we shall discuss these *truth values* further in Chapter 9.

2. It is necessary to ask the question of how the relational operators fit into the operator hierarchy discussed in Section 5.2.2, since relational expressions may contain both arithmetic and relational operators. The answer to the question is immediate. These operators must be lower in the hierarchy than any of the arithmetic operators because, for example, in the expression

A+B.GT.C

to interpret this as A plus B.GT.C is meaningless (even though some languages do try to impart meaning to the sum of an arithmetic quantity and a truth value).

3. The first Fortran statement, called the arithmetic IF, can always be replaced by two statements of the second form, called logical IFs. For example,

IF (X−Y * Z) 10,20,30

can be replaced by

    IF (X−Y * Z.GT.O.) GO TO 30
    IF (X−Y * Z.EQ.O.) GO TO 20
10 ---------------

This example should enable the reader to see how the arithmetic IF statement fits into the IF α THEN β ELSE γ format (Problem 26).

Table 5.5   Relational operators

Operator	Fortran	PL/I[†] 48-char. set	PL/I[†] 60-char. set	Cobol
<	.LT.	LT	<	IS LESS THAN
>	.GT.	GT	>	IS GREATER THAN
≤	.LE.	LE	< =	IS NOT GREATER THAN
≥	.GE.	GE	> =	IS NOT LESS THAN
=	.EQ.	=	=	IS EQUAL TO
≠	.NE.	NE	¬ =	IS NOT EQUAL TO

[†] PL/I also defines ¬<(NL) and ¬>(NG) as equivalent to > = and < =, respectively.

4. In the Fortran logical IF statement the *st* cannot be another logical IF (or certain other statements either). In Algol, the statement after **else** (but not the one after **then**), and, in PL/I, either of the statements in the IF, can be another conditional statement which permits unlimited nesting of these conditionals.[†]

For example, in Algol

      if re_1 **then** st_1 **else if** re_2 **then** st_2 **else if** re_3 **then** st_3 **else** ...

enables the execution of any one of a number of statements depending upon which of the same number of *re*'s is true first. (Why?)

5. In Algol any *st* can be a *block* (defined in Section 6.1.2) and in PL/I either *st* can be a BEGIN block (also defined in Section 6.1.2) or a DO-group (defined in Section 8.2).[††]

6. In Cobol the literal NEXT SENTENCE can appear once but not twice (Why?); in Section 6.1.2 we shall define the concept of *sentence* in Cobol.

7. None of the statements interior to IF statements need be GO TO statements. For example the PL/I statement

      IF $X < Y$ THEN I = 4; ELSE I = 5;

has two assignment statements.

    The conditional mechanism is therefore substantially more flexible and sophisticated in Algol and PL/I than in Fortran or Cobol. The two types of IF statements in Fortran exist only because the arithmetic IF, the only one available in early dialects of Fortran, proved too constraining and inconvenient in some cases.

    We have now covered enough of the four languages to write, with the exception of input and output, small programs in these languages.

Example 5.13

Write a program in each of the four languages, ignoring input and output and in Cobol ignoring the various *divisions* of the program other than the PROCE-

---

[†] Allowing the statement after THEN in PL/I to be another conditional gives rise to the "dangling ELSE" problem. For, if the conditional after THEN has the first form in Panel 5.9 but the parent conditional has the second form, the ELSE will seem to belong to the subconditional rather than to the parent conditional. This problem can be solved using BEGIN blocks or DO-groups (see 5. above).

[††] Normally it should be the latter; see Section 6.1.2.

DURE DIVISION (see Section 6.2), to find the largest of 10 numbers, stored as a one-dimensional array A in Fortran, Algol, and PL/I and in Cobol as a file with the structure

```
01  TABLE.
    02 A OCCURS 10 TIMES PICTURE 9999.
```

and to put this number in a location ALARGE (cf. Example 2.5, p. 38).

Panel 5.9   Conditional transfer statements

FORTRAN	*ALGOL, PL/I*	*COBOL*
	Syntax	
i) IF (ae) sl_1, sl_2, sl_3	Algol: i) if re then st;	IF re $\left\{ \begin{array}{l} st_1 \\ \text{NEXT SENTENCE} \end{array} \right\}$
ii) IF (re) st	ii) if re then st_1 else st_2;	ELSE $\left\{ \begin{array}{l} st_2 \\ \text{NEXT SENTENCE} \end{array} \right\}$
	PL/I: i) IF re THEN st; ii) IF re THEN st_1; ELSE st_2;	
	Semantics	
i) If $ae <$,=, or $>$ zero, respectively, next statement executed is one with first, second, or third sl ii) If re is true execute st; otherwise skip st	i) If re is true execute st; otherwise skip it ii) if re is true execute st_1 and skip st_2; otherwise skip st_1 and execute st_2	If re is true execute st_1 (or NEXT SENTENCE) and skip st_2; otherwise skip st_1 and execute st_2 (or NEXT SENTENCE)
	Examples	

IF (X−Y) 10, 10, 20
 IF (X.LE.Y) Y = X
	if $X < Y$ then $Y = X$;
	 IF X LE Y THEN GO
	    TO L1; ELSE GO
	    TO L2;
		IF X IS LESS THAN Y
		 GO TO L1 ELSE GO TO
		    L2

ae—arithmetic expression
re—relational expression
sl—statement label
st—statement (executable)

Fortran:

```
      ---
      ---
      ALARGE = A(1)
      I = 2
   20 IF (ALARGE.GE.A(I)) GO TO 10
      ALARGE = A(I)
   10 I = I+1
      IF (I.LE.10) GO TO 20
      ---
      ---
```

Algol:

```
      ---
      ---
      ALARGE := A[1] ; I := 2;
  L1: if ALARGE ⩾ A[I] then go to L2 else ALARGE := A[I] ;
  L2: I := I+1; if I ⩽ 10 then go to L1
      else ...
```

PL/I:

```
      ---
      ---
      ALARGE = A(1); I = 2;
  L1: IF ALARGE > = A(I) THEN GO TO L2; ELSE
      ALARGE = A(I);
  L2: I = I+1; IF I < = 10 THEN GO TO L1;
      ELSE ...
```

Cobol:

```
      ---
      ---
      MOVE A (1) TO ALARGE MOVE 2 TO I.
  LABEL 1. IF ALARGE IS NOT LESS THAN A (I) GO TO LABEL 2
      OTHERWISE MOVE A (I) TO ALARGE.
  LABEL 2. ADD 1 TO I. IF I IS NOT GREATER THAN 10
      GO TO LABEL1 ELSE ...
```

The varying physical formats of these four programs and the use of spacing and punctuation will be explained in Section 6.2.

We are now ready to look at the structure of programs and how they are written in some detail in order to apply the material already covered to actual problems. However, before going on with discussions of further statements of the various languages, in the next chapter we shall consider the rules of program structure and writing.

BIBLIOGRAPHIC NOTES

For the reader who has had little contact with algebraic laws and formalism, some valuable contact with these can be obtained from the first chapter of Birkhoff and MacLane (1949). A good elementary treatment of logarithms and exponentials can be found in Chapter VIII of Courant and Robbins (1948), a book which can be read with profit from cover to cover, particularly by those with limited mathematical backgrounds. Knuth (1969), Volume 1, contains much useful material for the mathematically unsophisticated. Volume 2 has the best and most complete treatment available of computer arithmetic.

The references at the end of Chapter 2 to books which discuss the various languages all contain thorough discussions of the assignment and decision statements. The reader will look in vain for discussions in these or other books for the rationale which led to these general forms. They developed as they did because in some sense they were natural.

Lee (1967) discusses in detail a particular Fortran compiler and Randell and Russell (1964) do the same for an Algol compiler. Both contain useful discussions of Polish notation and arithmetic scan techniques. Hassitt (1967) also contains some useful material in these areas.

Bibliography

Birkhoff, G., and S. MacLane (1949): *A Survey of Modern Algebra*, The Macmillan Company, New York.

Courant, R., and H. Robbins (1948): *What Is Mathematics?*, Oxford University Press, New York.

Hassitt, A. (1967): *Computer Programming and Computer Systems*, Academic Press, New York.

Knuth, D.E. (1968-69): *The Art of Computer Programming*, vols. 1 and 2, Addison-Wesley Publishing Company, Reading, Massachusetts.

Lee, J.A.N. (1967): *The Anatomy of a Compiler*, Reinhold Publishing Company, New York.

Randell, B., and L.J. Russell (1964): *Algol 60 Implementation*, Academic Press, New York.

PROBLEMS

Section 5.1

1. a) Show how floating-point underflow can result in failure of the associative law for multiplication and the distributive law to hold.

b) Give an example of failure of the associative law for addition because of floating-point overflow.

2. What aspect of the commutative laws, as opposed to the associative and distributive laws, results in their being satisfied for computer arithmetic?

3. Suppose the error in the two numbers on p. 156 is at most 1/2 in the least significant position. Show that their difference may be accurate to no more than one part in 10^4.

Section 5.2

4. Let M be the floating-point multiplication time on a computer, let L be the time required to compute a logarithm and E the time required to compute an exponential. What is the relation between M, L, and E from which you can determine when it is more economical to compute A**I as $eI \cdot \ln A$ or as $A*A* \ldots *A$?
    I factors

5. Explain why the equal hierarchy of double-precision and complex in Fortran in Panel 5.2 will not cause any ambiguity in practice.

6. What are the values of the following quantities, written using normal algebraic notation?

a) entier (-3.6) (i.e., $[-3.6]$)
b) $[-8.7]$
c) $[|-4.3|]$
d) $[3.7] - 5.9[1.8] + |[-2.1]|$

7. Show how integer division may be used to determine if one integer is a divisor of another.

8. a) Write Fortran expressions for the following algebraic expressions using the *minimum* possible number of parentheses:

   i) a^b c^d ef
   ii) (ab) c^d
   iii) ab^c / de f
   iv) $(a^b$ / $c^d)$ / efg

b) What changes, if any, must be made in the answers to part (a) for PL/I?

9.   Fill in the missing elements in the following Fortran BNF definitions which ignore the restrictions on mixing modes:

```
<ADD OP> :: = + | −
<MULT OP> :: = * | /
<EXP OP> :: = **
<PRIMARY> :: = <CONSTANT> | <UNSUBSCRIPTED VARIABLE> |
       <          VARIABLE> | ( <          > )
<FACTOR> :: = <PRIMARY> | <PRIMARY>        <PRIMARY>
<TERM> :: = <FACTOR> | <TERM> <          > <FACTOR>
<SIGNED TERM> :: = + <TERM> | − <TERM>
<SIMPLE ARITHMETIC EXPRESSION> :: = <TERM> | <SIMPLE
       ARITHMETIC EXPRESSION> <          > <SIMPLE
       ARITHMETIC EXPRESSION>
<ARITHMETIC EXPRESSION> :: = <SIMPLE ARITHMETIC
       EXPRESSION> | <SIGNED TERM> | <          > <ADD OP>
       <SIMPLE ARITHMETIC EXPRESSION>
```

How else could the definition of signed term be written?

10. Show how the definitions of the previous problem embody the rules of hierarchy and parentheses.

Section 5.3

11. Suppose the restrictions of Section 5.3 on using variables with a single letter and no constants in arithmetic expressions were removed. Draw a flow chart for an algorithm which scans an arithmetic expression as normally written from left to right and produces as output the variables and constants in the expression as sequences of coded binary characters. Retain the second and third assumptions on p. 170.

12. Draw a flow chart which would take an arithmetic expression stored in 6-bit characters of consecutive words in memory and would remove all spaces in the expression.

Section 5.3.1

13. a) Derive the PSN equivalent of

   (A/(B+C)) * D

   b) Derive the PPN equivalent of

   (A * X+B)/(C * X–D)

   c) Give an example of an expression containing no pluses or minuses which has more than one Polish representation.

14. Translate the following PSN expressions to normal algebraic notation first from right to left and then from left to right.

   a) ABC/E * +FGH * –/I *
   b) AB+CD * EF/GHI/ ** ——

15. a) Give a formal proof that a Polish string represents a unique arithmetic expression.

   b) Why would your proof fail if there were not a special representation of the unary minus?

Section 5.3.2

16. Use the arithmetic-expression-to-PSN translation algorithm to generate the strings of Problem 14.

17. Use the algorithm of Figure 5.3 to convert A*(–B–C) to PSN.

18. Use the notation of Table 5.3 and the algorithm of Figure 5.4 to "compile" the two PSN strings of Problem 14.

19. Draw a flow chart to combine the two algorithms of Figures 5.3 and 5.4 into one. That is, derive an algorithm which integrates the conversion to PSN and the compilation of the PSN string into one algorithm.

Section 5.4

20. Explain why Fortran requires no rule about subscript evaluation before expression evaluation in assignment statements analogous to the one for PL/I and Algol.

21. Suppose the = in assignment statements really meant equality so that statements of the form N = N+1 were not allowed. How could the effect of N = N+1 be implemented in this case?

22. Give plausible reasons for the prohibitions against certain conversions in Fortran as given in Table 5.4.

23. Could the Cobol statement in Example 5.12 be written using the verbs of Panel 5.4? Why?

Section 5.5

24. Discuss the statement "Labels in Fortran are syntactically no more restrictive than in Algol or PL/I but they do restrict the actual structure of the program as it gets punched on cards more than in Algol and PL/I."

25. a) Is the statement

GO TO (1,2,3,1,2,3), I

syntactically correct in Fortran? Why? Give an example of a case when you might like to use such a statement.
    b) Write Algol, PL/I, and Cobol equivalents of the above statement.

26. a) Prove or disprove that a logical IF statement in Fortran can always be replaced by an arithmetic IF.
    b) Show how both logical and arithmetic IFs in Fortran fit into the framework of

IF α THEN β ELSE γ

27. a) Draw a flow chart which illustrates the Algol conditional shown on p. 198.
    b) What kind of data structure does this flow chart remind you of?

28. Write programs in each of the four languages, ignoring input and output and the divisions of Cobol, to invert the order of 10 numbers stored as in Example 5.13 (i.e., make the last the first, next to last the second, etc.).

6

program structure, preparation, and testing

And the earth was without form.

Genesis 1:2

The proof of the pudding is in the eating.

Miguel de Cervantes in Don Quixote

This chapter is in the nature of an interlude before those chapters which discuss the truly significant features of P-O languages. With the completion of Chapter 5 we have discussed enough features of P-O languages to enable the reader to write simple programs. But we have not really said what a program *is,* nor have we discussed any aspects of input and output. In this chapter we will remedy these omissions and prepare in a natural way for the chapters which follow.

6.1 THE STRUCTURE OF PROGRAMS

We have said that the *statement* is the basic building block in all P-O languages. Generally, all programs are simply sequences of statements. But, in order that a program be a syntactically correct sequence of statements, there are various rules in the four languages which must be observed. Our purpose in this section is to define a program in each of the languages by stating and discussing these rules.

6.1.1 Special and Reserved Words

Most of the Cobol words we have used thus far in considering constructs in this language are called *reserved words,* which means they cannot be used as names.

Thus, for example, ELSE, EQUALS, IF, LESS, OF, TO, as well as almost two hundred other words in Cobol are reserved. Neither Fortran nor PL/I have reserved words (although some PL/I implementations do reserve a few words). In the latter the requirement of blanks in certain places (see Section 6.2.1) removes any possible ambiguity between names and words with special meaning in the language. In Fortran, even without blanks the syntax is unambiguous. For example, a statement which begins with

IF

could be a conditional transfer statement *or* an assignment statement with IF the variable name on the left side or part of the variable name. But this ambiguity is removed by the presence, absence, or placement of an equal sign in the remainder of the statement (Problem 1); an equal sign may appear in a logical IF only in an assignment statement following the parenthesized condition (see Panel 5.9, p. 199).[†]

Algol does not have reserved words but it does distinguish between words such as **if, then,** and **else,** which have special syntactic meanings in the language, and these same words used as variable names. In the publication of Algol programs this distinction is made, as we have already been doing here, by printing in boldface the words with special syntactic meanings when they are used with these meanings. Thus

if IF **then** THEN := ELSE **else** ELSE := THEN;

distinguishes between **if, then,** and **else** as special words and variable names. In implementations of Algol, of course, some other arrangement must be made. A common one is to use quotation marks around the special words. Thus the above sentence might be punched on a card

'IF' IF 'THEN' THEN = ELSE 'ELSE' ELSE = THEN.,

Note also the transliteration ; to ., in the above. It is good programming practice in Fortran, Algol, and PL/I not to use the special words of the languages as variable names in order to avoid confusion.

6.1.2   Program Structures Larger Than Statements

A number of different techniques are employed in the four languages to separate one statement from another, analogous to the separation of sentences by periods

---

[†]Although the official syntax does not allow it, many Fortran systems allow Hollerith constants (cf. Panel 4.5) in IF statements (e.g., IF(A.EQ.2H=1) ....), in which case the position of the equal sign with respect to parentheses removes the ambiguity.

in English. Fortran requires no punctuation between statements because, in preparing the program for input, it requires that every statement begin on a new card (see Section 6.2.1). The other three languages allow a freer format for program preparation. Algol and PL/I require that statements be separated by a semicolon while Cobol, with some exceptions to be discussed below, requires only that statements be separated by spaces.

We have mentioned previously that Cobol contains structures called sentences and paragraphs. A *sentence* is one or more statements followed by a period and space which the programmer wishes to group together for his own convenience. The statements in a sentence are separated by one or more blanks, and, optionally, by one of a number of *separators* including the semicolon, comma, and period. Thus, instead of

ADD A TO B MOVE B TO C.

we could write, for example,

ADD A TO B. MOVE B TO C.

or

ADD A TO B; MOVE B TO C.

We emphasize that the sentence has no special syntactic meaning; it is merely a convenience to the programmer.

However, a *paragraph* in Cobol does have special syntactic meaning. A paragraph is any group of sentences which is headed by a label. Therefore a paragraph is the smallest syntactic unit which can be referred to in a transfer of control statement. Of course, a paragraph can consist of a single statement or sentence but typically, as in natural language, a paragraph includes a group of sentences pertaining to the same "thought" (i.e., computation).

Cobol also allows structures called *sections.* A section is a group of paragraphs and is headed by a label called a section name followed by the word SECTION and a period. A section ends at the next section name or at the end of the program. The physical appearance of labels, sentences, paragraphs, and sections on coding forms or cards will be discussed in Section 6.2.

Fortran has no larger structure than a statement except a program itself (see Section 6.1.4) or subprograms (see Chapter 7). However, both Algol and PL/I define various structures larger than statements but normally smaller than a program itself. In PL/I a *compound statement* is any statement which contains another type of statement as a part of it. One example is the conditional statement (see Panel 5.9) because it includes other PL/I statements within it. The only other compound statement in PL/I is the ON statement (see Section 6.3). Algol also has a structure called a compound statement but it is a very different

Panel 6.1   Blocks

Syntax

ALGOL

sl_1: sl_2: . . . : sl_n:
  begin td_1 ; td_2 ; . . . ; td_m ;
  st_1 ; st_2 ; . . . ; st_r **end**

PL/I

sl_1: sl_2: . . . sl_n:
  PROCEDURE $(ar_1, . . . , ar_k)$;
  st_1 ; st_2 ; . . . ; st_m ;
  END sl;

or

sl_1: sl_2: . . . : sl_n:
  BEGIN; st_1 ; st_2 ; . . . ; st_m ;
  END sl;

Options

m and n may be zero; r must be at least 1; if $m = 0$ (i.e., td missing), structure is called a *compound statement*, otherwise a *block*.

n may be zero in BEGIN blocks but must be at least 1 in PROCEDURE blocks; k may be zero; m must be at least 1; sl after END is optional, but if it is included it must be one of labels before PROCEDURE or BEGIN (see text).

Examples

Compound statement:

```
L1:   begin
      if B * B-4. * A * C>0
      then REAPT := . . .
      else IMGPT := . . .;
      end
```

Block (with nested compound statement):

```
      begin
      integer array A[1 : 100] ;
      integer I, ALARGE;
L1:   ALARGE: = A[1]; I := 2;
      if ALARGE ⩾ A [I] then
      go to L2 else ALARGE := A[I] ;
L2:   begin I:=I+1; if I ⩽ 10
             then go to L1 else . . .
      end
      end
```

BEGIN block:

```
L1:   BEGIN;
      IF B * B-4. * A * C>=0
      THEN REAPT= . . .;
      ELSE IMGPT= . . .;
      END;
```

PROCEDURE block (with nested BEGIN block):

```
L3:   PROCEDURE;
      DECLARE (A(100),I,ALARGE)
      FIXED;
L1:   ALARGE=A(1); I=2;
      IF ALARGE > =A (I) THEN
      GO TO L2; ELSE ALARGE=
      A (I);
L2:   BEGIN; I=I+1; IF I < =10
      THEN GO TO L1; ELSE . . .
      END;
      END;
```

ar—argument
sl—statement label
st—statement
td—type declaration

211

structure from the one in PL/I and is more properly discussed under *blocks* below.

The block is basic to the structure of both Algol and PL/I and is one of the most important concepts in computer science. Panel 6.1 describes the Algol and PL/I block structures. Note also the following remarks:

1. Blocks in Algol and PROCEDURE blocks in PL/I must be headed by one or more labels; BEGIN blocks in PL/I may be labeled but need not be. The body of a block in both languages is a normal sequence of statements in the language. In Algol blocks these consist of declarations of all variables local to the block (i.e., not declared in any block containing this block; more later in this section). The main distinction between a compound statement and a block in Algol is that the former has no local variables and, therefore, no type declarations.

2. The PROCEDURE block in PL/I is more important than the BEGIN block. The latter serves only as a convenient way to group statements together in the normal sequential flow of the program in order to facilitate storage allocation and freeing. PROCEDURE blocks, on the other hand, are the basic building blocks of PL/I. As we shall see in Section 6.1.4, a program in PL/I is a PROCEDURE block. In Chapter 7 we shall see that all subprograms in PL/I are PROCEDURE blocks. Indeed, except for the PROCEDURE block which is the program itself, PROCEDURE blocks are not executed by having the sequential flow of the program reach them. They are activated only by being *called* from another portion of the program as we shall discuss in Chapter 7. The *arguments* (ar_i) of the PROCEDURE block as shown in Panel 6.1 have use in subprograms and, therefore, we shall postpone discussion of them to Chapter 7.

3. In Algol, **begin** and **end** are special words that denote the beginning and end of a block; in PL/I, BEGIN; and END; are statements like any other executable statements.

4. If a statement label appears after END in a PL/I block, this END statement terminates the block which has that *sl* as a label *and* all other blocks contained in that block. This obviates the necessity of writing the END statements to terminate the contained blocks. In the example in Panel 6.1, in place of the two end statements we could have written

END L3;

5. In Algol, semicolons after **end** cannot be used if the **end** precedes an **else,** need not be used if the **end** precedes another **end,** and must be used otherwise, for if not, what follows would be a comment (see Panel 6.5).

6. The Algol block syntax distinguishes between type declarations and statements because the former are not considered statements in Algol. But in PL/I all declarations are indicated via the DECLARE statement.

But why have a block structure at all? There are three reasons which we give in order of increasing importance:

i) It gives the programmer a convenient way to segment his program.

ii) It enables reference to a group of statements (analogously to reference to a paragraph in Cobol). The importance of this will be clearer when we discuss subprograms in Chapter 7 and iteration in Chapter 8.

iii) Most importantly, it provides a mechanism for control of storage allocation and variable naming. In most programs the reader will write, he will use a single variable name only once; indeed, he may have implicitly assumed that a given variable name could be used only once per program. In Fortran and Cobol this is true.[†] But in Algol and PL/I variable names can be reused. Each variable declared in an Algol or PL/I program has a *scope* which is defined to be that block in which the variable is declared, but excluding any blocks which are internal to the defining block in which the same variable name is declared. This situation is illustrated by the Algol program in Figure 6.1. The scopes of the variables are shown in Table 6.1. Thus, for example, the scope of the variable D declared in block L1 does not include the internal block L2 in which D is again declared. It follows then that in both Algol and PL/I a variable name can be reused any time a new block is defined. From Panel 6.1 we see also that all variables in a compound statement have a scope larger than the compound statement. (Why?)

But more important than the ability to reuse variable names is the control of storage allocation made possible by the block structure. In Section 4.4.2 we alluded to this mechanism, called *dynamic storage allocation,* which works a bit differently in PL/I and Algol.

In Algol, with one exception, an identifier is *assigned* memory space only when the program control enters the block in which the identifier is declared. This space is released (i.e., made available for the storage of other data) whenever program control leaves the block in which the variable is declared (i.e., by passing through **end** or by means of a transfer of control statement). Thus, referring to Figure 6.1, 10 memory locations are assigned to the array B when the block labeled L1 is entered. When L4 is entered these 10 locations are retained but they are not available (i.e., the programmer cannot refer to them) because of the use of B in L4. In L4 one location is assigned to the identifier B local to it. When the **end** in L4 is reached this one location for B is released and the 10 locations for B in L1 are again available. Finally, when control passes through **end** in L1, these 10 locations are released.

Normally in Algol, every time program control reenters the block L1 the values of the identifiers declared in this block are undefined. That is, once the

---

[†]For example, in Fortran the same identifier cannot be used for a subscripted and unsubscripted variable; but variable names can be reused in subprograms (see Chapter 7).

```
L1:      begin
         real A, C, D; real array B[1 : 10] ;
             L2:   begin
                   real D, E; real array F[-4 : 6, 1 : 12] ;
                       L3:   begin
                             real F, G;
                             |
                             end L3;
                       L4:   begin
                             real B, C, G;
                             |
                             end L4;
                   end L2;
         end L1;
```

Figure 6.1   Scope of variable names (labels after **end** are comments; see Panel 6.5).

program control exits from L1 nothing is retained for the next entry into the block. However, one exception to this rule occurs when the identifier is declared **own**. The **real, integer,** and **boolean** type declarations discussed in Section 4.3 can be preceded by **own**. Every time a block is reentered each identifier in the block declared as **own** retains the value it had on the previous exit from the block. Therefore, if in Figure 6.1 the declaration in block L2 had been

    real D,E;
    own real array F[-4:6,1:12] ;

the values of the array F would be retained after exit from block L2 and would be available again when L2 is reentered. Of course, because F is declared again in block L3, the array declared in L2 would never be available in L3.

In PL/I each variable has a storage allocation attribute, STATIC, AUTO-MATIC, or CONTROLLED so that, for example, one may write

    DECLARE A FIXED BINARY AUTOMATIC;

For the STATIC attribute, storage is assigned as in Fortran at the start of execution and is never released. This attribute is therefore analogous to **own** in Algol. The AUTOMATIC attribute results in storage allocation and release on block entry and exit just as in Algol. The CONTROLLED attribute allows the programmer to allocate and release storage himself using statements called ALLOCATE and FREE. For variables declared in the outermost block the

Table 6.1   Scope of names in Figure 6.1

Name	Label of defining block	Scope of name
A	L1	L1
B	L1	L1-L4
C	L1	L1-L4
D	L1	L1-L2
D	L2	L2
E	L2	L2
F	L2	L2-L3
F	L3	L3
G	L3	L3
B	L4	L4
C	L4	L4
G	L4	L4

Note:
L1-L4, for example, means those parts of the program in block L1 but *not* block L4.

default attribute is STATIC but, for those in any interior block, it is AUTO-MATIC. (Why?)

The above implies that in each block in Algol and PL/I there are two kinds of variables, those which are declared in the block and therefore are *local* to it, and those which are declared externally to the block and are *global* to it. Referring again to Figure 6.1, in block L3, F and G are local variables while A, B, C (in L1), D (in L2), and E are global to L3. D in L1 and F in L2 are also global but cannot be used in L3 because of the declarations of D in L2 and F in L3.

An important benefit of dynamic storage allocation is the ability to use variables in declaring the size of arrays. Since storage is normally not assigned until a block is entered in Algol and PL/I, all that is necessary is that the variables in array dimensions have values *when the block is entered.* Storage is then allocated and released as discussed above. In Fortran, by contrast, since all storage is assigned before any execution, there cannot be variable dimensioning (except in one special case to be discussed in the next chapter). Finally, we should note that neither Algol nor PL/I can have variable dimensions in the block at the highest level. (Why?)

6.1.3   Program Termination

All languages allow one or more legal ways of terminating the execution of a program. In addition, various *illegal* actions will terminate execution. Some of the latter are discussed in Sections 6.2.2 and 6.3. The legal means of terminating a program are shown in Panel 6.2. Note the following:

1. Many Fortran compilers implement a CALL EXIT statement which is functionally identical to STOP, and whose purpose is to indicate that termination of a program really calls a subroutine (see Chapter 7) which returns control to the computer operating system (cf. Chapter 11).

2. The PAUSE statement in Fortran is a carryover from the days when programmers ran and tested their own programs (cf. Section 6.3). Then it was sometimes useful to stop the program, check the output, and continue if things were going well. The only purpose of this statement now is to enable the computer operator to do something such as mounting or demounting a tape before the calculation continues. Other languages have alternate means (such as STOP in Cobol) to accomplish this.

3. In normal usage, a PL/I program will be a single procedure block (see Section 6.1.4) in which case the STOP and EXIT statements are identical. In PL/I jargon the program is called a *major task*. In order to achieve some parallelism in certain operations, PL/I defines an elaborate task structure involving subtasks of the major task. Most PL/I programmers will be able to ignore this structure.

The reader should be careful not to draw the conclusion that in a normal program which executes correctly the program will terminate with one of the statements in Panel 6.2. Another way for a program to terminate is to have it "run out of data."

Example 6.1

Indicate the structure of a Fortran program to compute the roots of a quadratic equation which would terminate by running out of data.

In the following program A, B, and C are the coefficients of the quadratic equation. The READ statement will be discussed further in Section 6.3 and the END statement in Section 6.1.4.

```
100 READ, A, B, C
    ┌──────────────┐
    │ Main body    │
    │ of program   │
    │ including    │
    │ printing of  │
    │ results      │
    └──────────────┘
    GO TO 100
    END
```

Panel 6.2   Program termination

FORTRAN	ALGOL	PL/I	COBOL
		Syntax	
STOP or PAUSE, either of which may be optionally followed by a positive integer of 1 to 5 digits	No specific statements; reaching the end of the highest level block terminates execution	STOP; or EXIT; or by reaching the END; of an external procedure block	STOP followed optionally by RUN or a literal
		Semantics	
STOP terminates the program so that it cannot be restarted; PAUSE stops execution but allows for restarting at the point of termination; the positive integer is included as part of the output and enables the programmer to distinguish which of his STOPs or PAUSEs terminated his program		STOP; and EXIT; both terminate *tasks* (see Section 6.1.3)	STOP or STOP followed by a literal end execution but permit restarting; the literal is printed out at the operator's console or displayed in lights at the console; STOP RUN terminates execution so that it cannot be restarted

Every time control returns to Statement 100 three more coefficients are read from cards. When there is no more data the next card will be the first card of the next program (see Section 6.2.2). This will be recognized as not being a data card and the above program will be terminated. Usually an error message to the effect that the program tried to read more data but none was available will be printed out as part of the output. Such a message is desirable because a common programming error is to not provide enough data (cf. Section 6.2.3). But in the case of a program designed as above to terminate when it runs out of data, the message does not really indicate an error. Since the programmer does not usually know beforehand how many sets of data his program will have to operate on, termination by running out of data is often a reasonable way to organize the program. However, we should note that many P-O language implementations allow the programmer to test for no more data by use of a statement like IF(EOF) GO TO *sl* [EOF for End of File(of data)] which transfers to the statement labeled *sl* (which might be STOP) only when there is no more data. This allows a positive test rather than the negative one of running out of data.

6.1.4   The Definition of a Program

Descriptions of programming languages, formal or informal, have as their goal the definition of the structure *program*. In this section we shall approach the definitions of a program informally; only in the case of Cobol will it be necessary to add substantially to our previous discussion.

In Fortran a program is any concatenation of syntactically correct statements terminating with an END statement.[†] But a program may or may not do what the programmer wants; syntactic correctness does not imply logical correctness (cf. Section 6.3). A program may not even *execute* because of logical errors. But a program will *compile.*

In Algol a program is a block. Thus, a program cannot contain two blocks, neither of which is contained in any other block (i.e., there must be one and only one block on the highest level). Schematically an Algol program may be defined as

$$\textbf{begin } d_1; d_2; \ldots; d_m; st_1; st_2; \ldots; st_n; \textbf{ end}$$

where the declarations (d_i's) can be type declarations as already discussed or *procedure declarations* to be discussed in Chapter 7. The type declarations must include all variables in the statements. This definition must be understood recursively in that each statement (st) may be replaced by a block, which will have its own declarations, or a compound statement. The PL/I situation is similar to that of Algol except that a PL/I program is a *sequence* of procedure blocks on the highest level. However, most PL/I programs will consist of only a single block on the highest level.

Cobol programs require quite a bit of formalism besides what we have discussed here already. They consist of four parts or *divisions*, each of which requires certain heading information. These are:

1. *The identification division,* whose purpose is to identify the program and author (see Figure 6.2*a*).

[†]Syntactic correctness implies not only that each statement be properly constructed but also that certain global properties be satisfied. For example, the statement numbers in an arithmetic IF statement must appear elsewhere in the program.

a)   Identification division

    IDENTIFICATION DIVISION.
    PROGRAM-ID. SAMPLE.
    AUTHOR. A RALSTON.
    DATE WRITTEN. 2 MAY 1969.

b)   Environment division

    ENVIRONMENT DIVISION.
    CONFIGURATION SECTION.
    SOURCE COMPUTER.   IBM-360 H40.
    OBJECT COMPUTER.   IBM-360 H40.
    INPUT-OUTPUT SECTION.
        (Information on peripheral device
        assignment follows)

c)   Data division

    DATA DIVISION.
    FILE SECTION.
    FD SAMPLE-DATA.
        (Physical organization information follows)
    01 DATA-LIST.
            02 ITEM1 PICTURE 9(6).
        (Followed by remainder of SAMPLE-DATA definition)
    FD COMPUTED-DATA.
        (Followed by physical organization of file and by definition of
        COMPUTED-DATA as above and then by any other file definitions
        (FD's) needed)
    WORKING STORAGE SECTION.
            77 J PICTURE 9(2) COMPUTATIONAL.
            77 SALES-TAX PICTURE V9(2) VALUE IS .04.
        (Followed by other definitions of temporary variables and constants
        (level 77) and by definitions of temporary files structured as in FILE
        SECTION)

d)   Procedure division

    PROCEDURE DIVISION
        (Followed by the program itself)

Figure 6.2   An example of Cobol program structure.

2. *The environment division,* which contains information about the computer to be used for compilation and execution (normally the same) and about the assignment of peripheral devices to the files which will be processed by the program (see Figure 6.2*b*). This information is used by the compiler to make the handling of peripherals, particularly magnetic tapes, as efficient as possible.

3. *The data division,* which describes the structure of the files to be used by the Cobol program as discussed in Section 4.4.3. This division in Cobol corresponds to the DIMENSION statements and type declarations in Fortran, the type declarations in Algol, or DECLARE statements in PL/I. It must be headed by a DATA DIVISION card (see Figure 6.2*c*) and contain these sections:

> a) the *file section,* headed by a FILE SECTION card and followed by a description of the structure of each file. Each of these descriptions is headed by some descriptive information about the physical organization of the file on the peripheral storage device (e.g., number of tape records per tape block; cf. Section 10.1.2.1).
>
> b) the *working storage section,* headed by a WORKING STORAGE SECTION card and describes the structure of the records needed for temporary storage during the course of the calculation. In it are listed the constants needed in the calculation.

4. *The procedure division,* which is the part of the program we have been discussing and which contains the program statements themselves. It must be headed by a single card punched with PROCEDURE DIVISION as shown in Figure 6.2*d*.

Thus the difference between the structure of a Cobol program and programs in the other three languages is not in principle but rather in the formalism of structure required.

The description above makes clear that the beginning of a Cobol program is indicated explicitly by the

IDENTIFICATION DIVISION

card as shown in Figure 6.2*a*. Similarly, the first **begin** in Algol and PROCEDURE in PL/I indicates the beginning of programs in these languages. In Fortran there is no explicit way of denoting the beginning of a program; rather, this is indicated implicitly by the first statement which appears after a certain *control card* which we shall consider in Section 6.2.2.

The end of a source program is also normally indicated by a control card (see Section 6.2.2). In Algol, of course, the end of the program is automatically indicated by the **end** which matches the first **begin.** But in PL/I there is no such simple rule. (Why?) Also, we note that in FORTRAN the first END statement does not necessarily denote the end of the source deck, as we shall see in Chapter 7.

Panel 6.3   Syntactical rules for blanks

Fortran	*Algol*	*PL/I*	*Cobol*
1. Are ignored by the compiler except in Hollerith constants (see Panel 4.5).	Allowed without restriction in reference language; in actual implementations, however, there are often some restrictions on their use (see Section 6.2) and some requirements on their use.	1. Not allowed in identifiers, constants, picture specifications and composite operators (e.g., $\neg=$).	1. Not allowed in identifiers and before various types of punctuation.
2. May be used freely except in single case of continuation card (see Section 6.2).		2. Needed as separators between identifiers, constants and keywords (e.g., IF A not the same as IFA).	2. Must appear as separators in many places (e.g., between a variable name and its subscripts).
		3. Allowed and not ignored in character-string constants.	3. More than one space treated as a single space except in nonnumeric literals.
		4. Otherwise ignored by the compiler.	4. No space allowed after + or – in numeric literal.

6.2   PREPARING THE PROGRAM FOR TESTING

The four languages we are considering vary considerably in their rules about how statements can be concatenated in the preparation of a program to be compiled and executed. Fortran requires a rigid format in program preparation, Cobol a somewhat less rigid format but a large number of specific rules, while Algol and PL/I allow relatively free formats.

6.2.1   Blanks, Comments, and Card and Console Formats

The first matter we shall consider in this context is the rules about *blanks* or *spaces* in programs. We mentioned this briefly in Section 2.5.1 when discussing the question of embedded blanks in names. Panel 6.3 considers this question more generally. The reader should understand the various motivations for these rules:

1. Compilers which *ignore* spaces, except perhaps in a very small number of special cases, normally collapse the input with spaces to strings inside the com-

IBM

FORTRAN Coding Form

X28-7327-6 U/M 050
Printed in U.S.A.

PROGRAM

PROGRAMMER

DATE

PUNCHING INSTRUCTIONS

GRAPHIC

PUNCH

PAGE OF

CARD ELECTRO NUMBER*

COMM.	STATEMENT NUMBER	CONT	FORTRAN STATEMENT	IDENTIFICATION SEQUENCE
1	2 3 4 5	6	7 8 9 10 11 12 13 14 15 16 17 18 19 20 21 22 23 24 25 26 27 28 29 30 31 32 33 34 35 36 37 38 39 40 41 42 43 44 45 46 47 48 49 50 51 52 53 54 55 56 57 58 59 60 61 62 63 64 65 66 67 68 69 70 71 72	73 74 75 76 77 78 79 80

*A standard card form, IBM electro 888157, is available for punching statements from this form

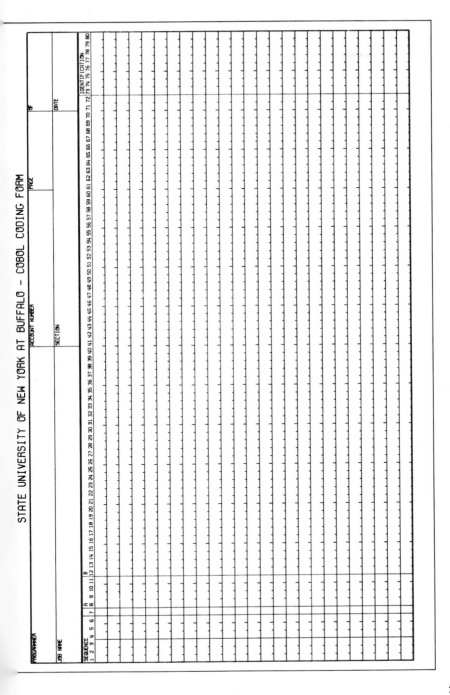

Figure 6.4 (Courtesy of IBM Corp.)

puter with no spaces; this speeds up compiling.

2. The ability to use spaces freely allows the programmer to produce a program which is easy for him to read.

3. Bans on using spaces in certain instances and requirements that they be used in others are to:

> a) assist the compiler in certain ways (e.g., if *embedded* blanks are not allowed in names, when the compiler scans P2Q followed by a blank it can assume P2Q is a name).
>
> b) prevent ambiguity. For example, if the statement

> IF ALEGTB THEN....

were allowed in PL/I (using the 48-character alphabet), it could not be determined whether the relational expression is ALE GT B or A LE GTB, assuming the four variables ALE, B, A, and GTB all appear in the program. Therefore, we must write either

> IF ALE GT B THEN ....

or

> IF A LE GTB THEN ....

Panel 6.4 considers the program format rules of the four languages. The panel assumes input is on punched cards but, for example, even if the input is from an on-line typewriter, the rules are similar. Figure 6.3 and 6.4 display the Fortran and Cobol programming forms on which the user may write his program prior to its being punched on cards. The correlation of these forms with Panel 6.4 is clear. Other comments relevant to Panel 6.4 are:

1. Statements in Fortran which are too long to put on one card may be continued on the next card by punching any character other than 0 or blank in column 6. The Fortran language allows unlimited numbers of continuation cards but most implementations restrict the number to from 10 to 20. Cobol requires a hyphen in column 7 any time a word must be continued from one card to the next (e.g., EQU in columns 70-72 of one card and ALS in columns 12-14 of the next). When a Fortran program is input not from cards but from an on-line typewriter, it is necessary to denote the end of a statement by a special character, such as a semicolon, so that the computer which accepts one line (i.e., card equivalent) at a time can know (by the absence of the special character) that there will be a continuation card without actually reading it.

2. Comments by the programmer which serve a mnemonic purpose for him or for other readers of the program, but are ignored by the compiler, can be inserted in various ways in the four languages as indicated in Panel 6.5. Note that

Panel 6.4 Program formats

Fortran

1. Each *statement* must begin on new card

2. Columns 1-5 used for statement labels

3. Column 6 must be blank or 0 except for continuation cards (see text)

4. Columns 7-72 used for statements

5. Columns 73-80 ignored

Algol, PL/I

1. Statements must be separated by semicolon; otherwise completely free format

2. Implementations usually restrict usage to columns 1-72 (Algol) or 2-72 (PL/I) of card

Cobol

1. Each paragraph (see Section 6.1.2) must begin on a new card

2. Columns 1-6 used for optional card sequence number

3. Column 7 must be blank except for continuation card (see text)

4. Paragraph names must begin in column 8

5. Except for first card of paragraph, all other cards must use columns 12-72 and not 8-11 for statements

6. Columns 73-80 ignored

7. Sentences must end with a period followed by at least one space. Statements may be separated by one or more spaces and, optionally, by one of a number of separators, including semicolon, comma, and period

comment cards in Fortran are an exception to some of the rules of Panel 6.4. Note also that the rule for comments in Algol indicates that a semicolon need not appear between two **ends** because the second **end** serves the purpose of terminating the (empty) comment after the first **end**.

3. One difference between PL/I and Algol not indicated in Panel 6.4 is that in the former any statement before ELSE must have a semicolon after it like any other statement. In Algol the semicolon must not appear before **else**. Thus,

PL/I: IF A $<$ B THEN N=2; ELSE N=3;

Algol: **if** A $<$ B **then** N:=2 **else** N:=3;

4. The sequence numbers in columns 1-6 of Cobol are a convenience to the programmer to give him a check that his cards are properly ordered.

6.2.2   Control Cards

One of the first things any user of a big computing system learns is that it is not enough to write a program and punch it and the data on cards. That is, in addition to these cards, the program deck used as input to the computer must contain certain other cards called *control cards*. These cards give information to the *operating system* (see Chapter 11) of the computer about the program. Control cards take on many and various forms and the information contained on them varies considerably from one installation to another, even sometimes when both use the same computer. By this time the reader has probably learned the control cards required for the system he is using. We shall not consider the format of such cards in detail here but rather we shall discuss the bare minimum of information normally required on control cards and the purpose of each item of information.

The basic control card required by all computer operating systems is the *job card*. This card may require a symbol such as $ in column 1 followed by JOB in columns 2-4 (see Figure 6.5a) and always contains certain other information discussed below.[†] The major purpose of the job card is to serve as a separator of different program and data decks (jobs) stored in the *input queue* of the computer. The input queue is a record, usually on magnetic tape or disk, of program and data cards read by the card reader (see Chapters 10 and 11). When the job card is read, it is recognized by the computer as the termination of one job and the beginning of another. Our example at the end of Section 6.1.3 pointed out that one way to end a program is to have it run out of data. When a program runs out of data the computer first tries to read the job card of the next job as the next data card, recognizes that it cannot be a data card and must, therefore,

---

[†]Job cards for some newer computing systems allow a much freer, less rigid format than that shown in Figure 6.5a.

Panel 6.5   Comments

FORTRAN	ALGOL	PL/I	COBOL

Mechanism

FORTRAN	ALGOL	PL/I	COBOL
Comment cards inserted in program deck	In comment statement or after **end**	Character string enclosed in /*...*/.	NOTE sentences in program

Rules

FORTRAN	ALGOL	PL/I	COBOL
C in column 1 followed by any characters in the remainder of the card; may be inserted anywhere in program	After **begin** or ;, **comment** followed by any sequence of characters except ; *or* any sequence of characters except ; or **end** or **else** after **end** (terminated by **end** or **else** or ;)	May be inserted any place a blank is allowed (except in character string)	Any combination of Cobol characters terminated by a period may appear after NOTE

Examples

Fortran:	C PROGRAM TO FIND LARGEST NUMBER
Algol:	**comment** PROGRAM TO FIND LARGEST NUMBER;
	or **end** PROGRAM TO FIND LARGEST NUMBER;
PL/I:	/ * PROGRAM TO FIND LARGEST NUMBER * /
Cobol:	NOTE PROGRAM TO FIND LARGEST NUMBER.

be a job card and then turns control over to the operating system to process this next job.

In addition, programmers often supply too much or too little data for their programs because, for example, of misapplication of the rules to be introduced in Section 6.2.3. Without a job card, the former case would make the extra data appear to be the start of the next program and the latter case would make the start of the next program look like the missing data of the first. The job card, therefore, serves as a means of catching input errors of this kind.

The following is a list of some of the other information which usually appears on the job card or on other control cards which immediately follow the job card:

1. *The designation of the language being used.*   Most computers allow programmers to write in more than one of the four languages being discussed here as well as in other languages; this item of information tells the operating system which language's compiler will be needed.

a) Job card

i) IBM 7044

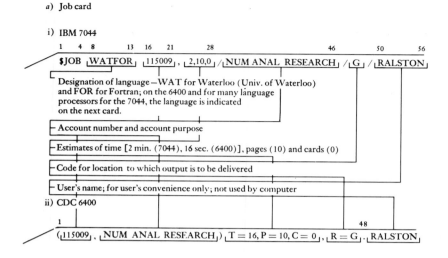

b) Program and data-separation card

i) IBM 7044 — **$ENTRY** in columns 1 through 6

ii) CDC 6400 — 7-8-9 punched in column 1 — called EOR (for End Of Record) card since it ends record consisting of program statements

Figure 6.5   Typical control cards for two computers.

2. *Accounting information.*   This typically includes the user's *account number* and may include his name or a designation of the purpose of his usage of the computer as well. This information is used to

a) determine if the user is authorized to use the computer, and

b) to keep a record of his usage of the computer

3. *Timing, memory usage, and output information.*   This normally includes upper estimates of how much central processor time the problem will require, how much core memory it will need, and the amount of output (printed pages and punched cards) that will be produced. These estimates are used

a) for scheduling purposes; long jobs, jobs which make severe demands on the memory of the computer, and jobs with a lot of output are often given a low priority or are put off to a night shift so as not to inconvenience other users, and

b) to terminate jobs; if the time, memory, or output estimates are exceeded, the computer system will terminate the job; without such a mechanism a single long computation or a job that got into a never-ending computational loop by a programming error could monopolize the computer system.

This list is by no means all-inclusive. Operating systems often require other information besides that above. In Figure 6.5*a* there is a job card for the IBM 7044 computer which contains all the information above as well as other information as indicated in the figure. This figure also contains a CDC 6400 control card containing the same information except for the designation of the language.

Finally, Fortran, Algol, and PL/I systems usually require a special control card (see Figure 6.5*b*) between the program statements and the data.

6.2.3   Free-Format Input and Output

Input-output facilities are often available in a form equivalent or similar to that discussed here in many implementations of Fortran and sometimes in Algol and PL/I. This is not so in Cobol because of its data structure requirements. The input and output statements we shall discuss first are

FORTRAN[†]:	PL/I:
READ, *list*	GET LIST (*list*);
PRINT, *list*	PUT LIST (*list*);

In Fortran the list is any sequence of identifiers separated by commas. The identifiers may be subscripted, in which case, if the subscript is a variable, it must have been previously set to a value by the program (see "defined" variables in Section 6.3). Also, an identifier in the list may be an array identifier without any subscripts in which case it refers to the entire array. In PL/I the list is also a sequence of elements separated by commas. For input (i.e., the GET statement) these elements must be identifiers but, on output (PUT), they may also be expressions.

Example 6.2

What is the correct interpretation of the following sequence of Fortran statements?

```
DIMENSION A(8), B(5,10)
I=7
READ, C, A(I),N,B
```

[†]And those Algol compilers which implement input-output like Fortran; for convenience we shall hereafter use the above Fortran statements in Algol examples.

The READ statement reads data into

1. the single memory location for C (since C is not an array variable)
2. the location of A(7)
3. the location of N
4. the 50 locations of the array B

The READ statement, therefore, instructs the computer to read a set of data from cards into specified variable locations and the PRINT statement instructs it to print a list of variable values on the printer. What is unanswered still is:

1. In what format does the computer expect to find the data punched on cards?
2. In what format will the printed data appear?

The answer to the first question in most implementations is that the data can be punched in any of the 80 columns of a card with each datum separated by at least one blank or a comma and zero or more blanks. No datum may be continued from one card to the next. If blanks are allowed as datum separators then, clearly, no embedded blanks are allowed in the data. This input format is called *free format* to distinguish it from the more constrained format rules to be considered in Chapter 10.

When a READ statement is encountered, a card is read by the computer and the data on the card are assigned sequentially to the variables in the list of the READ statement. If the list has more elements than the card has data, the next card is read and so on until the list is *satisfied*, that is, until all variables in the list have been assigned values. When the list is satisfied and more data still remain on the card being read, these may be saved for the next READ statement but, more commonly, when the list is satisfied, *all remaining data on the card are thrown away*.

Example 6.3

Given the statements

```
DIMENSION A(3),B(2,4)
READ, A,N
READ,B
READ,D
```

and the cards shown in Figure 6.6, what values are assigned to A,B,D, and N,

Card 1:	1.63	8.4E2	-5.9
Card 2:	18	-14	
Card 3:	2.0	3.0	4.0
Card 4:	.4629E1	.3758E2	.2739E-2
Card 5:	.6721E4	.9271	.2374
Card 6:	.647593		

Figure 6.6   Card data for Example 6.3.

assuming the remainder of the card being read is discarded when a list is satisfied?

```
A(1)=1.63
A(2)=8.4E2
A(3)=-5.9
N=18 (-14 discarded)
B(1,1)=2.0
B(2,1)=3.0
B(1,2)=4.0
B(2,2)=.4629E1
B(1,3)=.3758E2
B(2,3)=.2739E-2
B(1,4)=.6721E4
B(2,4)=.9271 (.2374 discarded)
D=.647593
```

Note that the two-dimensional array is read in column order.

When a PRINT statement is encountered the format of the printed output is a fixed format built into the compiler system. Typically, the elements in each list are printed out four to a line until the list is satisfied. Each PRINT statement always starts printing on a new line.

Example 6.4

What printed output results from the statements

```
PRINT,B,D
PRINT,A
PRINT,N
```

when the values of the variables are as given in Example 6.2?

```
0.20000000E 01      0.30000000E  01      0.40000000E 01      0.46290000E 01
0.37580000E 02      0.27390000E- 02      0.67210000E 04      0.92710000E 01
0.64759300E 00
0.16300000E 01      0.84000000E  03     -0.59000000E 01
18
```

Figure 6.7   Output for Example 6.4.

An answer is shown in Figure 6.7. Note that the output format causes each floating-point number to be printed out in the same format—decimal point followed by a specific number of decimal places (8 is most common)—followed by a 2-digit exponent. We should also note that in a binary computer, because of the decimal-to-binary conversion on input and then the binary-to-decimal conversion on output, the output might not precisely reproduce the input. For example, instead of .30000000E01 there might be printed

.30000001E 01

or

.29999999E 01

With the GET LIST statement in PL/I the input data format is just the same as with Fortran, except that a datum may be continued from one card to the next and data remaining on a card after the list is satisfied are not thrown away. Instead, they are read by the next GET LIST statement. The output format for PUT LIST statements is fixed as in the Fortran case but depends upon the declaration of the variable (or variables in an expression) in the program. We shall not discuss the details here.

The above discussion and examples indicate that "free format" is a misnomer as far as the output is concerned; fixed format would be more accurate. But "free format" does apply to the input and, for verbal convenience, is usually linked in Fortran to both input and output. In PL/I this form of input and output is called *list-directed.*

The output format described above for either Fortran or PL/I is clearly not satisfactory for all purposes. Furthermore, the input format will not always be convenient. But, for the beginning programmer—and for many applications programmed by an advanced programmer—free-format input and output serves all necessary purposes and is much easier to learn and use than the more sophisticated input and output techniques we shall discuss in Chapter 10. We shall use it in all examples until Chapter 10.

Some Fortran IV systems implement free-format input and output by means of the NAMELIST statement which has the form

NAMELIST/vn_1/$list_1$/vn_2/$list_2$/ . . . /vn_m/$list_m$

with $m \geqslant 1$. An actual example would be NAMELIST/L1/A,WHY,B/L2/ BECAUS,C,D. The variable names may be any valid identifiers and may not be subscripted. Normally these names may not be used in any other statements of the program except in input-output statements as described below. Each list is a sequence of variable names separated by commas, again with no subscripted variables allowed.

The variable names in the NAMELIST declaration may then be used in input-output statements to refer to all the elements of the associated list. Most Fortran systems only allow NAMELIST to be used in conjunction with the input and output statements to be discussed in Chapter 10. But for simplicity here, let us assume statements of the form

READ, *vn*
PRINT, *vn*

are possible, where the variable name is one of those which appear in a NAMELIST declaration. Thus, referring to the example above, we might have READ, L1, or PRINT, L2. The READ statement then looks for data on cards punched in columns 2 through 80 with the first item being a $\$^\dagger$ followed by the variable name in the READ statement. Following this, the data takes the form

vn_1 = *value(s)*

where the variable name vn_1 here is one of those in the *list* in the NAMELIST statement corresponding to the variable name *vn* in the READ statement. The value or values are those to be assigned to the scalar or array name, respectively. (Some Fortran systems with NAMELIST allow other possibilities than those we discuss here.) Successive values are separated by a comma and one or more blanks. All the variables in the NAMELIST need not be read in, and those that are need not be in the same order as in the list. The NAMELIST input cards are terminated by a single card with $\$END^\dagger$ in columns 2-5.

---

†In IBM 360 Fortran, & (available on the 29 keypunch) is used instead of $.

a) Input

Column
2

Card 1: $INOUT A = 1.63, 8.4E2, -5.9, N = 18,

Card 2: B = 2.0, 3.0, 4.0, .4629E1, .3758E2, .2739E-2, .6721E4, .9271,

Card 3: D = .647593,

Card 4: $END

b) Output

$INOUT

A = 0.16300000E 01, 0.84000000E   03, -0.59000000E 01,

N = 18,

B = 0.20000000E 01, 0.30000000E   01,   0.40000000E 01, 0.46290000E 01,
    0.37580000E 02, 0.27390000E- 02,   0.67210000E 04, 0.92710000E 00,

D = 0.64759300E 00,

$END

Figure 6.8 Use of NAMELIST.

234

Example 6.5

Illustrate the use of NAMELIST for the situation in Example 6.2.

In place of the statements in Example 6.3 we could have the following:

```
DIMENSION A(3), B(2,4)
NAMELIST/INOUT/A,N,B,D
READ, INOUT
```

with data cards which could be punched as shown in Figure 6.8.

When a PRINT statement is used, the output appears in a format very similar to the input format described above. This is illustrated in Figure 6.8 for the statement

```
PRINT,INOUT
```

added to those of Example 6.5. The PRINT statement always causes the values of all the variables in the list to be printed. NAMELIST then provides a free-format input and fixed-format output quite similar to that discussed at the beginning of this section, with the exception of the $ control words and the punching and printing of the variable names. This latter is, of course, quite convenient for reference purposes and can also be achieved using the format facilities to be discussed in Chapter 10.

In addition to the READ and PRINT statements usually available in Fortran implementations, PUNCH is generally also available with either free-format or NAMELIST output. For example, PUNCH, *list* causes the variables in the list to be punched on cards in a predetermined format. With NAMELIST, PUNCH is particularly convenient because the cards punched are automatically in the correct format for later input to the same or another program using NAMELIST.

As with free format, PL/I has an analog of NAMELIST. this is called *data-directed* input and output. The input and output statements have the form

```
GET DATA (list);
PUT DATA (list);
```

where the *list* may be empty in the GET statement. The rules for using these statements are quite similar to those for NAMELIST, the main differences being that $*name* is not required on input and is not printed. PL/I has one further input and output technique called *edit-directed* which is analogous to formatted input and output in Fortran. Both are discussed in Chapter 10.

In addition to the input and output facilities listed in this section, it is appropriate to mention here another data-directed technique in Fortran for assigning values to variables. This takes the form of a declaration rather than an input statement. It is called the DATA statement and has the form

DATA/*var list*$_1$/*value list*$_1$/,*var list*$_2$/*value list*$_2$/,.../,*var list*$_n$/*value list*$_n$/

where the variable lists are, as usual, variable names separated by commas. The variables may be simple variables, subscripted variables with integer subscripts, or array names. The value lists are the values, separated by commas, to be assigned to the variables in the corresponding list. Each element of the value list has the form

*integer * value*

where the integer indicates the number of times the value which follows it is to be repeated. Normally these values are fixed- or floating-point arithmetic constants. However, Hollerith constants (see Panel 4.5) are also allowed in the value list. These provide, among other things, an easy way to get titles or heading data for output into the computer memory which will later be printed using techniques to be described in Chapter 10. Such data cannot be printed using free-format input and output.

Example 6.6

What values are assigned to the variables by the following statements?

```
      DIMENSION A(3), B(2,4), E(6)
      DATA/A,N/1.63,8.4E2,-5.9,18/,B,D/2.0,3.0,4.0,
*     .4629E1,.3758E2,.2739E-2,.6721E4,.9271,.647593/
*     ,E/3*5.0,2*6.8E2,.27541/,F/4HWHAT/
```

Note the two continuation cards marked by asterisks in the DATA statement. The values assigned to A,B,D, and N are precisely those of Example 6.3. For E, the values assigned are

```
      E(1)=5.0
      E(2)=5.0
      E(3)=5.0
      E(4)=6.8E2
      E(5)=6.8E2
      E(6)=.27541
```

and F contains the coded (see Table 3.6) equivalent of WHAT [left justified (i.e., W in leftmost part of computer word) in most implementations].

PL/I provides a simpler and more powerful way of initializing identifier values through the INITIAL attribute, which is attached to a variable in a DECLARE statement.

To conclude this section we point out the value of immediately printing all data input to a program. This procedure, called *echo checking*, has the following advantages:

1. It provides a printed record as part of the output of all the input data.
2. It assures the programmer that his data was correctly read by the input device and stored in the memory of the computer.

PL/I provides a simple mechanism for echo checking via the COPY option in a GET statement. For example, GET LIST (N) COPY causes N to be printed after it is read.

6.3   PROGRAM TESTING

A good programmer is not merely someone able to write accurate statements which make effective, efficient programs when run on a computer. A good programmer must also be adept at finding errors in his programs. It is a law of programming, proved by its few exceptions, that no program of any complexity gives the desired results the first time it is run. This is because computer programming is an extremely complicated art. To write an errorless program requires the same combination of talent and luck required to bowl a 300 game by an expert bowler. Errors of various kinds can easily creep in. Indeed, great effort to insure that a program is errorless before it is run is probably poorly expended, because the computer itself will catch most errors. This is *not* an invitation to carelessness—meticulousness in programming is a most desirable attribute. It is meant to suggest that a reasonable balance should be struck between man and machine in the correction of programming errors.

Program testing is not usually a single step but a series of steps, each one of which consists of the correction of errors hidden by the previous errors which were corrected. Programming errors are of two types:

1. *Syntactic*, which are violations of the rules for the structure of programs and are detected at compilation, and
2. *Logical* or *semantic*, which cause calculations other than those which the programmer wanted done by the computer. These may result in errors such as overflow or the computation may proceed to its end but give wrong results.

In this section we shall consider various ways by which the computer can help the programmer find errors contained in his program. The process of finding errors is normally called *debugging,* an error being a "bug" in the program. A number of different techniques of debugging can be distinguished. We shall present them here in the order in which they are normally used, but it should be pointed out that the debugging process can often be lengthy and involved and may necessitate returning to a particular debugging technique again and again.

1. *Desk Checking.*   In line with our previous statements about good programming habits, before a program deck is submitted, a listing (i.e., the printed record of the program obtained whenever the compiler tries to compile it) of it should be checked for obvious syntactic (e.g., unmatched parentheses) and logical (e.g., failure to provide an exit from a loop) errors.

2. *Syntactic debugging during compilation.*   All compilers check for syntactic errors during compilation; this is necessary because only syntactically correct statements can be compiled. But compilers differ a great deal in

    i) the action they take when an error is discovered, and
    ii) how they present the error message to the user.

To illustrate these differences, let us consider the Fortran statement

    A=B+C(D- E/F)

Any compiler, when it scans the left parenthesis, will recognize that an error has been made.[†] At this point the compiler cannot tell which of a number of possible errors it could be. Among these are:

    i) A missing multiplication operator between C and (
    ii) An incorrect character in a variable name C(D
    iii) An incorrect addition or subtraction operator between C and D

(Can the reader find any others?) To the best of the author's knowledge no compiler in existence scans further to attempt to determine which error has been made. But among the different actions different compilers may take are the following:

1. Terminate the job and print out an error message.
2. Print the error message but continue to scan subsequent statements searching for further syntactic errors and make no further attempt to produce an object program.

[†]This is a simplification of the truth; in Chapter 7 we shall see why.

```
ISN
1              DIMENSION G(20), H(10,10)
2              READ, N,D,E,F
3              PRINT, N,D,E,F
4              G(1)=D-E/F
5              DO 4 I=2,N
6              G(I)=G(I-1)*E/F
7         4    H(I,I-1)=G(I)*D
10             B=G(N)*D
11             C=H(N,N-1)*G(N)**2
12             A=B+C(D-E/F)
13             IF(A.GT.B*C) GO TO 8
14             A=A*G(N)
15             N=N-1
16        8    DO 10 I=1,N
                    .
                    .
                    .
```

Figure 6.9   Program listing with Internal Statement Numbers.

3. Truncate the statement after C, thereby retaining a syntactically correct statement, A=B+C, print out an error message, and continue compiling. The rationale behind this is that, by so doing, an executable object program will result and often a user will get useful information from an executed program even if one statement is surely not what he intended.

4. Assume the error is in fact the missing multiplication operator, on the assumption that this is the most likely of the errors listed above, compile the statement

A=B+C * (D-E/F)

print out an error message, and continue compiling.

If the reader will agree that the most likely error in the statement is indeed the missing *, he will probably also agree that the last alternative above is the one that a good compiler would take. Indeed, the best compilers now being written have *default* conditions for all syntactic errors which attempt to correct the error in the most likely fashion, print out an error message, and then continue compiling.

But what of these error messages? They can take many forms, of which the examples below will illustrate the most common types and their pros and cons. They are based on the error in the statement considered above.

i) At the end of the listing of the program (provided by all compilers) the following message might appear:

ERROR 64 AT ISN 12

To understand this it is necessary to point out that, in the listing of the program, most compilers precede each statement by an *internal statement number* (ISN), usually in *octal,* to be used for reference purposes (see Figure 6.9). To interpret the message above, the user would look up ERROR 64 in a list of error messages which might say[†]

ERROR 64   MISSING OPERATOR

after which he would look in his listing at ISN 12

12   A=B+C(D-E/F)

to find the error. The ISN should not be confused with the statement label. If the statement were labeled, say 10, the listing would appear as

12   10 A=B+C(D-E/F)

ii) As an alternative to the above, the listing of the program might appear as:

12   A=B+C(D-E/F)
        ERROR OP-2

In this case the error message appears directly after the statement in error. ERROR OP-2 corresponds to ERROR 64 in the above example; the use of OP-2 illustrates the possibility of using mnemonic codes (OP for operator) to suggest the error to the user, which might obviate the need to look up OP-2 in the list of error messages. We also note that not all errors can be printed directly after the statement, since some cannot be ascertained until the whole program has been read (e.g., if there is an IF (A+B) 10,20,30 statement but no statement labeled 20, this is a syntactic error which cannot be determined until the end of the program has been reached).

iii) A better type of error message than either of the above is the following:

[†]Actually, this would not be the error message which would result from this error; in Chapter 7 we shall see why.

    12   A=B+C (D+E/F)
             *MISSING OPERATOR

This incorporates two features missing above:

    a) the asterisk marks the *position* of the error.
    b) the error message is part of the listing and thus it is not necessary to
    look up error codes in a separate list.

There are many variations on the above theme, some of which the reader may
be familiar with his own installation. The point we would stress here is the
importance of good diagnostic messages as an aid to debugging.

In addition to the error messages discussed above, some compilers give warning messages about possible or probable semantic errors during compilation. Two
examples will suffice to illustrate this:

i) Fortran does not officially allow mixed-mode expressions but many implementations do accept and compile mixed-real and integer-mode expressions by
converting all integer quantities to real (except for exponents and subscripts).
Such compilers also typically print out a message warning the programmer that
he has written a mixed-mode expression on the assumption that the user
possibly did not mean to write, for example,

    A + I

ii) None of the languages *require* that the statement following a GO TO statement be labeled. But, if it is not, control can never reach it. (Why?) Therefore, a
sequence in Fortran such as

    GO TO 64
    A = B

will trigger a warning message in many compilers on the assumption that the
programmer probably did not want to write statements which could never be
executed. This same warning is also appropriate after other transfer-of-control
statements (Problem 13).

3. *Test cases.*   At execution time, certain errors will be caught by the computer and appropriate error messages printed out. The most common of these
are attempts to violate one arithmetic rule or another. For example:

    i) Overflow (including division by zero) and underflow

ii) Attempts to compute

   0 * * 0 (indeterminate)

or

   (- X) * * Y   (X positive, Y not integral—result is complex)

Another common error, which many compilers find at execution time (but some do not!), is that of leaving a variable *undefined*. This is an attempt to use a variable on the right-hand side of an assignment statement, or elsewhere in an arithmetic expression, to which no value has been previously given either by its appearance on the left-hand side of an assignment statement or in an input statement. The position in memory assigned to this variable may contain zero or some meaningless combination of bits or digits. A good compiler will assure that such a situation is detected and the user is informed via an error message.

Good compilers also catch a variety of other errors at execution time, one example of which would occur if the FORTRAN statement

   GO TO (10, 20, 30), J

were executed with the variable J having a value of 4.

Sometimes, when an error is detected in execution, the computer will just print the error message and terminate the computation. In other cases it will print the error message, attempt to overcome the error (e.g., in underflow by taking the result as zero) and proceed with the computation.

Often a program will execute to completion but fail to give the desired results. But how do you know what the desired results are? The most obvious way is by running a test case with input data for which the correct answer is known, either from hand computation or perhaps from a previously known result. When a program executed with test data fails to give the correct results, this is a certain indication of error; the converse, however, is not true. Even for such a simple problem as computing the roots of a quadratic equation, a single set of test coefficients cannot test the cases of both real and complex roots. The correctness of the results for one case is no proof whatsoever of the correctness in the other. In some problems, therefore, it will be desirable to run more than one test case to test different possibilities. Still the reader should not be misled into thinking that the use of test cases is a good way to find all the errors in a program. One reason why it is not is indicated under 4. below. Another is that for very long, complex programs, test cases often just cannot be found which, on the one hand, test the entire, perhaps very intricate logic of the program and, on the other, can be hand-computed for comparison purposes without too much effort.

4. *Output of intermediate results.*   When the results of a test case are incorrect the form of the incorrect numbers (e.g., wrong sign or off by a factor of 2 or 10) may suggest the reason for the error, but often the wrong numbers will indicate no more than the existence of the error. Particularly in a long computation with many statements between the input and output, just knowing that an error exists is not much help in finding it. For this reason when debugging a program it is frequently a good idea to sprinkle PRINT statements in the program to print out intermediate results. By comparing these intermediate results with the hand calculation it will usually be possible to pinpoint the error accurately. Then, when the program has been debugged, these extraneous PRINT statements may be removed.† Note in this context the value of data-directed output since the appearance of the variable name with its value is a great convenience when debugging.

An alternative to printing out intermediate results is to break a large program into smaller pieces and attempt to check out each one separately. Chapter 7, in which subroutines are discussed, will indicate the way to do this.

5. *Dumps and traces.*   Sometimes all the above techniques will be to no avail. What then? Most compilers allow the user to request certain "post-mortem" actions when a program fails to execute to completion or even after execution has successfully taken place (in the sense of not producing a machine error, not in the sense of producing correct results). Such post-mortems usually take the forms of "dumps" of the contents of some specified portion of the main memory of the computer. These will typically be useful for debugging purposes only to those users who have a solid knowledge of machine language.

As a last resort there is the *trace.* Traces take various forms. All are initiated by a special control card or cards. The most common type of trace produces as output the result of every arithmetic statement in the program or in that part of the program indicated by the user on the control card. Some traces also print out the results of every conditional transfer of control statement. As a last resort traces can be useful. But they are prodigal of computer time and, unless very carefully used, can produce a great morass of numbers in which the user can drown. For these reasons fewer and fewer compilers have traces built into them. In any case, the brute-force nature of traces means that they should be used very

---

†Alternatively, in Fortran, for example, one might have a statement at the beginning ISWTCH=1 and each print statement for testing would appear as

IF (ISWTCH.EQ.1) PRINT,...

Then, to stop intermediate printing, it is sufficient to replace ISWTCH=1 by ISWTCH=0.

sparingly. With good programmers it is almost a matter of pride not to have to resort to tracing.

It is a melancholy fact, which all programmers learn sooner or later, that even if great care is taken in the original writing of a program, debugging may be more time consuming—and certainly more frustrating—than the original writing itself. This is why competence at debugging is an important measure of a good programmer. This competence requires that the programmer be aware of the debugging tools at his installation and know how to use them. We hope this discussion has made clear that a well-organized program can make testing easier; hence one should program with ease of testing in mind.

As a final note in this chapter we point out that many calculations run to successful conclusions only for certain combinations of input data. A simple example is the quadratic equation program in the case when the coefficients of x and x^2 are zero, in which case the equation has no solution. The reader should try to figure out what would happen in a program which ignored this possibility but was prepared for the case when only the coefficient of x^2 is zero. The obvious point we wish to make here is that programs should be written to handle all possible combinations of input data and to provide *error exits* when combinations occur which cannot be handled. These error exits are usually nothing more than little pieces of program which print out appropriate messages and then halt the program or, more normally, return to read more data.

Often it cannot be determined until after the computation has proceeded part way that a problem is insoluble in some sense. Arithmetic overflow or an attempt to divide by zero are two conditions which often indicate failure of the computation. In Fortran these usually result in termination of the computation and the printing of an error message. PL/I, on the other hand, provides a facility which is quite general and sophisticated through the use of the ON statement to test the internal hardware, which records such things as overflow and divide checks (attempts to divide by zero), and to transfer to a special bit of program which may make it possible to recover from the condition without terminating the computation.

PROBLEMS

Section 6.1

1. Is the following statement true or false: The first non-blank character after IF at the beginning of a Fortran statement determines if the statement is an assignment statement or a conditional transfer statement? Explain your answer.

2. a) Draw a flow chart to indicate the effect of the Algol statement on p. 208.

   b) Do the same for the first example in Panel 6.1.

3. a) Find and explain the syntactical errors in the following Algol block:

   L1:   **begin**
         real   A[-7:15], B, C[4:12, 3:6];

   L2:   **real** A, C[1:10], D;
               A[-5]:=B:=C[7];
            end;
         C[4,4]:=A;
   L3:   **begin**
            real B[-2:0], C[-2:2, 1:5];
               B[-1]:=C[7,3]:=A[-3];
            end
      end

   b) Give the scope of each of the variables in the program of part (a).

4. a) Indicate how the compiler might assign memory locations to the variables in Figure 6.1 so as to obtain the most efficient use of memory.

   b) Do the same for the program of Problem 3a.

5. Consider the situation of a *multiprocessor* computing system in which two or more processors (i.e., CPU's) can each independently execute programs. Explain why the PL/I program structure might enable certain computations to be carried out more efficiently on such a system than the Algol structure.

Section 6.2

6. Allowing blanks in variable names creates a problem for a compiler similar to that of parentheses in arithmetic expressions, namely a given variable name may consist of many different strings of characters (since 'blank' is a character). If you were designing that part of a compiler whose function was to scan program strings in memory to search for variable names, what is the first thing you might design this compiler to do?

7. a) What facilities might you like to have in input and output not provided by free format? What price might you have to pay for such facilities?

b) Compare the relative advantages of free-format input and output and NAMELIST.

8. Given the Fortran statements

```
    DIMENSION A(3,2), B(7)
    READ, N, A
    I=1
  2 READ, B(I), B(I+1)
    I = I + 2
    IF (I .LE. N+2) GO TO 2
```

and cards with data as follows:

Card 1:	5	6.3	7.2	1.0E7	3.92E-04
Card 2:	4.61	-3.72	-5.7E-04	2.1	
Card 3:	8.517	-2.1	6.3E02		
Card 4:	-7.4E03	1.7			
Card 5:	4.2E3	17.7	6.80		

what values are assigned to the variable N and the arrays A and B?

9. Rewrite the program of Problem 8 and indicate how the data cards might be punched to achieve the same values of the variables using NAMELIST.

Section 6.3

10. Syntactic errors in a program may be local (an error in a single statement) or global (an error which can only be discovered by looking at more than one statement of the program). Give as many examples of possible global errors as you can.

11. Semantic errors may be classified into two types—detectable ones, which can be found during execution by the computer, and undetectable ones. Give examples of the former and state the general property of the latter.

12. What are the possible syntactic errors in the following Fortran statements:

    a) N = J(I*2+3)
    b) A = B+C*- D/(E*F)

In each case display possible error messages which might be printed out by a *good* compiler.

13. In Fortran, can arithmetic or logical IF statements be used in such a way that a warning message such as discussed on p. 241 should be given by the compiler? Why?

14. For each of the examples of Section 2.4, devise sets of input data to be used in debugging programs to implement the flow charts. Remember that each test should give a result easily verifiable by hand computations.

15. Indicate where the flow charts of Section 2.4 require error exits which are not shown.

7

functions, subprograms, and procedures

Render therefore unto Caesar the things which are Caesar's; and unto God the things which are God's.

Matthew 22:21

. . . and to assume among the powers of the earth the separate and equal status to which the laws of nature and nature's God entitle them. . . .

Thomas Jefferson in the *Declaration of Independence*

Some features of computer languages enable the user to perform calculations that could not be done without these features. Other features do not add any more power to the language but make the accomplishment of certain tasks more convenient, so much more convenient that without them, some tasks, although theoretically possible, would not be undertaken because they would be so tedious to accomplish. The subject of this chapter falls in this latter category, but it is so important that the generic term for the languages we are considering—procedure-oriented—is derived from the material of this chapter. The language structures to be considered in this chapter add no theoretical power to P-O languages, but in total they represent the most significant features added to these languages since the original development of Fortran in 1954.

7.1 THE NEED FOR SUBROUTINES

Suppose you are writing a program which requires a specific calculation be done a number of different times at various places in your program. Examples of such a calculation might be finding a square root or computing compound interest. In such a case you would have two choices:

1. Write a program to do the calculation and insert it in your program in each place it is needed.
2. Try to make a single version of the program serve in all cases.

If the program to do the specific calculation contains more than a very few statements (or really, more than a very few machine-language instructions), the latter choice may save a great deal of memory space and a great deal of clerical work in preparing the program. A program to do a specific calculation which is needed at various places in a program is called a *subroutine*. There are two types of subroutines corresponding to the two choices above:

1. *Open* subroutines, in which the statements are inserted in the program whenever needed.
2. *Closed* subroutines, in which one copy of the subroutine is used many times.

The words "open" and "closed" refer to the fact that, in the former case, the subroutine contains only the statements required to perform the desired calculation, while in the latter case additional statements are required at each end to handle the problem of serving requests to execute the same set of statements from different parts of the program.

The use of closed subroutines is illustrated schematically in Figure 7.1. At three places in the *main program*, that is, the program written by the user which contains the main logic for his calculation, a subroutine is required to perform some calculation. As indicated by the arrows, each time this happens control is transferred to the subroutine, the subroutine calculation is performed, and then control is passed back to the main program. Each horizontal line in Figure 7.1 is best interpreted as a single machine-language instruction. The problem of transferring control to the subroutine each time and then coming back to the proper place in the main program is called the *linkage problem*. How the subroutine is "linked" to the main program is an important aspect of machine-language programming but it is not of concern to the user of a P-O language because the compiler takes care of establishing the linkage properly in each case.

The use of subroutines has other advantages besides saving memory space and clerical work. The most important of these are the following:

1. In two of the four languages (Fortran and PL/I) and occasionally in implementations of others, subroutines may be compiled separately from the main program. Thus the *object program for the subroutine* can be combined with

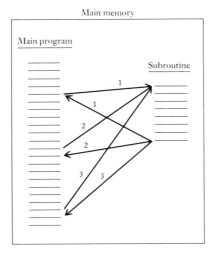

Figure 7.1   Closed subroutines.

various main programs, negating the need to compile the subroutine each time it is used (see Section 7.5).

2. The use of subroutines provides a convenient way of breaking a large program into smaller logical blocks. This has two advantages:

i) Even if subroutines cannot be compiled separately, it is often much easier to debug programs which are segmented into a number of logically separate blocks.[†]

ii) Separation of a program into a (perhaps quite small) main program and a number of subroutines provides the programmer with a very useful logical tool to aid his own thinking as he constructs the program. The result is likely to be a program with fewer errors when it is tested on the computer.

3. Putting common calculations, even quite lengthy ones, into subroutines facilitates the exchange of programs between users and installations.

Subroutines then are an extremely important weapon in the programmer's arsenal. They provide that vital aspect of all intellectual activity, namely, the ability to break complex structures into smaller units. In the remainder of the chapter we shall consider the various ways in which the subroutine concept is implemented in the four P-O languages.

———
[†] But, of course, the block structures of Algol and PL/I provide this feature without the use of subroutines.

Table 7.1   Intrinsic mathematical functions

Function	Mathematical definition	Fortran name	PL/I name	Algol name
Exponential	e^x	EXP DEXP CEXP	EXP	EXP
Natural logarithm	$\ln x$	ALOG DLOG CLOG	LOG	LN
Common logarithm	$\log_{10}x$	ALOG10 DLOG10	LOG10	——
Logarithm to base 2	$\log_2 x$	——	LOG2	——
Sine	$\sin x$	SIN DSIN CSIN	SIN SIND	SIN
Cosine	$\cos x$	COS DCOS CCOS	COS COSD	COS
Tangent	$\tan x$	——	TAN TAND	——
Hyperbolic sine	$\sinh x$	——	SINH	
Hyperbolic cosine	$\cosh x$	——	COSH	——
Hyperbolic tangent	$\tanh x$	TANH	TANH	——
Square root (always positive)	$\sqrt{x}$	SQRT DSQRT CSQRT	SQRT	SQRT
Arctangent	$\arctan x$	ATAN DATAN	ATAN ATAND	ARCTAN
Error function	$\operatorname{erf} x$	——	ERF	——
Error function complement	$\operatorname{erfc} x$	——	ERFC	——

Notes:
1. A blank implies the function is not intrinsic to the language.
2. For all Fortran functions in this table, the argument and result have the same type. Names

beginning with D are double-precision functions, names beginning with C are complex functions (except COS), and all others are single-precision floating point.

3. In PL/I function arguments are converted to floating-point mode and the results have floating-point mode. If the argument is complex, so is the result. (Some of the functions are defined for real arguments only.) The D at the end of a function name indicates an argument or result (as appropriate) in degrees instead of radians.

4. The definitions of erf x and erfc x are

$$\text{erf } x = 2 \sqrt{\pi} \int_0^x e^{-t^2} dt$$

$$\text{erfc } x = 1 - \text{erf } x$$

5. The Algol publication language uses lower case letters for function names but here and elsewhere we use upper case letters since this is general practice in all other languages and in Algol implementations.

7.2   INTRINSIC FUNCTIONS

Much of the material of this chapter will be concerned with how to refer to the various types of subroutines which can be used in P-O languages. All the languages and all the types of subroutines have in common that the normal function notation of mathematics is used. This consists of:

1. the *name* of the function, followed by
2. a *list* of *arguments* separated by commas and in parentheses.

In this section we shall consider subroutines, available only in Fortran, Algol, and PL/I, called *intrinsic* or *built-in* functions. Invoking these functions results in a calculation or manipulation that occurs so often, particularly in scientific calculations, that, rather than require the programmer to write programs for these calculations when he needs to do them, the compiler contains within itself these programs to be supplied to the user as needed. Thus, all the programmer has to do is name the program and its arguments.

The official Fortran and PL/I definitions specify an extensive list of intrinsic functions which the language should contain. Nevertheless, some implementations supplement even this list. Algol, on the other hand, suggests only a short list which should be available. The result is that Algol implementations usually provide a number of functions in addition to what is suggested.

The intrinsic functions are basically of two types:

1. Standard mathematical functions
2. Functions to implement common mathematical and data manipulations

Table 7.1 lists the standard mathematical functions in Fortran and PL/I and those suggested by the designers of Algol. All of these functions require one argument only. Thus, to compute the sine of a real variable X, we would write

SIN(X)

The allowable forms of the arguments are given in Panel 7.1 as well as the rules for determining what type of number results from an evaluation of the function. Other pertinent remarks on Table 7.1 and Panel 7.1 are:

1. All these functions as well as those in Table 7.2 may be used in any arithmetic expression where our previous definition allowed a constant or variable. Thus, statements of the form

A = B * SIN(X) − C ** EXP(B)

are valid. We must, however, consider how function evaluation fits into the hierarchy of operations discussed in Sections 5.2.2 and 5.5.3 because function evaluation acts, in effect, as an operator. Here, as with relational operators, the answer is obvious. Function evaluation must be *higher* in the hierarchy than any other operator because, in order to associate any meaningful interpretation to arithmetic expressions, the function name must be associated with its argument first. That is, the argument itself (see Panel 7.1), following the rule of parentheses, is first evaluated and then the function is evaluated (Problem 1).

2. Fortran and PL/I also allow a two-argument form of the arctangent routine to avoid the problem of principle values.

3. Note the use of A̲LOG and A̲LOG10 in Fortran because otherwise the leading L would result in an integer value.

Table 7.2 displays the functions in the second category, common mathematical and data manipulations:

1. The table is complete for Algol; Fortran provides some and PL/I provides a substantial number of other common manipulations.

2. Arguments in PL/I and Algol may have any mode except when this clearly violates mathematics or common sense. For example, MAX and MIN in PL/I cannot have complex arguments and ENTIER in Algol must have a real argument. (Why?)

3. The truncation and entier functions are not identical; the reader should understand the difference (Problem 2). PL/I contains a function related to FLOOR called CEIL which is the smallest integer not exceeded by the argument.

4. The MOD mnemonic for the remainder function is used because another mathematical notation for this function is:

x (modulo y)

FORTRAN	PL/I	ALGOL

Arguments

Can be *any* valid arithmetic (or, where appropriate in PL/I, string) expression.

FORTRAN	PL/I	ALGOL
Must have correct mode which always corresponds to first letter of name in Table 7.1 and is as indicated in Table 7.2	Converted to proper mode automatically; all arguments with FIXED mode for Table 7.1 converted to FLOAT; when function is defined for more than one mode, mode as given is used; see also below	All functions operate on real or integer arguments

Functions are defined only for those values of the arguments which are mathematically valid.

Values

FORTRAN	PL/I	ALGOL
Mode is determined by mode of function name considered as variable, except that in Table 7.1 leading D means double-precision and leading C means complex (except COS)	Mode is determined by function definition except where defined for more than one argument mode in which case mode of result is same as mode of argument. Units of value of trigonometric functions determined by function name; last letter D means degrees, otherwise radians	Mode is real for functions in Table 7.1

Arctangent and complex-valued routines give principle values.

Examples

FORTRAN	PL/I	ALGOL
EXP (X)	EXP (X)	EXP (X)
	EXP (I)	EXP (I)
COMPLEX, X, Y, A A = CSIN (X * X − Y)	DECLARE A, X, Y COMPLEX; A = SIN (X * X − Y);	
B = MAX1 (B,2.0,R, A6*3.0)	B = MAX (B,2,R, A6*3);	
C = AINT (X ** Y)	C = TRUNC (X ** Y);	C : = ENTIER (X↑Y);

255

Table 7.2 Intrinsic mathematical and data manipulations

Function	Mathematical definition	Fortran name	argument mode	PL/I name	Algol name
Absolute value	$|x|$	ABS IABS DABS CABS	Real Integer Double-prec. Complex	ABS	ABS
Sign	-1 if $x < 0$, 0 if $x = 0$, $+1$ if $x > 0$	--		SIGN	SIGN
Truncation	Sign of x times largest integer $< |x|$	AINT INT IDINT	Real Integer Double-prec.	TRUNC	--
Entier	Largest integer not greater than x	--	--	FLOOR	ENTIER
Remainder	$x - $ entier $(x/y) * y$ (if $y = 1$ gives fractional part of x); x first argument	AMOD MOD DMOD	Real Integer Double-prec.	MOD	--

			Mode of argument		
Maximum	Max $(x_1, x_2, \dots, x_n)$ for any n; value is maximum argument	AMAX0	Integer	MAX	—
		AMAX1	Real		
		MAX0	Integer		
		MAX1	Real		
		DMAX1	Double-prec.		
Minimum	Min $(x_1, x_2, \dots, x_n)$ for any n; value is minimum argument	AMIN0	Integer	MIN	—
		AMIN1	Real		
		MIN0	Integer		
		MIN1	Real		
		DMIN1	Double-prec.		
Float	Integer-to-real conversion	FLOAT	Integer	FLOAT	—
Fix	Real-to-integer conversion	IFIX	Real	FIXED	—

Mode of Results

Fortran—Indicated by usual default option on first letter of name except those that begin with D produce double-precision results

PL/I—Normally mode of argument

Algol—Real for ABS, integer for SIGN and ENTIER

5. If a complex argument has real part X and imaginary part Y, the complex absolute value is

$$\sqrt{X^2 + Y^2}$$

6. The purpose of the float and fix functions is not immediately obvious since

I = IFIX (X)

is the same as

I = X

because, as we have pointed out previously, mode conversion takes place across an equal sign. The purpose of these functions is to enable the user to accomplish in one statement certain things that otherwise would require two statements. For example, in Fortran the two statements

I = X
N = I * J+K

can be replaced by

N = IFIX(X) * J+K

7. When an intrinsic function is used in an arithmetic statement it is said to be *called*. If the arguments in the calling statement do not have the required mode—when a particular mode is required or forbidden—an error results, normally the program halts, and an error message is printed.[†] Also, except for the maximum and minimum functions which have a variable number of arguments, the *number* of arguments in the calling statement must agree, of course, with the defined number which is one for all other functions in Table 7.2 except the remainder function (i.e., AMOD(X,Y)).

Most programmers will find that very few programs require no use at all of intrinsic functions.

In addition to the discussion above on the intrinsic functions in Fortran, Algol, and PL/I, we close this section with some additional remarks:

1. Fortran compilers which allow mixed-mode expressions in arithmetic expressions normally allow them in argument expressions also.
2. Most of the intrinsic functions are implemented by means of closed subroutines, but some which require very few machine-language instructions are open subroutines. One example of the latter is the absolute-value function. In Fortran the MOD and AMOD functions are normally open subroutines but DMOD, which requires more instructions, is normally closed. The Fortran (but not the PL/I or Algol) definition specifies which functions should be implemented using

---

[†] PL/I has a technique which enables calling arguments with attributes which differ from those of the defining arguments to be used (see Section 7.3.2).

open and closed subroutines but given implementations may not follow the rules. Whether a given function is an open or closed subroutine does not directly affect the user.

3. PL/I contains many intrinsic functions not described here for a total of about 75. A number of these involve functions whose arguments are strings. In general, PL/I also allows function arguments to be arrays in which case the function operates on each element separately. Finally, PL/I has some special purpose functions of which the following two, neither of which requires an argument, are interesting examples:

DATE produces as value a character string of length six YYMMDD where:
> YY is the year
> MM is the month
> DD is the day
> > e.g., 690417 would be April 17, 1969.

TIME produces as value a character string of length nine HHMMSSTTT where:
> HH is hours
> MM is minutes
> SS is seconds
> TTT is milliseconds
> > e.g., 173627462 would be 5:36:27.462 P.M.

Both of these functions assume that the computer hardware and instructions allow the date and time to be automatically determined.†

4. Since some of the intrinsic functions can be formed using concatenations of others (Problem 4), one might ask how many and which ones should a language have. For any given user, the answer to this is probably that any function he uses a lot, he would like to make intrinsic. In fact, as we note in Section 7.5, there are ways at most computer installations for the user to effectively add to the intrinsic functions provided.

7.3 SUBPROGRAMS AND PROCEDURES

The material of this section represents the sharpest difference between Fortran and the other three languages which we will encounter. The means by which Fortran enables the user to incorporate subroutines written by him into his programs are substantially more complicated and less general than those pro-

---

† Functions like DATE and TIME in PL/I which require no arguments cannot be used as normal identifiers unless they appear in a DECLARE statement. Otherwise, for example, A=B+DATE; would cause the function DATE to be invoked and the value of the character string it returns would be added to B.

vided in the other three languages. Algol and PL/I in particular avoid most of the inadequacies in Fortran in their facilities for programmer-written subroutines.

Let us begin our discussion by going back to Example 2.9, the knight's tour problem. In three boxes, 4, 7, and 10 of Figure 2.15 (p. 47), the flow chart for this problem, is the requirement that a search be made for the possible moves which a knight can make from a given place on a chessboard, given the pattern of previous squares the knight has traversed. Here we have an obvious candidate for a subroutine, a calculation which must be performed at a number of different places in one program.

Example 7.1

Draw a flow chart for the subroutine to search for the moves available to the knight.

This flow chart is given in Figure 7.2 and is annotated as follows:

Input data: The two items listed are the information which must be known in order to determine the possible moves.

Box 1: This box hides a substantial amount of computation. The coordinates of the eight directions in which the knight can move (see Figure 7.3) are found by appropriately adding or subtracting 1 or 2, to or from the input coordinates even if a resulting coordinate is less than 1 or greater than 8.

Box 2: I is a counter of the number of possible moves; J is used to locate which of the eight possible moves is being considered.

Box 3: The row and column coordinates of a possible move are tested to see if both are ≥ 1 and ≤ 8.

Box 4: If so, the record of the tour thus far is tested to see if the knight has been at this location previously in the tour.

Box 5: If not, this is a possible move; therefore, counter is increased.

Box 6: Location of possible move coordinates is stored.

Box 7: Have all eight possibilities been tested?

Box 8: If not, J is increased and another move tested.

Output results: The program implementing this flow chart will produce as results both the number of possible moves and the coordinates of each. The reader should consider why the list of coordinates themselves is not enough.

The reader may also wish to go back to Example 2.9 and note that the flow chart in Figure 2.15 does not include an explicit recording of the move in an 8x8 array of a record of the tour. This is a failing of the flow chart of Figure 2.15 which should be corrected.

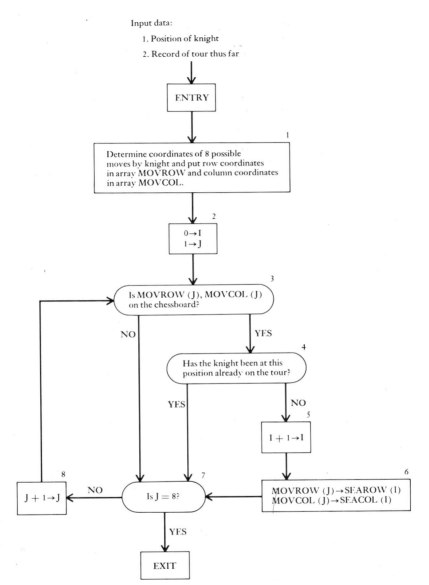

Input data:
1. Position of knight
2. Record of tour thus far

ENTRY

1
Determine coordinates of 8 possible moves by knight and put row coordinates in array MOVROW and column coordinates in array MOVCOL.

2
$0 \rightarrow I$
$1 \rightarrow J$

3
Is MOVROW (J), MOVCOL (J) on the chessboard?

NO

YES

4
Has the knight been at this position already on the tour?

YES

NO

5
$I + 1 \rightarrow I$

8
$J + 1 \rightarrow J$

NO

7
Is J = 8?

6
MOVROW (J) → SEAROW (I)
MOVCOL (J) → SEACOL (I)

YES

EXIT

Output results:
1. I which is number of possible moves.

2. Arrays SEAROW and SEACOL which contain coordinates of these moves.

Figure 7.2   Flow chart for Example 7.1.

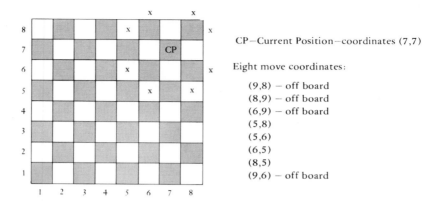

Figure 7.3   Possible moves by a knight.

What then are the lessons to be learned from this example? The chief one is that a subroutine, like the intrinsic functions of the previous section, is a calculation needed at various places in the program written by the user. Referring to Figure 7.1, the major difference between intrinsic functions and subroutines is that, in addition to the program normally written by the user—*the main program*—the user must also write the subroutine. By contrast, the intrinsic function subroutines are provided to the user by the compiler system.

In the succeeding sections we shall discuss first the syntax and semantics of programmer-written subroutines and then indicate the mechanisms by which these subroutines are invoked or *called* by the main program. Before commencing this discussion we note that all programmer-written subroutines are implemented as *closed* subroutines.

7.3.1   Language Structures for Subroutines

In Algol and PL/I, programmer-written subroutines are called *procedures*. In Cobol these subroutines are also called procedures and are just paragraphs or sections (see Section 6.1.2) of the PROCEDURE DIVISION of the program. In Fortran these subroutines are called *subprograms* or *arithmetic statement functions*. The latter have a structure specific to Fortran which we shall discuss in Section 7.4.1.

Unfortunately for the unwary reader, Fortran subprograms are subdivided into two classes, SUBROUTINE and FUNCTION subprograms, which brings the terminology full circle to our original use of subroutine. The reader should be aware that the terms subroutine, subprogram, and procedure are used nearly synonomously in much of the P-O language literature.

In Fortran and Algol the immediate thing that distinguishes subroutines from main programs is the *heading statement* which begins subprograms in Fortran and procedures in Algol. In PL/I a heading statement is needed but it is the same or nearly the same statement as that which heads the entire program. In Cobol, because of the integration of subroutines into the PROCEDURE DIVISION, there is no distinguishing heading for a subroutine. Panel 7.2 considers the structure of the heading statements in the various languages:

1. In Fortran these headings are statements—SUBROUTINE and FUNCTION statements—in the normal sense and occupy one card; in Algol and PL/I they are also statements and are incorporated in programs like any other statements of these languages.
2. PL/I allows, and some implementations require, certain additional information between the argument list and the semicolon (see Example 8.17).

As indicated in Panel 7.2, the function arguments serve two purposes. As with intrinsic functions, they serve as the input to the subroutine. In addition, they may also serve as one means, among others we shall discuss below, of communicating output results back to the main program. Indeed, an understanding of what the arguments are and how they are used is perhaps the key to understanding procedures. Panel 7.3 considers some of the important aspects of arguments in the subroutine (as opposed to *calling arguments*; see Panel 7.9). Regarding Panel 7.3:

1. The notion of dummy arguments is crucial. The reader must understand that these arguments are used only to *define* the subroutine in order to indicate what manipulation it is to perform. As we shall discuss below, these dummy arguments are replaced by the actual arguments when the procedure is called from the main program, just as the dummy argument in an intrinsic function is replaced by a calling argument.
2. Algol has a special facility to enable comments to be inserted in the argument list. This consists of replacing the comma separating the arguments by

) < LETTER STRING > : (

where the structure < LETTER STRING > is any length sequence of letters only. Thus, the example in Panel 7.2 could be written

   procedure SEARCH (ROW, COL) KNIGHTRECORD: (TOUR);

Some Algol systems do not implement this feature because, for one reason, it has the effect of substantially decreasing readability.

3. The reader may wonder how a subroutine could have no arguments. This will become clear in Section 7.3.4.

4. An argument of one procedure may be the name of another procedure. This may occur, for example, if part of the calculation of the procedure being called involves the evaluation of a function which would vary (e.g., sine one time, cosine another) on different uses of the procedure. Although we shall not discuss this further here, arguments which are procedures (or statement labels or switches) must appear appropriately in type declarations.

Panel 7.2   Heading statements for subroutines

FORTRAN	*ALGOL*	*PL/I*
	Syntax	
SUBROUTINE *id*	**procedure** *id* $(ar_1,$	*sl*: PROCEDURE $(ar_1,$
$(ar_1, ar_2, \dots , ar_n)$	$ar_2, \dots , ar_n);$	$ar_2, \dots , ar_n);$
or	optionally preceded	
FUNCTION *id*	by **real, integer,** or	
$(ar_1, ar_2, \dots , ar_n)$	**boolean**	
FUNCTION may be optionally preceded by IN-TEGER, REAL, DOUBLE PRECISION, LOGICAL, or COMPLEX.		

Semantics

The *id* is the *name* of the SUBROUTINE or FUNCTION and the *arguments* refer to input data and, for SUBROUTINEs, the output results; FUNCTIONs produce a single quantity as result; the mode of the result is determined by the word preceding FUNCTION if it is present or by the usual mode default option on the *id* if it is not; SUBROUTINES may produce multiple results.	The *id* is the *name* of the procedure and the *arguments* refer to input data and output results; if a type declaration word precedes **procedure**, the procedure is called a *function procedure* and produces a single result of the indicated mode.	The *sl* is called the *entry name* and serves as the name of the procedure; the *arguments* refer to input data and output results; certain procedures (see Section 7.3.1) called *function procedures* produce a single output result whose mode may be specified by the default option of the *sl* or by an attribute (e.g., FIXED, FLOAT) after the argument list.

FORTRAN	*ALGOL*	*PL/I*
	Examples	
SUBROUTINE SEARCH (ROW, COL, TOUR)	**procedure** SEARCH (ROW, COL, TOUR);	SEARCH: PROCEDURE (ROW, COL, TOUR);
FUNCTION COMPUT (A, C2, D, E)	**real procedure** COMPUT (A, C2, D, E);	COMPUT: PROCEDURE (A, C2, D, E,);

id—identifier
ar—argument
sl—statement label

Note:
In Cobol a procedure always begins with a paragraph or section.

Panel 7.3   Subroutine arguments

FORTRAN	*ALGOL*	*PL/I*

Dummy or formal arguments

All arguments are *dummy* in the sense that they serve only to define the calculation performed by the subroutine; when the subroutine is called from the main program (see Section 7.3.2) these dummy arguments are replaced by the *actual* arguments.

Form of arguments

Each argument may be any *identifier* (unsubscripted). These identifiers may refer to

scalar variables *or* subprogram names *or* arrays *or*, for SUBROUTINE only, Hollerith constants.	scalar variables *or* procedure names *or* arrays *or* statement labels *or* switches.	scalar variables *or* entrynames *or* structures *or* arrays *or* statement label variables or constants *or* string variables or constants.

Number of arguments allowed

For SUBROUTINES any number from zero up; for FUNCTIONS at least one.

           Any number from zero up.

5. The use of statement label constants and variables as arguments provides a mechanism to direct control to a point other than that from which the procedure was called after the completion of the procedure calculation by using the argument in a GO TO statement. We give an example of this in Section 7.3.2.

6. The ability to have Hollerith constants as subroutine arguments in Fortran enables, for example, special output headings or labels to be printed on separate calls of the subprogram. The PL/I facility allows this as well as a variety of other possibilities including actual manipulation of the string variable or constant in the procedure.

Example 7.2

Write a subroutine heading in Fortran, Algol, and PL/I for the search subroutine of Example 7.1.

The first example in Panel 7.2 seems to do this but it only provides for input and not output. Better examples are:

Fortran:
```
SUBROUTINE SEARCH (ROW,COL,TOUR,I,SEAROW,SEACOL)
```

Algol:
```
procedure SEARCH (ROW,COL,TOUR,I,SEAROW,SEACOL);
```

PL/I:
```
SEARCH: PROCEDURE (ROW,COL,TOUR,I,SEAROW,SEACOL);
```

ROW and COL represent the coordinates of the knight's position.
TOUR is an 8 x 8 array representing the record of the tour.
I is the number of possible moves found.
SEAROW and SEACOL are one-dimensional arrays which store the coordinates of these moves.

The last three arguments represent the output arguments and the first three the input arguments. This would be a most unlikely routine to program in Cobol but it could be done with a paragraph named SEARCH and a structure in the DATA DIVISION corresponding to the input and output arguments.

Following the heading statement, the structure of subroutines is essentially the same as that in main programs with a very few additional rules. Dimension declarations are required as in the main program for all variables *local* to the subroutine (i.e., declared in the subroutine; see Section 6.1.2) as well as for the arguments.

Panel 7.4 Type declarations in subroutines

FORTRAN	*ALGOL*	*PL/I*
	Arguments	
Any argument may appear in a type declaration; array arguments must appear in DIMENSION statements (but not necessarily with correct dimensions; see Section 7.3.1); also dimensions can be variables	All arguments must appear in type declarations immediately following semicolon after procedure heading; array arguments must appear without dimensions	Must appear in DECLARE statement (if not to be assigned by default); array arguments must appear with subscripts which have same values as in the invoking procedure *or* with subscripts replaced by asterisks (see Section 7.3.1)
	Local variables	
Any argument may be typed; array variables must appear in DIMENSION statement with correct integer dimensions	Must appear in type declarations after **begin** which starts procedure *or* after **begin** in some subblock of procedure	Must appear normally in DECLARE statements or be assigned by default
	Examples	
SUBROUTINE WHO (A,B,C) INTEGER A,E DIMENSION B (10, 10), D (7)	**procedure** WHO (A, B,C); **real** C; **integer** A; **real array** B; **begin real array** D [1:7]; **integer** E;	WHO: PROCEDURE (A, B,C); DECLARE B(*,*), D(7) (A,E) FIXED;
SUBROUTINE WHY (A,M,N) DIMENSION A (M,N)	**procedure** WHY (A); **real array** A;	WHY: PROCEDURE (A, N); DECLARE A (M,N) FLOAT; (M,N are FIXED by default)

Panel 7.4, in which type declarations in procedures are considered, indicates the one case in Fortran where variable dimensions—and these must be unsubscripted integer variables—can appear in a DIMENSION statement. The variable dimensions must be arguments of the subroutine.† The reason Fortran allows variable dimensions as arguments in subroutines is that *no storage is actually allocated to the array* because the subroutine uses the storage set aside by the main program. For a similar reason, constant dimensions in subroutine DIMENSION statements in Fortran need not always be true dimensions. In the next section we shall elucidate this further. In Algol procedures, all arguments and local variables must appear in type declarations, the former before the **begin** which starts the procedure body and the latter after it. Array arguments, however, cannot be dimensioned. Dimensioning is not necessary because storage is allocated in the block calling the procedure and the address of the array together with the necessary dimensioning information is transferred to the procedure when it is called. Similarly, in PL/I the dimension of array arguments is generally superfluous.†† But, since arrays are declared with the DECLARE statement as are simple variables (cf. **real** and **real array** in Algol), some information must be provided to the compiler that the variable is, indeed, an array variable. If normal subscripts are used, these must have the same values as in the main program which calls the procedure. Alternatively, normal subscripts may be replaced by asterisks to indicate that the array bounds will be provided from the calling program.

Panel 7.5 indicates the means by which computation is terminated in a subroutine and control is returned to the main program. Fortran and PL/I both allow more than one RETURN statement in a subroutine; whichever one is reached first returns control to the main program. Fortran requires at least one RETURN statement but PL/I does not because reaching the END statement at the end of the procedure block serves the same function as a RETURN statement. The reader should recall that while END is an executable statement in PL/I, in Fortran it is not and therefore cannot be used to return control.

PL/I, like Algol, also allows an exit from the subroutine using the END which terminates the subroutine. PL/I, Algol, and Cobol allow exit from a subroutine by means of a GO TO statement. In the case of Algol and PL/I the label or switch following the GO TO must have been an input argument of the procedure or be in the block containing the procedure. Because of the basically simpler structure of the procedure division in Cobol, the GO TO can transfer to any paragraph or

---

† But they can be implicit instead of explicit arguments: see Section 7.3.4.

†† But not always because PL/I has more sophisticated storage allocation facilities than Algol.

section name. Some Fortran implementations allow statement labels as arguments in SUBROUTINE subprograms and suitably modify the RETURN statement to allow varying exits from the subprogram.

If the procedure from which control is returned is not a function procedure,
then the results which are returned from the subroutine to the main program are
the values of the output arguments of the subroutine (but see also Section
7.3.4). For example, in Example 7.2, ROW, COL, and TOUR are input arguments transmitted to the subroutine from the main program but I, SEAROW,
and SEACOL are output arguments. The values given to the output arguments
by the subroutine are picked up by the main program after control is returned
from the subroutine to the main program. A given argument can be both an
input and an output argument if one of the purposes of the subprogram is to
take the value of this argument and use it to compute a new value of the
argument. In Cobol, of course, all subroutines and the main program use the
same data division from which they obtain input data and where they put all
output results.

As we shall discuss in the next section, function procedures in Fortran, Algol,
and PL/I are called from expressions in the same manner as intrinsic functions
and need to return a value to the expression from which they were called. The
inability to do this in Cobol is a major failing of that language. For example, the
Algol statement

    A := B+C * FUNCT(D,E);

calls the function procedure FUNCT with input arguments D and E and wants a
value returned so that the right-hand side expression can be evaluated. As Panel
7.6 indicates, Fortran and Algol use the same method of returning a value and
PL/I uses a somewhat different technique. Sometimes, in an Algol or Fortran
function procedure or in a PL/I function procedure, the name of the function
may appear more than once if various paths in the procedure can be followed,
depending upon the input data. In the example in Panel 7.6, if FUNCT only
appeared once on the left side of an assignment statement as shown, in which
case it would normally be the last statement executed before control was returned to the main program (Why?), then, in the PL/I program, the VALUE =
_____ statement could be deleted and its right-hand side could replace
VALUE in the RETURN statement. If the name of the function is used as the
expression after RETURN in PL/I, as in Panel 7.6, then the PL/I mechanism is
identical to that of Fortran and Algol. Therefore, the PL/I technique in its full
generality allows somewhat more flexibility than that of the other two languages.

Panel 7.5   Normal return of control from a subroutine to a main program

FORTRAN	*ALGOL*	*PL/I*	*COBOL*
By a statement consisting of the single word RETURN.	By coming to the end of the highest level block in the procedure.	For function procedures, by a statement consisting of RETURN followed by an expression in parentheses; for subroutine procedures, by a RETURN alone or by reaching the end of the procedure block (see Section 7.3.4).	By reaching the end of the paragraph or section whose name began the procedure or, if the THRU option is used (see Panel 7.8), by reaching the end of the procedure named following THRU.

Semantics

For procedures which are not function procedures, control is normally returned to the next statement after the statement which invoked the subroutine; for function procedures control is returned to the expression which invoked the procedure (see Section 7.3.1).

Panel 7.6   Returning function values

FORTRAN and ALGOL	*PL/I*
The *name* of the function must appear on the left-hand side of at least one assignment statement in the function. The last value assigned to this identifier is the value returned by the function.	When the RETURN statement is encountered, the expression in parentheses which follows it is evaluated and this value is the one returned by the function.

Examples

Algol

```
real procedure FUNCT (X,Y);
real X,Y;
begin
——
——
FUNCT: = _____ ;
——
——
——
end
```

```
FUNCT: PROCEDURE (X,Y);
DECLARE (X,Y,VALUE) FLOAT;
——
——
——
VALUE = _____ ;
——
RETURN (VALUE);
END;
```

270

The reader should be sure he understands the difference between a value returned by a function subprogram or procedure on the one hand, and a subroutine subprogram (Fortran) or non-function procedure (Algol or PL/I) on the other hand (see Example 7.7). Using Fortran as an example, subroutine subprograms return values by means of their output arguments so that the subprogram causes values of the variables in the main program to be changed (see Section 7.3.2 on name and value). Functions, on the other hand, cause a value to be computed and returned to the main program to be used directly in the expression from which the function was called.† This value may be inserted by the subprogram in a register in the arithmetic unit (from which the main program will retrieve it) or it may be put in a location set aside for this purpose in the main program. It is not used as in subroutines to change a variable value in the main program.

In the foregoing we have effectively described the syntactical structure of subprograms and procedures. In Panel 7.7 we have recapitulated the foregoing material and filled in some details not covered previously. The value part of Algol procedures is discussed in the next section. From this panel it is reasonable to infer that the PL/I structure is both the simplest logically and most general of the four languages. It conforms more closely to the block structure already adduced for PL/I than the Algol structure does. In Section 7.3.3 we shall consider how subroutines and procedures are embedded in the overall program structure.

7.3.2   Linking Subroutines to the Main Program

Writing a subprogram or procedure is one thing; using it is something else again. In Section 7.1 we considered the mechanism by which intrinsic functions are *called* in the main program. The corresponding mechanisms for calling subprograms and procedures seem almost equally simple and straightforward. But there are also some complications and subtle implications in calling subprograms and procedures which do not exist with intrinsic functions. These together with the calling statements themselves will be discussed in this section.

We noted in Panel 7.2 that Fortran, Algol, and PL/I all have some mechanism for distinguishing between

1. *function* procedures, which always compute a single value as their result, and
2. *subroutine* or normal procedures, in which many values may be computed.

---

† Function subprograms *can* also have output arguments in addition to the value returned directly to the arithmetic expression, but this facility is seldom used.

Panel 7.7   Structure of subprograms and procedures

FORTRAN	*ALGOL*	*PL/I*	*COBOL*

Name

| Subprograms | Procedures | Procedures | Procedures |

Syntax

A procedure heading as in Panel 7.2, followed by a procedure body which consists of

			A paragraph or
any syntactically correct sequence of statements terminating with an END statement and including at least one RE-TURN statement; for FUNCTION subprograms the name of the subprogram must appear as the left side of an assignment at least once.	the value part, if any (see Panel 7.10 and text), a type declaration for the procedure arguments, and any legal Algol single statement, compound statement, or block; if a block there may be sub-blocks; if the procedure is a function procedure the name of the procedure must appear as the left side of an assignment statement at least once.	any legal PL/I PROCEDURE block; function procedures must have a RETURN statement followed by an expression in parentheses	section name followed by any sequence of statements; ended by, respectively, the next paragraph or section name *or* the end of the procedure division; the paragraph or section name is called a *procedure name.*

This distinction would be artificial if it were not for the way function procedures can be called from the main program. Just as with the intrinsic functions of Section 7.2, a function procedure may appear in any arithmetic expression wherever a variable or constant is allowed.[†] Thus, using the example of Panel 7.2, we may write in Algol a statement such as

A := B+2.0 * C14/COMPUT(R,S,T,U);

Note that the argument variables are not the same as those in Panel 7.2. We shall

---

[†] Naturally, this refers only to function procedures whose type is real, integer, double-precision, or complex. We shall discuss the use of logical or Boolean procedures in Chapter 9.

consider below in detail the relation between the arguments in the *calling* and *defining* functions.

Procedures which return more than one value (or, as we shall discuss below, no values) clearly cannot appear in arithmetic expressions. Fortran, Algol, PL/I, and Cobol (which has no analog of function procedures) all, therefore, provide special statements in the language, called subroutine or procedure calls, to invoke these procedures from the main programs. These statements are summarized in Panel 7.8.

PL/I allows multiple entries to a procedure by use of the ENTRY statement anywhere in the procedure. For example, the statement

```
FIND: ENTRY(ROW,COL,TOUR);
```

somewhere in the procedure whose heading is given in Panel 7.2, would define another entry-name, FIND, to this procedure. Then,

```
CALL FIND(R,C,T);
```

would enter the procedure at the statement after the ENTRY statement. The arguments in the ENTRY statement need not be the same as those in the PROCEDURE statement. Some Fortran implementations allow a similar facility, also using an ENTRY statement, even though this is not an official part of the Fortran language.

The PERFORM statement in Cobol is more complex than indicated in Panel 7.8. In the first place, the procedure name following THRU need not be physically further down in the program than the first procedure name in the statement. It need only be possible to "reach" the second procedure name from the first by some path which can include the use of GO TO statements.

Example 7.3

Show how the statement

```
PERFORM L1 THRU L2
```

could be correct even if L2 appears earlier in the program than L1.

Figure 7.4 indicates one way in which this could occur. The PERFORM statement would transfer control to paragraph L1. The GO TO statement would transfer control to paragraph L3 and when the label L2 was reached, control would be transferred back to the statement following the PERFORM statement.

Panel 7.8   Subroutine call statements

FORTRAN	ALGOL	PL/I	COBOL

Syntax

| CALL followed by name of procedure followed by arguments in parentheses and separated by commas. | Name of the procedure followed by arguments in parentheses and separated by commas. | CALL followed by by entry-name of procedure followed by arguments in parentheses and separated by commas. | PERFORM followed by a procedure name and, optionally, by THRU and another procedure name; other options available also (see Section 7.3.2). |

Semantics

Each of these statements causes the subprogram or procedure to be invoked with the arguments specified as described in the text.

Examples

| CALL SEARCH (R,C,T,J,SROW, SCOL) | SEARCH (R,C,T, J,SROW,SCOL); | CALL SEARCH (R,C,T,J,SROW, SCOL); | PERFORM SEARCH |

Cobol also allows options in the PERFORM statement, following the optional THRU clause, whose effect is to enable certain iterative calculations to be done. This is properly the subject of Chapter 8 and we shall defer a discussion of these options until then.

We come now to the rules governing the arguments in subroutine calls and then to the mechanism by which arguments are transferred from the calling statement to the subroutine. The rules concerning arguments are quite analogous to those discussed in Section 7.2 for intrinsic functions. They are summarized in Panel 7.9. Note in particular that the calling argument may be subscripted if the defining argument is a scalar variable. Thus, to call the Fortran subroutine in Example 7.2 we could use

    CALL SEARCH (R(K),C(K),T,J,SROW,SCOL)

The subscript K must have been given a value when the CALL statement is reached and the arguments will then be the proper entries of the arrays R and C.

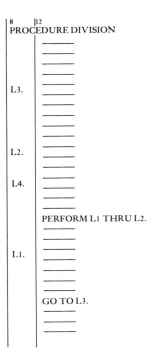

Figure 7.4   Scope of PERFORM statement in Cobol.

PL/I allows different types in the calling and defining arguments by use of the ENTRY attribute. Suppose, for example, that a procedure

    E1: PROCEDURE (A,B);
         DECLARE (A,B) FLOAT;

is defined and called by

    CALL E1 (M * N,D);

where M*N has the attribute FIXED. In the main program it would then be necessary to have the statement

    DECLARE E1 ENTRY (FLOAT,FLOAT);

which declares E1 to be a subroutine entry and declares the two arguments both to have attribute FLOAT. Then M*N would be converted to floating-point before control was transferred to the procedure E1.

Panel 7.9   Arguments in subroutine calls

FORTRAN	*ALGOL*	*PL/I*

Form

Any valid arithmetic expression *or* an array identifier *or* the name of another procedure *or*, for SUBROUTINEs only, a Hollerith constant.

Any valid arithmetic expression *or* an array identifier *or* the name of another procedure *or* a switch identifier *or* a string constant.

Any valid arithmetic (or other) expression *or* an array or structure identifier *or* the entry-name of another procedure *or* a statement label constant or variable *or* a string constant or variable.

Rules

The number of arguments in the calling statement must agree with the number of arguments in the defining statement. Each calling argument must *agree* with the defining argument in the sense that, if one is a procedure name, so must the other be, and similarly for strings and statement labels and arrays. Only if the defining argument is a scalar variable may the calling argument be any valid arithmetic expression (except for PL/I which allows array identifiers in expressions).

The type of the calling argument must agree with the type of the defining arguments.

The official language specifications do not require the types to agree but specific implementations may so require.

The types of the calling and defining arguments need not be the same but, if not, an ENTRY attribute must be used (see Section 7.3.2).

Array arguments must be similarly dimensioned in main and subprogram (except for exception noted in text).

Array arguments must be dimensioned in main program but not in procedure (see Panel 7.4).

Attributes of calling and defining arguments must agree when these are arrays or structures.

As noted in Panels 7.3 and 7.9, PL/I allows statement labels as arguments in procedures. For example, the procedure

```
TEST: PROCEDURE (A,B,JUMP);
      DECLARE (A,B)FLOAT, JUMP LABEL;
      ———

      ———

      GO TO JUMP;
```

might be called with the statement

CALL TEST (X,Y * Z,TRANS);

with TRANS a variable declared as a label in the main program. Then the GO TO JUMP statement in the procedure TEST would cause control to be transferred to the statement in the main program whose label is the *current value* of the statement label variable TRANS.

To really understand the rules in Panel 7.9 it is necessary to consider the actual mechanism by which arguments are transferred from the main program to the subroutine. Few beginning P-O language programmers understand what happens inside the computer when they invoke a subroutine in their programs. This lack of comprehension is a source of many programmer errors.

In Section 4.3 we considered briefly the distinction between the name of a variable and its value. The name-value distinction is also an important concept here because there are two ways in which arguments are transferred from the main program *to* a subroutine. These are known as calling by *name* and calling by *value*. In the former, sometimes known as calling by *address*, or calling by *reference*, the *location* of the argument in the computer memory is made available to the subroutine, and in the latter the *value* of the argument itself is made available. This is illustrated in Figure 7.5. ZZ is a subroutine with a single dummy argument A which we assume to be a scalar variable. It is called from the main program with the actual argument B whose value is stored, somewhere in the main program, in a memory word with address L(B). When calling is by name, before control is transferred from the main program to the subroutine, the address of B—that is, the location of the word holding the value of the name B—is transferred to a location in the subroutine at which the subroutine expects to find this address when reference is made to A in the statements of the subroutine. Thus the machine-language code compiled in the subroutine for the statement

C = A * A

will be such that the address of A will be picked up from the location to which L(B) was transferred.

By contrast, when calling by value, the value of the name B and not its location is transferred to the subroutine, and in C=A*A, the value of A will be picked up directly from this location.

Now which of these two methods is to be preferred? At first, calling by name may seem more cumbersome because it is necessary to first pick up the location of B and then the value of B. However, in almost all computers the machine-language repertoire makes it no more difficult to do this than pick up B directly. Moreover, Figure 7.5 does not really give a true picture of how calling by value is

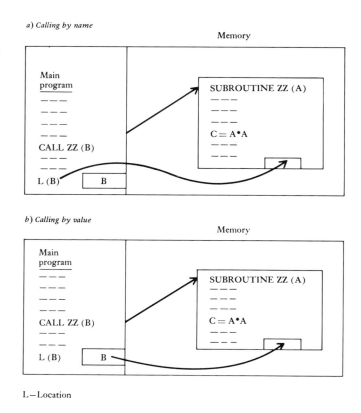

a) Calling by name

b) Calling by value

L—Location

Figure 7.5   Calling by name and value.

usually implemented. In fact, when a parameter is called by value, its value is normally put in some temporary memory location (external to the subroutine) and the address of *this* location is transmitted to the subroutine. Thus, even in the case of call-by-value, first an address must be picked up and then the value itself.

More significantly, calling by name is much to be preferred in the common case when the argument is an array name. Suppose the dummy and real arguments A and B in Figure 7.5 were 10 x 10 arrays, and suppose the statement in the subprogram was C=A(I)*A(I). Then the values of the elements of the array would be stored in 100 locations in the main program. When calling by name, still all that would be transferred would be a single address, the location of the first element of B, B(1,1). But when calling by value all 100 elements of B would have to be transferred to the subroutine. This is not good for two reasons:

1. 99 more locations would be needed in the subroutine for data storage than when calling by name.

2. The computer time to transfer 100 values will be greater than that to transfer just one address.

For the reasons noted above, Fortran, Algol, and PL/I do almost all their argument transference by name. The exceptions are noted in Panel 7.10. But this panel does hide some subtleties. In Fortran and PL/I calling by value takes place, as indicated previously, by evaluating the argument, placing it in some temporary memory location, and transmitting the name of that location to the subprogram. In Algol, however, the language specifies a *copy rule* for calling by name which requires that every occurrence of the formal argument in the procedure be replaced by the actual argument. Thus, a calling argument A+2.3*B corresponding to a formal argument C would cause C to be replaced by A+2.3*B wherever C appears in the procedure. In actual implementations the copy rule is usually followed by constructing an internal procedure to evaluate the calling argument; this internal procedure is then called wherever C appears in the procedure.

The value specification in Algol allows the value itself to be transmitted even when the calling argument is an identifier. The usefulness of this is that it allows changing the value of the argument within the procedure without changing the value of the calling argument. The reason why arguments which are not variable names are normally transferred by value is illustrated by the following example.

Example 7.4

What is printed at the end of the following Fortran main program and subroutine?

Main program	*Subroutine*
CALL SWAP (5,6)	SUBROUTINE SWAP (J,K)
I = 5 − 6	L = J
PRINT, I	J = K
STOP	K = L
END	RETURN
	END

The RETURN statement returns control to the main program (see below). The purpose of the SWAP subroutine is to interchange the values of J and K. At first glance it would appear that, since SWAP does not affect I, the answer is −1. But if the call is by name, the address of J in the subroutine is the location of the constant 5 and that of K is the location of the constant 6. Thus L = J puts 5 into the location of L, J = K puts 6, the value of K, into the location of J [i.e., replaces the constant 5 by 6(!)], and K = L puts 5, the value of L, into the location of K [i.e., replaces the constant 6 by 5(!)]. The result, therefore, is to swap the constants 5 and 6 in the main program. As a result, I = 5−6, which refers to the *original* locations of 5 and 6 for its values, really computes 6−5 and the answer is +1! Of course, for *output* arguments *this is just what procedures are supposed to do*, namely, compute new values of variables. But, normally, the programmer will not want *input* arguments to be changed by the subprogram. Sometimes, however, as in the case of Example 7.4, some or all parameters are both input *and* output arguments. In this example, if the call was by value, −1 would be printed out.

The example above is completely unrealistic in the sense that, if one wrote a subroutine to interchange two variables, it would never be called with constant arguments. But this example should teach the reader that any formal argument which appears on the left-hand side of an assignment statement will cause a change in the value of the calling argument when that argument is called by name. (Why?) Of course, as noted above, for *output* arguments this is just what procedures are supposed to do.

The discussion above implies the reason for the note in Panel 7.3 about why it is not necessarily required to have the same dimensions for calling and defining arguments which are arrays. The purposes of the dimensioning in the main program are:

1. To enable the computer to assign storage to the array
2. To give the compiler some information on how to handle the variable since it will appear subscripted in expressions

But, when argument transfer is done by name, only the latter reason is operative in the subroutine, since no storage is assigned for the array. Now, what kind of information does the compiler need about a subscripted variable in order to compile references to it properly?

We assume that arrays are stored by column as they are in Fortran and usually in Algol. Consider first a one-dimensional array A. If L(A) is the location of A(1), then the location of A(I) is

L(A)+(I−1)

which does not depend on the dimensions of A at all. But, if A is two-dimensional with row dimension N1 and column dimension N2, and L(A) is the location of A(1,1), then the location of A(I,J) is

$$L(A)+(I-1)+(N1)(J-1)$$

Similarly, for a three-dimensional array dimensioned $A(N1,N2,N3)$, the location of $A(I,J,K)$ is

$$L(A)+(I-1)+(N1)(J-1)+(N1)(N2)(K-1)$$

From these examples it is easy to see (Problem 11) that the *last* dimension is immaterial in the calculation of the location of the element of an array (but the others most certainly are needed). For this reason, in some compilers it is immaterial which dimension appears as the last one in arrays in subroutines. Still it is good programming practice to include the correct dimensions (i.e., the same dimensions as in the main program).

Our discussion of argument transfer also explains why, even though Fortran has no dynamic allocation of storage, variable dimensions are allowed in Fortran in subroutines if the array is an argument of the subroutine. For, since no storage is assigned to an array which is an argument, there is no difficulty in handling variable dimensions which are used only to locate elements in the array as described above. On the other hand, arrays in subroutines in Fortran which are *local* to the subroutine must have integer constant dimensions because storage is allocated to them.

Panel 7.10 Rules for calling by name and value

FORTRAN	*ALGOL*	*PL/I*
All calling is by name except when the		
argument is an arithmetic expression other than a single variable name, unsubscripted or not	arguments appear after **value** before the type declaration in the procedure heading.	argument is an entry name or an arithmetic expression other than a single variable name, unsubscripted or otherwise

Example

procedure R1 (B,C);
value B; **real** B,C;

7.3.3 Program Structure with Subroutines

Perhaps the greatest contrast between Fortran on the one hand, and Algol and PL/I on the other, in the area of procedures is how they are put together with the rest of the program. Cobol has a very simple structure as regards procedures since they merely become paragraphs or sections in the procedure division.

```
C     MAIN PROGRAM
      ----
      ----
      CALL SUBPR1 (A,B,C)
      ----
      ----
      D = B + C * FUNCT1 (A,E)
      ----
      ----
      CALL SUBPR2 (H,I * I)
      ----
      ----
      END

C     SUBPROGRAM 1
      SUBROUTINE SUBPR1 (X,Y,Z)
      ----
      ----
      Y = X + FUNCT2 (COS (X) )
      Z = X + FUNCT2 (Y + SIN (X) )
      ----
      ----
      RETURN
      END
```

```
C     SUBPROGRAM 2
      SUBROUTINE SUBPR2 (X,J)
      ----
      ----
      ----
      RETURN
      END

C     FUNCTION 1
      FUNCTION FUNCT1 (X,Y)
      ----
      ----
      ----
      FUNCT1 = ----
      RETURN
      END

C     FUNCTION 2
      FUNCTION FUNCT2 (X)
      IF (X * X - 25.) 10, 10, 20
  10  ----
      ----
      ----
      FUNCT2 = ----
      RETURN
  20  ----
      A = X + FUNCT1 (25.,X)
      ----
      ----
      FUNCT2 = ----
      RETURN
      END
```

Figure 7.6 Fortran program schematic.

```
begin real A, B, C; integer I, J; real array F[−1:10, 0:10] ;
      ————
      ————
      ————
  begin integer J, K; real N;
    real procedure PROG1 (R, S);
      real R; real array S;
        begin
        ————
        ————
        ————
        PROG1 : = ————;
        ————
        ————
        ————
        end;
  C : = PROG1 (A, F) * A * (B/C);
      ————
      ————
      ————
    begin real G, H;
      procedure PROG2 (X); real X;
        begin
        ————
        ————
        end;
                          PROG2 (B);
                          ————
                          ————
                          PROG2 (H);
                          ————
                          ————
                          ————
                          G : = H * B + PROG1 (EXP (B), F);
                          ————
                          ————
                          ————
                          end;
                          ————
                          ————
                        end;
                      begin real N, Q, T;
                          ————
                          ————
                          ————
                        begin
                          ————
                          ————
                          ————
                        end;
                          ————
                          ————
                        end;
                          ————
                          ————
                          ————
                      end
```

Figure 7.7   Algol program schematic.

283

Panel 7.11   Program structure with procedures

FORTRAN	*ALGOL*	*PL/I*	*COBOL*
Each subprogram is a logically separate entity with its own declarations and END statement; a Fortran program is a main program as described in Section 6.2, followed by any number of subprograms; the data for the program follows the last subprogram.	All procedures in Algol are part of some block; the procedures in each block follow the type declarations for that block.	A PL/I program is a set of (in almost all cases relevant here—just one) procedure blocks on the highest level called external procedures; within an external procedure, procedure blocks may be interspersed at will as long as no two blocks overlap.	Procedures are just additional paragraphs and sections added anywhere in the procedure division.

Panel 7.11 contains the definition of the program structure of procedures in each of the four languages. To understand these structures better, we have schematic examples of programs in the four languages in Figures 7.6—7.9. We shall discuss each of these figures in turn.

Remarks on Figure 7.6

1. This Fortran program consists of a main program, two subroutine subprograms, and two function subprograms. Both subroutine subprograms and one of the function subprograms are called from the main program. The other function subprogram is called from one of the subroutines and this function in turn calls the other function. This illustrates the ability to call subprograms from subprograms and to make multiple use of one subprogram.

2. The arguments in each subprogram are dummy arguments. Therefore, there is no connection between the X's used in each one as dummy arguments.

3. The calling arguments can be any expression as illustrated in subprogram 1 and these expressions can include calls to other function subprograms or, as in this case, to an intrinsic function.

4. The second function illustrates the ability to have multiple RETURN statements. But whenever there are multiple RETURNs, all but one can be removed as follows (although there is no good reason to do this): Give one RETURN a label L and replace all the others by GO TO L (where L, of course, is an integer constant in Fortran).

```
L1:   PROCEDURE;
      DECLARE B FIXED, (A, C) FLOAT;
      ———
      ———
      ———
      L2:   BEGIN;
            ———
            ———
            ———
            END L2;
      L3:   PROCEDURE (X, Y);
            DECLARE (X, Y) FLOAT;
            ———
            ———
            ———
            END L3;
      L4:   BEGIN;
            DECLARE A FIXED;
               ———
               ———
               ———
               L5:   PROCEDURE (Y);
                     DECLARE Y FLOAT;
                     ———
                     ———
                     ———
                     RETURN (Y * Y − A);
                     END L5;
               ———
               ———
               ———
            B = L5 (C) − 2 * A;
               ———
               ———
               ———
            END L4;
      ———
      ———
      ———
      CALL L3 (A, B * C);
      END L1;
```

Figure 7.8   PL/I program schematic.

Remarks on Figure 7.7

1. This program, like all Algol programs, is a single block at the highest level. Within this block are two main subblocks. Within both of these, there is one subblock. There are two procedures in the first main subblock, one of which is defined at the start of the block and the other at the start of its subblock.

2. The reader should be able to determine the scope of all variables (Problem 12).

3. Since the first procedure is a function procedure, it is called in an assignment statement, but the second is not a function procedure and is called in a statement by itself.

Remarks on Figure 7.8

1. The thing to understand about this program is the flow of control. Starting at L1, the flow continues through the BEGIN block L2 but then skips over procedure L3 because, as in Algol, procedures are only entered by *calls* from the program. Flow then passes to BEGIN block L4, procedure L5 is skipped, and then blocks L4 and L1 are completed.

2. The second procedure is a function procedure which returns the value Y*Y−A. Note, that since this procedure is internal to block L4, all variables declared in L4 are "known" in the procedure; see Section 7.3.4. Procedure L5 cannot be called from outside block L4 because it is internal to this block. *In both Algol and PL/I, control can never be transferred from outside a block to a point internal to it.*

3. The call of L5 uses as argument C, which is declared in PROCEDURE block L1 and is, therefore, "known" in L4; see Section 7.3.4.

Remarks on Figure 7.9

1. The normal flow in this program is from paragraph START to NEW, CONTIN, and OLD because of the PERFORM and then to CONTIN, OLD, and NEXT. Paragraphs NEW, CONTIN, and OLD together form a procedure.

2. The PERFORM statement causes the execution of all of paragraph OLD.

Example 7.5

Write Fortran and Algol programs for the subroutine of Example 7.1, as given in the flow chart of Figure 7.2.

Fortran

```
          SUBROUTINE SEARCH (ROW,COL,TOUR,I,SEAROW,SEACOL)
          DIMENSION TOUR(8,8), SEAROW(8), SEACOL(8), MOVROW(8),
       *      MOVCOL(8)
          INTEGER ROW, COL, SEAROW, SEACOL, TOUR
C         COORD IS A SUBROUTINE TO COMPUTE THE EIGHT POSSIBLE
C             MOVES
          CALL COORD (ROW, COL, MOVROW, MOVCOL)
```

```
         I = 0
         J = 1
C        ROW AND COLUMN COORDINATES TESTED TO SEE IF THEY
C               ARE ON BOARD
    14   IF ((MOVROW(J)−1) * (8−MOVROW(J))) 4,2,2
     2   IF ((MOVCOL(J)−1) * (8−MOVCOL(J))) 4,6,6
C        ASSUME TOUR(I,J) = 1 IF SQUARE (I,J) HAS BEEN REACHED
C               ALREADY AND TOUR(I,J) = 0 OTHERWISE
     6   II = MOVROW(J)
         JJ = MOVCOL(J)
         IF (TOUR(II,JJ)) 4,8,4
     8   I = I + 1
         SEAROW(I) = MOVROW(J)
         SEACOL(I) = MOVCOL(J)
     4   IF (J−8) 10, 12, 10
    10   J = J + 1
         GO TO 14
    12   RETURN
         END
```

Algol

```
procedure SEARCH (ROW, COL, TOUR, I, SEAROW, SEACOL);
   integer array TOUR, SEAROW, SEACOL; integer ROW, COL, I;
   begin
      integer array MOVROW[1 : 8] , MOVCOL[1 : 8] ; integer J;
      COORD (ROW, COL, MOVROW, MOVCOL);
      I := 0;   J := 1;
      L1: if (MOVROW[J] −1) * (8−MOVROW[J] ) < 0 then go to L2 else
          if (MOVCOL[J] −1) * (8−MOVCOL[J] ) < 0 then go to L2 else
          if TOUR[MOVROW[J] ,MOVCOL[I] ] = 1 then go to L2 else
             begin
                I := I + 1;
                SEAROW[I] := MOVROW[J] ;
                SEACOL[I] := MOVCOL[J] ;
             end;
      L2: if J−8 ≠ 0 then
          begin J := J + 1; go to L1 end
          else
   end
```

IDENTIFICATION DIVISION.
— — —
— — —
— — —
ENVIRONMENT DIVISION.
— — —
— — —
— — —
DATA DIVISION.
— — —
— — —
— — —
PROCEDURE DIVISION.
START.
        — — —
        — — —
        — — —
        PERFORM NEW THRU OLD.
        — — —
        — — —
        — — —
        GO TO CONTIN.
NEW.
— — —
— — —
— — —
CONTIN.
— — —
— — —
— — —
OLD.
— — —
— — —
— — —
NEXT.

Figure 7.9   Cobol program schematic.

We leave to the reader the programming of the subroutine COORD (Problem 15). The technique for programming iterative calculations (to be discussed in Chapter 8) should suggest to the reader another way of organizing the calculation of this subroutine.

7.3.4   Local, Global, and Common Variables

Fortran, Algol and PL/I all provide a mechanism for transferring arguments back and forth between subroutines and calling routines [†] other than that already

---

[†] We have been denoting the calling routine as the main program, but, since we have seen that one subroutine can be called from another, we shall hereafter use *calling routine*.

discussed. In Algol and PL/I this mechanism is inherent in their block structure. In Fortran it is the result of a specially provided statement.

In Algol and PL/I the notion of local and global variables introduced in Section 6.1.2, provides a method for transference of arguments. Any variables in a block in which a procedure is defined, or in a block global to the defining block, are "known" to the procedure. Thus, for example, referring to Figure 7.7, the procedure PROG2(X) can make use of all variables declared in the block which contains it (G,H), or the two blocks global to it (J,K,N; A,B,C,I,F). Note, however, that the variable J defined in the outermost block is not available to the procedure because the reuse of J in the next block makes the original J unreachable. Similar examples could be given for PL/I using Figure 7.8 (Problem 16).

The reader may wonder the reason to have an argument X at all in PROG 2. Why not just declare it in a block global to the procedure? The answer is that X is truly a parameter of the procedure since the procedure is called from two different places with different arguments (B and H). Therefore, the general rule concerning when a variable must be used as an argument and when it can be merely a global variable is as follows:

> Any parameter—input data or output results—whose calling name varies from one call of the procedure to another *must* be an argument of the procedure; any other parameter can be (but need not be) transferred implicitly from a global block.

For convenience in writing procedures and calling statements, it is clearly desirable to have as few arguments as possible. From the above rule it follows, in particular, that a subroutine which is called only once in a program need have no arguments. (Such a subroutine could, of course, be part of the calling program, but it is often convenient in writing programs to write them in pieces even if it means a subroutine will be called only once.)

In Fortran transference of arguments without reference to them is accomplished by means of the COMMON statement which is described in Panel 7.12. The usefulness of the COMMON statement follows from the fact that common blocks with the same labels in the main program and subroutines are stored in precisely the same places in main memory. Thus, for example, if we have

Main program	*Subprogram 1*
COMMON/C1/A,B,C/ /D(10),E	SUBROUTINE S1 (X)
CALL S1 (R)	COMMON/C1/Y,Z (2)
CALL S2 (S,T)	*Subprogram 2*
	SUBROUTINE S2 (Y,Z)
	COMMON R (11)

then the memory locations of A,B, and C in the main program correspond precisely to Y,Z(1) and Z(2) in the first subprogram, and D(1),D(2),...,D(10),E in the main program correspond to R(1),...,R(11) in the second subprogram. Therefore, for example, all references to Y,Z(1) and Z(2) in S1(X) use the values of A,B, and C from the main program. Without the use of common storage, S1 would need arguments X,Y, and Z and the first calling statement would need to be

    S1(R,A,B)

where now B would be a two-element array in place of the old B and C. Common storage, therefore, provides a convenient way of transferring arguments between calling routines and subroutines. The reader should now be able to see why a Fortran subroutine need have no arguments of its own (Problem 17). Many different subprograms can, of course, refer to the same common block. There are many complexities involving common storage in Fortran, particularly in connection with its interaction with the EQUIVALENCE statement, but we shall not discuss them here because our purpose has been to indicate only the use of common storage for argument transfer.

   In the next section we shall introduce some other subroutine features of Fortran, Algol, and PL/I and then in Section 7.5 we shall compare the subroutine facilities of the various languages.

7.4   OTHER SUBROUTINE FEATURES OF FORTRAN, ALGOL, AND PL/I

With two exceptions, Section 7.3 covers all the salient aspects of subroutine usage in the four languages. These two exceptions—statement functions in Fortran and recursive procedures in Algol and PL/I—are considered in this section.

7.4.1   Statement Functions in Fortran

In one particular instance Fortran allows incorporation of subroutines as part of the main program in a manner analogous to that allowed in Algol and PL/I. The subroutines thus defined are called arithmetic statement functions and are described in Panel 7.13. The statement function definitions must appear in any main program or subroutine *before* the first executable statement of that routine. This rule is analogous to the Algol rule about defining procedures at the beginning of a block.

   The parameters in the arithmetic expression on the right-hand side of the definition may be any variables in the routine in which the statement function is

Panel 7.12 The COMMON statement

Syntax

COMMON / id_1 / $list_1$ / id_2 / $list_2$ / ... / id_n / $list_n$

where each list is a sequence, separated by commas, of identifiers or array names, optionally followed by the dimensioning information of the array; each *id* is an identifier or, in at most one case, empty; if the first identifier is empty the first two slashes may be omitted.

Semantics

The elements in each list are assigned to a specific block of storage in main memory which is referred to by the identifier preceding the list; if there is no identifier, the area assigned is called *blank common.*

Examples

	Notes
COMMON A,B(10),C	12 locations assigned in blank common
COMMON / C1 / F, G (12)	13 locations in block C1,
/ / R (4), I / C2 / M, N	2 in block C2, and 5 in blank common
DIMENSION A (5, 10)	51 locations in blank common
COMMON A, B / C1 / D, E, F (10)	and 12 in block C1

id—identifier

Note:
When an array name *with* dimensions appears in a COMMON statement, it must not appear in a DIMENSION statement.

defined. This corresponds in Algol or PL/I to a procedure making use of variables in the block in which the procedure is defined. Some implementations relax the ban on the use of subscripts by allowing them in parameters but, of course, not in dummy arguments. (Why?)

Statement functions are called just as function subprograms by their appearance in an arithmetic expression. As Panel 7.13 indicates, they act exactly like a function subprogram whose subroutine body consists of a single assignment statement followed by RETURN and END. The rules on the actual calling arguments are precisely the same as those for function subprograms.

Since the arguments in statement functions are dummy arguments, these same arguments can be used as normal variables elsewhere in the program. This produces an interesting anomaly. In order that statement functions can use variables and produce results of type double-precision and complex, as well as real and integer as determined by the default option, the dummy arguments and the name can appear in type statements. But this means, of course, that any identifier used as a dummy argument and as a variable must have the same type. The conclusion to be drawn is that it is good programming practice never to use the same identifier as a dummy argument and as a variable elsewhere in the program.

Example 7.6

Write a function subprogram and an arithmetic statement function in Fortran to compute the angle in radians opposite the first of three given sides of a triangle.

To do the calculation we use the *law of cosines*

$$\cos \alpha = (b^2 + c^2 - a^2) / 2bc$$

where α is the angle opposite the side a. We also need the relationship

$$\cos^2 x = 1/(1 + \tan^2 x)$$

The function subprogram then is

```
      FUNCTION ANGLE (A,B,C)
C     A,B, AND C ARE THE SIDES OF THE TRIANGLE
      COSANG = (B * B+C * C-A * A)/(2. * B * C)
      ANGLE = ATAN(SQRT(1.-COSANG * COSANG)/COSANG)
      RETURN
      END
```

The reader should decide whether any arithmetic checks against errors in the data or any specific kind of result are needed (Problem 20). To do the same calculation using a statement function, we compress the two assignment statements above into one using a continuation card as follows:

```
      ANGLE(A,B,C) = ATAN(SQRT(1.-((B * B+C * C-A * A)
     * /(2. * B * C)) ** 2)/((B * B+C * C-A * A)/(2. * B * C)))
```

Alternatively, we could use two statement functions:

```
      ARCCOS(X) = ATAN(SQRT(1.-X * X)/X)
      ANGLE(A,B,C) = ARCCOS((B * B+C * C-A * A)/(2. * B * C))
```

Note that ARCCOS must be defined *before* it is used in ANGLE.

Panel 7.13   Statement functions in Fortran

Syntax

$id (ar_1, ar_2, ..., ar_n) = ae$

where the dummy arguments are non-array identifiers (i.e., no subscripts) and the expression may contain variables other than those in the argument list although these cannot be subscripted; the expression may also contain references to intrinsic functions, to previously defined statement functions, and to function subprograms.

Semantics

The statement function is useable in precisely the same way as a function subprogram with name *id*, arguments $ar_1, ..., ar_n$ and a procedure body consisting of

> *id* = *ae*
> RETURN
> END

and where all variables in the *ae* which are not arguments of the subprogram appear in COMMON statements in the main program and subprogram.

Example

STAFUN (A, B, C) = EXP (A * B) − T ** C

ae—arithmetic expression
ar—argument
id—identifier

Example 7.7

Indicate how the arithmetic statement functions and the function subprogram of the previous example could be used in a main program and, in addition, how a subroutine subprogram could be used for the same task.

The function subprogram might be called by a statement in the main program

> SUM = ANGLE(A1,A2,A3) + ANGLE(A2,A3,A1)

to compute the sum in radians of two angles of a triangle.

Similarly, precisely the same statement could be used in a main program with either of the arithmetic statement functions defined in the previous example.

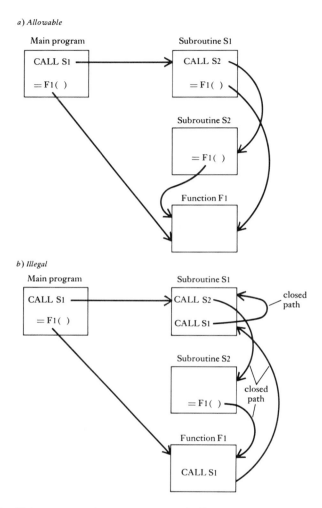

Figure 7.10   Main program-subprogram structure in Fortran.

The following SUBROUTINE subprogram could be used:

```
SUBROUTINE TRIANG (A,B,C,ANGLE)
COSANG = (B * B+C * C—A * A)/(2. * B * C)
ANGLE = ATAN(SQRT (1.—COSANG * COSANG)/COSANG)
RETURN
END
```

Here ANGLE is an output argument since subroutines do not transfer their results back to the main program by the subroutine name. To use this subroutine as above in the main program we could use the following:

```
CALL TRIANG (A1,A2,A3,ANGLE1)
CALL TRIANG (A2,A3,A1,ANGLE2)
SUM = ANGLE1 + ANGLE2
```

7.4.2 Recursive Procedures in Algol and PL/I

It was implicit in Panel 7.11 and explicit in the examples which followed this panel that subprograms and procedures can be called from the main program or other subprograms and procedures with great generality. In Algol and PL/I there is essentially complete generality in this, but not in Fortran. The restriction in Fortran can be stated in two equivalent ways:

1. After one reference (call) of a subprogram there can be no further references to that subprogram until a RETURN statement has been executed in the subprogram.

2. If arrows are drawn as in Figure 7.10, from each call of a subprogram to the subprogram called, then starting from the tail of any arrow it must not be possible to trace a closed path coming back to this tail. Figure 7.10 illustrates both a legal situation and one in which there are two illegalities, one in which a subroutine calls itself and a second in which there is a closed path from S1 to S2 to F1 and back to S1.

When a subprogram or procedure calls itself, this is called *pure recursion* and, when there is a closed path involving more than one subprogram or procedure, this is called *indirect recursion*.

In Chapter 8 we shall discuss the problems of implementing recursion at some length. But briefly consider the following example:

```
FUNCTION XYZ(A)
———
———

B = XYZ(C)
———
———
———
XYZ = ———
RETURN
END
```

Now what would happen if the above were allowed? When the statement B=XYZ(C) is encountered, control would have to be transferred from that statement in the subprogram XYZ *to the subprogram XYZ itself.* If the complications of doing this are not obvious here, they will be made more clear in the next chapter. Because of these complications, it is not surprising that Fortran does not allow recursion explicitly (although it can be simulated; see Section 8.3). Then is it surprising that both Algol and PL/I do allow recursion? Recursion has thus far found little application in P-O languages (although, in the class of languages known as list-processing languages, recursion is a quite useful technique). Algol and PL/I do allow recursion because there is increasing reason to believe that recursion will find a substantial number of applications in P-O languages. In Sections 8.1 and 8.3 we shall discuss various examples of the use of recursion.

7.5   A COMPARISON OF THE SUBROUTINE CAPABILITIES OF THE FOUR LANGUAGES

As we pointed out at the beginning of this chapter, the ability to use subroutines and procedures does not add any additional capability to any of the four languages. The only exception to this is the provision for recursive procedures in Algol and PL/I. Otherwise, all subprograms and procedures could appear as open subroutines in line with the rest of the program whenever needed. The programmer could write programs for the intrinsic functions and include them in line as needed. Still, if the reader does not yet fully grasp the immense practical value of subprograms and procedures, he will not have to do very much programming before he realizes that without them many calculations using P-O languages would be totally impractical.

In assessing the capabilities of the four languages in this area Cobol is clearly in a class by itself. The rigid program format of Cobol, with its procedure division and data division, means on the one hand that argument transfer between calling and called procedures is no problem but, on the other hand, the overall procedure capability of the language, particularly the lack of function procedures, is far less than for the other three.

Among Fortran, Algol, and PL/I, the latter two have such similar procedure mechanisms that we may consider them as one. Algol and PL/I clearly have a simpler, more elegant way of implementing subroutines than does Fortran. The complications of having FUNCTION and SUBROUTINE statements as well as statement functions, while needing to use COMMON statements to transfer arguments implicitly, do not exist in either of the other two languages. The relative simplicity of the use of procedures in Algol and PL/I is a direct consequence of the block structure of these two languages. As has perhaps been clear all along, the design· of both Algol and PL/I has corrected much of the clumsiness of Fortran with more elegant and useable structures.

One significant advantage of Fortran is the physical separation of a Fortran program into a main program and a sequence of separate subroutines. This makes it possible to compile each subprogram separately and to intersperse compiled object program card decks with source program decks. In PL/I each external procedure block must be compiled as a single source program entity, but previously compiled procedures can be loaded together with source program statements if they appear as additional procedure blocks at the highest level. Since an Algol program is always a single block at the highest level, normally Algol programs must be compiled as a single entity entirely in source language.[†]

The reader may wonder how subprograms in Fortran (or any other P-O language) can be compiled "separately," since the location of a subprogram in memory and, therefore, the addresses in its instructions depend upon how much memory space the main program requires. Also, how can the main program know to where to transfer address names or values, unless the subroutines are compiled with the main program? The answer is that subroutines are compiled with all addresses internal to the subroutine *relative* to the location of the first word of the subroutine in memory. In the main program all addresses which depend upon subroutine locations are flagged. Then at *object time*, that is, the time when the object programs are loaded into memory for execution (in contrast to *compile time*), the subroutine locations are determined and all addresses in the subroutines are appropriately set and all flagged addresses in the main program are filled in using the now known subroutine locations. Such subroutines are said, therefore, to be *relocatable*.

Compiling subroutines separately from the main program has two beneficial results:

1. Once any part of the total program—main program or subprogram—has been debugged it need not be recompiled as further testing of the entire program proceeds. This is so because it is possible to intermix compiled program decks (i.e., object program decks) and source decks. This is illustrated in Figure 7.11, where we have assumed the complete program is a main source program and three subprograms, two already compiled and one in source form. The compilation process then ignores the object programs for subprograms 1 and 3 (except to note that they exist, since they are called from the main program or subprogram

---

[†] Some Algol systems (e.g., on CDC 6000 series computers) allow separate compiling of procedures.

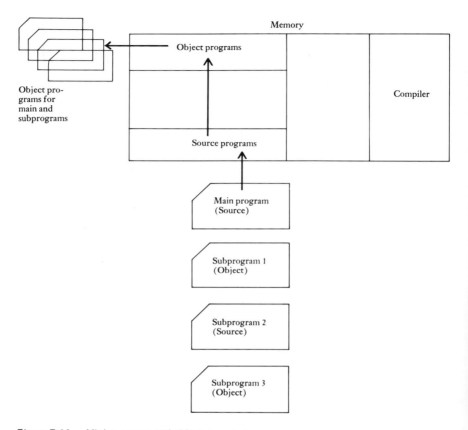

Figure 7.11   Mixing source and object programs.

2). If there are no syntactical errors in the main program and subprogram 2, then object programs for these will be produced; otherwise, the usual error messages will be printed. In most computer operating systems, if all parts of a program compile, then execution can proceed as well as the punching of object decks.

2. Any debugged subprogram may be used by *any* programmer as part of his program. Debugged subprograms which are of substantial general use can be made part of the operating system and can be called from other programs without the need of actually inserting the object deck for the subprogram as part of the user's program deck. In this way a *library* of programs can be built up to serve all the users of a computing installation and, indeed, users at other installations as well.

The latter advantage can also be attained in Algol and PL/I implementations by effectively adding to the list of intrinsic functions and allowing non-function intrinsic procedures also, but the first advantage is easily available only in Fortran. It is a significant advantage but not significant enough to outweigh the basic language advantages of Algol and PL/I.

BIBLIOGRAPHIC NOTES

Virtually all books on computer programming discuss subroutines and procedures in some detail because of their great importance in P-O languages as well as in other computer languages. For example, see Chapter 10 of Sherman (1963), Chapter 6 of Stein and Munro (1964), Chapter 6 of Hassitt (1967), and Chapters 15-20 of Dijkstra (1962).

The mathematically-oriented reader may be interested in how the elementary mathematical functions are approximated in computers. An introduction to this area will be found in Chapter 7 of Ralston (1965). Books devoted exclusively to approximations for computers are the recent books by Fike (1968), Hart et al. (1968), and the pioneering but difficult work by Hastings (1955).

Bibliography

Dijkstra, E.W. (1962): *A Primer of Algol 60 Programming*, Academic Press, New York.

Fike, C.T. (1968): *Computer Evaluation of Mathematical Functions*, Prentice-Hall, Inc., Englewood Cliffs, New Jersey.

Hart, J.F., et al. (1968): *Handbook of Computer Approximations*, John Wiley & Sons, Inc., New York.

Hassitt, A. (1967): *Computer Programming and Computer Systems*, Academic Press, New York.

Hastings, C. (1955): *Approximations for Digital Computers*, Princeton University Press, Princeton, New Jersey.

Ralston, A. (1965): *A First Course in Numerical Analysis*, McGraw-Hill Book Company, Inc., New York.

Sherman, P.M. (1963): *Programming and Coding Digital Computers*, John Wiley & Sons, Inc., New York.

Stein, M.L., and W.D. Munro (1964): *Computer Programming—A Mixed Language Approach*, Academic Press, New York.

PROBLEMS

Section 7.2

1. What is printed out in each of the following:

    a) PI = 3.14159265
       I = 13
       A = SIN(PI/FLOAT(I/3))
       PRINT, A

    b) X = 256.
       A = LOG2(SQRT(X))
       PRINT, A

2. a) Draw graphs of the entier and truncation functions.
    b) Draw a graph of the remainder function for $y=1$.

3. a) What is the value of N in the following?

    A = 2.5
    N = IFIX (A * FLOAT(IFIX(A * FLOAT(IFIX(A)))))

    b) Write a single assignment statement to find the fractional part of a floating-point number without using the remainder function.

4. a) PL/I contains all the functions listed in Table 7.1. What is the smallest number of intrinsic functions in Table 7.1 which would have to be included in PL/I, so that all the other functions in Table 7.1 could be calculated as combinations of these?
    b) Answer the same question for Table 7.2.

Section 7.3

5. a) Any function subprogram in Fortran can be replaced by a subroutine subprogram together with appropriate changes in the main program. Prove or disprove this statement.
    b) Prove or disprove the statement above with the words "function" and "subroutine" interchanged.

6.   a) Explain why subscripted variables are not allowed as dummy arguments in subprograms and procedures.

   b) Why is there no corresponding restriction in the calling statement?

7.   Suppose you were going to write a subroutine to compute the sine function and were going to proceed as follows:

   i) The argument in radians, which could be any real number, would first be transformed into an equivalent argument (i.e., an argument with the same sine) between plus and minus π.

   ii) Then the series

   $$\sin x = x - x^3/3! + x^5/5! - x^7/7! + x^9/9!$$

   was to be used to compute the sine.

   a) Show how (i) above would be accomplished.

   b) Write a subprogram or procedure in any P-O language for this function evaluation.

   c) Suppose you wished to use this same procedure with only minor modifications to compute the cosine also. Show how you could do this by providing an alternate entry for the cosine to the main one used for the sine. (Do not use square roots.)

(Note: The above technique is similar to the way sines and cosines are actually computed, except that a more sophisticated approximation to the sine than the series above is normally used.)

8.   Under what circumstances can a calling argument in Fortran not be an arithmetic expression? Why?

9.   If all subprogram arguments were called by value, which of the following would not be possible and why?

   a) Variable dimensions in Fortran subprograms

   b) Dimensions in Fortran subprograms which were not the same as those in the main program

   c) Array variables as procedure arguments

10. If you are using a compiler for a P-O language and do not know whether or not arguments are called by name or value, explain why no dummy input argument which is not also an output argument should ever appear on the left-hand side of an assignment statement in the subprogram.

11. a) Verify the equations on p. 281 for the locations of elements in two- and three-dimensional arrays.

b) How would these equations be changed if arrays were stored by row instead of by column?

c) With arrays stored by row, which dimension becomes immaterial if arrays are called by name? Explain.

12. Indicate the scope of all variables in Figure 7.7.

13. Write subprograms or procedures for the following intrinsic functions:

   a) Max
   b) Min
   c) Sign

14. a) Write a subprogram for the truncation function assuming the existence of a program for entier.

b) Do the same for entier assuming the existence of truncation.

15. Write a subprogram for the subroutine COORD in Example 7.5 which, given any position on a chessboard, returns the eight possible places a knight could move, including those which are, in fact, off the board.

16. What is the scope of all variables in Figure 7.8?

17. Explain why common storage in Fortran and the local-global variable structure of Algol and PL/I makes it possible for some subprograms or procedures to have no arguments.

Section 7.4

18. Explain why arithmetic statement functions in Fortran are syntactically more like procedures in Algol and PL/I than the normal subprogram capability of Fortran.

19. Using any other intrinsic functions you wish, write an arithmetic statement function to implement the absolute value function (see Table 7.2).

20. Why is the subprogram of Example 7.6 incomplete?

8

iteration and recursion

A rose is a rose is a rose.

Gertrude Stein

O! Thou hast damnable iteration. . . .

Henry IV, Part 1 (Act 1)

If you don't say anything, you won't be called on to repeat it.

Calvin Coolidge

If a program to find the roots of a single quadratic equation required 15 statements, but one to find the roots of ten quadratic equations required 150 statements, it would be safe to say that the computer revolution of the past two decades would never have occured. Absolutely crucial to the value of digital computers is their ability to be programmed to execute the same statements again and again (maybe millions of times in a single computation!) on different input data or on the same variables as they change values during a computation. In this chapter we shall consider the two basic theoretical techniques for doing this repetitive type of calculation and how these are implemented in Fortran, Algol, PL/I, and Cobol.

8.1   DEFINITIONS AND EXAMPLES

The two basic techniques of repetitive calculation mentioned above are *iteration* and *recursion*. While the two have many features in common, there are comparatively few problems for which one has a choice of which to use. Iteration is

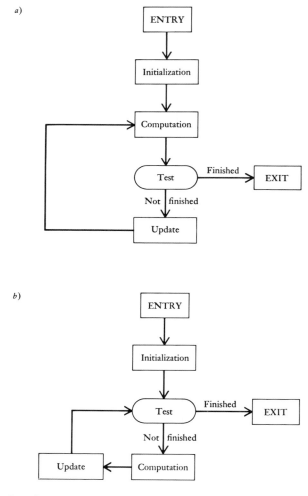

Figure 8.1   Iteration.

by far the more common of the two techniques. There are few strictly numerical applications for which recursion can be used and fewer still for which it is efficient. But recursion is becoming increasingly important in nonnumeric, symbol manipulation applications.

An iteration or *iterative calculation* normally consists of four separately identifiable sections, as shown in the flow chart of Figure 8.1*a* (see p. 308 for a discussion of Figure 8.1*b*). The functions of the four boxes are as follows:

1. *Initialization.*   a) To set the parameters or arguments of the computation to their initial values (e.g., setting "current largest number" to maximum value in search for the largest of a set of numbers (Example 5.13, p. 198), or setting the initial value in the iterative solution of an equation), and b) to set the counter or test parameter to be used in the *test box* for determining when to exit from the iteration loop.

2. *Computation.*   As its name implies, this box refers to the computation which is the basic part of the iteration.

3. *Test.*   Every iteration or *loop* must have some way of exiting from it or else the program would endlessly remain "in a loop." Tests for when to exit from a loop are basically of two types:

> a) Counter tests, in which the exit occurs after a given number of cycles, the number being determined before entry into the iteration (e.g., the counter might record the number of items in a list to be alphabetized).
>
> b) Tests involving a specific property (e.g., magnitude) of some quantity involved in the computation (see Example 8.1 below).

Sometimes when it is not certain that a condition of the type (b) will ever be satisfied, a counter is also used so that the exit will be reached one way or another.

4. *Update.*   When going from one cycle of a loop to the next it is necessary to update certain quantities involved in the calculation, such as a) the counter of the number of cycles through the loop, and b) the values of certain variables involved in the calculation. For example (see Example 8.1 below), if the computation box computes X2 as some function of X1, say

$$X2 = .5 * (X1 + A/X1)$$

the next stage of the iteration may be to compute X2 again, using as X1 the X2 computed in the previous stage. Thus an update statement of the form

$$X1 = X2$$

is required.

Updating may be thought of as *reinitializing* the loop for the next stage.

Example 8.1

A common method of computing square roots on a computer is the following iteration. Let A be the positive number whose square root is desired and let X_0 be an initial nonzero guess for the $\sqrt{A}$. Then we compute

$$X_{i+1} = 1/2 \ (X_i + A/X_i) \qquad i = 0, 1, \ldots$$

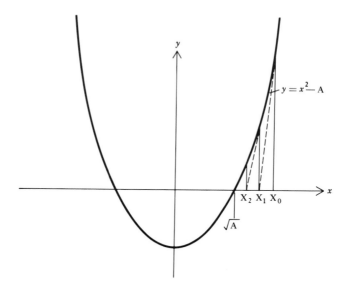

Figure 8.2   Square root iteration.

A rationale for this formula is indicated in Figure 8.2. The point X_1 is the intersection of the straight line which is tangent (i.e., just touches) to the parabola $y = x^2 - A$ at the point $X_0^2 - A$ and the x-axis. The formula above is an algebraic statement of the fact that the $i + 1$ point is the intersection of the tangent at the ith point on the curve with the x-axis. Successive tangents intersect the x-axis closer and closer to the point $x = \sqrt{A}$. This iteration is a special case of the *Newton-Raphson iteration.*

Figure 8.3 is a flow chart for a computer program to compute $\sqrt{A}$. Remarks:

1. Each of the four parts of the iteration occupies one box of the flow chart; in more complicated iterations the computation part will occupy a number of boxes.

2. EPS [mnemonic for the commonly used Greek letter ϵ (epsilon)] represents a *tolerance,* such that when two successive approximations differ by less than EPS, the latest approximation will be sufficiently accurate and the iteration will be terminated.

3. Reading in X_0 could be avoided by using A as the initial approximation.

4. Note that no subscripts are used in the iteration. From the equation above one might expect each *iterate* to be stored in an array X. But this would be wasteful of storage. Only the latest two iterates are needed for the test.

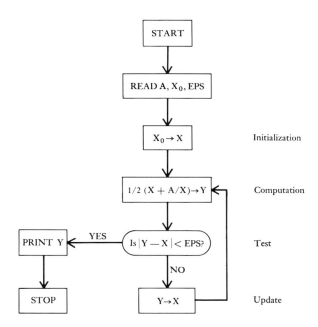

Figure 8.3   Flow chart for square root calculation.

5. Since it can be proved mathematically that this iteration always converges (i.e., successive iterates will approach arbitrarily closely to $\sqrt{A}$), the test will always be satisfied at some point. Still there is a subtlety here. No matter how many times the iteration is carried out, roundoff may prevent Y and X from ever being equal. Therefore, if EPS is chosen too small the test might never be satisfied.[†]

Example 8.2

In Examples 2.5 and 5.13 we considered the problem of finding the largest of a set of numbers. Here we draw a flow chart for a program to find and print out the largest of some number N (greater than 1) of positive numbers which we assume have been stored in an array A.

The flow chart is shown in Figure 8.4. The reader should be able to identify the four parts of the iteration (Problem 2). He should also be able to ascertain

---

[†]This does not mean the computer would stay in the loop forever; it would only stay in until the time estimate on the job card was exceeded, at which point the operating system would terminate the computation.

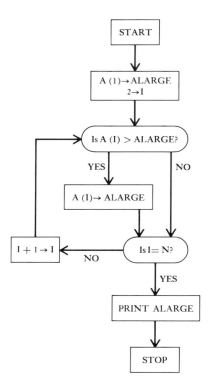

Figure 8.4 Flow chart for largest-number problem.

how the update part could have been done before the test (Problem 2). It is generally possible to interchange the test and update boxes in Figure 8.1*a*. One of the most common errors in programming iterations is to test a counter for a value which would have been the correct one if the update has been before rather than after the test (or vice versa). We note finally that it is also generally possible to do the test *before* the computation as shown in Figure 8.1*b*. This has the merit of *enabling the computation box to be entirely bypassed* if the exit test is satisfied initially. We shall return to this point in Section 8.2.

Example 8.3

Suppose, using the language of PL/I, that a sequence of K words are stored as character strings in an array WORD and suppose further that a keyword KEY is read into the computer. We wish to find if there is a word in WORD which

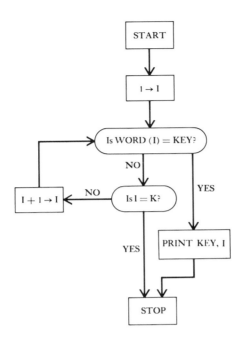

Figure 8.5   Flow chart for word-matching problem.

matches (i.e., is identical to) KEY and, if so, to print it out together with its
position in WORD and, if not, to do nothing.

A flow chart for this problem is given in Figure 8.5. This example illustrates
the case of two tests for exit from the iteration, one if the keyword is matched
and another if the entire list of words is searched without a match.

A *recursive calculation* is one in which a procedure calls itself either directly
or indirectly (e.g., when a routine calls another which in turn calls the first). But,
whereas flow charts provide an effective vehicle for introducing iteration, it is
very difficult—some would say well nigh impossible—to get the full flavor of
recursion from a flow chart representation. Recursion is a more subtle, less
palpable concept than iteration. Still, in Figure 8.6 we have attempted a flow
chart representation of recursion. At best, the reader should obtain some intuition rather than a full understanding from this flow chart and the discussion
below. Supplementing this discussion, the examples in this section and those in
Section 8.3 should be helpful. Remarks on Figure 8.6:

1. From the point of view of understanding recursion, the key box is the call-of-procedure box. The dotted line exit is meant to imply, as the examples below will indicate, that this box has the effect of initiating a call to the procedure *from within that same procedure*. The normal solid line exit is taken after this so-called *recursive call* has returned control back to this box. Consider for a moment one of the implications of this. Suppose the procedure in Figure 8.6 uses a variable X as a local variable. When the call of procedure box is invoked, this variable will have a value which must be saved because it may, for example, be needed in the final computation box. But when the procedure is *reentered—* the essence of recursion—this variable X will be used again as a local variable. How is the old value—or old values, if the procedure is reentered many times—to be saved? We shall return to this briefly at the end of Section 8.3.

2. The function of initialization in recursion is taken care of in the process of calling the procedure.

3. The two computation boxes are always present in recursion and have quite different functions. The partial computation box may be combined with the procedure call box as Example 8.4 will illustrate.

4. The test in recursion is always on the basis of the value of a counter.

5. As with iteration, the flow chart for recursion involves a loop, but in recursion the loop is closed by the *procedure calling itself*, a very different mechanism from that employed in iteration.

Example 8.4

Show how

$$n! = n(n-1)(n-2)\ldots 3\cdot 2\cdot 1 \qquad n \text{ an integer} \geqslant 1$$

can be computed iteratively and recursively.

The flow chart of Figure 8.7a illustrates the iterative approach. The four parts of the iteration are clearly delineated in this flow chart. In Figure 8.7b the corresponding flow chart for the recursive computation of $n!$ is shown. An understanding of this flow chart and its contrast to that of Figure 8.7a is basic to an understanding of recursion.

One way to approach Figure 8.7b is to consider a particular case. Let N = 3. Then, after the call of the procedure FACT with N = 3, the calculation proceeds as follows using the box numbers in Figure 8.7b.

Box	Effect	Comments
1	$N \neq 1$	
3	Call of FACT(2)	NFACT is to hold final result; at this point nothing is put into NFACT awaiting the calculation of FACT(2).

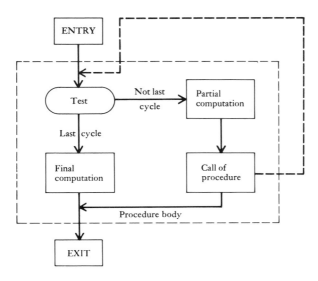

Figure 8.6   Recursion.

1	N ≠ 1	
3	Call of FACT(1)	Still, the memory location NFACT has had nothing stored in it.
1	N = 1	
2	NFACT = 1	NFACT now contains a 1 and control proceeds out of the procedure (but see discussion which follows).

When control exits from the procedure FACT(N) at the last step above, it does not proceed to the print box *because this exit is from the call of FACT in Box 3 by the procedure itself with N = 2.* Control, therefore, passes back to Box 3 with N = 2 and the result is to put 2*FACT(1) = 2·1 = 2 into NFACT. Now the procedure exits again, but still not to the print box, but rather back again to Box 3 because FACT(2) was called from there by FACT(3). This time 3*FACT(2) = 3·2 = 6 goes into NFACT and control passes to the print box. Thus, by a mechanism which we shall consider in Section 8.3, the computer must somehow *stack* and keep track of the various recursive calls of the procedure by itself, so that it knows where to pass control to when each of these recursive calls is completed.

This example illustrates the meaning of the various boxes in Figure 8.6. It also suggests the basic difference between iteration and recursion. The former is

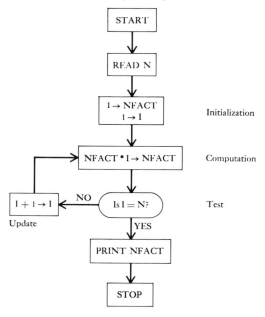

a) *Iterative flow chart for n!*

START	
READ N	
1 → NFACT 1 → I	Initialization
NFACT • I → NFACT	Computation
Is I = N?	Test
I + 1 → I (Update)	
PRINT NFACT	
STOP	

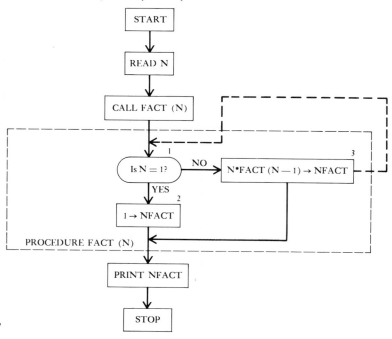

b) *Recursive flow chart for n!*

START

READ N

CALL FACT (N)

PROCEDURE FACT (N)

Is N = 1?

1 → NFACT

N•FACT (N — 1) → NFACT

PRINT NFACT

STOP

Figure 8.7

essentially a *bottom-up* procedure, starting from nothing and building up the result step by step. Thus, to compute $n!$ we start with 1 and multiply by successive integers until we have the result. By contrast, recursion is a *top-down* procedure in which the thing we wish to compute is successively broken down into its components. Thus to compute $n!$ we start by saying

$$n! = n \cdot (n-1)!$$

and then

$$(n-1)! = (n-1) \cdot (n-2)!$$

and so on until we get to $1! = 1$. For the mathematically inclined, we may state this difference in simplified form as follows: If our object is to compute some function $Q(N)$ of an integer N, then iteratively we have

$$Q(i + 1) = f(Q[i]) \qquad i = 1, 2, \ldots, N-1$$

where f is some known function. By contrast, recursively we compute

$$\begin{aligned}
Q(N) &= g(N) \cdot Q(N-1) \\
&= g(N) \cdot g(N-1) \cdot Q(N-2) \\
&\quad --- \\
&\quad --- \\
&\quad --- \\
&= g(N) \cdot g(N-1) \cdot \ldots \cdot g(1) \qquad Q(0) = 1
\end{aligned}$$

where again g is some known function. The reader should try and relate this notation to Example 8.4 (Problem 3). The following example will further clarify the notion of recursion.

Example 8.5

The most common method of evaluating a polynomial

$$p_n(x) = a_0 x^n + a_1 x^{n-1} + a_2 x^{n-2} + \ldots + a_{n-1} x + a_n$$

is by the technique variously known as *nesting, synthetic division,* or *Horner's method.* This is an iterative technique in which we proceed as follows:

$$\begin{aligned}
b_0 &= a_0 \\
b_{i+1} &= x \cdot b_i + a_{i+1} \qquad i = 0, 1, \ldots, n-1
\end{aligned}$$

from which it follows that $b_n = p_n(x)$. Alternatively we may write

$$p_n(x) = x \cdot p_{n-1}(x) + a_n$$

where

$$p_{n-1}(x) = a_0 x^{n-1} + a_1 x^{n-2} + \ldots + a_{n-2} x + a_{n-1}$$

which is a recursive statement of the problem. The reader should be able to draw flow charts for either iterative or recursive polynomial evaluation analogous to those in Figure 8.7 (Problem 4).

The reader may think from the above examples that any computation which can be defined recursively can also be defined iteratively. Practically, this is almost always true, but there are exceptions as Example 8.17 in Section 8.3 will illustrate.

We have not yet considered some of the specific problems of recursion—such as the stack referred to above—and as well we have made no attempt yet to compare the relative efficiency of doing a computation iteratively or recursively when both are possible. We shall, however, consider these questions as we proceed in this chapter to consider how iteration and recursion are implemented in P-O languages.

8.2   ITERATION

Our approach in this section will be to synthesize the iteration statements in the four languages by considering each part of the language structures for iteration and then putting them all together. In order to orient the reader, however, we shall begin by briefly discussing what the end product looks like.

The main component of the iteration structure in any P-O language is a heading statement which

1. indicates that the statement is indeed an iteration statement (e.g., through a verb such as DO), and
2. indicates how many times the iteration is normally to be carried out, typically by defining an index or *control variable* and an initial value, final value, and increment for this variable (e.g., DO INDEX = INITIAL VALUE TO FINAL VALUE BY INCREMENT). The examples of the previous section should imply the need for this.

In addition, some mechanism is needed to indicate which statements following the heading statement are included in the iteration. This may take the form of

1. a label in the heading statement as in Fortran and Cobol (e.g., DO 20 I=1, 10), which indicates the *last* statement to be included in the iteration, or

2. the use of the block structure of the language, as in Algol and PL/I, so that the block following the heading statement is the structure included in the iteration. (This is done in a slightly different way in Algol and PL/I; see below.)

With the above as introduction, we may proceed to consider the various parts of iteration structures and then put them together into a single whole.

Panel 8.1   Iteration verbs

FORTRAN	ALGOL	PL/I	COBOL
		Name of verb	
DO	do	DO	PERFORM
		Comments	
Part of DO statement	Part of **for** statement	Can be part of larger DO statement or, followed by semicolon, statement by itself	Part of previously discussed PERFORM statement

Panel 8.1 introduces the "verbs" of the iteration statements in the four languages. Three of the four languages use the verb DO. Only in PL/I can it be a statement by itself:

DO;

More usually in PL/I, and always in Fortran and Algol, the verb is part of a larger statement. Cobol uses the PERFORM statement, which we have seen previously is used for subroutine calls, to specify iterations also.

The four languages have different ways of specifying which statements are to be "done" or "performed" as the computational part of the iteration. Panel 8.2 considers these. As mentioned above, Algol and PL/I both make use of their block structure, but in somewhat different ways. In PL/I the DO itself replaces the BEGIN statement at the start of a block, so that DO; . . . END; which forms the DO-group, acts like a block itself.[†] The purpose of the restrictions on the last

---

[†] One major difference between a BEGIN block and a DO-group is that storage allocation (via DECLARE statements) is made in the former but not the latter.

statement of the range of a DO statement in Fortran will become clear later in this section.

As indicated in Panel 8.2, Fortran, Algol, and PL/I all allow further iteration statements within the basic structure following the DO statement. This *nesting* of iterations is important in performing many computations, as some of the examples later in this section will indicate. The Algol syntax, since it is based on the block structure of Algol, guarantees that if the block following one **for** statement contains another **for** statement, then the block following the second **for** statement will be wholly contained in the block following the first. In general this assures that the computational parts of two iterations *will not overlap each other.* Two sets of statements are said to *overlap* if

1. there are some statements common to both sets, and
2. all the statements of one set are not contained in the other.

Therefore, in order that two sets of statements should not overlap, they must either

1. contain no statements in common, or
2. all the statements in one set must be contained in the other.

Similarly in PL/I, the "program-elements" which make up the DO-group can include other DO statements and DO-groups but if so they must include the entire DO-group, thereby again eliminating overlap. In Fortran, to prevent such overlap we need the specific requirement that *the ranges of two DO statements cannot overlap each other.* This requirement is illustrated in Figure 8.8 in which each of the ranges is indicated by brackets.

Now we are ready to consider the most complex part of iteration statements, namely, how they accomplish counting, updating, and testing. As the reader should by now expect, Algol and PL/I have very similar mechanisms here. Fortran, Algol, and PL/I allow the iteration to be carried out for a set of indices starting with a certain value of an identifier and continuing by specified increments of that identifier until some final value is reached. This is illustrated in Panel 8.3. The structures described in this panel and the next two are all parts of the DO or **for** or PERFORM statements previously mentioned. The complete syntax is considered later in Panel 8.6. Remarks on Panel 8.3:

1. The three quantities after the = in all three languages are called, respectively, the initial value, the final value, and the increment of the variable on the left-hand side. In Fortran, all three must be positive at execution time. Since the left-hand side integer variable will often be a subscript in the range of the DO statement, the rules on the values of Fortran subscripts are sufficient motivation

Specification of computational structures in iteration

			COBOL
	ALGOL	*PL/I*	

FORTRAN

ALGOL *PL/I* *COBOL*

Name of Structure

| *Range* of the DO statement | *Block* following **for** statement | DO-*group* | Procedure specified by PERFORM statement |

Syntax of structure

| Following DO there must be an *sl*; the range is the *first* executable statement following the DO statement up to and including the executable statement with label *sl*. | The "block" following the **for** statement may be a single statement or a normal block delimited by **begin** and **end**. | The sequence of program elements (i.e., statements and blocks) including the DO statement and those following it which terminate with an END statement. | The procedure specified by the procedure name or names following PERFORM (see Panel 7.8). |

Comments and restrictions

| The statement labeled *sl* may not be any GO TO or IF, RETURN, STOP, PAUSE, or another DO.

The range of a DO statement may contain other DO statements (see text). | The block may contain other blocks within it and may include other **for** statements. | The program elements may contain other DO statements and their associated DO-groups. | The procedure called may itself call other procedures with the iteration form of the PERFORM statement; last statement of procedure may not be a GO TO. |

sl—statement label

317

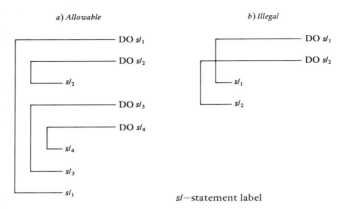

a) Allowable   b) Illegal

sl—statement label

Figure 8.8   Nesting of iterations.

for restricting the values of this variable to be positive. The required positivity of the increment, however, is a feature of the Fortran language which exists only for the convenience of the compiler writer. In Algol and PL/I, initial values, final values, and increments can be negative and, therefore, the test to see if the final value has been reached must involve the sign of the increment. (Why?)

2. In Algol and PL/I the variable on the left side, which is called the *control* variable (since it controls the number of times the block or DO-group is executed), need not be an integer. Even if the identifier is an integer the arithmetic expressions need not be. If they are not, mode conversion across the = or := sign takes place as usual. Thus, for example, in Algol, the following is syntactically correct.

   real R,S; **integer** I;
   for I := 1 **step** R**2 **until** SIN(S)*10 . . . .

3. In Fortran, neither the control variable nor any variables appearing on the right-hand side of the iteration structure may be *redefined* in the range of the DO statement. That is, none of these variables may appear on the left-hand side of assignment statements. For example,

   DO 2   I = 1,N
   — —
   — —
   — —
   I = I- 1
   — —
   2 — —

Panel 8.3   Increment parts of iteration statements

FORTRAN	ALGOL	PL/I

Syntax

$$iv_1 = \left\{\begin{matrix} iv_2 \\ int_1 \end{matrix}\right\} , \left\{\begin{matrix} iv_3 \\ int_2 \end{matrix}\right\}$$

$$\left[\left\{\begin{matrix} iv_4 \\ int_3 \end{matrix}\right\}\right]$$

$id := ae_1$ **step** ae_2
until ae_3

$id = ae_1$ BY ae_2
[TO ae_3]

or

$id = ae_1$ TO ae_3
[BY ae_2]

Semantics

The statements of the structures described in Panel 8.2 are each executed once,

with iv_1 set equal to $\left\{\begin{matrix} iv_2 \\ int_1 \end{matrix}\right\}$

and then incremented by $\left\{\begin{matrix} iv_4 \\ int_3 \end{matrix}\right\}$

or 1, if the former is omitted, as long as iv_1 does not exceed $\left\{\begin{matrix} iv_3 \\ int_2 \end{matrix}\right\}$

with id set equal to ae_1 and then incremented ("stepped") by ae_2 as long as $(id-ae_3) \times$ sign (ae_2) is not positive; if TO ae_3 is omitted in the first PL/I increment part, the iteration continues until stopped by some other statement (see Remark 5 for this panel and Panel 8.4); if BY ae_2 is omitted in the second PL/I increment part, ae_3 is assumed to be 1

Examples

I = 1, J, K	I := 1 **step** K **until** J	I = 1 BY K TO J
I = M2,N6Z	I := M2 **step** 1 **until** N6Z	I = M2 TO N6Z
	I := 1 **step** R **until** Q	I = 1 TO R BY Q

ae—arithmetic expression
int—integer
iv—integer variable

is incorrect (although some implementations allow it). One reason for this is that, if the statement I = I- 1 were executed in every pass through the range, I would remain constant at the start of each pass and the loop would never terminate. Another reason for not allowing redefinition of the loop parameter is the difficulties that allowing it would mean in compilation, since loop parameters are often handled in special hardware registers, called *index registers.* For this latter reason the other parameters in the Fortran increment structure also cannot be redefined in the range of the DO statement. In Algol, although there is no explicit restriction on redefining the control variable, it should be avoided. In PL/I the control variable may be redefined but only very rarely will this be useful. In neither Algol nor PL/I is there any restriction on redefining variables which appear on the right-hand side of the iteration structure.

4. An interesting question arises when the final value of the control variable is less than the initial value (assuming the increment is positive). Should the computation statements be executed once or not at all? In Fortran the official language specifications require that the computation be executed at least once because the test of iv_1 against $\begin{Bmatrix} iv_3 \\ int_2 \end{Bmatrix}$ only takes place *after* the range of the DO statement is executed. PL/I and Algol, on the other hand, require the test to be made *before* the DO-group or block is executed and, therefore, it is possible that the computational statements will not be executed at all. A few Fortran compilers now implement the Algol-PL/I idea. Referring back to Figure 8.1, Fortran implements Figure 8.1*a* (with the test and update boxes interchanged), while Algol and PL/I implement Figure 8.1*b*. Unquestionably the latter is the superior technique.

5. Despite the semantics in Panel 8.3, the computational statements need not necessarily be executed for each value of the identifier indicated by the increment structure. This is because one of the computational statements can be a conditional or unconditional transfer of control *out of* the range or block or DO-group, and thus may terminate the iteration before the identifier has taken on all its possible values. It should be noted that when such a transfer of control occurs, the value of the control variable is *available*, that is, it can be referred to, later in the program. However, if the iteration is terminated in a normal manner, then usually the value of the control variable is not available. This lack of availability is explicit in Fortran and Algol. The reason is (similar to that in 3. above) because an index register is often used to store the iteration parameter and it is usually inconvenient or impossible to recover the value of this parameter when the iteration terminates normally.

Example 8.6

This example illustrates when the control variable is and is not available in Fortran after exit from the iteration.

i) *Available*

        K = 7
        ‒‒
        ‒‒
        DO 6 I = 1, 10
        ‒‒
        ‒‒
        IF(I‒K) 6,8,8

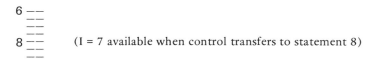

$$6 \; -- \\ -- \\ 8 \; -- \qquad (I = 7 \text{ available when control transfers to statement 8}) \\ --$$

ii) *Not available*

K = 11

followed by the same DO-loop as above, since in this case the loop terminates normally.

Incremented iteration of the type shown in Panel 8.3 is the only type possible in Fortran. But Algol and PL/I allow various other possibilities. One of these, which corresponds to the only type of iteration in Cobol, involves a termination test which depends upon the truth or falsity of a relational expression.[†] Incrementing of an identifier may or may not be involved in this case. In PL/I there need not even be an identifier involved. Panel 8.4 considers these structures.
Remarks:

1. The first example in the panel indicates how PL/I and Cobol can duplicate the Fortran structure of Panel 8.3 by using a relational expression to test when the final value has been reached.
2. Algol, PL/I, and Cobol all allow structures which could lead to non-terminating computations[††] (e.g., if the *re* after **while** in Algol remains true; Problem 7). Indeed, the structures described in Panel 8.3 also allow non-terminating computations for Algol and PL/I but not for Fortran. (Why?)
3. In Panel 8.4, as in Panel 8.3, it is clear that in PL/I we can do anything possible in any of the other languages.
4. The Algol structure and the first two PL/I structures in Panel 8.4 both have no requirement that there be any incrementing of a variable. Therefore, neither would be used without some statement in the block or DO-group which changed the value of some variable in the relational expression.
5. Cobol allows iterations to be nested by appending to the VARYING clause one or two clauses of the same form as the VARYING clause, except that VARYING *id* is replaced by

    AFTER *id*

[†]Actually a Boolean expression; see Chapter 9.
[††]Of course the operating system would terminate the computation when the time on the job card was exceeded.

Panel 8.4   Iteration terminated by a relational expression

ALGOL	PL/I	COBOL

PL/I

Syntax

i) WHILE (*re*)

or

ii) *id* = *ae* WHILE (*re*)

or

iii) *id* = *ae*$_1$ BY *ae*$_2$ WHILE (*re*)

or

iv) *id* = *ae*$_1$ BY *ae*$_2$ TO *ae*$_3$ WHILE (*re*)

or

v) *id* = *ae*$_1$ TO *ae*$_3$ [BY *ae*$_2$] WHILE (*re*)

Semantics

Continue executing the DO-group as long as the *re* is true before executing the first statement in the DO-group.
In addition, for (ii), (iii), (iv), and (v) set *id* = *ae*$_1$ at first entry and for (iii), (iv), and (v) increase it by *ae*$_2$ at each successive entry; also, for (iv) and (v) cease executing the DO-group if (*id*−*ae*$_3$) × sign (*ae*$_2$) is ever positive; in (v), if BY *ae*$_2$ is missing, increment is 1.

COBOL

VARYING *id*$_1$ FROM

$\begin{Bmatrix} id_2 \\ int_1 \end{Bmatrix}$ BY $\begin{Bmatrix} id_3 \\ int_2 \end{Bmatrix}$

UNTIL *re*

The procedure is first executed with *id*$_1$ equal to $\begin{Bmatrix} id_2 \\ int_1 \end{Bmatrix}$ and then successively with *id*$_1$ increased each time by $\begin{Bmatrix} id_3 \\ int_2 \end{Bmatrix}$ as long as the *re* is *not* true at entry into the procedure.

ALGOL

id := *ae* while *re*

Continue executing the computational statements with the *id* equal to the *ae* as long as the *re* is true before the first computational statement is executed.

I := J*J **while** L $<$ M

Examples

I = 1 BY K
WHILE (I$<$ = J)

I = J*J BY 0 WHILE
(L $<$ M)

I = 1 BY K TO J
WHILE (L $<$ = M)

VARYING I FROM 1
BY K UNTIL I IS
GREATER THAN J

VARYING I FROM 1 BY K
UNTIL I IS GREATER THAN J OR L
IS NOT LESS THAN M

ae—arithmetic expression
id—identifier
int—integer
re—relational expression

The identifiers after VARYING and AFTER normally serve, of course, as subscript names like the control variables in Fortran DO-loops. When AFTER clauses are used, the last identifier is varied first and, then, if there are two AFTER clauses, the second identifier and finally the identifier following VARYING. With two AFTER clauses, this acts like three nested DOs in Fortran. For example,

> PERFORM SORT VARYING I FROM 1 BY 2 UNTIL I IS GREATER
> THAN J AFTER I1 FROM 1 BY 3 UNTIL I1 IS GREATER
> THAN 10 AFTER I2 FROM 7 BY 2 UNTIL I2 IS GREATER
> THAN 11

is the Cobol analog of

> DO 2 I = 1,J,2
> DO 2 I1 = 1,10,3
> DO 2 I2 = 7,11,2

in Fortran. Note that if IS EQUAL TO were used instead of IS GREATER THAN in the Cobol statement, then the Fortran statements would not be equivalent to the Cobol statement because Cobol tests the end condition on *entry* into the loop, while Fortran tests on *exit* from the loop.

In addition to the structures of Panels 8.3 and 8.4, Algol and PL/I allow one further structure for controlling iterations which is shown in Panel 8.5. This is simply a list of arithmetic expressions whose values are given successively to an identifier at each entry into the block or DO-group. In fact, the structures in Panels 8.3 and 8.4 for both Algol and PL/I, with the exception of that labeled (i) in Panel 8.4 for PL/I, may also appear as elements of a list following the := or =, respectively. That is, the structures of Panels 8.3, 8.4, and 8.5 may be put together in a single iteration control. Using some examples in these panels we could write, for example, in Algol:

> I := 1 **step** K **until** J, M2 **step** 1 **until** N62, J * J **while** L < M, 1, V * W, 16,N

and in PL/I:

> I = 1 BY K TO J, M2 TO N62 BY 1, J * J BY 0 WHILE (L < M), 1,
> V * W, 16, N

In both cases the computation statements are executed first under control of the first element of the list and then successively under control of the other elements of the list.

Panel 8.5   Iteration lists

<table>
<tr><td>ALGOL</td><td>PL/I</td></tr>
</table>

Syntax

ALGOL:

id := *list*

where

list ::= ae | ae, list

PL/I:

id = *list*

where

list ::= ae | ae, list

Semantics

The block or DO-group is executed once with the *id* set equal to the *ae* for each *ae* in the list.

Examples

I :=1,V*W, 16,N

I = 1,V*W,16,N

ae—arithmetic expression
id—identifier

Nothing in the previous discussion is affected by nested iterations in Fortran, Algol, or PL/I. When one iteration is nested within another, the parameter values in the first are not affected by the inner iteration. Of course, this implies that the control variable in an inner iteration should always be different from those in any outer iterations of which it is a part.

We are now ready to put all the elements of this section together to describe the complete syntax of iteration in the four languages. This syntax is given in Panel 8.6 and is almost self-explanatory in light of the previous discussion. In Fortran, the same statement label can terminate one or more nested DO-loops as well as the outer one. The reader should be warned, however, that Fortran has rules restricting when transfer statements in nested DO-loops may refer to the statement label at the end of the range†. In PL/I the END terminating the DO-group may be followed by a statement label, in which case this END terminates the DO-group whose DO has a matching label *and* all DO-groups contained in this one (cf. multiple closure of blocks on p. 212.)

Fortran does not allow the last statement of the range to be one of those listed in Panel 8.2, in order to avoid confusion between transferring control back to the beginning of the iteration and transferring out to some other statement. It is not uncommon, however, for a programmer to wish the last statement of the

---

†Whose implementation varies from one computer to another.

Panel 8.6 Language structures for iteration

FORTRAN

DO *sl ip*

⎡ Range of
⎣ DO
statement

where the *ip* is given in Panel 8.3

With the identifier in the *ip* varied as described in Panel 8.3, the range is executed once for each value of the identifier.

ALGOL

for *ip* **do** followed by statement or block

where the *ip* is an *id* := followed by a list, separated by commas, of the forms given in Panels 8.3, 8.4, and 8.5

For each value of the identifier in the *ip*, the statement or block after **do** is executed.

PL/I

Syntax

i) DO; *or*
ii) DO WHILE (*re*); *or*
iii) DO *ip*;
in each case followed by a
DO-group

where the *ip* is an *id* = followed by a list, separated by commas, of the forms given in Panels 8.3, 8.4, and 8.5

Semantics

(i) The DO-group is executed once;
(ii) The DO-group is executed successively as long as the *re* is true;
(iii) For each value of the *ip*, the DO-group is executed.

COBOL

PERFORM statement as in Panel 7.4, followed by *ip* as given in Panel 8.4

The procedure named after PERFORM is executed once for each value of the identifier subscript name in the VARYING clause.

In each case, however, an unconditional or conditional transfer of control statement can terminate execution of the range, block, DO-group, or procedure.

Examples

DO 10 I=1,N

for I := 1 **step** 1
until N **do**
for I := N **while**
M < K **do**

DO I=1 BY
1 TO N;
DO I = N WHILE
(M < K);

PERFORM L1 THRU
L2 VARYING I
FROM 1 BY 1
UNTIL I IS
GREATER THAN N

ae—arithmetic expression
id—identifier
ip—increment part
re—relational expression
sl—statement label

computational part of an iteration to be an IF statement, which would cause continuation of the iteration in one case, but transfer out to some other part of the program if another condition is satisfied. The following example illustrates this situation.

Example 8.7

We consider a problem analagous to that of Example 8.3. Let NUMBER be a list of integers and let KEYNUM be a key number which we wish to match against the list to see if KEYNUM is in the list. If it is, we print its position in the list and KEYNUM. If not, we do nothing.

Here is an almost complete Fortran program for this problem:

```
        DIMENSION NUMBER (100)
        READ, K, (NUMBER(J), J = 1,K), KEYNUM
C       THIS STATEMENT INTRODUCES ANOTHER USE OF
C       FREE FORMAT INPUT—IF THE SIZE OF NUMBER IS
C       KNOWN ONLY TO BE NO GREATER THAN 100, THE ACTUAL
C       SIZE K IS READ FIRST AND THEN ** NUMBER ** IS READ
C       BY MEANS OF ** AN IMPLIED DO-LOOP ** WHICH
C       APPLIES THE BASIC SYNTAX OF DO STATEMENTS TO
C       READ IN ARRAYS
        DO 2 I = 1,K
        IF (KEYNUM-NUMBER(I))2,4,2
    2 ———
        GO TO 6
    4 PRINT, I, KEYNUM
    6 STOP
        END
```

But what should the statement labeled 2 be, since all we wish to do at this point is go on to the next value of I in the DO statement? (Note that the DO statement itself *cannot* be labeled 2.) One possibility would be to insert as statement 2 any *null* statement, that is, a statement which effectively produces no change in the state of the computer. Such a statement might be

```
    A = A  (Fortran)
    A := A;  (Algol)
    A = A;  (PL/I)
    COMPUTE A = A  (Cobol)
```

but, since these actually cause machine-language code to be compiled and operations to take place [A would be sent from its memory location to the arithmetic unit and then stored back in L(A)!], they are inefficient ways to indicate the null operation. The reader can undoubtedly devise other ways of expressing the null operation in the four languages (Problem 8). To avoid using a null statement such as above, Fortran includes a statement called a continue statement which consists of a single word CONTINUE and whose effect is null, that is, the program just continues with the next statement to be executed. Thus, to complete the program at the beginning of the example, statement 2 would become

```
2 CONTINUE
```

Example 8.8

The largest-number problem of Example 8.2 provides another good illustration of the usefulness of the CONTINUE statement. Here is a program to implement the flow chart of Figure 8.4:

```
DIMENSION A(100)
READ, N, (A(I),I = 1,N)
ALARGE = A(1)
DO 2 I = 2,N
IF(A(I).LE.ALARGE) GO TO 2
ALARGE = A(I)
2 CONTINUE
PRINT, ALARGE
STOP
END
```

In this example, the continue statement provides a labeled statement to be jumped to when part of the range is to be skipped.

From the above it should be clear that, although syntactically correct, we would almost never expect to see a continue statement without a label (Problem 8).†

Cobol, as indicated in Panel 8.2, has a restriction similar to that in Fortran in that the last statement of a procedure cannot contain a GO TO statement.

---

†Some Fortran implementations require a label on all continue statements.

"Contain" is the key word in the previous sentence, since IF statements often contain GO TO statements within them. The Cobol analog of the CONTINUE statement is the EXIT statement, which consists of the single word EXIT and is used just like the Fortran CONTINUE statement.

Algol and PL/I have no restrictions on the last statements in iterative computations and, therefore, no need for analogs of the CONTINUE or EXIT statements, because the **end** in Algol or END in PL/I always terminates a block and can be labeled, thereby avoiding the reference problems of Fortran and Cobol. However, it is often convenient in other contexts than iterations to have a null statement whose only purpose is to place a label to be referred to from somewhere else. The CONTINUE statement can be used for this in Fortran, but not the EXIT statement in Cobol, which can be used only at the end of a procedure and in this sense is more like the RETURN statement in Fortran. Algol and PL/I both define null statements which have an empty statement part followed by a semicolon and are normally preceded by a label or labels. Thus in Algol one could replace

        L1: A := B;

by

        L1:   ;
           A := B;

This might be convenient if there was a reasonable chance that in a later version of the program a statement would need to be inserted before the assignment statement.

Since all transfers in Cobol are to labels, which may be thought of as procedure names, it is not possible to transfer into the middle of an iteration. But in Fortran, Algol, and PL/I we must consider what might happen if control was transferred into the range of a DO statement, the block following a **for** statement, or a DO-group, respectively. In Algol this is implicitly forbidden because the language specifications state that any such transfer is undefined. In PL/I it is also forbidden except when the DO statement is that given under (i) in Panel 8.6, for in this case no iteration is defined. If the reader will consider a moment, he will surely realize that such transfers into an iteration are forbidden because of the obvious difficulties that might occur with the iteration parameters. In Fortran, too, transferring into the range of a DO is forbidden except in one special case when Fortran allows a DO to have an *extended range* including statements outside the normal range to which control can be transferred by a

GO TO or IF from within the range, and which ends with a GO TO or IF which can transfer control back into the normal range. For the details the reader is referred to the American Standard Fortran reference at the end of Chapter 2.

We conclude this section with some examples which illustrate the use of iteration statements.

Example 8.9

Show how iteration statements could be used in the programs of Example 7.5 (p. 286).

For the Fortran program we would replace the

    J = 1

statement by

    DO 4 J = 1,8

and then the statements

    4 IF(J–8) 10,12,10
    10 J = J + 1
       GO TO 14

would be replaced by

    4 CONTINUE

The statement label 14 could then be removed.

In the Algol program the

    J := 1;

statement would be replaced by

    for J := 1 **step** 1 **until** 8 **do begin**

and then the statement labeled L2 would be replaced by

    L2: **end;**

Finally, the label L1 could be removed.

Example 8.10

Write Fortran, Algol, and PL/I programs using the iteration structures of this chapter for the square root calculation of Example 8.1 and Figure 8.3.

Fortran

```
       1 READ,A,X0,EPS
C        NEXT STATEMENT IS ECHO CHECK
         PRINT,A,X0,EPS
         X = X0
         DO 2 I = 1,100
         Y = .5 * (X + A/X)
         IF(ABS(Y-X).LT.EPS) GO TO 4
       2 X = Y
       4 PRINT, Y
         GO TO 1
         END
```

Remarks:

1. The DO statement is really less convenient for the implementation of this iteration than use of an IF statement.

2. The 100 in the DO statement is much larger than the expected number of iterations before the IF statement will transfer control out of the loop.

3. Note that the program ends by returning to the beginning to read more data.

Algol

```
    begin
        real A,X0,EPS,Y,X; integer I;
    L1: READ, A,X0,EPS; PRINT, A,X0,EPS;
        X := X0; Y := 100.;
        for I := 1 while ABS (Y-X) ≥ EPS do
            begin
                Y := X; X := .5 * (X + A/X);
            end;
        PRINT, X; go to L1;
    end
```

Remarks:

1. Because the semantics of the **for** statement causes the relational expression to be tested before entry into the iteration, the arrangement of the computation is

a little different from the Fortran program in that Y is the saved value from the previous iteration and X is the new value.

2. The I := 1 following the **for** is there to satisfy the syntax only; it has no effect on the computation.

3. Y = 100. is an arbitrarily chosen starting value for Y. In this and the PL/I program below we have implicitly assumed that X is small so that ABS (Y-X) will be large the first time through.

PL/I

```
SQRT: PROCEDURE;
    DECLARE (A,X0,EPS,Y,X) FLOAT, I FIXED;
L1: GET LIST (A,X0,EPS) COPY;
    X = X0; Y = 100.;
    DO WHILE (ABS(Y- X) > = EPS);
        Y = X; X = .5 * (X + A/X);
END;
PUT LIST (X); GO TO L1;
END;
```

Remark: The copy option on the GET statement causes an echo check and is simpler than PUT LIST (A,X0,EPS).

Example 8.11

Write Fortran, Algol, and PL/I programs for the iterative calculation of $n!$ as in Example 8.4.

Fortran

```
1 READ, N
  IF (N) 1,1,3
3 NFACT = 1
  DO 2 I = 1,N
2 NFACT = NFACT * I
  PRINT, N, NFACT
  GO TO 1
  END
```

Remarks:

1. The IF statement assures that the calculation will only be performed for positive N.

2. The statement labeled 2 is redundant when I = 1 but we cannot restate the DO statement as

$$DO\ 2\ I = 2,N \qquad (Why?)$$

3. In order to avoid the error message which would occur when there were no more values of N to be read by READ, N, many implementations of Fortran provide a statement such as (cf. p. 218)

    IF (EOF) GO TO *sl*   (EOF—End-of-file)

which would be placed after READ,N and which directs control to the statement (usually STOP) labeled *sl,* if there are no more data, and continues in sequence if there are more data. In this example STOP would be placed after GO TO 1.

Algol

```
begin
   integer N,I,NFACT;
L1: READ, N;
   if N ≤ 0 then go to L1 else
      begin
         NFACT := 1;
         for I := 1 step 1 until N do NFACT * 1;
         PRINT, N, NFACT; go to L1;
      end
end
```

PL/I

```
FACT: PROCEDURE;
   DECLARE (N,I,NFACT) FIXED;
   L1: GET LIST (N);
   IF N <= 0 THEN GO TO L1; ELSE
      BEGIN;
      NFACT = 1;
           DO I = 1 TO N;
           NFACT = NFACT*I;
           END;
         PUT LIST (N,NFACT);
            END;
   END;
```

Example 8.12

Write Fortran, Algol, and PL/I programs for the polynomial evaluation of Example 8.5.

Fortran

```
      DIMENSION A(50), B(50)
      READ, N
      M = N + 1
      READ, (A(I), I = 1,M)
      PRINT,N, (A(I), I = 1,M)
   10 READ, X
      PRINT, X
      B(1) = A(1)
      DO 20 I = 2,M
   20 B(I) = X * B(I-1) + A(I)
      PRINT, B(M)
      GO TO 10
      END
```

Remarks:

1. Since Fortran does not allow zero subscripts, the coefficients of Example 8.5 were renumbered from 1 to N + 1.

2. This calculation is ended by trying to read another value of X on the assumption that it is more reasonable to assume the same coefficients are going to be used for a number of values of X than to assume a new set of coefficients for each value of X. (See also Remark 3 after the Fortran program in Example 8.11.)

Algol

```
      begin
      real array A[0:50], B[0:50]; real X; integer N,I;
      READ, N; PRINT, N;
      for I := 0 step 1 until N do
         begin READ, A[I]; PRINT, A[I]; end;
      L1: READ, X; PRINT, X;
      B[0] := A[0];
      for I := 1 step 1 until N do
         B[I] := X * B[I-1] + A[I];
      PRINT, B[N];
      go to L1;
      end
```

PL/I

```
POLY: PROCEDURE;
    DECLARE (A(0 : 50),B(0 : 50),X) FLOAT,(N,I) FIXED;
    GET LIST (N) COPY;
        DO I = 0 TO N;
        GET LIST (A(I)) COPY;
        END;
L1: GET LIST (X)COPY;
    B(0) = A(0);
        DO I = 1 TO N;
        B(I) = X * B (I- 1) + A(I);
        END;
    PUT LIST (B(N));
    GO TO L1;
    END;
```

Example 8.13

Example 8.2 is a trivial example of searching through a set of data for a datum with a particular property. A more practical problem, which arises often in business data processing problems, is the need to order or *sort* a set of data according to some particular criterion such as size or alphabetical order. Let us consider the problem of sorting N numbers into decreasing order. One approach to this problem would clearly be to use the algorithm of Example 8.2 to first find the largest number, then somehow eliminate it from the list, then find the largest number remaining, eliminate it, etc. We leave this approach to Problem 10 and consider here a more efficient (but by no means the best!) means of solving this problem.

The technique we consider here is called the *method of interchanges*. We proceed as follows:

1. At the Mth stage of the process the head of the list contains the M- 1 largest elements in decreasing order.
2. The remaining N- (M- 1) elements are searched by successively comparing the Mth element with each other element of the list. Anytime an element larger than the Mth is found, this element and the Mth are interchanged. The result after N-M comparisons is to have the next largest element in the Mth position. (Why?)
3. After N- 1 stages the list will be in order of decreasing magnitude. (Why?)

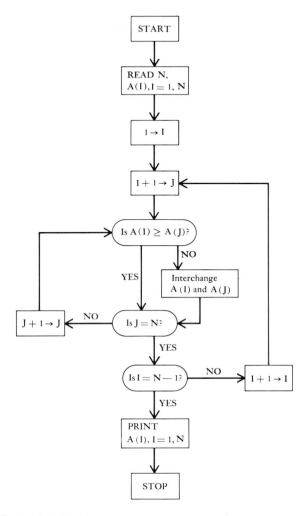

Figure 8.9   Sorting by interchanges.

Figure 8.9 is a flow chart for this technique. The following are programs in the four languages to implement this flow chart:

Fortran

```
     DIMENSION A(1000)
20 READ, N, (A(I),I = 1,N)
```

```
      K = N-1
      DO 10 I = 1,K
      KK = I + 1
      DO 10 J = KK,N
      IF(A(I).GE.A(J)) GO TO 10
      TEMP = A(I)
      A(I) = A(J)
      A(J) = TEMP
   10 CONTINUE
      PRINT, (A(I),I = 1,N)
      GO TO 20
      END
```

Remarks:

1. Note the use of TEMP. Why is it needed?

2. This is an example of two nested DO loops, both ending with the same CONTINUE statement.

Algol

```
begin
real array A[1:1000] ; real TEMP; integer I,J,N;
L2: READ, N; PRINT,N;
   for I := 1 step 1 until N do
       begin READ, A[I]; PRINT, A[I]; end;
   for I := 1 step 1 until N - 1 do
       begin
           for J := I + 1 step 1 until N do
           begin
             if A [I] ⩾ A[J] then go to L1
             else
                 begin
                     TEMP := A[I]; A[I] := A[J]; A[J] := TEMP;
                 end;
           L1: end
       end
   for I := 1 step 1 until N do PRINT, A[I];
   go to L2;
end
```

Remarks:

1. Note that in Algol two nested loops never end on the same **end**. Thus the L1 label must be on the **end** which completes the block which starts with the **if** statement.

2. Note also that, since Algol allows expressions in **for** statements, no analogs of the K = N-1 and KK = I + 1 statements in the Fortran program are needed.

PL/I

```
SORT: PROCEDURE;
    DECLARE (A(1000), TEMP) FLOAT, (I,N) FIXED;
L2: GET LIST (N) COPY;
    DO I = 1 TO N;
    GET LIST (A(I)) COPY;
    END;
L3: DO I = 1 TO N – 1;
    DO J = I + 1 TO N;
    IF A(I) > = A(J) THEN GO TO L4; ELSE
    DO;
    TEMP = A(I); A(I) = A(J); A(J) = TEMP;
    END;
    L4: END;
L2; END L3;
    DO I = 1 TO N;
    PUT LIST (A(I));
    END;
END;
```

Cobol

```
IDENTIFICATION DIVISION.
PROGRAM–ID.INTERSORT.
AUTHOR. A RALSTON.
DATE WRITTEN. 1 DECEMBER 1968.

ENVIRONMENT DIVISION.
CONFIGURATION SECTION.
SOURCE COMPUTER. IBM-360 H40.
OBJECT COMPUTER. IBM-360 H40.
```

```
INPUT-OUTPUT SECTION.
FILE-CONTROL.
     SELECT OLD-DATA ASSIGN TO 'SYS005' UNIT RECORD 2540R.
     SELECT SORTED-DATA ASSIGN TO 'SYS006' UNIT RECORD 1403.
DATA DIVISION.
FILE SECTION.
FD OLD-DATA
     RECORDING MODE IS F
     LABEL RECORDS ARE OMITTED
     DATA RECORD IS NUMBER-LIST.
01 NUMBER-LIST.
     02 NUMBERX PICTURE 9(10).
FD SORTED-DATA
     RECORDING MODE IS F
     LABEL RECORDS ARE OMITTED
     DATA RECORD IS PRINTREC.
01 PRINTREC.
     02 SORTED-ITEM PICTURE 9(10).
WORKING STORAGE SECTION.
     77 N PICTURE 9(10) VALUE IS 0.
     77 I PICTURE 9(10) VALUE IS 0.
     77 J PICTURE 9(10) VALUE IS 0.
     77 TEMP PICTURE 9(10) VALUE IS 0.
01 SORTLIST.
     02 A OCCURS 1000 TIMES PICTURE 9(10).


PROCEDURE DIVISION.
BEGIN.
     OPEN INPUT OLD-DATA OUTPUT SORTED-DATA.
     READ OLD-DATA AT END GO TO INVALID.
     MOVE NUMBERX TO N.
     NOTE N IS NUMBER OF RECORDS WHICH HAVE TO BE
     SORTED.
GET-NEXT.
     PERFORM READLIST VARYING I FROM 1 BY 1 UNTIL I
     GREATER THAN N
     GO TO SORTX.
INVALID.
     DISPLAY 'INPUT FILE CONTAINS NO RECORDS'.
     STOP RUN.
```

```
READLIST.
    READ OLD-DATA AT END GO TO SORTX.
    MOVE NUMBERX TO A (I).
SORTX.
    PERFORM PRE-ORDER VARYING I FROM 1 BY 1 UNTIL I
    EQUAL TO N.
    GO TO WRITEOUT.
PRE-ORDER.
    PERFORM ORDER THRU ORDER-EXIT VARYING J FROM 1
    BY 1 UNTIL J GREATER THAN N.
ORDER. IF A (I) GREATER A (J) GO TO ORDER-EXIT.
    MOVE A (I) TO TEMP. MOVE A (J) TO A (I). MOVE TEMP TO
    A (J)
ORDER-EXIT. EXIT.
WRITEOUT.
    MOVE N TO SORTED-ITEM.
    WRITE PRINTREC.
    PERFORM WRITELIST VARYING I FROM 1 BY 1 UNTIL I
    GREATER THAN N
    CLOSE SORTED-DATA, OLD-DATA. STOP RUN.
WRITELIST.
    MOVE A (I) TO SORTED-ITEM
    WRITE PRINTREC.
```

Remarks:

1. This program assumes, for simplicity, that the data to be sorted are initially on cards and then are printed, although normally magnetic tape would be used for input and output in sorting. The program assumes that the first item of data is the number of items to be sorted.

2. The reader unfamiliar with Cobol should ignore the items in the FILE SECTION just after OLD-DATA and SORTED-DATA.

3. The PICTURE 9(10) at various places in the program indicates that the data item in question is numeric (9) and that it is a 10-digit number.

8.3 RECURSION

While our description of the language structures for iteration required a considerable amount of discursive presentation, recursion requires virtually no discussion whatsoever. Of the four languages, only Algol and PL/I allow recursion, and both do so in precisely the same way; namely, by allowing procedures to call themselves or, indirectly, by allowing one procedure to call another which calls the first. In both languages any procedure can contain a statement in which the procedure itself is invoked. If the recursive procedure is a function procedure, a call to the procedure will appear in an arithmetic expression within the procedure. For non-function procedures the invocation will be by naming the procedure with arguments in a statement by itself in Algol, or in a CALL statement in PL/I. These will be illustrated in the examples below. Algol requires no other indication of recursion. PL/I requires that the procedure statement which heads the recursive procedure have the attribute RECURSIVE as will be illustrated below. This attribute provides information to the compiler about the procedure, which Algol compilers only discover for themselves when the statement invoking the procedure recursively is encountered.

Example 8.14

Write recursive programs in Algol and PL/I for the computation of $n!$.

Algol

```
begin
integer N,NFACT;
real procedure FACT(N);
integer N;
if N- 1 ≤ 0 then FACT := 1;
else
FACT := N * FACT(N- 1);
L1: READ, N;
if N < 0 then go to L1
else
NFACT := FACT(N);
PRINT, N,NFACT;
go to L1;
end
```

Remark: Note that the procedure body is a single statement, not a block.

PL/I

```
FACTR: PROCEDURE;
    DECLARE (N, NFACT) FIXED;
    FACT: PROCEDURE(N) RECURSIVE;
```

```
                DECLARE (N,NF) FIXED;
                IF N-1 < = 0 THEN NF = 1;
                ELSE
                    NF = N * FACT (N-1);
        RETURN (NF);
        END FACT;
        L1: GET LIST (N);
            IF N < 0 THEN GO TO L1;
            ELSE
                NFACT = FACT(N);
            PUT LIST (N,NFACT);
            GO TO L1;
            END;
```

Remarks: These programs also compute 0! = 1 which is the usual mathematical definition (Problem 11). Note that execution of each program starts at label L1; the procedure FACT is *defined* above the label and then *used* (i.e., called) in the statements following the label.

Example 8.15

Write recursive Algol and PL/I programs to evaluate the polynomial $p_n(x)$ of Example 8.5.

Algol

```
begin
real XVAL,VAL; real array A[0:100]; integer I,N;
    real procedure POLY (A,X,N);
    value N;
    integer N; real array A; real X;
    if N = 0 then POLY := A[0]
    else
    POLY := X * POLY(A,X,N-1) + A[N];
READ,N,XVAL;
PRINT, N,XVAL;
for I := 0 step 1 until N do
    begin READ, A[I]; PRINT, A[I]; end;
VAL := POLY(A,XVAL,N);
PRINT, VAL;
end
```

Remarks:

1. The array A is declared in the main block with constant bounds since variable subscripts can only include variables in a block *global* to the block in which they appear.

2. The arguments in the procedure could all have been omitted and just transferred from the main block as global variables. As another alternative they could have been given different names in the procedure.

3. When POLY is called recursively the array used always has N+1 elements but the third argument changes. This causes no problems because nothing in POLY itself assumes that A contains one more element than the third argument.

4. POLY could also be written as a recursive non-function procedure (Problem 14).

PL/I

```
POLYR: PROCEDURE;
    DECLARE (X,VAL,A(0 : 100)) FLOAT,(I,N) FIXED;
    POLY: PROCEDURE (A,X,N) RECURSIVE;
    DECLARE (X,VAL, A(0 : N)) FLOAT, N FIXED;
    IF N = 0 THEN VAL = A (0);
        ELSE
        VAL = X * POLY(A,X,N- 1) + A(N);
    RETURN (VAL);
    END;
GET LIST (N,X) COPY;
    DO I = 0 TO N;
    GET LIST (A(I)) COPY;
    END;
VAL = POLY (A,X,N);
PUT LIST (VAL);
END;
```

Remarks: Note the two ways in which VAL is used. On the one hand it is the value returned by the procedure. On the other, it is the left-hand side of an assignment statement. Therefore, the statement

VAL = POLY(A,X,N);

returns the value of the *dummy* variable VAL to the main procedure, which then sets the identifier VAL equal to this value.

Example 8.16

Pascal's triangle is well known to anyone who has learned the binomial theorem. It may be written as follows:

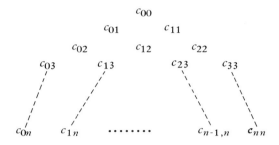

where the binomial coefficient c_{jk} is defined as

$$c_{jk} = k!/(j!(k-j)!) \qquad k \geqslant j$$

Using the definition above it is easy to show that

$$c_{jk} = c_{j-1, k-1} + c_{j, k-1} \qquad k \geqslant 1, j \neq 0, k$$

Thus, for example, with $n = 3$ the triangle is

```
            1
         1     1
      1     2     1
   1     3     3     1
```

The following is an Algol program to generate Pascal's triangle for a given value of n:

```
begin
integer array A[0 : 50,0 : 50] ; integer I,J,NN;
    procedure PASCAL (TRIANGLE,N);
    integer N; integer array TRIANGLE;
    begin
    integer I;
    if N = 0 then TRIANGLE [0,0] := 1
    else
        begin
        PASCAL (TRIANGLE, N- 1);
```

```
        TRIANGLE[N,0] := TRIANGLE[N,N] := 1;
        for I := 1 step 1 until N-1 do
            TRIANGLE [N,I] := TRIANGLE[N-1,I-1] + TRIANGLE [N-1,I] ;
        end
    end;
READ,NN;
PRINT, NN;
PASCAL(A,NN);
for I := 0 step 1 until NN do
for J: = 0 step 1 until I do
    PRINT, A[I,J] ;
end
```

All three foregoing examples of recursion have one important thing in common. The use of recursion in each case is much less efficient than the use of iteration, which we have seen is possible in the first two examples and is equally possible in the third (Problem 15). The major reason for the inefficiency of recursion in these cases is that it involves essentially the same amount of computation as iteration, and also requires a substantial extra amount of "bookkeeping" to keep track of where in the recursion one is. There is, in fact, for almost all scientific and business problems, no good reason to use recursion instead of iteration when both are feasible. For these reasons valid objections can be raised to even including the facility for recursion in languages such as Algol and PL/I. However, recursion can be a valuable tool, and for some strictly computational problems it is more efficient than iteration. To illustrate this we shall consider the following classical example.

Example 8.17

Ackerman's function is defined as

   i) A $(0,n) = n + 1$
   ii) $A(m,0) = A(m-1,1)$
   iii) $A(m,n) = A(m-1,A[m,n-1])$

where m and n are nonnegative integers. Thus, to compute $A(m,n)$ for any given pair of nonzero integers, m and n, we must first apply (iii). Since the second argument of the right-hand side of (iii) involves another evaluation of Ackerman's function, the reader may be able to see that normally a great many terms appear before the value of $A(m,n)$ is found. For example, with $m = n = 2$ we compute $A(2,2)$ as follows (the notations at the right refer to which of the three equations above has been used):

$$A(2,2) = A(1,A(2,1)) \tag{iii}$$
$$A(2,1) = A(1,A(2,0)) \tag{iii}$$
$$= A(1,A(1,1)) \tag{ii}$$
$$A(1,1) = A(0,A(1,0)) \tag{iii}$$
$$= A(0,A(0,1)) \tag{ii}$$
$$= A(0,2) \tag{i}$$
$$= 3 \tag{i}$$
$$A(2,1) = A(1,3)$$
$$= A(0,A(1,2)) \tag{iii}$$
$$A(1,2) = A(0,A(1,1)) \tag{iii}$$
$$= A(0,3)$$
$$= 4 \tag{i}$$
$$A(2,1) = A(0,4)$$
$$= 5 \tag{i}$$
$$A(2,2) = A(1,5)$$
$$= A(0,A(1,4)) \tag{iii}$$
$$A(1,4) = A(0,A(1,3)) \tag{iii}$$
$$A(1,3) = A(0,A(1,2)) \tag{iii}$$
$$= A(0,4)$$
$$= 5 \tag{i}$$
$$A(1,4) = A(0,5)$$
$$= 6 \tag{i}$$
$$A(2,2) = A(0,6)$$
$$= 7 \tag{i}$$

From this example the reader will probably realize the vast amount of computation required to compute $A(m,n)$ for sizable m and n. In fact, it can be shown using analytic techniques that

$$A(0,N) = N + 1$$
$$A(1,N) = N + 2$$
$$A(2,N) = 2N + 3$$
$$A(3,N) = 2^{N+3} - 3$$
$$A(4,N) = 2^{2^{2^{.^{.^{.^2}}}}} \overbrace{}^{N+2} - 3$$

so that even for $m=4$ the values rapidly become astronomical as n increases (Problem 16). From the definition of $A(m,n)$ it should be clear that it is made to order for recursive calculation. Here are Algol and PL/I programs to calculate $A(m,n)$.

Algol

```
begin
integer MM,NN,K;
    integer procedure ACKER (M,N);
    value M,N;
    integer M,N;
    begin
    if M = 0 then ACKER := N + 1
    else
        if N = 0 then ACKER := ACKER (M-1,1)
        else
        ACKER := ACKER (M-1, ACKER(M, N-1));
    end
READ, MM,NN;
PRINT, MM,NN;
K := ACKER(MM,NN);
PRINT, K;
end
```

Remark: MM and NN are used in the main block and M and N in the procedure purely for readability. M and N could have been used in both places.

PL/I

```
ACKERR: PROCEDURE OPTIONS (MAIN);
    DECLARE (MM,NN,K) FIXED;
        ACKER: PROCEDURE (M,N) RECURSIVE;
            DECLARE (A,M,N) FIXED;
            IF M = 0 THEN A = N + 1;
            ELSE
                IF N = 0 THEN A = ACKER (M-1,1);
            ELSE
                A = ACKER (M-1,ACKER(M,N-1));
            RETURN(A);
            END;
    GET LIST (MM,NN) COPY;
    K = ACKER(MM,NN);
    PUT LIST (K);
    END;
```

Remark: The OPTIONS (MAIN), included here for the first time in the PROCEDURE statement, indicates to the operating system (see Chapter 11) that this procedure is the first one to be executed. OPTIONS is part of PL/I itself, while MAIN is an installation-defined parameter.

The simplicity of the above Algol and PL/I programs illustrates powerfully the usefulness of recursion in this example. To emphasize this point further, we present now a Fortran program to compute Ackerman's function[†]:

Fortran

```
            DIMENSION STACK(200)
C           THE ARRAY STACK CONTAINS VALUES OF THE
C           FIRST ARGUMENT FOR WHICH FUNCTION VALUES
C           NEED TO BE CALCULATED
            INTEGER STACK,ACKER
       100 READ,M,N
            PRINT,M,N
C           INDEX IS A POINTER TO A LOCATION IN THE ARRAY STACK
C           WHEN INDEX = 0 AFTER A VALUE
C           HAS BEEN GIVEN TO ACK, THEN CALCULATION IS
C           COMPLETE
            INDEX = 0
C           CASE M = 0
         8 IF(M.NE.0) GO TO 2
C           ACKER WILL CONTAIN VALUE OF ACKERMANS
C           FUNCTION FOR VARIOUS ARGUMENTS, ITS FINAL
C           VALUE WILL BE ACKER(M,N)
            ACKER = N + 1
            IF(INDEX.NE.0) GO TO 4
            PRINT,ACKER
            GO TO 100
C           CASE N = 0
         2 IF(N.NE.0) GO TO 6
            M = M- 1
            N = 1
            GO TO 8
C           CASE M AND N BOTH NONZERO
C           VALUE OF M STORED IN STACK. THEN GO BACK
C           TO COMPUTE ACKER(M,N- 1)
         6 INDEX = INDEX + 1
            STACK (INDEX) = M- 1
            N = N- 1
            GO TO 8
```

[†]This program is due to Morris (1969).

```
C        AFTER ACKER HAS BEEN GIVEN A VALUE. SET N
C        EQUAL TO THIS VALUE AND M EQUAL TO LAST
C        ENTRY IN STACK AND DELETE THIS ENTRY.
C        THIS IS IN ACCORDANCE WITH DEFINITION
C        A(M,N) = A(M-1,A(M,N-1)) SINCE LAST ENTRY
C        IN STACK WILL BE THE M-1 TO BE USED
C        WITH ACKER = A(M,N-1)
      4 M = STACK(INDEX)
        N = ACKER
        INDEX = INDEX-1
        GO TO 8
        END
```

Not only is this program longer than the Algol and PL/I programs but it is logically more complicated. The reader will find that understanding this program is not easy. One important thing the reader should note is that this program is a direct implementation of the recursive function A(M,N). That is, we do not compute Ackerman's function in Fortran by replacing the recursive definition with an iterative one.[†]

The Fortran program in the example above implements explicitly the data structure known as a push-down list, which was introduced in Section 5.3.2. In the Fortran program the array STACK simulates such a list. Each time an (M,N) pair is found for which M and N are both nonzero, the pointer INDEX to the next position in the array STACK is increased, and then the value of M is added to STACK. Whenever a zero value of M is reached and a value of ACKER is computed, the next value of M is taken from the stack and that entry is, in effect, deleted by reducing INDEX by 1 (i.e., the list is popped up). A disadvantage of this procedure, besides the necessity of the explicit implementation of the push-down list as part of the program, is the need to specify in the dimension statement the maximum length of the list. The reader should find it instructive to work through this Fortran program with M = N = 2 and compare the ordering of the calculation with that on p. 347.

By contrast, the Algol and PL/I programs do not explicitly implement the

---

[†]In general it is true that a doubly recursive function such as Ackerman's (i.e., loosely speaking, the right-hand side of the definition for A(m,n) contains the function itself twice) cannot be expressed in any practical computational fashion in iterative terms. However, in the particular case of Ackerman's function a fairly simple iterative technique does exist and is given in Rice (1965).

push-down list, and, moreover, the length of this list is restricted only by the available storage in the computer memory and not by any dimensioning information.[†]

At the start of execution of the Algol or PL/I program, the computer automatically sets up push-down lists[††] for M and N associated with the block in which the recursive procedure is called because it has recognized that ACKER is a recursive procedure. Then, each time ACKER is called recursively, the current values of M and N together with other control information are inserted at the top of the push-down list. Every time the **end** (or END) statement in ACKER is reached, the list is popped up by removing the top elements. This type of operation is possible in both Algol and PL/I because both assign storage dynamically and, therefore, have knowledge of the available memory at any time and so can allocate it efficiently and effectively.

BIBLIOGRAPHIC NOTES

As the first paragraph of this chapter states, iteration is a crucially important technique in the effective use of digital computers. It is, therefore, discussed in one form or another in any book on programming, including all those in the bibliographies of previous chapters. Recursion, on the other hand, is neither so widely used nor so well understood as iteration. Even in books on languages like Algol and PL/I it may not be mentioned at all or, if it is, only cursorily. Recursion is more important in computer languages other than P-O languages, in particular, in list- and string-processing languages. One of the earliest and widely used list-processing languages is IPL-V (for Information Processing Language 5). The reader will find a useful discussion of Ackerman's function in the IPL-V Manual (1961). As mentioned earlier, the "recursive" Fortran program for Ackerman's function may be found in Morris (1969) and an iterative program (although not quite correct) may be found in Rice (1965). Some other useful examples of recursion may be found in Lynch (1965).

[†]Another language which allows recursion is MAD, but in this case there are two explicit statements, SAVE and RESTORE, which can be used, respectively, to insert elements on a push-down list, and to pop them up.

[††]These lists are sometimes called LIFO (last-in, first-out) stacks.

Bibliography

Lynch, W. C. (1965): Recursive Solution of a Class of Combinatorial Problems, *Communications of the Association for Computing Machinery*, vol. 8, pp. 617-620.

Morris, J. (January 1969): Programming Recursive Functions in Fortran, *Software Age*, pp. 38-42.

Newell, A., et al. (1961): *Information Processing Language-V Manual*, Prentice-Hall, Inc., Englewood Cliffs, New Jersey.

Rice, H. G. (1965): Recursion and Iteration, *Communications of the Association for Computing Machinery*, vol. 8, pp. 114-115.

PROBLEMS

Section 8.1

1. Show how the flow chart of Figure 8.3 could be modified to assure that the calculation would never stay indefinitely in the computation-test loop.

2. a) Identify the four parts of the iteration in Figure 8.4.

b) Show how to modify the flow chart so that the update will be performed before the test.

3. a) Indicate what boxes in the flow chart of Figure 8.7b are executed, as on pp. 310-311, when $N = 5$.

b) Show how the notation on p. 313 relates to $n!$ for both the iterative and recursive cases.

4. Flow chart both iterative and recursive polynomial evaluation.

Section 8.2

5. a) Discuss the advantages of the block structure of Algol and PL/I over what is required in Fortran for nesting of iterations.

b) Although Fortran allows two or more nested DO-loops to end on the same statement, it does not allow the statement label of this statement to be referred to in an IF or GO TO statement unless that statement is in the innermost loop. Can you see a reason for this restriction?

6. Consider a one-dimensional array which is dimensioned for one more element than it contains. Suppose it is desired to move all the elements from some point M on up to one higher location in the array (i.e., the Mth element becomes the M+1st, the M+1st, the M+2nd, etc.) and to replace the Mth element with zero. Show why it would be useful in Fortran to be able to use negative increments in DO statements, that is, to be able to count down instead of up.

7. Explain which of the iteration structures in the various languages could lead to infinite computations, if there were no test of time such as that on the job card, by the operating system.

8. a) Which of the following statements or groups of statements are null (i.e., when they are executed they leave things precisely as they were before execution)? Explain your answers.

i) A = A
ii) IF (A.EQ.B) GO TO 10
10 ....
iii) A := (A + 1.0) * A– A ↑ 2;
iv) I = 3
    J = 2
    DO 6   K = I,J
6 CONTINUE

b) Can you think of any situation in which an unlabeled null statement in a program would be useful?

9. a) Show how the iteration statements in Fortran, Algol, and PL/I can be replaced by IF statements.

b) Rewrite one of the programs of Example 8.10 without using a DO statement.

10. Write a program in any P-O language to perform the calculation of Example 8.13 by making use of the algorithm of Example 8.2.

11. Rewrite any one of the programs of Example 8.11 so that it works for any nonnegative n and gives 0! = 1.

12. a) Write a program in a P-O language for the problem of Example 8.2.

b) Do the same for Example 8.3.

13. Rewrite the following Fortran statements using IF instead of DO statements. Are the two programs precisely equivalent?

```
    DO 4 I = 1,5
    J = I * I
    DO 4 K = J,30
    L = I + K * I
    DO 4 M = L,200
  4 N(I,K,M) = I * L-K**I
```

Section 8.3

14. Write an Algol program equivalent to that in Example 8.15 in which POLY is a recursive non-function procedure.

15. a) Write an iterative program to calculate Pascal's triangle.

b) Using Algol or PL/I, compare the running time of iterative and recursive programs to calculate Pascal's triangle.

16. a) Use the definition of Ackerman's function to calculate A(3,1).

b) Use the formulas on p. 347 to calculate A(4,1).

17. Use Algol or PL/I to compare the running time of a recursive program to compute various values of Ackerman's function and a program which uses the technique of the Fortran program of Section 8.3.

9

logic, logical design, and logical variables and statements

Logic is logic. That's all I say.

Oliver Wendell Holmes in *The Deacon's Masterpiece*

Mathematical logic impinges on and overlaps computer science from a number of directions. We have already noted or footnoted in a few places the presence of logical quantities in P-O languages. Particularly when considering relational expressions, we have pointed out that these were members of a larger class called logical or Boolean expressions which have as values truth and falsity. Our discussion of the binary nature of many computing devices and binary arithmetic in Chapter 3 indicates another area where concepts from computer science and logic are closely related. In this chapter we shall consider the explicit use of concepts from mathematical logic in the design of digital computers and then discuss the explicit implementation in our P-O languages of constructs in logic. But first we shall briefly introduce a branch of mathematics whose development was essential to the formalization of logical concepts and which is of great use in various aspects of computer science.

9.1 BOOLEAN ALGEBRA

George Boole (1815-64) was an English mathematician and logician who realized the lack of a mathematical formalism in which to express the concepts of symbolic logic. He set about to remedy this. The result was an algebraic system known as Boolean *algebra* which has found much wider application than Boole ever dreamed.

355

The term *algebra* in mathematics refers to a mathematical system in which certain rules called *postulates* are defined concerning how quantities in a certain *domain* may be manipulated. An algebra is a *deductive system* in that it is a body of knowledge deduced from the application of the postulates to the domain of the algebra.

In the algebra learned in high school, these postulates are implicit and concern how arithmetic operations may be performed on real numbers, the domain of ordinary algebra. Normally, in an algebra one defines *variables* to be quantities which can take on any value in the domain. In ordinary algebra the variables are usually denoted by lower case italic letters such as x and can take on any real value.

In Boolean algebra the domain of values on which the algebra operates consists of only two quantities, which we shall denote by 1 and 0.[†] Another common notation is T (true) and F (false). The variables in Boolean algebra, which we shall denote by upper case letters, can then take on only these two values. It is useful to consider these variables as representing *propositions* which can be either true (1) or false (0). For example, the variable A might represent the proposition:

The man is bald.

and would have the value 1 if a given man is bald and 0 if he is not.

The operations of Boolean algebra will be familiar to any reader with some background in symbolic logic. There are three operations; their names and notation are given in Table 9.1. The *definitions* of these operations, that is, the postulates concerning their effect on variables and constants, are shown in Table 9.2. In this table, A and B represent Boolean variables, each of which can take on the values 0 or 1. The tables in Table 9.2 give the results when the three operators are applied to Boolean variables. As is obvious from the tables, conjunction and disjunction are binary operators and negation is a unary operator.

The reason for sometimes denoting the operators by AND, OR, and NOT is easily seen from Table 9.2. A · B is true (i.e., equal to 1) if and only if both A *and* B are true. A + B is true if either A *or* B is true, and $\overline{A}$ is true only if A is *not* true.

The use of the + and · notation, more commonly used for ordinary addition and multiplication, will be motivated in the next paragraph. But, because this notation is reasonable, conjunction and disjunction are often called, respectively, *logical multiplication* and *logical addition*.

[†] More precisely, such a Boolean algebra is called a *two-element* Boolean algebra; more general Boolean algebras have 2^m elements, $m > 1$.

Table 9.1 Operations of Boolean algebra

Name	Notation in this book	Other common notations
Conjunction (or logical product)	·	$\wedge$ or AND
Disjunction (or logical sum)	+	$\vee$ or OR
Negation	— (overbar over variable)	$\sim$ or $\neg$ or NOT

Table 9.2 Definitions of Boolean operators

A·B				A + B				$\overline{\text{A}}$	
A\B	0	1		A\B	0	1		A	$\overline{\text{A}}$
0	0	0		0	0	1		0	1
1	0	1		1	1	1		1	0

In Boolean algebra, as with the ordinary algebra with which the user is familiar, the commutative, associative, and distributive laws of arithmetic may be stated (cf. Section 5.1):

Commutative laws
Addition: $A + B = B + A$
Multiplication: $A \cdot B = B \cdot A$

Associative laws
Addition: $(A + B) + C = A + (B + C)$
Multiplication: $(A \cdot B) \cdot C = A \cdot (B \cdot C)$

Distributive law
$(A + B) \cdot C = A \cdot C + B \cdot C$

These are the precise analogs of the corresponding laws of ordinary algebra and explain why we used the + and · notation. But, of course, stating the above laws does not prove them. They are true, but rather than prove them here, we shall leave the proofs to Problem 1. Instead, we shall indicate some techniques for proving Boolean theorems by stating and proving another distributive law for Boolean algebra which has no analog in ordinary algebra. This law is

$$(A + B) \cdot (A + C) = A + B \cdot C \tag{9.1}$$

Table 9.3   Truth table for $(A + B) \cdot (A + C) = A + B \cdot C$

A B C	A + B	A + C	$(A + B) \cdot (A + C)$	B · C	A + B · C
0 0 0	0	0	0	0	0
0 0 1	0	1	0	0	0
0 1 0	1	0	0	0	0
0 1 1	1	1	1	1	1
1 0 0	1	1	1	0	1
1 0 1	1	1	1	0	1
1 1 0	1	1	1	0	1
1 1 1	1	1	1	1	1

The first method of proof we shall use is called the *truth table* method. A truth table is nothing more than an exhaustive test of every possible set of values of the variables which can occur. This is possible in Boolean algebra—and practical when the number of variables is small—because each variable is limited to two values. The truth table for the theorem above [i.e., the distributive law labeled (9.1)] is given in Table 9.3. The first three columns are necessary to this truth table for they express all possible combinations of the three variables A, B, and C. If there are n variables, the number of possible combinations is 2^n. (Why?) The reader should note that the eight combinations in Table 9.3 are written in such an order that they denote the first eight binary integers.

The next three columns in Table 9.3 represent the calculation of the left side of the theorem. As one develops expertise in Boolean manipulations, he would probably omit the first two of these columns. The last two columns are a similar calculation for the right side. Since the last and second from last columns are identical, the left and right sides are the same for all values of the variables and thus the theorem is proved.

Boolean theorems can also be proved by techniques more analogous to familiar proofs in algebra and geometry as we shall indicate below.

Boolean variables, constants (0 and 1), and operators can be combined to form *Boolean functions* in a fashion similar to the way algebraic variables are combined to form, for example, polynomial functions such as

$$x^3 + 4x^2 - 2x + 7$$

Three common and important Boolean functions are the following:

Implication function
$$\overline{A} + B$$

If A is true and this function is true, then B is true (Why?); thus A *implies* B,

Table 9.4 Truth table for Example 9.1

A	B	C	AB + AC + BC	$\bar{A}BC + A\bar{B}C + AB$
0	0	0	0	0
0	0	1	0	0
0	1	0	0	0
0	1	1	1	1
1	0	0	0	0
1	0	1	1	1
1	1	0	1	1
1	1	1	1	1

which is usually denoted by

$$A \rightarrow B$$

Note that, if A is false, the function is always true, which is a variant of the old rule that anything can be proven with false hypotheses.

Equivalence function
$$A \cdot B + \bar{A} \cdot \bar{B}$$

This function is true if and only if A and B have the same truth value (Why?); that is, if A and B are *equivalent.*

Tautology function
$$A + \bar{A}$$

A tautology is a statement which is true irrespective of the truth of its components, which is clearly true for the function above.

Boolean functions can be further combined to form more complicated functions which in turn can be used as parts of Boolean theorems.

Example 9.1

Prove or disprove, using truth tables, the Boolean theorem

$$AB + AC + BC = \bar{A}BC + A\bar{B}C + AB$$

Note that we have adopted the convention here, as in ordinary multiplication, of dropping the multiplication dot.

The truth table is given in Table 9.4. Since the last two columns are identical, the theorem is true.

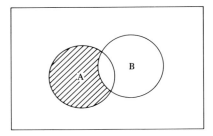

Figure 9.1   Venn diagram for A · B̄.

As we stated above, Boolean theorems can also be proven using more standard techniques. To illustrate these techniques we again prove the second distributive law (9.1):

$$(A + B) \cdot (A + C) = A + B \cdot C$$

The proof is as follows with comments at the right:

$(A + B) \cdot (A + C) = A \cdot (A + C) + B \cdot (A + C)$	First distributive law
$= (A + C) \cdot A + (A + C) \cdot B$	Commutative law
$= A \cdot A + C \cdot A + A \cdot B + C \cdot B$	First distributive law
$= A + A \cdot B + A \cdot C + B \cdot C$	Commutative law and $A \cdot A = A$
$= A \cdot 1 + A \cdot B + A \cdot C + B \cdot C$	$A \cdot 1 = A$
$= A \cdot (1 + B + C) + B \cdot C$	First distributive law
$= A + B \cdot C$	$1 + 0 = 1; 1 + 1 = 1;$ therefore, $1 +$ anything $= 1$

Remarks:

1. The theorems used in the fourth and fifth lines of the proof ($A \cdot A = A$ and $A \cdot 1 = A$) are both trivial (Problem 2).

2. In the next to last line, as in ordinary arithmetic, we have extended the first distributive law to

$$A \cdot (B_1 + B_2 + \dots + B_n) = A \cdot B_1 + \dots + A \cdot B_n$$

The reader should be able to prove this extension (Problem 2).

Another way of proving simple Boolean theorems is by means of *Venn diagrams*. In a Venn diagram each variable is represented by a circle and all circles must overlap all other circles. The area *inside* the circle for a given variable

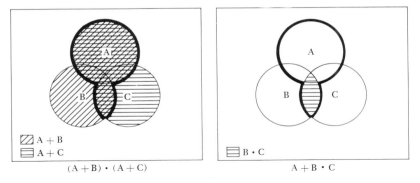

$$(A + B) \cdot (A + C) \qquad\qquad A + B \cdot C$$

Figure 9.2   Venn diagrams for $(A+B) \cdot (A+C) = A+B \cdot C$.

represents a one value; the area outside represents a zero value. For example, the shaded portion of Figure 9.1 represents $A \cdot \bar{B}$ since $\bar{B}$ is everything outside of the circle for B. Note that we have enclosed the two circles in a square in Figure 9.1. This square is called the *universe* and is used to facilitate indicating complements, since a complement of a variable is "everything outside" the circle for the variable. Figure 9.2 contains Venn diagrams for the distributive law (9.1). The regions corresponding to the two sides of (9.1) are outlined in heavy lines.

Our purpose in introducing these very basic concepts of Boolean algebra has not been just to teach the algebra itself, although a deeper study of Boolean algebra is of great mathematical interest. Rather, our purpose is to use it as a tool in discussing some basic aspects of the logical design of digital computers in the next section.

9.2   LOGICAL DESIGN

Three distinct steps in the hardware design of any digital computer can be distinguished:

1. The *system* design which begins at the conception of the computing system and carries this forward to the hardware specifications of the system, including such things as

> machine-language instruction repertoire
> size and speed of main memory
> auxiliary memories—size and speed
> input and output units—types and characteristics

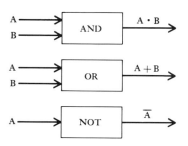

Figure 9.3   Basic logical circuitry.

2. The *logical* design in which these specifications are reduced to logical state-ments about what is required to implement the *functional* part of the systems design (as opposed to, for example, aspects of circuit speed).

3. The *electronic* design in which the systems design and logical design together are implemented in electronic circuitry to satisfy the speed and other aspects of the systems design and the functional aspect of the logical design.

Our interest here is in the second of the above and in particular how tech-niques of Boolean algebra can be applied to it.

Just as circuit design requires the use of standard modules of electronic circuits, logical design makes use of standard logic circuits. Of these, the three most basic, and virtually the only ones we shall require for our discussion in this section, are illustrated in Figure 9.3. Each of the boxes in this figure is to be interpreted as accepting the input or inputs on the left and producing as outputs the Boolean functions indicated by the names in the boxes (cf. Table 9.1). With these logical circuits as building blocks we can design many of the basic elements of a digital computer. We begin with a simple example to illustrate the tech-niques involved and then give a more complicated example which is obviously of direct interest in the design of digital computers.

9.2.1   Design of a Complementer

In Section 3.2.2 we considered how negative numbers can be stored in a com-puter memory. One of these techniques was by using nines complements in a decimal computer or ones complements in a binary computer. The latter is more commonly used since most present-day computers are binary. However, the decimal case results in a better illustration of logical design so we shall focus our attention on it. If negative numbers are to be stored as nines complements, then, clearly there is a requirement for circuitry which can take as input a decimal

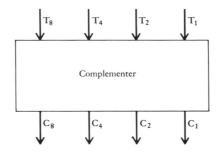

Figure 9.4 The decimal-complementer problem.

number and produce as output its nines complement. For example, to implement the Fortran statement

$$I = -I$$

we would want to have available machine-language instructions of the form:

| Clear and Subtract L(I) | (i.e., bring the negative of I into the arithmetic unit) |
| Store L(I) | (i.e., store this back in L(I)) |

To implement the first of these in hardware in a decimal computer a (nines) complementer is required. In this section we shall consider how to design a complementer, not of a whole number, but of a single decimal digit.

Since computer circuit elements are basically binary devices, we considered in Section 3.1.4 how decimal integers could be coded in a binary computer. The most natural coding is BCD (for binary-coded decimal) (cf. Table 3.1) and, therefore, we shall assume here that the decimal integer we wish to complement is stored in binary-coded decimal form. Our problem is illustrated in Figure 9.4. T_8, T_4, T_2, T_1 [T for true and the subscripts denoting the values of the binary digits (cf. Table 3.4)] are the 4 BCD bits of the decimal digit and C_8, C_4, C_2, C_1 (C for complement) are the 4 bits of the complement. Our problem is to design the circuitry in the complementer box.

In Table 9.5 we have given the BCD code for the 10 decimal digits and the corresponding complemented digits. Using Table 9.5, we would like to discover relationships between T_8, T_4, T_2, and T_1, and C_8, C_4, C_2, and C_1 which would enable us to design the logical circuitry in the box in Figure 9.4. We note the following:

Table 9.5   Nines complements in BCD

Decimal digit	BCD equivalent				BCD equivalent of nines complement				Nines complement of digit
	T_8	T_4	T_2	T_1	C_8	C_4	C_2	C_1	
0	0	0	0	0	1	0	0	1	9
1	0	0	0	1	1	0	0	0	8
2	0	0	1	0	0	1	1	1	7
3	0	0	1	1	0	1	1	0	6
4	0	1	0	0	0	1	0	1	5
5	0	1	0	1	0	1	0	0	4
6	0	1	1	0	0	0	1	1	3
7	0	1	1	1	0	0	1	0	2
8	1	0	0	0	0	0	0	1	1
9	1	0	0	1	0	0	0	0	0

1. C_1 and T_1 have different values for each digit.
2. C_2 and T_2 are always the same.
3. $C_4 = 1$ if, and only if, T_2 or T_4, but not both, is one.
4. $C_8 = 1$ if, and only if, T_2, T_4, and T_8 are all zero.

Only the third of these rules requires more than the simplest observation. These four rules translate easily into Boolean terms as

$$C_1 = \bar{T}_1$$
$$C_2 = T_2$$
$$C_4 = (T_2 + T_4)(\bar{T}_2 + \bar{T}_4) \qquad (9.2)$$
$$C_8 = \overline{T_2 + T_4 + T_8}$$

The reader should not think that these are the only possible Boolean equations connecting the true and complemented bits (Problem 8), but they are a set which can be used to complete the logical design. Neither should the reader think that the intuitive approach embodied in looking at Table 9.5 and then deducing the rules above is the only possible route to deriving the equations (9.2). Formal procedures exist for deriving such equations; they are considered briefly in Problem 9.

The equations (9.2) are the first step of the logical design, namely, expressing the problem in Boolean terms. The second and final step is converting the Boolean equations to logical circuitry, using the logical circuits of Figure 9.3. Since the equations (9.2) are so simple, this can be done almost by inspection and results in the logical circuit of Figure 9.5, which, in effect, completes Figure 9.4.

Before going on to the second design problem we shall discuss, let us consider for a moment an important problem in all logical design, namely, whether or not a particular logical circuit is the "simplest" possible. We have put simplest in quotes because there is often no easy way of determining which of two logical circuits is simpler. But, generally speaking, it should be intuitive that one should aim at logical circuits with the smallest possible number of boxes, since these will be the most economical to implement in actual electronic circuitry. The process of taking logical equations such as those in equation (9.2) and reducing them to a form which can be implemented using fewer logical circuits is called *minimization of Boolean functions* and is a very important aspect of logical design. We shall do no more here than illustrate the process with an example.

Example 9.2

Simplify the Boolean function

$$f = \bar{A}BC\bar{D} + \bar{A}B\bar{C}\bar{D} + AB\bar{C}\bar{D} + ABC\bar{D}$$

We proceed as follows:

$$\bar{A}BC\bar{D} + \bar{A}B\bar{C}\bar{D} + AB\bar{C}\bar{D} + ABC\bar{D} = \bar{A}B\bar{D}(C + \bar{C}) + AB\bar{D}(C + \bar{C})$$
$$= \bar{A}B\bar{D} + AB\bar{D}$$
$$= (\bar{A} + A)(B\bar{D})$$
$$= B\bar{D}$$

which is clearly much simpler than the original function.

Because of the important economic advantages of implementing the simplest circuit, methods for the minimization of Boolean functions are an important area of research. Substantial advances in this area have been made since the advent of digital computers. The most commonly used technique in this area is called the *Quine-McCluskey method.*

9.2.2   The Design of Adders and Accumulators

The problem we shall consider in this section is the design of a logical circuit to add two n-bit binary integers as shown in Figure 9.6. For simplicity, we assume both numbers are positive. Circuitry to accomplish this addition is, of course, basic to fixed-point arithmetic in a computer. In Figure 9.6 the two numbers to

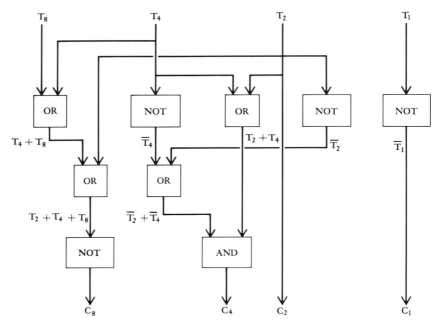

Figure 9.5   Logical circuit for complementer.

be added are represented by two arrays. A_i and B_i are, respectively, the ith bits from the right of the integers A and B. The sum is represented by an array S where S_i is the ith sum bit. Of course, two n-bit integers can produce an $(n + 1)$-bit result. This is a condition in a computer which we have previously called overflow (assuming, as we shall, that the word length in our computer is n bits plus sign). Again for the sake of simplicity, we shall ignore overflow in this discussion.

The array of carry bits represents the carry from the next lowest position to the position indicated. Thus C_i is the carry generated by the addition of A_i, B_i, and the carry from the previous stage C_{i-1}. Our assumption in the previous paragraph requires that $C_n = 0$.

As a first step toward the solution of our problem we shall design a *half adder*, a term used to designate a logical circuit which accepts two binary inputs and produces two outputs, one representing the units position of the sum of the 2 bits and the other the "tens" or carry position. Figure 9.7 illustrates the general problem and Table 9.6 gives a truth table relating the inputs and outputs. In Figure 9.7 we have denoted the sum and carry by lower case letters in order

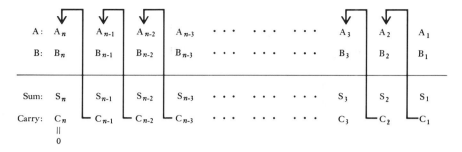

Figure 9.6 The binary addition design problem.

to distinguish them from the sum and carry bits in Figure 9.6. (Why are s_i and c_i not generally equal to S_i and C_i?) Note that the two right-hand columns in Table 9.6 are the binary sum of the two left-hand columns in reverse order. (Why?)

From Table 9.6 we easily deduce that:

1. s_i is 1 if, and only if, A_i or B_i but not both is 1 (cf. the rule for C_4 in previous section).
2. c_i is 1 if, and only if, both A_i and B_i are 1.

The Boolean equations which relate s_i and c_i to A_i and B_i are, therefore,

$$s_i = (A_i + B_i)(\overline{A}_i + \overline{B}_i)$$
$$c_i = A_i B_i$$

(9.3)

and from these we design the box labeled H in Figure 9.7 as shown in Figure 9.8.

Now, whereas a half adder accepts two inputs and produces their sum and carry, a *full adder* accepts three inputs (2 sum bits and the carry from the previous stage) and produces their sum and carry as shown in Figure 9.9. The full adder truth table is given in Table 9.7. Also shown in this table are half adder outputs corresponding to each A_i, B_i pair and an additional column C'_i which we shall discuss below.

Table 9.6   Half adder truth table

A_i	B_i	s_i	c_i
0	0	0	0
0	1	1	0
1	0	1	0
1	1	0	1

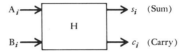

Figure 9.7   The half adder problem.

We could now proceed as before to deduce Boolean equations which relate S_i and C_i to A_i, B_i, and C_{i-1}, but, instead, we shall use our design above of the half adder to deduce directly the design of a full adder. We note first that S_i bears the same relationship to s_i and C_{i-1} that s_i does to A_i and B_i. That is, S_i is 1 if, and only if, s_i or C_{i-1}, but not both, is 1. Therefore, if s_i and C_{i-1} are inputs to a half adder, one output will be S_i. The other output, as shown in Figure 9.10a, we shall call C_i'. The last column of Table 9.7 is the truth table for C_i'. (Why?)

Now, if we combine the circuits of Figures 9.7 and 9.10a, we get the circuit of Figure 9.10b. To complete the design we now note from Table 9.7 that C_i is 1 if, and only if, C_i' or c_i or both (a condition which never occurs) is 1. Therefore, the design of the complete full adder is given in Figure 9.10c.

Now our task is to take the design of the full adder for each bit of our n-bit word and use this to design an *adder* to add all n-bits. Conceptually, the simplest such design is that of a serial adder which is illustrated in Figure 9.11. Serial addition is a synchronous operation in which, at a sequence of n equally-spaced intervals of time Δt, the n bits of A and B, shown stored in words in the computer memory, are successively sent to two inputs of a full adder with successive sum bits going to a register labeled sum, and successive carry bits being fed back to the third adder input after a delay Δt. That is, at time t_0 the two least significant bits of A and B, A_1 and B_1, are sent to the adder and S_1 goes to the sum register. At the time $t_0 + \Delta t$, A_2 and B_2 are sent to the adder together with C_1 as it emerges from the delay unit to produce S_2 and C_2, etc.

Table 9.7   Full adder truth table

A_i	B_i	C_{i-1}	S_i	C_i	s_i	c_i	C_i'
0	0	0	0	0	0	0	0
0	0	1	1	0	0	0	0
0	1	0	1	0	1	0	0
0	1	1	0	1	1	0	1
1	0	0	1	0	1	0	0
1	0	1	0	1	1	0	1
1	1	0	0	1	0	1	0
1	1	1	1	1	0	1	0

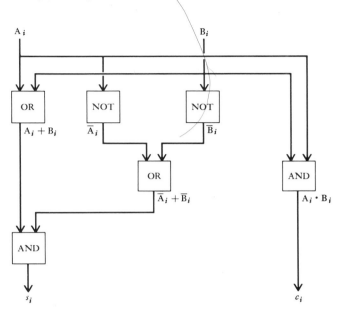

Figure 9.8 Logical circuit for half adder.

The sum register could be a register in the arithmetic unit of the computer or could be one of the memory words in which A or B were stored. That is, if the sum of A and B is to replace, say, A, then the sum bits could be successively inserted into the left-hand side of A, since the process of sending the bits of A to the full adder would be accomplished by successively shifting all the bits of A one position to the right. When the sum replaces one of the inputs, we call the register in which the sum is placed the *accumulator* register and typically the entire device is called an accumulator.

The carry output of the full adder goes to a delay unit which delays the transmission of C_i one time interval and then feeds the carry to the full adder as its third input. The timing is illustrated in Table 9.8. Note that at time t_0 the carry will be C_0 which must be forced equal to zero by the circuitry.

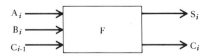

Figure 9.9 The full adder problem.

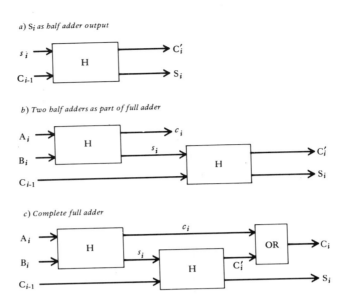

a) S_i as half adder output

b) Two half adders as part of full adder

c) Complete full adder

Figure 9.10   Full adder logical design.

The advantages of serial addition are its logical simplicity and, therefore, its economy. Its major disadvantage is its slowness, since it takes $n-1$ of the basic time intervals of the computer (called the *cycle time*) to complete the addition. For this reason serial addition is seldom used in digital computers and then only for the slowest computers. Instead, most computers use *parallel* addition which we shall now consider briefly.

Parallel addition is generally performed using an accumulator in which the augend is in the accumulator and the addend is in another register in the arithmetic unit to which it has been transferred from memory. The term parallel refers to the fact that, instead of one full adder as in Figure 9.11, there will be an equivalent piece of circuitry, usually more nearly a half adder than a full adder, for each of the n bits of the word.

In order to justify the cost of n replications of the same circuit we must be able to reduce the $n-1$ time intervals of Table 9.8 to a small number. Since with n circuits the corresponding bits of addend and augend can be added simultaneously at time t_0, the problem lies in handling the carries. One way to handle carries is indicated schematically in Figure 9.12. Each arrow indicates the transfer of n bits in parallel so that for example, the AND unit represents n such units in parallel. Whenever a pulse appears on the add-pulse line, the contents of the addend register are added bit by bit to the accumulator register, the result is sent

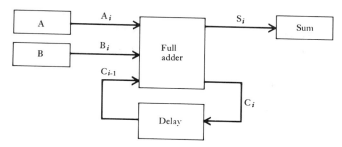

Figure 9.11   Serial adder.

back to the accumulator register, and the carries produced are sent back to the cleared addend register. In effect, the logical circuitry would be a half adder for each bit position. Then, at successive time intervals, the process would be repeated until no more carries were produced. In the worst possible case $n-1$ time intervals would be required (Problem 10), but it can be shown that on the average for, say, 36-bit numbers, about four carry cycles will be needed after the original addition of the addend to the accumulator. However, this situation can be substantially improved upon as we shall now indicate.

Among the various ways of implementing rapid processing of carries, the one we shall present is not quite as effective as some others but it is much better than the method of Figure 9.12 and is probably the simplest to explain. The logical circuit is shown in Figure 9.13. This logical circuit contains two features not contained in any of our previous logical circuits:

1. The storage elements which make up the addend and accumulator registers. They can store a 0 or 1. An input to the element causes it to change from 0 to 1 or 1 to 0. If a 1 is stored, an output line from 1 produces a steady signal and similarly for an output line from 0 when a 0 is stored. Such a device is often called a *flip-flop*.

Table 9.8   Timing for serial addition

Time	Full adder inputs	Full adder outputs
t_0	$A_1, B_1, C_0 = 0$	S_1, C_1
$t_0 + \Delta t$	A_2, B_2, C_1	S_2, C_2
$t_0 + 2 \Delta t$	A_3, B_3, C_2	S_3, C_3
$--$	$--$	$--$
$--$	$--$	$--$
$--$	$--$	$--$
$t_0 + (n-2) \Delta t$	$A_{n-1}, B_{n-1}, C_{n-2}$	S_{n-1}, C_{n-1}
$t_0 + (n-1) \Delta t$	A_n, B_n, C_{n-1}	S_n, C_n

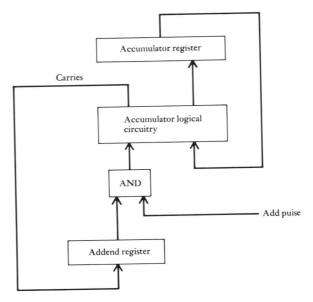

Figure 9.12   Parallel accumulator — Solution 1.

2. The fact that the lower left AND unit has three inputs and one output. In general, an AND unit with k binary inputs produces a 1 as output if, and only if, all k input lines have 1s on them.

The circuit in Figure 9.13 operates as follows:

1. At time t_0 a pulse is applied to the add-pulse line. At any stage where the addend register contains a 1, this pulse passes through the lower right AND and the upper OR of each stage and switches the accumulator storage element to 0 if it contained a 1 and to 1 if it contained a 0. In effect, each stage acts as a half adder for the accumulator and addend bits.

2. At time $t_0 + \Delta t$ a pulse is applied to the carry-pulse line. If the addend register contains a 0 at any stage, then the carry pulse is stopped at the lower left AND unit as it should be, since the previous half addition could not have generated a carry.

3. At $t_0 + \Delta t$, if, at the ith stage, the addend bit is 1 and the accumulator bit is 0, then at t_0 the accumulator bit was 1 and the add pulse resulted in a switch of the accumulator bit from 1 to 0 so that a carry needs to be generated to the $(i + 1)$st stage. In this case the carry pulse gets through the lower left AND, then through the OR, DELAY, and another OR and finally switches the accumulator bit at the $(i + 1)$st stage.

4. At the same time the carry goes to the DELAY, it also goes to the upper

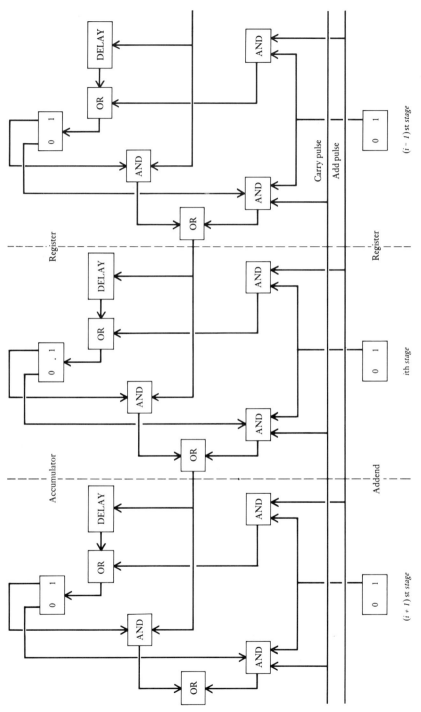

Figure 9.13 Parallel accumulator — Solution 2.

AND at the next higher stage. If the accumulator bit at the $(i + 1)$st stage is a 1 after the application of the add pulse, then this carry should generate a further carry to the next stage, which it does by passing through the upper AND and the OR which follows it at the $(i + 1)$st stage. Note the importance of the DELAY box. This allows the carry to get through the upper left AND *before* the accumulator bit changes from 1 to 0.

5. In fact, once the carry pulse gets through the lower left AND at one stage, it passes through successive ORs and ANDs at higher stages as long as the accumulator bit is 1. The delays enable the carry to propagate as far as it should. The carry is said to "ripple through" from one stage to the next.

Therefore, the result is that the addition is completed at time $t_0 + \Delta t$ plus at most one delay time (which is normally much less than Δt). Thus, this example makes clear why parallel accumulators are used in virtually all computers where speed is of the essence.

9.3 LOGICAL VARIABLES AND STATEMENTS

The use of logical structures in computer languages is normally unconnected with the logical design of computers. Rather, some of the same reasons which make Boolean algebra and related concepts useful in logical design also make them useful in writing computer programs. Just as electronic elements are binary devices, so, as indeed we have seen, are decisions in computer programs often binary in nature. Therefore, it is often useful to introduce the processes and

Panel 9.1   Logical constants

FORTRAN	*ALGOL*	*PL/I*
Called *logical*	Called *Boolean*	Special case of bit-string constant
	Syntax	
.TRUE. or	**true** or	'1' B or
.FALSE.	**false**	'0' B
	Semantics	
		'1' B corresponds to true and '0' B to false

Note:
Logical constants are not allowed in Cobol.

Panel 9.2   Logical operators

Boolean name	FORTRAN	ALGOL	PL/I	
			48-character set	60-character set
Conjunction	.AND.	∧	AND	&
Disjunction	.OR.	∨	OR	|
Negation	.NOT.	¬	NOT	¬

variables of mathematical logic directly into computer calculations. This latter fact was not recognized when Fortran was first developed. However, logical structures are quite fully developed in Fortran IV, PL/I, and Algol, although hardly at all in Cobol. In this section we shall discuss the facilities for the use of logical structures in the four languages.

In Section 4.2 we mentioned the existence of logical constants in addition to arithmetic and string constants in Fortran, Algol, and PL/I. The syntax of logical constants is shown in Panel 9.1. As would be expected since quantities in Boolean algebra are restricted to take on only two values, logical constants in the various languages have only two possible forms. Some Fortran systems allow .T. and .F. as well as .TRUE. and .FALSE. .

In Chapter 4 (Panel 4.6) we indicated that type declarations of LOGICAL in Fortran and **boolean** in Algol could be used to specify variables. Such variables, of course, are constrained to take on only the values indicated in Panel 9.1. In PL/I, since logical constants are a special case of bit-string constants, no special type declaration is needed.

Just as arithmetic variables and constants and arithmetic operators could be used together to form arithmetic expressions, so can logical variables and constants and logical operators be used together to form logical expressions. In fact, as we shall see, arithmetic expressions can also appear in logical expressions, although the converse is not true.

The logical operators of Fortran, Algol, and PL/I are shown in Panel 9.2. Not surprisingly, this panel bears a close resemblance to Table 9.1 which contains the operators of Boolean algebra. The Algol symbols are publication-language symbols which must be transliterated in actual implementations. In addition to the operators shown in Panel 9.2, Algol allows two additional logical operators: ⊃ corresponds to the implication function discussed in Section 9.1, and ≡ corresponds to the equivalence function.

A logical expression consists of *any combination of logical constants, variables, operators, and other expressions with logical values which conforms to the rules of Boolean algebra.* Except for the phrase "and other expressions with logical values," this definition is the precise analog of the definition of arithmetic expressions in Section 5.2. Ignoring for the moment the implications of this phrase, this definition allows us to use the logical operators of Panel 9.2, as well as the additional ones mentioned above for Algol, in the normal fashion for Boolean algebra.

Example 9.3

What are the values of the following logical expressions where A and B are logical variables, using Algol notation?

> i) A ∧ B
> ii) A ∨ B
> iii) ¬ A
> iv) A ⊃ B
> v) A ≡ B

For conjunction, disjunction, and negation the answers are given in Table 9.2. For implication and equivalence the truth tables are as follows:

	⊃			≡	
A\B	0	1	A\B	0	1
0	1	1	0	1	0
1	0	1	1	0	1

As with arithmetic expressions, we wish to be able to join simple expressions into more complicated ones such as

A ∧ B ∨ C ∧ ¬ D ⊃ C ∨ E ≡ A ∧ F

where A, B, C, D, E, and F are all logical variables. But is this expression to be interpreted as

> 1. ((A ∧ (B ∨ C)) ∧ (¬ D)) ⊃ ((C ∨ E) ≡ (A ∧ F))   or
> 2. (((A ∧ B) ∨ (C ∧ (¬ D))) ⊃ (C ∨ E)) ≡ (A ∧ F)   or
> 3. ((A ∧ (B ∨ C)) ∧ ((¬ D) ⊃ (C ∨ E))) ≡ (A ∧ F)

or does it have various other possible interpretations which the reader might find (Problem 14)? The answer clearly depends on the hierarchy of operators which we set up analogous to that in Section 5.2.2 for the arithmetic operators. In Algol this hierarchy is

high ¬
Λ
V
⊃
low ≡

In Fortran and PL/I the hierarchy is the same for the first three operators, the latter two not being directly available in either (Problem 15). Thus the correct interpretation of the expression above is the second one given.

Since each hierarchy level contains only one operator and since conjunction and disjunction are associative, there is no need for a left-to-right rule with logical expressions. However, we do again have a parentheses rule which over-rides the hierarchy. Thus, to obtain the first possibility in the list of three alternatives above it would be sufficient to write

$$A \wedge (B \vee C) \wedge \neg D \supset (C \vee E \equiv A \wedge F)$$

But the above discussion does not give us the full generality of logical expres-sions in any of the three languages. In Section 5.5.3 we defined relational expres-sions and discussed how they were used in conditional transfer statements. At that time we pointed out that the value of any relational expression was true or false. Therefore, such expressions can be made part of logical expressions in an obvious and convenient fashion. The rule is that any place a logical variable or constant can appear in a logical expression, a relational expression as defined in Section 5.5.3 can also be inserted. Thus, for example, in Algol we can write

$$A \wedge B < C$$

where B and C are now arithmetic variables and A is a logical variable. As a similar example in Fortran, we can have

A.NE.B.OR.C

where A and B are now arithmetic variables and C is a logical variable. It follows from this that a relational expression itself is a special case of a logical expression since, for example, the logical variable

A

which is itself a logical expression could be replaced by

B.NE.C

where B and C are arithmetic variables.

Table 9.9   Operator hierarchy

	Fortran	Algol	PL/I
High	**	↑	¬ ** − (unary)
	− (unary)	/ * ÷	/ *
	/ *	+ − (binary	+ −
	+ −	and unary)	‖
	Relational	Relational	Relational
	operators	operators	operators
	.NOT.	¬	&
	.AND.	∧		
	.OR.	∨	
		⊃	
Low		≡	

In Fortran and Algol there is no need to state explicitly an overall hierarchy which relates arithmetic, relational, and logical operators, although Algol does this and some Fortran texts do also. The reason no such hierarchy is needed is that arithmetic operators must be applied first, then relational operators, and finally logical operators. This is because

1. in an expression containing relational as well as arithmetic operators, if the relational operators were applied first, the result would be an expression with *logical values* and *arithmetic operators*, which has no meaning, and

2. in an expression with relational and logical operators, if the logical operators were applied first, the result would be *relational operators* with *logical operands*, which also has no meaning.

The situation in PL/I is not as simple. In principle, PL/I allows arithmetic variables to be operands of logical operators and logical (i.e., bit-string) variables to be operands of arithmetic operators.† PL/I defines precisely the conversion from data of one type to data of another type which must take place when an operator requires a data type different from the type of the operand. Therefore, a precise definition of the hierarchy involving arithmetic, relational, and logical operators is necessary. With one exception, this PL/I hierarchy is precisely that implied in Fortran and Algol, namely, that arithmetic operators have highest precedence, then relational operators, and then logical operators. The exception is that the negation operator has the same precedence as the exponentiation and unary minus operators and, as with these, evaluation of operators of equal precedence proceeds from right to left. The reader should see why this is reason-

---

† Character-string variables are also allowed as operands of arithmetic operators.

able (Problem 16). Of course, the reader should realize that the ability in PL/I to use an operand of a type different from that required by an operator, while it achieves a level of generality not possible in Fortran and Algol, is not likely to be invoked very often.

Table 9.9 summarizes the operator hierarchy for Fortran, Algol, and PL/I. The only thing in this table not discussed previously in this book is the ‖ operator. It is called the *concatenation operator* and its function is to take two strings and concatenate them into a single string. For example, if A is '01010' and B is 'WHY', then A ‖ B is '01010WHY'. The usage of this operator is clearly confined to nonnumerical types of applications. Originally lowest in the PL/I hierarchy, concatenation was moved to its position in Table 9.9 in order that A‖B = C‖D have its natural meaning. (What is this?)

Just as arithmetic expressions were used to form the right-hand sides of arithmetic assignment statements, so do logical expressions form the right-hand side of *logical assignment statements*. The structure of these statements is given in Panel 9.3. Logical assignment statements, as defined in Panel 9.3, are therefore seen to be the precise analog in each of the three languages of arithmetic assignment statements. In Fortran and Algol this discussion, together with the discussion in Chapter 5 of arithmetic assignment statements, tells the whole story about assignment statements. But this is not so in PL/I. In PL/I assignment statements of the form

$$var_1 = var_2 = \text{---} = var_n = exp$$

are allowed where each variable var_i may be of any type whatsoever and the expression on the right may be logical or arithmetic. PL/I defines explicitly, although we shall not go into this here, how the conversions between character-

---

Panel 9.3   Logical assignment statements

FORTRAN	*ALGOL*	*PL/I*
	Syntax	
$lv = le$	$lv_1 := lv_2 := \ldots := lv_n = le$	$lv_1, lv_2, \ldots, lv_n = le$

Semantics

The logical variable or variables on the left are set equal to the value of the logical expression on the right.

le—logical expression
lv—logical variable

string, bit-string, and arithmetic quantities are to be performed. Indeed, even the above expression is not the most general type of assignment statement allowed in PL/I, but we shall not consider any of the other possibilities. We repeat a remark we made above, that this added generality in PL/I will find only very limited application.

Example 9.4

The purpose of the following Fortran program is to compute and print out all prime numbers between 1 and an input value N. It illustrates the usefulness of logical variables and statements.

```
          LOGICAL P(100)
          READ, N
          PRINT, N
C         SET ARRAY TO TRUE. AT END OF COMPUTATION
C         ELEMENTS OF ARRAY WHICH ARE STILL TRUE
C         ARE PRIMES
          DO 10 I = 2, N
    10    P(I) = .TRUE.
C         OUR TECHNIQUE SHALL BE TO TAKE
C         INTEGERS STARTING WITH 2 AND DELETE (I.E.
C         SET TO FALSE) EACH MULTIPLE OF THE INTEGER.
C         IT IS ONLY NECESSARY TO TAKE INTEGERS UP TO
C         THE SQUARE ROOT OF N (WHY?).
          XN = N
          K = SQRT (XN)
          DO 12 I = 2, K
C         IF P(I) IS FALSE ITS MULTIPLES NEED NOT
C         BE CONSIDERED (WHY?).
          IF (.NOT. P(I) ) GO TO 12
C         FIRST MULTIPLE CONSIDERED IS TWICE INTEGER
          L = 2 * I
          DO 14 J = L, N, I
    14    P(J) = .FALSE.
    12    CONTINUE
          DO 16 I = 2, N
          IF (.NOT. P(I) ) GO TO 16
          PRINT, I
    16    CONTINUE
          STOP
          END
```

Example 9.5

Logical statements can of course be used directly to do problems in Boolean algebra. As an example, we give here an Algol program to prove the distributive law (9.1). The program generates all eight combinations of truth values for A, B, and C, calculates the left and right sides of (9.1) for each set of values, and checks that they are equal.

```
begin
boolean A,B,C,TRUTHL,TRUTHR,VALUE;
    A := B := C := VALUE := true;
L1: TRUTHL := (A V B) ∧ (A V C);
TRUTHR := A V (B ∧ C);
comment NEXT STATEMENT TESTS THAT LEFT AND RIGHT SIDES
        HAVE SAME TRUTH VALUE;
if (TRUTHL ∧ TRUTHR) V (¬ TRUTHL ∧
        ¬ TRUTHR) then go to L2
        else begin VALUE := false; go to L4; end;
comment THE NEXT STATEMENT ASSURES THAT THE OTHER SEVEN
        COMBINATIONS OF A, B, C WILL BE GENERATED;
L2: if C then C := false else
        if B then begin B := false; C := true; end
        else
        if A then begin A := false; B := C := true; end
        else
            go to L4;
    go to L1;
    comment IF THEOREM IS TRUE OUTPUT IS TRUE AND IF FALSE
            OUTPUT IS FALSE;
L4: PRINT, VALUE;
    end
```

As a final note in this chapter let us recall the discussion of IF statements in Section 5.5.3. In Algol, PL/I, and in one of the forms in Fortran, the quantity tested was a relational expression, defined there as an expression involving relational operators and arithmetic variables. But clearly it would make sense to allow any logical expression in place of the relational expression since, as mentioned in the previous section, relational expressions are just special cases of logical expressions. This is indeed allowed in all three languages, so Panel 5.9 should be restated with the *re* for relational expression replaced in each instance by *le* for logical expression. Actually, in PL/I an arithmetic expression is allowed also (e.g., IF I THEN ....) with the interpretation that a 0 value is false and any nonzero value is true.

BIBLIOGRAPHIC NOTES

There are a number of good books which treat the logical design of digital computers. In particular, Phister (1958) and Gschwind (1967) also have some good introductory material on Boolean algebra, including a discussion of the minimization of Boolean functions mentioned in Section 9.2.1. Other recommended books in this area are Richards (1955) and Ledley (1962). Korfhage (1966) contains an introduction to Boolean algebra and uses this material to develop a variety of related material on the properties and structure of algorithms.

Bibliography

Gschwind, H.W. (1967): *Design of Digital Computers: An Introduction*, Springer-Verlag, New York.

Korfhage, R.R (1966): *Logic and Algorithms*, John Wiley & Sons, Inc., New York.

Ledley, R.S. (1962): *Programming and Utilizing Digital Computers*, McGraw-Hill Book Company, Inc., New York.

Phister, M. (1958): *Logical Design of Digital Computers*, John Wiley & Sons, Inc., New York.

Richards, R.K. (1955): *Arithmetic Operations in Digital Computers*, Van Nostrand Company, Inc., Princeton, New Jersey.

PROBLEMS

Section 9.1

1.   Use truth tables to prove the Boolean associative, commutative, and distributive laws given on p. 357.

2.   Prove the following Boolean theorems:

   a) $A \cdot A = A$
   b) $A \cdot 1 = A$
   c) $A \cdot (B_1 + B_2 + \ldots + B_n) = A \cdot B_1 + A \cdot B_2 + \ldots + A \cdot B_n$

3.   a) Using any proof technique, show that

   i) $\bar{A}B + A\bar{B} = (A + B)(\bar{A} + \bar{B})$
   ii) $\bar{A} + \bar{B} = \overline{AB}$

b) Use these results to prove the theorem of Example 9.1, using deductive techniques.

c) Prove this theorem using Venn diagrams.

4. One of *De Morgan's Theorems*, $\overline{A} + \overline{B} = \overline{AB}$, was introduced in Problem 3a. The other of these important and useful theorems is

$$\overline{A + B} = \overline{A}\overline{B}$$

Prove this theorem using both the truth table and Venn diagram approaches.

5. Prove or disprove that

$$B = C$$

if

$$A + B = A + C$$

and

$$AB = AC$$

6. There are other Boolean operators sometimes used besides the "and," "or," and "not" operators. One of these is the "Sheffer Stroke" operator, which is usually written | (i.e., A|B) and whose truth table is

A\B	0	1
0	1	1
1	1	0

a) Prove that $A + B = (A|A) | (B|B)$
b) Prove that $AB = (A|B) | (A|B)$
c) Find a theorem relating $\neg$ to some combination of A and the Sheffer Stroke and thus show that all three of our operators can be expressed using just the Sheffer Stroke.

Section 9.2

7. Find a weighted 4-bit code which has the same binary configuration for the digits 0, 1, 2, 3, 4 as BCD and which, in addition, is self-complementing; that is, the complement of each digit is found by changing 1s to 0s and 0s to 1s.

8. a) Use De Morgan's theorems (see Problem 4) to find new expressions for C_4 and C_8 in equation (9.2).

b) Use the distributive law to simplify the expression for C_4 in (9.2).

9. a) Use the following algorithm to derive equations for C_8, C_4, C_2, and C_1 in Table 9.5. Consider the column for some C_i:

i) Whenever a 1 appears in this column write a term in T_8, T_4, T_2, and T_1, which is the product of four factors, one for each T_i, as follows. Consider the row in which the column has a 1. If the value of T_i in this row is 1 the factor is T_i and, if it is 0, $\overline{T_i}$. For example, for C_2 there is a 1 in the third row and the corresponding term is $\overline{T_8}\ \overline{T_4}\ T_2\ \overline{T_1}$.

ii) Form the sum of all these terms.

b) Use any Boolean theorems in the text or in the previous problem to simplify these expressions to come as close as possible to the form of equation (9.2) or one of the forms derived in the previous problem.

10. a) Show that the parallel accumulator shown in Figure 9.12 could require as many as $n-1$ time intervals to add two n-bit numbers.

b) Give an intuitive argument that, on the average, two 36-bit numbers would only need about four time intervals before all carries had been handled.

11. Assuming a time t between the add pulse and the carry pulse and a time t_d for passage through a delay box, and ignoring any time of transmission along wires or switching of flip-flops, what is the maximum time after the add pulse that the correct sum will appear in the accumulator in the circuit of Figure 9.13?

Section 9.3

12. Suppose Fortran allowed only the Sheffer Stroke operator in the form .SS. instead of .AND., .OR., and .NOT. Write function subprograms AND(A,B), OR(A,B), and NOT(A) to implement the .AND., .OR., and .NOT. operators.

13. Write a function subprogram SS(A,B) to implement the Sheffer Stroke in Fortran.

14. List any other possible interpretations of the expression on p. 376, other than those given, which would be possible without a rule of hierarchy.

15. Write function subprograms in Fortran to implement the equivalence and implication functions.

16. Explain why the PL/I operator hierarchy has the negation operator on the same priority level as exponentiation and the unary minus.

17. Fill in the missing quantities in the following BNF definition of a logical expression in Fortran:

```
<LOGICAL PRIMARY> ::= ( <———> ) |
       <RELATIONAL EXPRESSION> | <LOGICAL ———> |
       <LOGICAL VARIABLE> | <LOGICAL FUNCTION CALL>
<LOGICAL FACTOR> ::= <LOGICAL PRIMARY> |
       . ——— . <LOGICAL PRIMARY>
<LOGICAL TERM> ::= <LOGICAL FACTOR> |
       <LOGICAL TERM> . ——— . <LOGICAL TERM>
<LOGICAL EXPRESSION> ::= <LOGICAL TERM> |
       <LOGICAL EXPRESSION> . ——— . <LOGICAL EXPRESSION>
```

10

input and output

We have postponed our main discussion of the input and output features of P-O languages until almost the end of this book for two reasons. One is that the free-format (i.e., list-directed) and NAMELIST (i.e., data-directed) input and output features discussed in Section 6.2.3 are sufficient for the needs of beginning computer science students. This is particularly true for scientific data processing, where sophisticated input and output is usually only a luxury. For business data processing it must be admitted that full use of the input and output facilities of the language is often needed for quite elementary applications.

The other reason for postponing our discussion of input and output to the end is that, in an important sense, it lies outside the main orientation of this book, which is toward *communication* with computers. This may seem paradoxical, since, after all, the input to and output from a computer are the basic means of communication between man and computer. But our emphasis on communication is at a different level from the physical communication between man and computer; we have been concerned with the processes of communication and the language structures by which these are achieved. The specific techniques of getting data into the computer and results out are therefore not of prime importance to us. Algol, in particular, recognizes this by providing no explicit input and output features in the language. These are supposed to be provided as convenient by each using installation. It would, however, be pure pedantry in a

387

Figure 10.1   CDC 405 card reader. *(Courtesy of Control Data Corp.)*

book such as this to avoid discussion of input and output on the above grounds. Pragmatically speaking, users must know about these features. More significantly, as the user does more sophisticated programming, he often finds the use of the full range of input and output features to be very convenient and profitable.

To begin our discussion of input and output we shall first consider the hardware devices by which input and output are accomplished. Too often programmers misuse or fail to use these devices to their full advantage because of lack of understanding of the physical structure of the hardware.

10.1   HARDWARE CHARACTERISTICS

Input-output devices generally fall into two classes:

1. Those associated directly with the input of the user's program and data and the output of his results.

Figure 10.2   IBM 29 keypunch. *(Courtesy of IBM Corp.)*

2. Those used for intermediate storage of results during the execution of the program.[†]

Of the two classes it turns out that the hardware characteristics of the first are of much less concern to programmers than the characteristics of intermediate storage devices. This is because the first class typically has little effect on the writing of programs. By contrast, the characteristics of intermediate storage devices often significantly affect program structure. Therefore, we shall first discuss briefly the input-output devices which accept the programmer's data and instructions and give him his results, and then discuss intermediate storage devices in more detail.

10.1.1   Basic Input-Output Devices

Users of P-O languages employ a variety of *input* devices depending upon the computer they are using and the particular hardware configuration of that com-

---

[†] Those used for intermediate storage are often also used for the storage of *resident files*, that is, previously written programs and data which the user can invoke without reloading a card deck; we shall not discuss these further here.

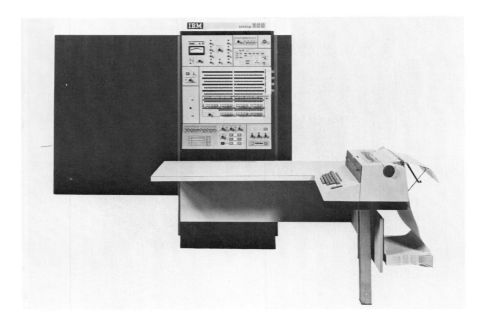

Figure 10.3   IBM 360 console with IBM 1052 console typewriter. *(Courtesy of IBM Corp.)*

puter. As we shall see in Section 10.2, the language structures for input are generally oriented toward the use of punched cards. However, devices other than those which read punched cards can be used for input. The most common input devices together with their relevant characteristics are:

1. *Card readers.*   Card readers (see Figure 10.1) read 80-column (i.e., IBM) cards at a variety of speeds ranging up to a maximum of about 1200 cards per minute. As far as the user of a P-O language is concerned, he need only understand that such readers read all 80 columns of a card and translate the punches in each column to a code which is transmitted to the memory of the computer. One example of such a code is given in Table 3.4 and another in Table 3.6. Normally, card readers will translate any combination of punches which results from pressing any key on a 26 or 29 keypunch, as well as certain other combinations which can be punched using the *multiple punch key* of the keypunch (Figure 10.2). These latter are sometimes needed for control card purposes. The reader should be aware that certain combinations of multiple punches will cause a reader error and result in the failure to process the user's program.

2. *Typewriters or teletypewriters.*   Most computers have typewriters attached to their console (see Figure 10.3) through which input may be transmitted to the computer. However, only on the slowest available computers are these type-

Figure 10.4   IBM 2741 remote typewriter terminal. *(Courtesy of IBM Corp.)*

writers available to the user as an input device, and even on such computers a card reader is the more normal mode of input. Our orientation here is toward typewriters and typewriter-like devices, such as teletypewriters, through which input to a computer can be entered from a point remote (perhaps a long distance) from the central computer and connected directly to it via some communications medium, most commonly a telephone line. The use of such devices (see Figures 10.4 and 10.5) for the input of programs is becoming increasingly common for P-O language programs. The user of such a device must learn some simple rules about its operation, but basically he types on it as if it were a keypunch with every key stroke corresponding to a card column. Although there is no physical card to tell the device when a given line is complete, the carriage return key, which signals the end of each line, usually serves to separate one "card" from the next.

These two devices account for the overwhelming majority of program and data input for P-O language users. A few computers allow input from punched paper tape which is prepared on devices analogous to card key punches. Optical scanning devices which can read typewritten copy directly are now becoming available, but these too, if used to read programs or data, would, in effect, treat each character position on the paper as a card column.

Figure 10.5   Teletype Model 33. *(Courtesy of Teletype Corp.)*

Direct input from magnetic tape is available on some computers from tapes produced by striking keys on a typewriter-like device, but again, as far as the user is concerned, it is essentially as if he were striking keys on a keypunch. More commonly there is direct magnetic tape input to computers from tapes which have been produced by a small auxiliary input-output computer which has taken data from cards and transmitted it to magnetic tape (see Figure 10.6). As far as the user is concerned, he is preparing input to be read by a card reader. He should realize, however, that the purpose of the organization shown in Figure 10.6 is to achieve the higher reading speeds of magnetic tape as compared to card readers in sending input to the main, fast computer. This technique was quite common a few years ago but is much less so now because current hardware and, more importantly, software allows computers to read at the same time they compute. In any case, it is more appropriate for us to defer discussion of magnetic tape to Section 10.1.2, in which its main use as an auxiliary storage device is discussed.

There is a wider variety of *output* devices in use than input devices. The most common of these are:

1. *Line printers.*   Printers (see Figure 10.7) are available at speeds up to about 1500 lines per minute; printers with even higher speeds are available at a very few installations. Two characteristics of printers of which the user should be aware are

> i) the maximum number of characters per line allowed, since, as we shall discuss in Section 10.3, the user can specify how much he wants printed on each line; the most common maximum numbers are 120 and 132, although occasionally as many as 144 is allowed.

> ii) the use of the first print column for carriage control; in most Fortran implementations the control of the carriage on the printer (e.g., double spacing, triple spacing, skipping to next page, skipping a certain number of lines) is controlled by a character which would print in the first column (but does not—it is only used to control the carriage); therefore, the pro-grammer should avoid having any results print in the first column. PL/I, however, handles carriage control directly in the output statement; see Section 10.2.

2. *Card punches.*   For later data processing use, it is sometimes desirable to have the output results punched into cards rather than printed (although it is

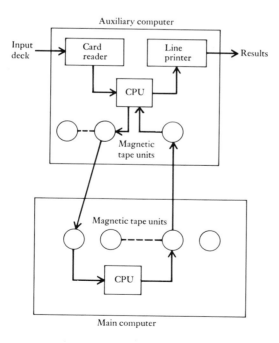

Figure 10.6   Use of auxiliary computer for input-output.

Figure 10.7   CDC 512 line printer. *(Courtesy of Control Data Corp.)*

more common in this case to store the results on magnetic tape or disk; see Section 10.1.2). Card punches (see Figure 10.8) operate at speeds up to about 300 cards per minute. The user typically specifies in which columns of the card he wishes his data (see Section 10.3), but aside from knowing there are 80 columns in a card he need know nothing else about these devices.

3. *Typewriters or teletypewriters.*   Just as input can be achieved on such devices by pressing keys and getting printed copy as well as transmission of signals to the computer, so can the computer transmit signals to the typewriter or teletypewriter which activate the printing mechanism so that printed output results. Because of the slow speed of these devices, they are normally used for output only when the volume is quite small. As far as the programmer is concerned, these devices act just like line printers except that the number of characters per line is normally limited to a smaller number than is allowed for printers.

We should also mention that visual display devices are becoming increasingly important for computer output purposes. The most common type of device of this kind (Figure 10.9) displays only *characters* (i.e., numbers and letters, as opposed to curves). In effect, the character display replaces the printing part of a typewriter or teletypewriter. The keyboard shown in Figure 10.9 is available for

Figure 10.8   CDC 415 card punch. *(Courtesy of Control Data Corp.)*

input as with typewriters but in addition to being transmitted to the computer, the typed input is displayed on the screen. Sometimes these character displays are attached to auxiliary printers so that "hard copy" may be obtained. Occasionally they have camera equipment associated with them which can be activated by the user to record the display. Without some recording device, visual displays are most practical only for output of intermediate results which can be used to check the course of the computation. As far as the user of character displays is concerned, they operate like printers except that he must know the maximum number of characters per line *and* the maximum number of lines on the screen at any one time.

Some computer installations have more sophisticated visual displays available which can plot curves. They usually have camera equipment associated with them and sometimes can accept input from *light pens*. Such displays are not normally directly available to the P-O language programmers. If available at all to such users, it is only through use of a special battery of subroutines written especially for this device by the installation. The language structures to be discussed later in this chapter cannot be used for output on these devices. Similar remarks also apply to the plotters available as on-line or off-line devices at many

Figure 10.9   IBM 2260 character display terminal. *(Courtesy of IBM Corp.)*

computer installations (see Figure 10.10) and which can only be used by calling one or more of a set of installation-provided subroutines.

Our previous remarks with respect to the use of magnetic tape as an input device also carry over to output, as illustrated in Figure 10.6.

As a final point, we note that all the input and output devices considered here, not only typewriters and teletypewriters, can be located remotely from the central computer and connected to it by communication lines. Indeed, most computers can have attached to them several readers, printers, punches, etc.— some remotely and some centrally located. The location of the input or output device does not affect the programmer at all in his use of a P-O language. However, the user should be aware of the options open to him, normally speci- fied on the job card (see Section 6.2.2), of using devices at different locations for input and output. For example, a program with an input deck numbering only some hundreds of program and data cards could be submitted at a remote location where the card reader might be slower than at the central location. But, if many thousands of lines of output were anticipated, it would make sense to print the results out on the high speed central computer printer (and then have them mail- or messenger-delivered) rather than at the slower remote printer.

Figure 10.10   Calcomp 565 plotter. *(Courtesy of California Computer Products Corp.)*

Some installations automatically force large amounts of output to be printed at the central installation so as not to tie up the slower remote printer unnecessarily.

10.1.2   Auxiliary Memory Devices for Input and Output

All programmers must be aware to some degree of the need to *manage* the storage available to them. This need arises because of the limited size of all computer storage media. The major purpose of the EQUIVALENCE statement in Fortran and the dynamic allocation available in Algol and PL/I is to increase the efficiency of main (i.e., magnetic core) storage utilization over what would be obtained if, in Fortran, no storage were shared, and, in PL/I and Algol, if storage were all assigned before execution time. Despite these techniques for making more efficient use of main memory, there is just not enough such memory available on any computer to satisfy the entire needs of all programs. Because of this it is necessary at times to store intermediate results on auxiliary memory devices and then read them back into main memory at a later point in the program. In addition it is sometimes necessary, for example, with large matrices or arrays of other kinds, to store part of the array in main memory

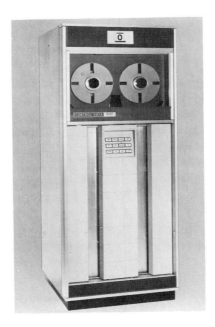

Figure 10.11   CDC 607 magnetic tape unit. *(Courtesy of Control Data Corp.)*

and part on some auxiliary device. The language structures to be discussed later in this chapter enable the programmer to read and write data to and from main and auxiliary storage. But, to use these structures effectively and efficiently, the user should understand some aspects of the physical characteristics of these auxiliary devices. In the remainder of this section we shall discuss the relevant characteristics of the most important auxiliary memory devices.

10.1.2.1 Magnetic tapes.   To the user the two most significant characteristics of magnetic tape storage are

1. it offers potentially unlimited storage (since a tape reel may be removed from a tape unit and replaced by another), and
2. it is a *serial access* device, as we shall describe below.

A typical magnetic tape unit is shown in Figure 10.11. The most usual length of the tape reel is 2400 feet, although shorter reels are sometimes used. Data is stored in *tracks* or *channels* on the tape, the most common number of tracks being 7 or 9 (see Figure 10.12). Each point on a track may be magnetized or unmagnetized and therefore can store one bit. Each line across the tape stores

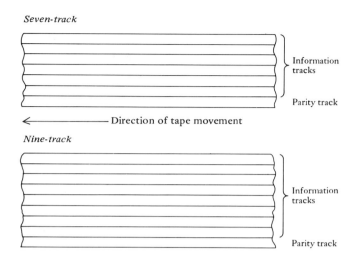

Seven-track

Information tracks

Parity track

← ——————————— Direction of tape movement

Nine-track

Information tracks

Parity track

Figure 10.12   Magnetic tape formats.

one *character*. Seven-track tape is most commonly used with computers which store characters in a 6-bit code (see Section 3.1.5). The seventh track is for *parity checking*. The bit in this track is set to 1 or 0 so that the total number of 1 bits in each line is odd. This serves to check that data has not been lost or that extraneous bits have not found their way onto the tape. Odd parity is used so that, if the tape is accidentally erased (i.e., 0 bits everywhere), the parity check will be violated. (Most computers also have parity checking in main memory locations.) Analogously, nine-track tapes are used mainly on computers where characters are stored as 8-bit bytes, with the ninth track used for parity.

Example 10.1

Indicate how the following computer words would normally be stored on magnetic tape:

1. From a 36-bit word computer (e.g., IBM 7000 series)

   | 100111 001101 100010 110110 010000 111011 |

2. From a 60-bit word computer (e.g., CDC 6000 series)

| 101101 001010 111110 110111 000100 110011 000101 011001 100011 100100 |

3. From an 8-bit byte computer with 4 bytes per word (e.g., IBM 360 series)

| 10110011 | | 00010100 | | 00111011 | | 10111001 |

In the first two cases the words are divided, as shown, into sets of 6 bits and each is stored, with the parity added, on seven-track tape as shown in Figure 10.13. In the third case, each byte is stored as one character, again as shown in Figure 10.13.

It should be noted that when computer words from main memory are written on magnetic tape, this is not always done by a direct transcription of the binary digits in main memory to magnetic tape. Often a transformation is first performed in which, for example, the fixed- or floating-point number in main memory is transformed into its binary-coded decimal (see p. 79) equivalent as a decimal number and then written onto tape (see Section 10.2.2).

The density of data on a magnetic tape is expressed in terms of the number of bits per inch (bpi) stored in a single track. On most magnetic tape units this density is 556, 800, or 1600 bpi, with the second being the most common today. Thus, a magnetic tape with data stored at 800 bpi on each track stores 800 characters per inch on the tape as a whole. Therefore, on a 2400-foot reel of magnetic tape with storage density of 800 bpi,

$$2400 \times 12 \times 800 = 23,040,000$$

characters or almost 4 million 36-bit words can be stored.

The speed of movement of magnetic tape is usually about 75 inches per second, so in one second 60,000 characters pass under the reading/writing heads of the tape unit on an 800 bpi tape. This figure of 60,000 characters per second is called the *transfer rate* of the tape unit and expresses the rate at which information can be transferred to and from magnetic tape and main memory.[†] While transfer rates as high as 120,000 characters per second are available, this number is still substantially less than the rate at which computers can shift data around inside the main memory. This latter may run as high as 10 million characters per second. But more important is the fact that, at 75 inches per second, it takes 38 seconds to go from one end to the other of a magnetic tape. The only way to get from one place to another on a magnetic tape is by having the tape pass under the read/write heads; this is what we mean by serial access. Therefore, if the tape is positioned a long way from the information to be

---

[†] A transfer rate of 60,000 characters per second is often written as 60KC, K for thousand and C for character.

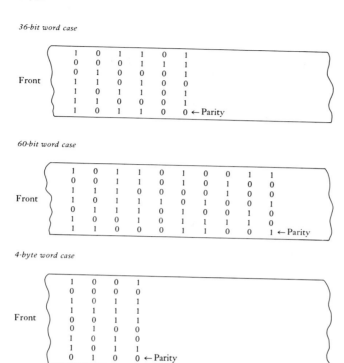

36-bit word case

60-bit word case

4-byte word case

Figure 10.13   Tape formats for Example 10.1.

written, there is a substantial waste of time in properly positioning the tape. The efficient use of magnetic tape by P-O language programmers requires that the programmer organize his usage to minimize the time wasted in getting from where the tape is to where he wants it. Some aspects of tape positioning will be covered in Section 10.2.2; here we shall consider some further aspects of data storage on magnetic tape with which the user should be familiar.

The normal organization of data on magnetic tapes is for a number of characters or words to be grouped together into a *record* with records separated by *interrecord gaps* (see Figure 10.14).† The size of the interrecord gap is about 3/4 inch and is chosen so that the tape will be accelerated to full speed when it reaches the record itself. (Of course, the interrecord gap, since it contains no data, reduces the effective transfer rate and available volume of storage.)

---

† Some special applications use so-called *gapless tape*, in which the entire tape is in effect one record.

When the programmer calls for a set of data from main memory to be written on a magnetic tape, this data is normally written on the tape as a set of records of equal length, except for the last which usually is shorter. For example, a record length of 256 words, with 1 word being for control purposes, is quite commonly used. Suppose a programmer wishes to write a group of 1000 words, which logically form a single group, on tape. These 1000 words are called a *logical* record. But the command to write this logical record on tape will result in three records of 256 words (765 data words) and one record of 236 words on the tape (see Figure 10.14). The four records on the tape are called *physical records*.

The control word in each physical record will normally be unused except in the last record of the logical record. In this record the fact that it is the last record will be indicated together with the number of words in the record. Sometimes, on the other hand, logical records are very short (e.g., names and addresses) and it is desirable to put a number of logical records into one physical record (Problem 5). When a number of logical records is put into one physical record, that physical record is called a *block* and the tape is said to be *blocked*.

Often a programmer receives data on magnetic tape (e.g., telemetered data from a satellite in orbit or output from a previous computer run) that he wishes to process using a P-O language program. (In this case, of course, the magnetic tape data is the primary input medium to the program.) It is vital in such a case that he know how the data was recorded on the tape. For example, he must know how many physical records there are in a logical record or how the tape was blocked when he uses the input statements considered in Section 10.2 to read data from tape for use by his program.

10.1.2.2 Magnetic disk storage.

Storage of information on magnetic disks rather than magnetic tapes has three advantages to the computer user. It allows more total data storage, it enables faster transfer rates between main and auxiliary memory, and, often most importantly, it provides much faster access to the data. A magnetic disk file typically consists of some five to twelve magnetized disks, each usually 6 to 12 inches in diameter, but sometimes as much as 4 feet in diameter, all mounted on a single axis as in a juke box, except that the axis is normally vertical. Since data can be stored on either side of the disk, the number of *disk surfaces* is twice the number of disks. In a disk file the disks themselves may be

1. permanently mounted on the axis (see Figure 10.15), or
2. removable (see Figure 10.16) and replaceable by other disks.

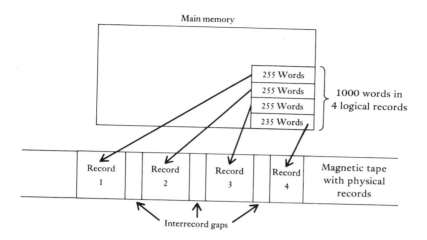

Figure 10.14 Logical records and physical records.

In the former case the amount of disk storage is strictly limited by the capacity of each disk (see below), but in the latter case the removable disks, called *disk packs*, provide effectively unlimited storage analogously to magnetic tape storage.

Each disk or cylinder contains a number of separate circular *tracks* like a phonograph record, except that each track is distinct from and unconnected to any other. Although the track may be the basic unit of storage on a disk which can be accessed, more usually tracks are further divided into *sectors* as shown in Figure 10.17. The *switching gap* shown in Figure 10.17 is an area on the disk where no data is stored and has the purpose of allowing the read/write head to switch from one track to another. Many disk drives provide one read/write head for each disk surface which must be positioned over the track to be read or written. In some of the larger disk units more than one such head is provided for each surface, each head taking care of the reading and writing from one *zone* (or group of tracks) of the disk.

Data on a magnetic disk is stored as bits sequentially on each track of each surface. The number of bits stored on a single track ranges from about 25,000 to 50,000 and the number of tracks on a disk from two to five hundred. Thus a given surface may store from 5 million to 25 million bits or, approximately, 1 million to 4 million characters. An entire disk file may store from about 7 million to 100 million characters. With disk pack drives, a single disk system may contain as many as eight separate disk drives (i.e., axes with disks). The maximum storage available at one time on any single physical disk storage mechanism

Figure 10.15   CDC 814 magnetic disk unit. *(Courtesy of Control Data Corp.)*

today is about a quarter-billion characters.[†] A single disk drive, therefore, in general provides substantially more storage than a single magnetic tape unit.

Magnetic disks rotate continuously on their axes while the read/write head remains fixed in angular location. The rotation speed of a disk drive is of the order of 15 to 40 revolutions per second. The numbers of bits per second which can be read ranges from about half a million to two million. Some disk drives store successive bits of a character or word on different disk surfaces and read or write these in parallel, thus increasing the number of bits read or written each second. Taking all these things into account, the transfer rate of most disk files is between 100,000 and 400,000 characters per second.

But, as we stated at the start of this section, to the user, often the most important aspect of magnetic disk storage is the speed of access of this type of storage. The time it takes from the instant the command is given to read from or write on a given place in a disk file until the data actually can be read or written depends on three factors:

[†] Although some with two or three times this amount of storage are about to become available.

Figure 10.16   IBM 2314 magnetic disk unit. *(Courtesy of IBM Corp.)*

1. the time required to select (electronically) the disk surface from which the reading or writing is to be done; this is called *head-switching* time.

2. the time to position (mechanically) the head at the track to be read or written; this is called *seek* or *head-positioning* time.

3. the time required for the location at which the data is to be read or written to rotate under the read/write head; this is called *latency* time.

Of the three, head switching requires much the least time, normally taking a few microseconds. Seek time is usually the largest of the three with a maximum value typically between 100 and 300 milliseconds. The maximum latency is the time required for one complete disk rotation, which would be 25 milliseconds for a disk rotating at 40 rps and 66 2/3 milliseconds for a rotation speed of 15 rps. The *average latency* is half the maximum latency. (Why?) The maximum access time, that is, the sum of the maxima of the three times, is on the order of 125 to 400 milliseconds and the average access time is about half the maximum.

Therefore, when data is to be read in an order different from that in which it was written, disk storage is far superior to tape in terms of the access time to get from one record to another. Of course, even when data is read in the order in which it was written or when it is written on sequential tracks, the faster transfer rate of disk is another advantage over tape.

The interrecord gap on magnetic tape is about 3/4 inch. Therefore, at 75 inches per second it takes 10 milliseconds to go from the end of one record to the beginning of the next. On disk there is no gap between records. But the discussion above might lead to the conclusion that there is substantial delay when switching from one track to the next, even when the tracks are being read or written sequentially. In fact, such switching from one track to an adjacent track is normally accomplished in the millisecond or less required for the rotation of the heads over the switching gap. On some disks the tracks are numbered

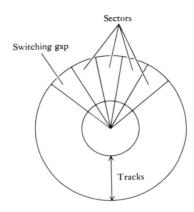

Figure 10.17   Magnetic disk organization.

in such a way that track 1 is on one surface, track 2 is in the same radial position on the second surface, track 3 is in the same radial position on the third surface, etc. With this scheme the switching from one track to the next is generally accomplished electronically in microseconds because no mechanical movement is required. Also, in this case no switching gap is required.

Another term sometimes used and worth mentioning in connection with disk storage is *half track*, which refers, of course, to half of one track on a disk. It is often convenient to store a sequence of records on alternate half tracks so that some processing of the data or determination of whether to read or write more data can be made while the other half track rotates under the read/write head.

Logical and physical records have much the same meaning with disk as with tape storage. A given logical record may reside on part of a track or on more than one track. Physical records are always of a size less than the capacity of a track and each physical record normally is stored all on one track. As with tapes, logical records can be blocked into physical records. Consecutive logical or physical records may or may not be stored on consecutive tracks of the disk. But this need not concern the user. The operating system of the computer remembers where there is empty space on the disk, stores new data in this space, and then remembers where it is stored so it can later be retrieved.

In sum then, disk storage provides a storage medium with substantial advantages over tape storage, particularly if the data are to be read in an order different from that in which it was written. Of course, there is a price that must be paid for this advantage. Disk storage, even on disk packs, is substantially more expensive than tape storage. Therefore, disks should be used for permanent

Figure 10.18   IBM 2301 magnetic drum unit. *(Courtesy of IBM Corp.)*

storage of results only when these are going to be needed often, that is, when having them available on-line or on disk packs is a distinct advantage. P-O language users will sometimes have a choice between use of disk or tape for storage of large files of results. When they have such a choice there will usually be a price tag attached to each to prevent everyone from using disk storage indiscriminately. Alternatively, each user may be assigned a maximum amount of permanent disk storage to use as he pleases. For storage of intermediate results, systems which have permanent disk storage normally use some of it for so-called *scratch-pad* purposes, which can be used by any P-O language program being executed.

10.1.2.3 Other mass storage devices.   Currently tapes and disks are the only two mass storage devices directly available to the P-O language programmer. But there are some other devices which store large amounts of data about which the reader should be aware, either because they are part of current computer systems (though they may not be available to him directly), or because they are just coming into use on large computer systems and may soon be available for use with P-O languages.

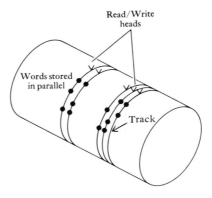

Figure 10.19   Data storage on magnetic drums.

A *magnetic drum* (see Figure 10.18) is a cylinder on which data is stored in *tracks*, where now a track is a circle around the cylinder (see Figure 10.19). Usually, but not always, magnetic drums have one read/write head for each track, the data coming under the head as the cylinder rotates at high speed (3000 or more rpm). Often the data is stored in parallel so that all the bits of a word come under the read/write heads at one time (see Figure 10.19). This enables substantially higher transfer rates than from disk, with rates of 1 million characters per second not uncommon. Also, because drums normally rotate more rapidly than disks and because there is no mechanical movement required to position the heads, the maximum and average access times are much less than for disk, 10 milliseconds being a typical average access figure. On the other hand, the storage capacity of drums is much less than disks, 1 to 8 million characters being the range available. And drum storage is much more expensive than disk storage. For this reason it is seldom available for use by the P-O language programmer. Rather, it is usually used to store programs which are often needed in main memory. For example, the Fortran, Algol, PL/I, and/or Cobol compilers might be stored on a drum to enable them to be read into main core memory quickly when they are needed. Also, commonly used subroutines, which the user of a P-O language might wish to call upon (e.g., subroutines to compute trigonometric functions), might be on the drum. In addition, the operating system of the computer may use part of the drum to shuttle parts of the system in and out of core memory.

In addition to disk, tape, and drum there are two mass storage devices which are just coming into use. They are at opposite ends of the spectrum in terms of

Table 10.1 Characteristics of auxiliary memory devices

Device	Access characteristics	Transfer rate	Capacity
Magnetic tape	Serial and slow	40 to 120KC	15 to 45 million characters/reel
Magnetic disk	125 to 400 ms maximum	100 to 400KC	Up to a quarter-billion characters
Magnetic drum	30 ms or less maximum	Up to 1000KC	1 to 8 million characters
Data cell	Slow, sometimes as great as 1 sec	About 100KC	Up to a half-billion characters
Large-core storage	Very fast; 3 to 8 μs	Very fast; up to 10,000KC	Up to 10 million characters

capacity, access time, transfer rate, and cost. One of these is *data cell* or *strip* storage, which is an inexpensive storage medium based on the use of magnetized strips which can store very large amounts of data (up to half a billion characters) at a cost per character substantially less than that of magnetic disk. Access to data stored in data cell storage can be quite slow, requiring up to a second, and the transfer rate is slow compared to disk. But, for large amounts of data which will be used regularly and are, therefore, needed on-line, data cell offers a very attractive storage medium which will undoubtedly prove of substantial use to P-O language programmers.

The other storage medium mentioned above is called *extended-core* or *large-core storage*. It consists of magnetic cores just like the main memory of the computer but in larger quantity than the main memory (quantities from 125,000 to 2 million words are in use) and fabricated at lower cost. Sometimes it is possible to execute instructions in this auxiliary core as in main core memory. But, more usually, the auxiliary core is used like a magnetic drum to store temporarily programs and data which are needed often and quickly in main memory. Access to words or characters in this core is not as fast as in main core, but the 3 to 8 microsecond access which is common is far faster than that for drums. Moreover, very high transfer rates, up to 10 million words per second, are possible with some large-core storage. For multiprogrammed, and particularly for time-shared systems (see Section 11.3), large-core storage will play a very important role in many computer systems. Table 10.1 summarizes the typical characteristics of the auxiliary memory devices we have discussed.

One of the problems which now faces the P-O language programmer is when to use disk and when to use tape. With the addition of data cell storage and the

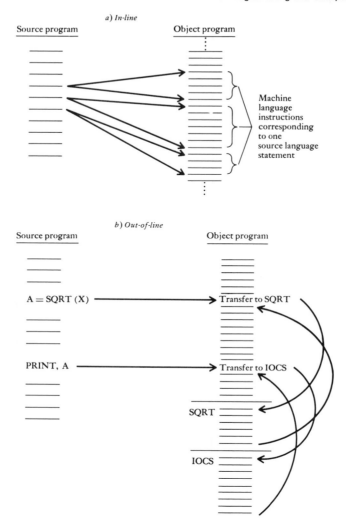

Figure 10.20   In-line and out-of-line compilation.

possible use of drum or auxiliary large core, the problems of *storage manage-ment* could easily become much greater. Fortunately for the programmer, var-ious automatic storage management schemes are now under development which will relieve the programmer of the burdens of storage management. These auto-matic schemes will normally store a new program or data file on magnetic disk. If the file is not used regularly the system will automatically move it to the next lower level of storage, which might be data cell or tape. In general, the location of the file at any time will depend on how often it is used. Therefore, the file is said to *migrate* from one auxiliary store to another. The migration of files from higher to lower level stores and vice versa is often called *trickle* and *percolate*, respectively.

10.2   LANGUAGE STRUCTURES FOR INPUT AND OUTPUT

The four languages we have been discussing offer substantial contrasts in their facilities for input and output. Fortran and Cobol have some quite different facilities, PL/I includes the facilities of both Fortran and Cobol, while Algol has no input or output facilities whatsoever in its definition. The developers of Algol assumed that input and output requirements were likely to be quite specific by installation and therefore thought it would be best to have them installation-supplied. The result is that most Algol systems use Fortran or Fortran-like input and output.[†]

When sequential statements in a P-O language program are compiled into groups of machine-language instructions in the object program which are sequential in main memory during execution, this is called *in-line* compilation (see Figure 10.20). Most of the language structures we have discussed thus far result in in-line compilation. On the other hand, invocation of subprograms or procedures results in *out-of-line* compilation of the subprogram or procedure which is transferred to by an in-line transfer of control instruction. For example,

A = SQRT (X)

does not result in in-line coding of the square root function, but rather in a machine-language transfer of control to the statements of the square root sub-routine (Figure 10.20). The reader might easily guess that input-output statements would result in in-line object code but this is not so. Before discussing the input-output statements themselves we shall point out why they do not.

10.2.1   Input-Output Control Systems

Like the compiler of a source-language program, the input-output control system (IOCS) is a complex machine-language program which the computer system puts at the disposal of the user. Whereas the compiler exists in core memory at, of

[†] However, a number of Algol compilers now use the input-output scheme proposed in A Proposal for Input-Output Conventions in Algol-60, *Communications of the Association for Computing Machinery*, May 1964.

course, compile time, IOCS is in memory at execution time (indeed, all the time, since the compiler uses it also). Our purpose here is not to discuss the spectrum of routines which make up the IOCS systems. Our intention is to point out some of the reasons why a separate input-output system, rather than in-line coding of input-output statements, is desirable.

One reason for IOCS is that many of the input and output functions are naturally carried out by subroutines, so that it would be wasteful to do input and output in-line. If, to print out the values of A, B, and C or to read from magnetic tape the values of A, B, and C, all that was required was to generate machine-language input and output statements with the addresses of A, B, and C, then in-line coding would be sufficient. But typical input or output operations require more than this. Two examples will illustrate this:

1. We indicated in Section 10.1.2.1 that physical records on magnetic tape normally contain a control word containing certain information about the contents of the record. Such control words are also used on disks. Reading, writing, and interpreting such control words is clearly a job for a subroutine.

2. Records on tape or disk usually have a standard maximum size because all input and output is accomplished by putting the data to be written in an *output buffer* and reading data from auxiliary memory into an *input buffer*. There are normally separate input and output buffers for tape and disk. A *buffer* is an area in memory, usually main memory, set aside to facilitate input and output. On most large computers a combination of software and hardware allows other instructions to be executed after an input or output instruction has commenced execution, but before the transmission of all the data has been completed. Thus input and output is said to be *buffered* from other instructions. Buffers are normally twice the length of the maximum record size allowed on the auxiliary storage medium, so that, for example, if 256 words were a maximum tape record size, the tape buffers would be 512 words in length. Such a double-length buffer is used as follows for a write-on-tape operation when a logical record contains more than one physical record:

   i) the data to be written is transferred to the buffer; when the first 256 locations are filled, a machine-language write-operation is given to write these 256 words on tape.

   ii) while the write-operation is proceeding the remaining 256 words of the buffer are filled; when the writing of the first 256 words is completed another write operation empties the remainder of the buffer; then the first 256 words of the buffer are refilled and so on.

This "Ping-Ponging" between the two halves of the buffer allows efficient handling of the input-output operations. To organize and handle the buffers properly is one of the jobs of IOCS and clearly is one which requires routines separate from the user's program.

The above discussion may motivate the need for IOCS when auxiliary memory is being used. But, if the programmer wants only, say, to print the values of A, B, and C, why should IOCS be needed? The answer to this question depends upon an understanding of the relation between the internal speed of a computer and the speed of its input-output devices. Without going into the details here (Problem 8), it should be clear that a computer which can manipulate numbers internally in a few microseconds can produce numbers much faster than even a 1500-line per minute printer can print them. Potentially then, one user could slow up the operation of the entire computer considerably by requesting a great deal of printing, which could cause the rest of the computer to wait while the numbers to be printed were sent to the printer. Considerations such as this become much more complicated when dealing with multiprogramming and time-sharing systems; see Sections 11.1.2 and 11.3. Here we wish only to point out that to avoid these problems it is common not to send the user's printed output directly to the printer, but rather to put it first on, say, a disk and then to print it later. To see the ramifications of this it is necessary to understand the distinction between logical and physical units.

The *logical* unit is that input or output unit from which the programmer *wishes* his input to be read or to which he wishes his output to be sent. The *physical* unit is the one from which the data is *actually* read into core memory or to which the data is sent from core memory. Two examples will elucidate this:

1. In the case discussed above the physical print unit might be some portion of a disk. All data to be printed would be sent ("spooled") to disk and would then be printed from disk. Since data can be sent from main memory to disk much more rapidly than to the printer, such a *spooling system* enables the print load to be smoothed out. Of course, if over an extended period of time users try to print faster than the speed of the printer, the area on disk reserved for printing will be filled and the computer will again have to wait upon the printer.

2. When the user wishes to read card data into main memory from a card reader (the logical unit), the computer system may in fact read the cards onto a physical unit, which may again be a disk, and, while this is being done, execute some other user's program. When the input data has all been read onto disk, the computer will return to the first user's program and read the data from the disk into main memory. In this way the system need not wait as it would if a user's data were read from the relatively slow card reader directly into main memory.

The correspondence between logical and physical units (which is of no concern to the user) and the handling of the spooling to and from disk or tape is another of the functions of IOCS. It explains why even the simplest input and output statements make use of IOCS (instead of being compiled in-line).

Our discussion has only touched upon the intricacies of IOCS which are better left to a more advanced course. Hopefully it will help to give the reader at least a feeling for what actually happens when he writes the input and output statements to be discussed below.

10.2.2   Input and Output Statements

Most input and output statements consist basically of three parts:

1. The verb which describes the operation such as READ or WRITE.
2. A specification of the *data* involved in the input and output.
3. A specification of the *format* of the input or output data.

In addition, some input and output statements require an indication of the input or output unit (e.g., card reader or printer). The only input and output statements which do not contain these parts explicitly or implicitly are those which are concerned with positioning, logically or physically, some external storage medium. In this section we shall discuss the first two aspects of input and output statements listed above and in Section 10.3 we shall discuss specification of format.

There is a distinct difference between the types of input and output statements in Fortran and Algol (as normally implemented) on the one hand, and Cobol on the other. PL/I, since it is oriented toward both scientific and business data processing problems, includes both types. Using PL/I terminology, the scientific languages perform input and output on *data streams* where the stream is a sequence of values of a list of variables. Normally the data undergoes some kind of transformation (e.g., conversion from decimal to binary or vice versa) between the external and internal storage media. For business applications, the input and output units are *records*, as discussed previously in this chapter. That is, they are groups of values going from or to an internal storage medium (usually a buffer in main memory) to or from some external storage medium with no transformation being performed. In the case of card input or output, a record is normally a single card. For printed output a record is usually a single line of printing.

Panel 10.1 lists the verbs used in Fortran, PL/I, and Cobol for input and output. The *basic verbs* are the ones which actually perform the input and output.

GET and PUT in PL/I have the same general meaning as READ and WRITE in Fortran. The bracketed verbs in Cobol have similar meanings. PRINT and PUNCH are not official parts of the Fortran language but are available at many installations. They may be used in place of WRITE to avoid specifying a *unit number* as described below.

The auxiliary verbs typically have the purpose of preparing data for input and output by properly positioning an input or output unit, or by performing some initializing task. We shall only describe them briefly here without detailing the specific syntax of the statements:

1. OPEN and CLOSE, respectively, prepare a file to be read and do some final processing after use of it has been completed. For example, files of data are often headed by *labels* which contain certain identifying information. These labels are read by an OPEN statement and, if necessary, updated by a CLOSE statement.

2. The REWIND statement in Fortran positions the unit, referred to in the statement, at its logical beginning. This repositioning may be physical, as when a tape reel is rewound, or logical, as when the pointer to a position on disk is reinitialized, or both, as when the read/write heads on the disk must also be

Panel 10.1   Input-output verbs

FORTRAN	*PL/I*	*COBOL*
	Basic verbs—Stream data	
READ	GET	
WRITE	PUT	
PRINT		
PUNCH		
	Basic verbs—Record data	
	READ	READ
	WRITE	ACCEPT
		WRITE
		DISPLAY
	Auxiliary verbs	
REWIND	OPEN	OPEN
BACKSPACE	CLOSE	CLOSE
ENDFILE		
	REWRITE	
	LOCATE	
	DELETE	
	UNLOCK	

moved. ENDFILE in Fortran is a statement which writes a record at the end of a file which can later be recognized as the end. BACKSPACE in Fortran repositions a tape or changes a pointer to disk so that the record prior to the one previously pointed at is ready to be processed. If the unit is already "rewound," no action takes place.

3. REWRITE in PL/I enables a given record in a file to be replaced by another. LOCATE allows an area in memory, other than the normal buffer, to be set up in which a record for a particular file can be assembled. DELETE allows a record in a file to be erased and UNLOCK makes a file available for reading and writing which had been previously "locked" (i.e., protected from all reading and writing) by an option on another input-output statement.

The detailed syntax for all the statements whose verbs are given in Panel 10.1 may be found in the language descriptions cited in the bibliography at the end of Chapter 2. In PL/I most of the statements allow a substantial number of options for performing various auxiliary input-output tasks.

Panel 10.2 describes the syntax of the data stream input and output statements. Note the following:

1. In Fortran, formatted input and output normally involves binary-coded decimal characters. Thus, for example, for printed output, if the logical unit is magnetic tape, the characters on tape are the BCD equivalents of the characters to be printed on the printer. In unformatted input and output, on the other hand, the characters are the precise binary equivalents of the internal memory representation. When auxiliary memory units are used for intermediate storage during a computation, it is most efficient to use unformatted binary input and output statements (Problem 9).

2. Unit numbers are required in Fortran but not in PL/I because the latter assumes that the computer system knows where the data is. This is because it has assigned each data set to a particular unit from information elsewhere in the PL/I program (which we shall not consider here), or by default to the normal input and output devices.

3. The GET and PUT statements have, in fact, more general forms than those shown in the panel. They allow the user to specify, instead of the system input or output medium, a string or file which is to be transferred from one place to another.

4. There are no options available with the form of the GET statement given in the panel. In another form, which allows naming a file to be input, a COPY option is available which has the effect of *echo-checking* the input by sending it to the standard system print file (cf. p. 333). To accomplish the same thing in Fortran a WRITE statement must follow a READ. The PUT statement has a number of options of which we mention only the PAGE option, which has the effect of starting the printing on a new page, and the SKIP option, which causes the next data item to be printed on a new line.

The specification of what quantities are involved in input and output is indicated by means of some type of list as indicated in Panel 10.2. Panel 10.3 considers some elements of the syntax of lists in Fortran and data specification lists in PL/I. Concerning Panel 10.3:

1. For DATA and LIST in PL/I the format of the data was discussed in Section 6.2.3. Only DATA in PL/I may be followed by an empty list but, when the list after DATA is *not* empty, every name in the data stream must be in the list (but not vice versa). In Fortran the list may also be empty; see Section 10.3.

Panel 10.2   Data-stream input and output statements

FORTRAN	*PL/I*

Syntax

i) $\left\{ \begin{array}{l} \text{READ} \\ \text{WRITE} \end{array} \right\}$ (un, fn) list $\qquad$ $\left\{ \begin{array}{l} \text{GET} \\ \text{PUT} \end{array} \right\}$ *data specification list options*

or

ii) $\left\{ \begin{array}{l} \text{READ} \\ \text{WRITE} \end{array} \right\}$ (un) list

where *list*, which may be empty, is described in Panel 10.3

where *data specification list* is described in Panel 10.3 and the *options* are discussed in the text

Semantics

One item of data corresponding to each element in the list is read from or written on unit *un*, under format control by the statement numbered *fn* in the first case and unformatted in the second case.

One item of data corresponding to each element in the data specification list is obtained from the system input medium (normally the card reader) or put on the system output medium (normally the printer); format control is contained in or referred to in the data specification list.

Examples

READ (5, 100) A, B, C
WRITE (6, 100) A, B, C

GET LIST (A, B, C);
PUT DATA (A, B, C);

fn—format number
un—unit number

Panel 10.3   Input—output lists

FORTRAN

PL/I

Syntax

A sequence of elements separated by commas where an element may be

i) a subscripted or unsubscripted variable name, or

ii) an array name, or

iii) a *repetitive specification* (see Panel 10.4).

A heading word which may be

LIST or DATA or EDIT

followed by, in parentheses, a sequence of elements separated by commas where each element may be

Input:

i) an unsubscripted variable name, or

ii) a subscripted variable name (not allowed if DATA is used), or

iii) an array name, or

iv) a repetitive specification (see Panel 10.4—not allowed if DATA is used), or others including structure names which we shall not discuss here. If DATA is used this list may be empty.

Output:

The same except that, if LIST or EDIT is used, variable names may be replaced by expressions and, when DATA is used, repetitive specifications are allowed. With the EDIT heading each data list must be followed by a *format list* (see Section 10.3) which may in turn be followed by further pairs of data and format lists.

Semantics

Data are input or output for each element of the list (see text and Panel 10.4) in the format specified by the FORMAT statement with statement label *fn* (see Section 10.3) or unformatted in binary if there is no *fn*.

Data are input or output for each element of the list (see text and Panel 10.4) in a format determined by the attributes of the data for DATA and LIST lists (cf. Section 6.2.3); since data names appear as part of the input for DATA lists, the list itself can be omitted.

Examples

A, B, C
A (I), B (1), C

DATA (A, B, C)
LIST (A(I), B(1), C)
EDIT (A(I), B(1), C) (*format list*)
EDIT (A(I), B(1)) (*format list*)
    (C, D) (*format list*)

fn—format number

2. When array variables appear in lists without any subscripts, the entire array is meant to be input or output. On input the current values of the dimensions are used and all elements of the array are expected to be input. In Fortran, on both input and output the elements are in *column* order; that is, the first subscript is varied most rapidly. Conversely in PL/I, arrays are transmitted in *row* order, the last subscript being varied most rapidly.

It remains now to discuss the repetitive specification mentioned in Panel 10.3. This specification is nothing more than a mechanism for implying iterations without using the structures described in Chapter 8. These repetitive specifications are generally known as *implied DO-loops* in Fortran (cf. Example 8.7). Panel 10.4 describes these specifications. Note the following:

1. As indicated in the second example, repetitive specifications can be nested to a depth which is installation-specified. The syntax implies this, since it allows any list element (e.g., another repetitive specification) to be part of a repetitive specification.

2. The syntax allows a repetitive specification of the form

$$(A, I = 1, 10) \text{ (Fortran) or } (A \text{ DO } I = 1, 10) \text{ (PL/I)}$$

where A can be either a scalar or an array variable. On input, such a specification is of no interest since it implies that A (or all the elements of A, if it is an array)

Panel 10.4   Repetitive specification

FORTRAN   PL/I

Syntax

Any list, as described in Panel 10.3, followed by a comma and then a structure of the form of Panel 8.3, the whole enclosed in parentheses.

Any sequence of elements separated by commas, as described in Panel 10.3, followed by DO followed by a structure of the forms of Panel 8.3 or (ii) through (v) of Panel 8.4.

Semantics

For every value of the incremented identifier, the entire list is input or output as described in Panel 10.3.

Examples

(A(I), B(I), I = 1, 10)
((C(I,J), I = 1, 11, 2), J = 1, 10)

(A(I), B(I) DO I = 1 TO 10)
((C(I,J) DO I = 1 BY 2 TO 11)
DO J = 1 TO 10)

Panel 10.5   Record input and output statements

PL/I   *COBOL*

Syntax

READ FILE (*filename*) [INTO *id*]   READ *filename* RECORD
  options   [INTO *id*] *options*
WRITE FILE *(filename)* FROM   WRITE *filename*
  (id) options   [FROM *id*] *options*

Semantics

Next logical record of the filename referred to is read or written to or from main
memory according to the various options specified (see text)

Examples

READ FILE (INPUT) INTO PAYROLL;   READ INPUT RECORD INTO
                                        PAYROLL

WRITE FILE (OUTPUT) FROM ACCT;   WRITE OUTPUT FROM ACCT
                                        WRITE OUTPUT

id–identifier

should be read in 10 times, which would result in only the tenth datum of the
set of data actually appearing in memory. (Why?) However, on output, such a
specification might be used to achieve a desired output format, by say, heading a
number of columns all with the same value.

Both PL/I and Cobol allow data to be input and output in the form of
records. Panel 10.5 gives the basic syntax of the statements which accomplish
this. Note the following:

1. It is clear from Panel 10.5 that PL/I record input and output is directly
patterned after the Cobol equivalents. Both languages assume the computer
operating system knows where the files named can be located so that no unit
numbers are needed.
2. In Cobol, any file which is to be read *must* be preceded by an OPEN statement which prepares it for reading; in PL/I, if the OPEN statement has not been
given, the file will automatically be opened by the READ statement.
3. In both PL/I and Cobol, reading and writing takes place to or from the input
and output buffer areas described in Section 10.2.1. The only option on READ

listed in Panel 10.5 occurs in both languages and consists of INTO followed by an identifier. When this option is used, not only will the input appear in the input area for the filename but it will also be placed in the storage area corresponding to the identifier. On output, PL/I requires that the identifier from which output is to be written be specified in the statement; Cobol writes the record from the output area for filename unless the FROM option is used.

4. The word RECORD in the Cobol READ is meant to emphasize the record nature of the input.

We shall not discuss the various error conditions, such as tape or disk parity errors and reaching the end of a tape reel, which can occur during input and output. However, the user of a P-O language who is going to make use of auxiliary memory devices should be aware of the possible errors, and the action the language or the implementation takes when such errors occur.

Panel 10.6   Format statements

FORTRAN

PL/I

Syntax

sl FORMAT *format list*

$sl_1 : ... : sl_n$: FORMAT *format list;*

where the *format list* is a sequence of *format elements* (examples in Panel 10.7) separated by commas and the whole enclosed in parentheses.

Semantics

The format statement is used to direct the input or output for a READ or WRITE statement whose format number *fn* (see Panel 10.2) equals the statement label *sl*; each element of the list in the READ or WRITE statement is input or output according to the corresponding element in the format list.

The format statement is used to direct the input or output for a GET or PUT statement with edit-directed input or output, which contains in its format list a *remote specification* (see Panel 10.8) with a statement label corresponding to elements in the format list specifications.

Examples

100 FORMAT (2E16.8,5X,I7)

L1: L2: FORMAT (2E(16.8), X(5),I(7));

sl—statement label

10.3   FORMAT

Many users of computers for scientific purposes care little for how pretty their output looks or for the ability to prepare their input in a variety of fashions. But these matters are of interest to virtually all users of computers for business data processing purposes as well as to an increasing number of scientific users. It is paradoxical then, that at first glance Fortran and the part of PL/I input and output specially aimed at scientific users have the most extensive and complex language structures for formatting input and output. The paradox disappears for Cobol, however, when it is realized that the specifications of file structures in Cobol itself provides the format for input and output. In particular, the PIC-TURE attribute discussed in Section 4.3 together with other facilities in Cobol allow the format of a file to be specified for input and output. In PL/I the format facilities of Fortran have been carried over and expanded so that the business data processing user would normally use these for output on preprinted

---

Panel 10.7   Format list elements in PL/I and Fortran

FORTRAN   *PL/I*

1. Data format example

Syntax

sFw.d   F(w,d,s)
where s, w, and d are integers;   where w, d, or s can all be expres-
s may be absent   sions which are evaluated and
                                                         converted to integers; ,d, s or ,s
                                                         may be absent

Semantics

The data item occupies a maximum   The data occupies a maximum of
of w positions with (on input) d   w positions with (on input) d
digits after the decimal point *if*   digits after the decimal point *if*
no decimal point appears (if there   no decimal point appears (if
is a decimal point, d is ignored) and   there is a decimal point, d is
(on output) d digits after a printed   ignored) and (on output) d
decimal point; the internal number   digits after the printed decimal
is floating-point; s is a scale factor   point (unless d = 0 in which
which represents a power of 10 to   case the decimal point is not
multiply the datum by on input or   printed); s is a scale factor
output.   which represents a power of
                                              10 to multiply the datum
                                              by on input or output.

forms or on blank forms on which he could produce his own titles. In this section we shall discuss the format facilities in Fortran and PL/I and in so doing we shall also consider how Cobol achieves formatted input and output.

Format enables the programmer in Fortran or PL/I (and normally in Algol input-output implementations) to accomplish the following types of things:

Panel 10.7   Format list elements in PL/I and Fortran (Continued)

FORTRAN   *PL/I*

2. Character format example

Syntax

Aw

where w is an integer

A(w)

where w is an expression which is evaluated and converted to integer

Semantics

The external field contains w Hollerith characters; the internal field contains the number of characters r assigned to the variable name in the input or output statement.

Input

If $r \leqslant w$, the rightmost r characters are input; if $r > w$, $w-r$ trailing blanks are inserted.

If $r \leqslant w$, the leftmost r characters are input; if $r > w$, $w-r$ trailing blanks are inserted.

Output

If $r < w$, $w-r$ blanks precede r characters; if $r \geqslant w$, the leftmost w characters are output.

If $r < w$, $w-r$ blanks follow r characters; if $r \geqslant w$, the leftmost w characters are output.

3. Control format example

Syntax

nX

where n is an integer

X(n)

where n is an expression which is evaluated and converted to integer

Semantics

On input the next n characters of the input stream are skipped; on output n blanks are inserted in the output stream.

Panel 10.8   Unique PL/I format elements

1. Remote format element

Syntax

R(*sl*)

Semantics

The format list in the statement with label *sl* is used to direct the input or output of the next elements in the data list; this element can appear *only* in a format list in a GET or PUT statement.

2. Picture specification

Syntax

P'*picture specification*'

Semantics

The picture specification as discussed in Chapter 4 governs the input or output of the next item in the data list.

sl—statement label

1. Alphabetic or alphanumeric data for titles, headings, and labeling of results can be output with the results and placed where desired on the printed page.† In PL/I, however, such output can be obtained without format also [e.g., PUT LIST ('THIS IS A TITLE')].

2. Output results can be placed where desired on the page.

3. The number of digits in each number may be controlled and, for floating-point numbers, output can be with or without an exponent part.

4. In Fortran numbers can be converted from internal binary not only to decimal, but also to other forms such as octal or BCD.

Panel 10.6 describes the overall structure of format statements in Fortran and PL/I. The format list in the PL/I format statement is identical to the format list which appears in edit-directed lists in Panel 10.3. In PL/I the format list may either be part of the GET or PUT statement itself or may be in the format statement as described in Panel 10.6. It is referred to by a special format list element (see below) in the GET or PUT statement format list.

---

† Format can also be used for output on punched cards or auxiliary storage media, but we shall orient our discussions here to printed output which is where format finds its main use.

Format list elements may take on many different forms. We shall consider only a few representative examples in Fortran and PL/I, first, of some of the types of list elements which appear in similar forms in both languages, and then some which are unique to PL/I. Panel 10.7 considers the former category. In all three examples, the syntax and semantics are quite similar with, as usual, somewhat greater generality characteristic of the PL/I elements.

Panel 10.8 considers two specifications unique to PL/I. The second one is the picture specification which corresponds to the "picture" used in Cobol to describe elements in the Cobol Data Division.

Fortran uses a slash (/) in the format list (which may replace a comma) to skip to the next line. PL/I provides two related format list items, SKIP and LINE, to accomplish line skipping. (Both of these can also appear as options in the PUT statement.)

Both languages allow repetition of format elements by use of an integer preceding the element, or preceding a group of elements in parentheses such as

6 (F7.2,A7) (Fortran) or 6 (F(7,2),A(7)) (PL/I)

PL/I also allows an expression, in parentheses, in place of the repetition integer which is converted to integer form.

BIBLIOGRAPHIC NOTES

Depending upon his own interests and the kind of problems with which he is involved, the reader will have to decide how deeply he wishes to understand input-output hardware. A good source of material similar to that in this chapter is Hassitt (1967). Ware (1963) has a good and much more detailed discussion of various input-output hardware.

The intricacies of IOCS are of concern to few P-O language programmers. Hassitt (1967) contains a brief discussion of IOCS and Fisher and Swindle (1964) a more detailed discussion, but the reader should also refer to the IOCS manuals provided with the software for most computers.

For the details of input, output, and format statements available to him, the reader should always consult the P-O language manual for his computer as well as the input-output modifications which have been made at his installation. In addition, the references at the end of Chapter 2 on particular languages are good sources of information.

Bibliography

Fisher, F.P., and G.F. Swindle (1964): *Computer Programming Systems*, Holt, Rinehart & Winston, New York.

Hassitt, A. (1967): *Computer Programming and Computer Systems*, Academic Press, New York.

Ware, W.H. (1963): *Digital Computer Technology and Design*, vol. 2, John Wiley & Sons, Inc., New York.

PROBLEMS

Section 10.1

1.   a) Object card decks from compiled P-O language programs are normally punched as *binary cards* with, for example, on a 36-bit word computer, 72 columns in all 12 rows punched with each row containing 2 machine words. For cards punched in this way, how many characters per second can be read by a 1200 cpm reader?

b) Discuss, therefore, why the use of magnetic tape for input, as in Figure 10.6, is more desirable in all cases than direct card input, if the computer is not buffered, so as to be able to do other calculations while cards are being read.

2.   a) Approximately what is the input speed in characters per second which could be achieved by a good typist at a typewriter-like console?

b) How many times faster an output device is a 1000 lpm printer printing 132 characters per line than a typewriter-like console which prints at 15 characters per second? .

3.   a) What are the transfer rates of a magnetic tape unit which moves at 75 inches per second and has data stored at the following densities?

   i) 556 bpi
   ii) 800 bpi
   iii) 1600 bpi

b) How fast would a tape unit have to move to achieve a 90KC transfer rate for data stored at a density of 800 bpi?

4.   a) Consider a seven-track magnetic tape unit which moves at 75 inches per second and has data stored at a density of 800 bpi. If the interrecord gap is 3/4

inch and each record consists of the contents of one 36-bit word, what is the effective transfer rate of the tape unit?

b) If instead, each record is 100 words, what is the effective transfer rate?

c) Repeat for the case when each record is 1000 words.

5. Suppose a seven-track tape unit and a 3/4-inch interrecord gap with data stored at 800 bpi is positioned at the first of 100,000 logical records, each of which consists of five 36-bit words. Suppose further that the tape unit moves at 75 inches per second and ignore the time required to accelerate to full speed.

a) If each logical record is also a physical record, how long does it take the tape to move to the position of the 50,000th record?

b) If there are ten logical records in each physical record, what is the answer to (a)?

c) Repeat for the case of 100 logical records per physical record.

6. Consider a magnetic disk storage unit with the following properties:

i) Rotation speed of 25 rps
ii) One read/write head per disk surface
iii) Time for movement of the head from the inner track to the outer track of a surface or vice versa is 200 milliseconds

Ignoring head-switching time and assuming the head seeks a track at constant speed (i.e., ignoring acceleration and deceleration),

a) what is the maximum access time?
b) what is the average access time?

7. For a magnetic drum which rotates at 2500 rpm with one head per track and negligible head-switching time, what is

a) the maximum access time?
b) the average access time?

Section 10.2

8. Suppose a computer is being used to produce a table of square roots where the output will be a sequence of lines, each of which will contain an argument and its square root. Assume the calculation of each square root including the incrementing to get the argument, the square root computation itself, and all "bookkeeping" (e.g., testing to see if all arguments have been used, preparation

of the output) requires 200 microseconds. What is the ratio of the speed at which output lines can be produced to

a) the rate at which they can be printed on a 1200 lpm printer?

b) the rate at which they can be written on a tape unit with a 90KC transfer rate (assuming the argument contains 6 characters and the square root contains 12 characters)?

c) the rate at which they can be written on a disk with a 200KC transfer rate?

9. Explain why data which is being written on magnetic tape for auxiliary storage during the course of a computation and which will, later in the computation, be read back into main memory, is more efficiently written in pure binary than as a sequence of BCD characters.

10. a) Show how READ statements using the implied DO-loops of Panel 10.4 could be rewritten as ordinary DO-loops which contain a READ statement in the range.

b) Assuming that, when the list following a READ statement is "satisfied" (i.e., exhausted), all remaining data on the card being read are discarded (cf. Section 6.2.3), do implied DO-loops or the DO-loops of part (a) allow greater flexibility of input data preparation?

Section 10.3

11. In any P-O language, write formatted output statements equivalent to those of Example 6.4 (p. 231) to achieve the output of Figure 6.7.

12. a) Write formatted input statements to read only the data of Example 6.3 as shown in Figure 6.6 (p. 231). Assume the first datum on each card is in columns 1-10, the second in columns 11-20, etc., with the 18 on card 2 in columns 2-3.

b) Then write formatted output statements to achieve precisely the output of Figure 6.8.

11

operating systems and time sharing

[In a multiple access computer system] one of the peripheral devices which must be connected to a computer is now seen to be a console with a human operator working at it, and knowledge of the operator's characteristics is as important to the system designer as a knowledge of the characteristics of, say, a magnetic tape.

M. V. Wilkes in *The Computer Journal* (May 1967)

This has been a book about computer programming. It has, with the exception of Chapter 10, ignored *computer hardware*. It has also ignored *computer software*—the complex of machine-language programs which organize the work of a computer and enable P-O languages to be used efficiently. Together the hardware and software form a *computer system*. It is becoming increasingly difficult to separate hardware and software as one delves deeply into computer systems. But, at the level of this book, it is possible to consider them separately and make some useful points. To beginning computer scientists and particularly to P-O language programmers there are some facts about computer software which are useful to know. In this chapter we shall discuss some of the features of operating systems—which are the heart of computer software—in general, and of remote computing and time-sharing systems, in particular, because of their increasing importance.

11.1 THE FUNCTIONS OF AN OPERATING SYSTEM

If he thinks about it at all, the beginning computer programmer often looks at the process by which his source deck produces results on a computer as sheer legerdemain. Some understanding of how computer memories are organized and what a compiler is helps, but it does not really explain what happens to his job, particularly as regards control cards, from the time his cards are read by the card reader until his results are printed. He dimly realizes perhaps that a great deal more occurs than just the compilation and execution of his program—but how does it all work, how are many different users' programs all kept track of inside the computer?

To do this general job of organization is the function of the *operating system* of the computer. The operating system is a complex, often very complex set of programs which make up the major portion of the software of a computer system. In Section 11.3 we shall consider briefly some of the components of the operating system, but first, in this section we shall indicate what it does. Since the functions of an operating system vary considerably, depending upon the general milieu in which the computer operates, we shall consider two separate situations here—batch processing and multiprogramming—and then later in this chapter we shall consider a third—time-shared operation.

11.1.1   Batch Processing

Until quite recently most large computer centers were so-called batch processing installations. Although "batch processing" does not mean a specific mode of operation, it refers in general to a computer system in which a "batch" of jobs—that is, the program and data decks with control cards—from a number of users are input, executed, and output as a group, one after another. The usual batch situation is illustrated in Figure 11.1:

1. The card reader and printer and the tape or disk on which the reader puts the input, and from which the printer gets the output, are often not part of the main computer. They can be part of an auxiliary computer used just for input and output. When this is so, it is usually possible to manually switch the tape or disk unit from the small input-output computer to or from the main computer so that a given tape or disk unit will at one time be logically attached to one computer and at a different time to another. In some cases it is necessary to physically carry a tape reel or disk pack to (from) the small computer from (to) a corresponding unit on the main computer (cf. Figure 10.6).

2. The purpose of using tape or disk as the input and output medium for the CPU is, as discussed in the previous chapter, to achieve a better match of input-output speeds and central processor speeds. Normally in batch operation, despite the buffering discussed in Chapter 10, the central processor is slowed somewhat while the program and data for a given job are read into main memory and, to a lesser extent, while the results are output from main memory. Since data can be

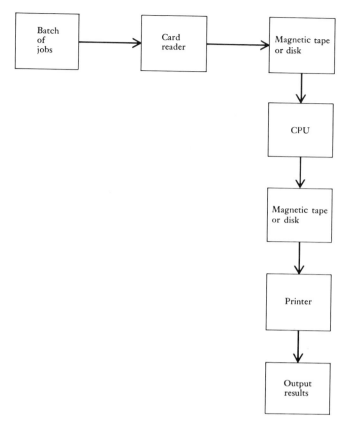

Figure 11.1 Batch processing operation.

read from and written on tape or disk much more rapidly than can be done using card readers or line printers, the procedure described in Figure 11.1 results in substantial savings of CPU time.

Let us then orient ourselves to the situation in which a batch of jobs is on magnetic tape or disk and the central processor is finished with its previous work and ready to read in the jobs and perform the processing requested. The operating system is normally too large to be able to reside entirely in main memory. Some of its parts which are used comparatively seldom may themselves reside on tape or disk (but on a different reel of tape or portion of disk than the batch of jobs) or, perhaps, on a magnetic drum because of its faster input and output speeds. At the instant we are focusing on here, the main portions of the operating system are in main memory. (Later, as we shall indicate, even some of

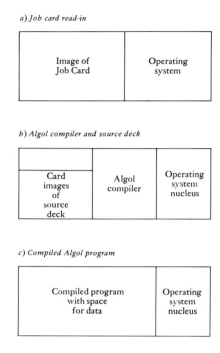

Figure 11.2   Contents of main memory at various stages of a batch processing run.

these portions may be written out to tape, disk, or drum.) Figure 11.2*a* illustrates the situation. The subsequent operations are generally (omitting some details) as follows:

1. The card image on the magnetic tape or disk of the first card of the first job is read into main memory. This should, of course, be the *job card* for the first job. (All operating systems have routines within them to detect errors in program decks, e.g., a missing job card, and to take certain action when this occurs. In our discussion here we shall assume all program decks are properly structured.)

2. The job card is checked to make sure the proper accounting and identification information is available. In some systems the job card will also indicate what compiler or other parts of the system the program deck will need. More commonly this is indicated on the second card of the deck. In any case, after reading the first or second card into memory, the operating system knows something about the requirements of the program deck to follow, including which language is being used. Let us suppose, for example, that the program to follow is an Algol program.

3. The operating system then causes the Algol compiler to be read into memory from tape, disk, or drum, typically over part of itself (see Figure 11.2b). The part of the operating system remaining in memory is normally that part which is always resident in main memory and is called the *nucleus*.

4. The Algol compiler then takes control, reads in the source deck, recognizes the end of the source deck either by a control card or by the language syntax, compiles the program, and normally puts it on disk or tape as it compiles. This latter is done so that the object program can later (see below) occupy main memory space, including that which the source deck and compiler occupy during compilation.

5. Assuming that the control card which caused the Algol compiler to be invoked also called for execution of the compiled program (this is usually an option), after the completion of compilation control is returned to the operating system which reads in the compiled object program and turns control over to it (see Figure 11.2c). The object program in turn reads the necessary data off the tape (using IOCS, which is part of the nucleus; see Section 11.2), performs the computation, sends the output to the system output tape or disk, and finally, at the end of the computation, turns control back to the operating system.

6. Normally then, the operating system reestablishes itself to the status of Figure 11.2a, performs various accounting functions, and then reads the job card for the next job. It continues then to process each job on the input tape or disk until all have been completed. By this time, a new tape or disk has been made from the next batch of input and the process repeats itself. At the end of each batch the output tape or disk is switched to the input-output computer and the results are printed out.

The above description by no means gives the full flavor of the functions performed by an operating system. Other features worth discussing are the following:

1. At many installations, particularly universities, the P-O language used for most applications has two compilers† in the system. One is the normal system compiler, which operates as described above for Algol. (The situation discussed here most commonly exists, however, at Fortran installations.) The other is usually called a *student compiler* or an *in-core compiler* or a *debugging compiler*. It is particularly efficient for very short jobs which require little execution time. This is a characteristic of almost all student jobs and all jobs which are being debugged (and, therefore, execute not at all or very little). If the procedure discussed for Algol earlier in this section were used, the compiler would need to be read in anew for each job, even if every one of a sequence of jobs were an Algol job. With an in-core compiler the compiler is read in for the first job and then remains in main memory (i.e., in core) as a sequence of jobs for that compiler are read in. The in-core compiler takes over part of the function of the

---

†Or, as they are often called today, *language processors*.

operating system in that it handles the reading of control cards for successive jobs. This type of compiler reads the source decks, compiles them in core rather than putting the object program on tape or disk, and then executes them. It returns control to the operating system only when a job appears which requires some other compiler or system program. The use of this compiler rather than the normal system compiler is indicated by a special control card. In order to utilize efficiently an in-core compiler it is, of course, necessary to arrange the input so that all jobs requiring this compiler are together on the input tape or disk. Such compilers can save large amounts of CPU time at busy installations, but they have the disadvantage of cutting down severely on the amount of main memory available for the object program because the compiler and nucleus are always kept in memory.

2. The job card usually contains an estimate of the running time and amount of output (printed pages and punched cards); in the absence of such estimates the operating system inserts standard estimates. During the execution of any program the operating system *monitors* the problem program by

> i) keeping track (using IOCS) of the amount of output, and
>
> ii) receiving a signal from a timer (set to zero by the operating system at the beginning of each job) when the time is exceeded.

When the time estimate is exceeded, the operating system will normally terminate a job, whether or not it has been completed, or, when the output estimate is exceeded, no more results will be output, except perhaps those in the output buffer when the execution is completed.

3. All software systems have as part of their facilities a *library* of programs available to the user. Some of these may be invoked in P-O language programs by using subroutine or function call statements. They are then the subroutine or procedure analog of built-in functions. Others are special programs which would not be part of another program, but rather would be called using a special control card and specially prepared data. The function of the operating system in relation to the library is not only to interpret the control cards, but also to use its *catalog* of library programs to find the desired program on some auxiliary memory device and make it available. For example, a library program called by the Algol program discussed earlier in this section would become part of the object program in memory shown in Figure 11.2c.

4. When a programmer gets a P-O language program debugged he will often, if he intends to use this program many times, get an object deck punched out. This deck is usually called a *binary deck* (cf. Problem 1 of Chapter 10), since it is a direct binary map of the object program in storage. The operating system must, when necessary, handle in a single Fortran job, for example, a succession of main programs and subprograms, some of which may be in source language and need compiling and others which may be binary decks requiring only relocation and loading.

5. Often programs have their data not on cards originally, but on tapes or disk packs saved from previous computer runs or obtained in some other fashion. Not only are control cards required to indicate this but, in addition, the operating

system must keep track of the various available physical units and assign them by messages to the operator so that he can load tapes and/or disk packs.

6. Another feature of the operating system is the ability to allow *chaining* or *overlays*. In the former, object programs too large to fit into main memory are split into parts (by the programmer) and then called into memory, one after the other, by invocation of a subroutine call in each part of the program. In the latter, parts of a program too large to fit into memory can be called from the main program by the programmer and written over (or *overlaid*) some part of the main program in main memory. One or both of these facilities is often provided in Fortran systems, in which case the various parts of the chain or the successive overlays communicate with each other through common storage (see Section 7.3.4).

In general then, the operating system in a batch processing environment carries on a multitude of tasks, only some of which have been covered here. It is typically a quite complex set of computer programs which the manufacturer delivers with the computer. But batch processing, while a distinct advance over earlier operational environments in which jobs were run one at a time and there was machine operator intervention between each job, still falls short of providing the ideal operating environment. Why this is true, and how some of the problems with batch processing can be overcome is the subject of the next section.

11.1.2 Multiprogramming

One easily understood failing of most batch processing systems is their relatively slow *turnaround time*. Turnaround time is most simply defined as the time which elapses from the instant the user drops off his card deck at the computing center to the time his printed results are available to him. Components of turnaround time are indicated in Table 11.1. Typically, at some time t_1 before the end of execution of the previous batch of jobs is expected, most[t] jobs submitted since the previous batch was prepared are inserted in the card reader, read, and put on tape or disk. Even though jobs are normally executed in the sequence, or nearly the sequence, in which they are submitted, it is nevertheless true that the nearer to t_1 the job is submitted, the smaller will be the turnaround time. This is because, at most computing centers, the printed results of a job in the batch are not available until the results for *all* jobs in the batch have been printed.[tt] Still,

---

[t]Most batch processing computer centers are scheduled so that jobs requiring more than some minimum amount of CPU time or printed output are run during second shift (4 P.M. to midnight) or third shift (midnight to 8 A.M.) so as to give short jobs as many turnarounds during prime shift (8 A.M. to 4 P.M.) as possible.

[tt]Often the input batch of jobs and the batch printed are not the same due to the way output is organized on tape and the need to schedule the printer efficiently; we shall ignore this here.

the important lesson here is that the turnaround time is determined by the time taken to run all the jobs in a batch—which may number 50 to 100—rather than the running time of the single job itself. Batch processing installations of the type we have discussed here have typical turnaround times of one to four hours for short jobs, and sometimes one or two days for long jobs.

Another failing of batch processing systems, but not such an obvious one is that, despite the buffering of input and output discussed in Chapter 10, substantial amounts of CPU idle time results because, if a program requires a large amount of input or output while it is running, the buffering system inevitably cannot keep up with the demand and the CPU is idle for periods of time while the system is said to be *input-output bound*. In addition, CPU time is lost in batch processing systems when a program requires, for example, that a magnetic tape be mounted or dismounted during a run. While the operator does this, often the system stands idle. Finally, time is lost between batches because of the time required to set up and start into execution one batch of jobs after the completion of another. (That is, the two events listed for t_2 in Table 11.1 are never simultaneous and often involve some seconds of elapsed time.)

The idle CPU problem could be alleviated:

1. if, on input-output bound jobs, there was some simple mechanism of executing *another* job while the first was waiting for input or output, and
2. if the hardware-software system lessened the need for operator intervention and, when intervention is required for one program (e.g., mounting a tape), allowed some other program to be executed while the first was waiting.

Reduction of idle CPU time would, of course, also result in some improvement in turnaround time. But, for real improvement in turnaround time, particularly for very short jobs, the following are necessary:

1. A reduction in the time from job submission to the time when the job is put into execution.

2. A mechanism which allows jobs to be executed in an order other than that in which they are loaded onto tape or disk.

Table 11.1　Batch processing turnaround time

Time	Event
t_0	Card deck delivered to computing center
t_1	Deck, as one of batch, read by card reader and transferred to tape or disk
t_2	Execution of previous batch of jobs ended; execution of new batch begun
t_3	End of execution of batch; start of printing of results
t_4	Printed results available

In fact, the conditions for improvement of both the idle CPU problem and turnaround time are provided by the hardware-software concept known as *multiprogramming.*

Multiprogramming refers to that mode of using a computer in which more than one user's program resides in main memory at the same time.[†] Before discussing this concept and its implications in more detail, let us first point out that, in Figure 11.2 and in our previous discussion of batch processing, it was implicit that only one user's program was in main memory at any given time. But why should that be so? There are both hardware and software answers to this question. The hardware answer is concerned with the *protection* of one users's program from another. When a user's program is completely debugged it will only use that part of main memory which has been assigned to it. But, when a program has not been debugged—often, even when the user thinks it has been—one of the most common things that happens is for the program to attempt to use memory space other than that which it has been assigned. For example, it is not uncommon for a program to attempt to *clear* memory, that is, set the contents of all words to zero. Now if this happens when only the user's program is in memory, the most that can happen is that the nucleus of the operating system will be affected and there are standard restart procedures when this happens. But, if another user's program is also in memory, and particularly if it is part way through execution and, therefore, if damaged must be restarted from scratch, it is intolerable to allow one user's program to damage another.

Despite the restart procedure mentioned above, it is inconvenient and wasteful to have to restart when the nucleus is damaged. For this reason, in the mid 1960s computers were provided with a *memory protection* feature which allowed one area of memory—typically that in which the nucleus resided—to be protected so that no other program could use this area of memory.[†] But, having established the principle of memory protection, it was then comparatively easy to visualize a situation in which every program in main memory would be protected from every other for writing or reading, or both, by restricting each

---

[†]Buffering, as discussed in Chapter 10, might be called proto-multiprogramming because two parts of the same user's program are executed simultaneously—the input or output operations *and* execution of that part of the program which can take place before the input or output is completed. We should also note that our definition of multiprogramming is a bit more restrictive than is really necessary; it is sufficient to require that more than one user's program be *active* in the system since, while one program is being executed, other active ones may be temporarily transferred to some auxiliary storage medium.

[†]Often this protection was just *write protection,* that is, the area could not be written into, but not *read protection,* since no harm could come to the nucleus by having another program attempt to read from its area of memory.

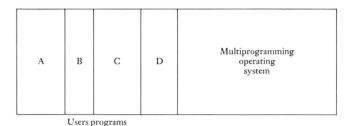

Figure 11.3 Main memory during multiprogramming operation.

program to use *only* that portion of memory assigned to it. And indeed, almost all large computing systems now provide memory protection of this nature.

With memory protection then, the main hardware barrier to multiprogramming was removed. But, to take advantage of the possibility of multiprogramming, the operating system has to be provided with substantial new capability. To begin, let us first orient ourselves properly to the overall operation of a multiprogramming system. At a particular instant of time the main memory of the computer might look as depicted in Figure 11.3. At the instant shown, four user programs and the multiprogramming operating system (or more precisely, its nucleus) are in memory. It should be emphasized that, at any given instant, only one program can be in actual execution, for example, program B or the operating system itself. Now, referring to this figure, let us consider what the multiprogramming operating system must be able to accomplish in order to execute all four user's programs, as well as the others awaiting execution on the *job queue* in some auxiliary storage medium:

1. Suppose program B is in execution. At some time it will either

    a) have run to completion, or
    b) need to wait for input or output.

When one of these happens the operating system must immediately switch to the execution of another program. But, to do this, the operating system must be made "aware" of the end of execution or the request for input or output. Many computers achieve this through hardware by having certain machine-language instructions, always including the input and output instructions, classified as *privileged,* which means that they can only be executed by programs in the so-called *supervisor mode.* The only program which operates in the supervisor mode is the operating system itself. The effect is that, any time a user's program calls for input or output or wishes to halt, the result is not the desired action but an *interrupt* which immediately transfers control to the supervisor program (i.e., the operating system), which then does the desired action for the user's program. [Other computers achieve the same result by having the operating system reside mainly in a small, peripheral computer which constantly *monitors* each of the programs in main memory to see what their *status* is (e.g., completed, waiting for input or output, etc.).]

2. When the operating system gains control it must decide which user's program to put into execution next. To do this, two things are required of the operating system:

a) it must know the current status of every user's program in memory (e.g., Is it still waiting for input or output? Is it ready to execute?), and

b) it must have some kind of *priority* scheme or, in more sophisticated systems, *a scheduling algorithm* to determine which program to put into execution next.

Most systems give a higher priority to jobs with shorter estimated running times, smaller required amounts of main memory, and smaller output volumes. Some systems usually increase the priority as a function of the time a job has been waiting to execute.

3. All the programs in memory use the same arithmetic unit and the same set of control registers. Therefore, every time a program is interrupted in its execution, the contents of all registers (e.g., the accumulator) must be saved. In addition, a record must be kept of the place where the program stopped execution. Recording of this information by the operating system is part of what was referred to above as keeping track of the status of the program.

4. In most multiprogramming systems jobs are read by the card reader as they are received and put on a job queue on some auxiliary storage device. (This, by the way, typically requires better input-output buffering than is usually available in batch processing computers.) When a job in main memory finishes execution, the operating system must decide which job to bring into memory. This depends on two factors:

a) the priority of the jobs in the job queue, and

b) the main memory space available and that required by each job.

This involves the operating system in a memory scheduling function as well as the aforementioned time scheduling. Some multiprogramming operating systems avoid the problem entirely by establishing *fixed-size* memory modules or *partitions,* each of which can hold one user's program of the size or smaller than the size of partition. But clearly, the inflexibility of such a system is undesirable. Rather, we should like to have the operating system allow variable-size partitions and *manage* memory to make the most efficient possible use of it. To see some of the aspects of this, suppose, for example, that job B in Figure 11.3 terminated, but there was no job in the job queue which would fit in this space. Or, suppose there was a job of very high priority which would not fit; can and

Figure 11.4   IBM 2260 character display terminal. *(Courtesy of IBM Corp.)*

should the operating system decide to wait until more memory becomes available, rather than bring in another job of lower priority which would fit? If the answer is yes, then, at a later time, job D might terminate and the operating system would wish to make the two non-contiguous areas of memory, B and D, available to a program in the job queue. It might perform this *dynamic memory reallocation* function by *relocating* C next to A. Or on some systems it might use a device called *paging* to avoid this reallocation problem. We shall return to paging in Section 11.3.4.

5. Multiprogramming computers have come along at just the time when computer hardware can support remote access to computers via telephone lines from small computers or from typewriter-like or keyboard-visual display consoles (see Figures 11.4 and 11.5). The operating system must typically keep track of the status of each remote unit and react as needed to requests for service from these units, while at the same time handling the jobs entering through the card reader as usual.

Multiprogramming, then, involves a substantially more sophisticated operating system than batch processing as previously described. It allows more effective use of the resources of the computer by, for example, enabling two programs, one with little requirement for input and output but a lot of computing and the other requiring much input and output and little computing, to

Figure 11.5   CDC 218 character display terminal. *(Courtesy of Control Data Corp.)*

be resident in main memory together. Whenever the latter requires input or output, execution can be switched to the former, thus reducing to a minimum the time the CPU stands idle waiting for completion of input or output. Good multiprogramming operating systems, therefore, provide much better turn-around time and achieve much higher CPU utilization than batch processing systems. However, there is a limit to the percentage of CPU time that *can be used by the users' programs.* This limit is, with any operating system, the result of *software overhead,* that is, the CPU time spent executing the operating system itself. It should be evident intuitively to the the reader that the more complex the operating system and the more functions it must perform, the higher the software overhead. Therefore, while multiprogramming systems do increase the percentage of CPU time used by users' programs, they also have a higher overhead than batch processing operating systems.

Finally, we should note that, despite the improved service to the user afforded by multiprogramming systems, they are still essentially "job-processing" systems in the sense that the user submits a job and later receives results as in batch operation. There is no *interaction* between the user and computer during the execution of his job. Part of Section 11.3 is concerned with interactive computer systems. First, however, we shall consider briefly the various parts of operating systems.

11.2   THE COMPONENTS OF AN OPERATING SYSTEM

We have noted already that an operating system is a large complex of programs suitably interconnected to perform the various necessary functions of the system. In this section we shall discuss, without presenting very much detail, some of the major components of a multiprogramming operating system.

1. Supervisor.   Sometimes also called the *monitor* or *executive,* this is the main control program of the operating system. Indeed, it is to the operating system software what the control unit of the computer is to the rest of the hardware. It has the basic responsibility of organizing the work of the operating system and scheduling what happens when the computer is executing inside the operating system. In addition, some of the other components discussed below are sometimes considered to be part of the supervisor.

2. IOCS.   This has already been discussed in Section 10.2.1. In a computer system with privileged instructions, IOCS must be an integral part of the operating system, since only the latter can execute the privileged instructions, among which are always the input and output instructions.

3. Loader.   The loader has the task of taking users' programs and library programs (as well as components of the operating system itself not in the nucleus) from some auxiliary storage medium and loading them into main memory. The reason this task is not generally trivial is because a given job may consist of a number of programs and subprograms, which may have been compiled separately, as well as certain programs from the library. Each program must, therefore, have its addresses relocated according to where it is going to be placed in memory. A still more difficult problem is the insertion, in one program or subprogram, of addresses which refer to quantities in another program or subprogram.

4. Scheduler.   As discussed in the previous section, the scheduler has the task of deciding, among those jobs in main memory, which job to put into execution when, and in addition, which program in the job queue to bring into main memory when one job completes execution.

5. Interrupt handler.   Interrupts may be external—from an input or output device or a remote terminal—or internal—from a user's program which requires some service from the supervisor. The function of the interrupt handler is first, to determine the cause of the interrupt (i.e., its source) and second, to inform the supervisor or other part of the operating system (see 6. below) what to do to service the interrupt.

6. Error-control routines.   One of the major functions of the operating system is to interpret errors in users' problems which result in interrupts and to decide what to do about them. For this purpose there is a battery of error routines in the operating system, each of which has the function of handling a particular kind of error.

These have been brief discussions of some of the major components of a multiprogramming operating system. In addition to the components above, such an operating system will contain a multitude of smaller programs to perform various of the housekeeping, bookkeeping, and general service functions required of the operating system. Although not really a part of the operating system, there are, of course, also the compilers, other language processors, and all the library programs which, together with the operating system, make up the total software system of the computer.

11.3   REMOTE COMPUTING, INTERACTIVE COMPUTING, AND TIME SHARING

Batch processing and multiprogramming systems are almost always operated on a *closed shop* basis, in which all operation of the computer is done by a full-time operations staff. In closed shop operation the user normally drops his card deck off at an input-output station at the computing center and receives his printed results back at this station. In some instances he may actually place his card deck in a card reader and pick up his printed results at a printer. But even in this case the card reader-printer is usually remote—at least, not in the same room—from the central computer.

By contrast, in *open shop* operation each user operates the computer himself. For multiprogramming systems open shop operation is clearly out of the question (Why?) but, in any case, it is a very inefficient way to operate a computing center. This is not simply because users are not as efficient operators as full-time trained personnel. Rather, it is because open shop users tend to do "console debugging"; that is, when something goes wrong with their program they attempt to fix it then and there, either by running to punch some corrected cards while the machine sits idle or by using the console buttons, switches, and other facilities to fix up the program directly in main memory. And this, as can be easily imagined, results in very inefficient use of the CPU.

Before the existence of batch processing and multiprogramming systems, open shop operation was the rule rather than the exception. Despite its inefficiency—each individual user usually does not care a great deal about the overall operating efficiency as long as he gets his job done—it was very popular. While its popularity was based partly on false values—the sheer joy of button pushing and switch throwing—it was also based on some real ones. One was that direct contact with the computer is psychologically more satisfying than coldly efficient closed shop operation with the user buffered away from the computer. A more important one is that direct contact with the computer lessens the turnaround time for a given program measured from the time the computer starts to be used until the results are available. (Of course, open shop operation may result in long waiting times to get on the computer.) Another advantage of open shop operation, and in some cases the most important one, is that there is real value to the user in being able to *interact* directly with the computer, to see what is going right and wrong with his calculation as it happens rather than later on a printed page. To have the positive values without the inefficiencies—that is the major purpose of *remote job entry, interactive* computing, and *time sharing.*

11.3.1   Remote Job Entry

We mentioned above the possibility of having input-output devices such as card reader-printers located remotely from the central computer. This situation is depicted in Figure 11.6. This type of operation is usually called *remote batch* or *remote job entry* (RJE). There is little to distinguish it from batch or multi-programming operation as described in Section 11.1. True, the operating system must recognize where the input came from so that it can direct the output back to the same place (or to some other place as specified by the user), but this is a comparatively minor problem. Rather, our emphasis here is on the remote type-writer-like or keyboard-visual display terminals† of the type illustrated in Figure 11.4 and 11.5. To begin our discussion of the ways in which such terminals can be used, we consider a mode of operation in which there is little or no immediate interaction between the user and the computer. Such systems may be called terminal RJE systems, although they provide various facilities besides remote job entry. Their aim is user convenience and efficiency. First, we shall describe the more important kinds of facilities available at a terminal.

1. *Remote job entry.*   Instead of punching a deck of cards on a keypunch, the

---

†We shall use *terminal* to refer to typewriter or visual display devices and not to card reader-printer devices, although the latter are sometimes called *batch* terminals.

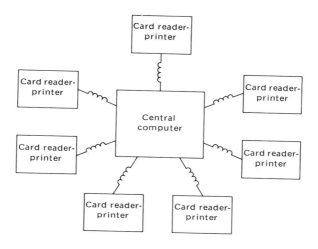

Figure 11.6 Batch terminal remote job entry.

user may type his program directly at the keyboard and have it transmitted to the computer. There are at least two potential advantages in doing this:

i) Simple errors such as pressing the wrong key can typically be corrected at a terminal by backspacing and retyping, whereas at a keypunch the whole card must be repunched. In addition, it is easier to spot such an error at a typewriter or on a display screen than it is by reading the printing on a card.

ii) Since these terminals are much less expensive than card reader-printer terminals, they can be distributed much more widely and may, therefore, be placed in offices, laboratories, dormitories, and even homes, thereby making access to the computer much more convenient to the user.

In addition, on interactive terminal systems there are other advantages to this method of source program input (see Section 11.3.2).

2. *Compilation.* The user of a terminal such as we are describing communicates his needs to the computer by a *command language* which consists of a variety of instructions that can be given by the user at the terminal. In effect, the command language replaces the control cards used with a deck of cards. One command always available to the user is a command to compile a program already entered. On some very high speed computers compilation is so fast that the user of an RJE system will, unless his program is very long, receive in a few seconds notification that his program has been compiled or a list of error messages, if any syntactic errors were found.

3. *Editing.* But what happens when these error messages are typed out or displayed? Does the user have to retype his whole program? No, instead he must merely *edit* his source program, which has been stored somewhere by the

system, normally on disk storage. This editing is accomplished by using the *line numbers* for each statement which are usually printed out or displayed at the terminal before each statement is typed. By referring to the proper line number, the user can delete or change a statement. And, by using line numbers in between those assigned by the computer (which usually are in steps of 10) statements may be inserted between those already entered. Some systems also allow *context editing* in which, for example, the user may request that *all* occurrences of a particular variable name be changed to some other name.

After editing, the user may again request compilation. The editing and compilation will continue until no further error messages are printed, at which time the program will have been compiled and an object program stored with the source program on disk.

It should also be noted that this editing procedure may be used to modify data or old working programs which have been saved by the system (see below).

4. *Execution.*   When requesting a compilation the user may, in some systems, also request execution if the program compiles. Alternatively in other RJE systems, again using the command language, the user may request execution of his previously compiled program. Data may be entered from the keyboard at execution time or, in some systems, may have been prestored in a personal data file on disk. Output may be printed or displayed at the terminal or, particularly if there is a lot of it, directed to a printer at the central installation or at some remote site. If the program does not execute because of some logical error or if incorrect answers indicate such an error, the user may, as above, use the editing procedure to correct the program and then try executing it again.

If, for short compilations and executions, the user receives his output very quickly (say, in a matter of seconds or at most a few minutes), then we may call the system *instant batch* RJE to emphasize the point that, while the terminal operation offers few, if any, facilities not available from the normal batch processing operation, it does give the user almost instant turnaround.

5. *Saving of programs.*   Good systems of the kind we are describing enable users to save both source and object programs as well as data and results on some auxiliary storage medium, usually disk, and to recall and use these at some later time. Normally a user will either be assigned a fixed amount of space on the disk or be charged for what he uses or both; therefore, only programs which are really likely to be useful again should be stored for any sizable length of time.

Terminal RJE systems, then, when they are well designed, give the user a convenience of operation not available from a normal batch processing operation. Indeed, good instant batch RJE systems satisfy the needs of most—but not all—remote terminal users. The next section considers interactive remote terminal systems and the additional user services available from them.

11.3.2   Interactive Terminal Systems

Time sharing is a term that has come to have a variety of meanings and shades of meaning. Sometimes RJE systems as described in the previous section are called time-sharing systems for reasons we shall discuss below. In this section we shall consider one further important connotation of this term and then in Section 11.3.4 we shall discuss yet one more.

An interactive terminal system allows the user, in addition to the facilities discussed in the previous section, to have much closer, immediate contact with his program as it is entered, compiled, and executed. Some of the facilities commonly provided by interactive systems are the following:

1. *Immediate syntax checking.* Rather than wait for the error messages from the compiler at the time the entire program is compiled, interactive systems normally provide line-by-line syntax analysis whereby any local[†] syntactic error in a statement is immediately displayed at the terminal and can be corrected before typing further statements. For example, using the same case as described in Section 6.3 (p. 238), after typing

12   A = B + C (D– E/F)

and then the carriage return (which in terminal systems indicates the end of the "card"), the computer would immediately (3 seconds or less in good systems) type[††]

*MISSING OPERATOR

Then, using the editing facility, the statement could be corrected before proceeding. Thus, when the program has been completely entered, it will be locally syntactically correct. Many interactive terminal system users are much enamored of this facility, but some people feel that the immediate line-by-line response is distracting, particularly if they are "composing" the program at the terminal rather than copying it from a programming form. Such people feel that, if the response of the computer when the whole program is compiled is fast enough, it is better to get the error messages all at once rather than line by line.

2. *Incremental compilation.* An important feature of many interactive systems is the ability to compile and test part of a program as it is being entered from the console. In this way logical debugging of small pieces of the program can be done in a convenient fashion. As an aid in this process the user can often interrogate the computer to find out the current value of a particular variable at the end of a test run.

3. *Execution time control.* Perhaps the most valuable aspect of interactive

---

[†]As opposed to a global syntactic error, such as referring to a statement label that does not appear anywhere.

[††]Of course, the reader should by now realize that this statement is not syntactically incorrect. C *could* be a function subprogram or an arithmetic statement function and D – E/F could be its argument. Therefore, in actual practice the compiler should accept this statement and should give a global error message after compilation of the entire program is attempted only if there is no subprogram or arithmetic statement function C.

computing is the ability to "monitor" the program during execution and interact with it when necessary. Often, when using a normal batch processing system, a computer user does more computation than is necessary (e.g., tests many values of a parameter) because he has no way of checking the progress of the computation until it is over. Some interactive facilities provide the user with the ability to interrupt a program which is executing to interrogate the value of a variable, to change the value of a parameter, or to terminate the computation if results already printed or displayed indicate there is no point in continuing.

Although the above discussion is by no means an exhaustive survey of the features of interactive systems, it has hopefully given the reader a feel for the possibilities of having almost instant control of the composition, compilation, and execution of programs. Of course, such facilities are quite expensive but, for some problems, the improvement in user efficiency is so great as to make the expense well worthwhile. Such systems also make possible otherwise impossible applications which require continuous man-machine interaction (e.g., psychological learning experiments). In general, we may say that interactive systems sharply reduce the *total problem turnaround time,* that is, the time from problem conception to the time when computer results are obtained.

To be fair, we should point out two negative features of interactive systems. One is that all the additional services provided by the operating system may result in more total computing time being used for the problem. On the other hand, the efficiency of the man-machine interaction may prevent certain errors and false starts from being made and thereby reduce the total time. The evidence on this question is not yet conclusive.

A more serious objection is that the more convenient the access to the computer is, the more frivolous the calculations that will be performed, calculations for which a computer is not necessary or which should not be done at all. This danger is real because too many people use computers as a substitute for thinking. However, we believe it does not outweigh the very real advantages of such a system.

The reason the systems described in this section as well as, sometimes, the RJE systems described in the previous section are called *time-sharing* systems is that a number of users at the terminals all have access to the computer simultaneously. "Simultaneously" is the key word here. It is not meant to imply that the CPU executes the users' programs simultaneously; a single CPU can only execute one program at a time. Rather, it is meant to imply that each user at his terminal is getting service from the computer such that in many instances *he seems* to have the whole computer at his beck and call. This, the reader should realize, is the hallmark of any *utility,* namely, that the user of the utility gets or at least seems to get the service he desires quite independently of how many others are requesting service at the same time. As an example of this, when you wish to make a telephone call, you could not care less how many other people are making calls at the same time, as long as your call goes through promptly. Time sharing then is an attempt at achieving a *computer utility.*

Now the reader should understand that, unless the program execution time is very short—a second or less—the system will fail to act as a utility in that it will not respond very quickly to the user. It must be remembered that other users may also be requesting execution. If 10 users each request execution of programs requiring one second of CPU time, then someone will have to wait at least ten seconds. This example should suggest that the type of terminal user-computer interaction we are describing here has its main value during debugging when the execution, if any, is likely to be very short. How longer runs (i.e., runs over, say, one second!—but remember, one second of computer time on a very high speed computer will allow over 1 million operations) are handled on such a system is described in the next section.

11.3.3   Scheduling for Time Sharing

Let us consider the type of operation discussed in the previous section but in the context of a computing system which must also service "batch" users, that is, users who will submit jobs at the central computer or at remote card reader-printers, perhaps for debugging runs, but more particularly for execution, which may require substantial amounts of computer time. This situation is depicted in Figure 11.7. How is the operating system going to schedule the demands on it so

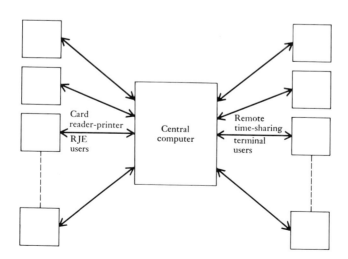

Figure 11.7   A total time-sharing system.

as to give the various users the kind of service they wish? There are two general answers to this question but these two may be combined into a great variety of scheduling procedures.

The first answer is by means of a priority system such as was discussed briefly in Section 11.1.2. The operating system must decide which jobs to bring into main memory from the job queue and which job in main memory to put into execution after an interruption. If it does this by a priority scheme which gives highest priority to jobs with shorter running time, less output, and smaller main memory requirements, then this will favor the time-sharing terminal users because most of their entry requests and compilation and debugging runs are short, small jobs. Therefore, such a priority scheme will tend to give the terminal user the rapid response he wishes. But there are two problems here:

1. If a long-running job gets into execution, there must be some way for it *to be interrupted,* for otherwise the higher priority jobs which are waiting for execution will not get a chance until the long-running job runs to completion or requests input or output.
2. On the other hand, if a mechanism does exist for interrupting a lower priority job to put a higher priority one in execution, the danger then exists that the terminal users may monopolize the system and no one may get a chance to execute even quite short running jobs, say 10 seconds or so.

The first problem is usually solved by using the *interval timer* in the computer. This can be set by the operating system monitor to provide an interrupt after a fixed interval of time which automatically interrupts the program in execution and returns control to the monitor. Another way of solving this problem is exemplified by the CDC 6000 series of computers in which the monitor program resides in a peripheral processor which has the ability to interrupt any central processor program and put another central processor program in execution. Thus, by monitoring the priority of all jobs in main memory and in the job queue, this monitor peripheral processor can always get the high priority jobs into execution.

But neither of these approaches by themselves solves the second problem. One way to attempt this is by establishing a *cycle time* of, say, three seconds, which is to be divided more or less equally between terminal time-sharing users and all other users. During one portion of the cycle time only terminal users would be serviced and during the other part the batch users would be serviced. In this way no type of user would be shut out entirely. The length of the cycle time is chosen so that, if a terminal user is serviced during each cycle, the response time will not make him impatient. Three to five seconds seems to be about the level at which impatience starts.

In this mode of operation the terminal users are often called *foreground* users and the others *background* users. The background operation may be thought of as a normal multiprogramming operation as described previously. The split of the cycle time between foreground and background can be preset or can be adjusted dynamically by the scheduler depending upon how much demand there is from each type of user. It should be clear, without going into details, that the scheduling and memory allocation problems for the operating system are substantially more difficult in this type of operation than in the multiprogramming type of operation described in Section 11.1.2. We should note, however, that time sharing as we have been discussing it is an extension of multiprogramming, rather than a completely different type of operation.

At this point an example of the operation of the type of system we have been describing is in order.

Example 11.1

Consider the situation in which ten terminals users, T_1, T_2, . . . , T_{10}, are actively requesting service as are three batch users, B_1, B_2, B_3, with lower subscripts representing higher priority. Suppost a cycle time of three seconds is to be divided about equally between the two sets of users. Indicate how the CPU time might be allocated.

A possible answer is indicated in Figure 11.8 for four cycle times of operation. Note the following remarks:

1. It is assumed in this figure that the operating system remembers which terminal users got no chance to execute during one cycle time and so gives them a chance at the beginning of the next cycle. The execution for each user is terminated either by the completion of the task (e.g., entering a single statement) or by an interrupt (e.g., a request for input or output).

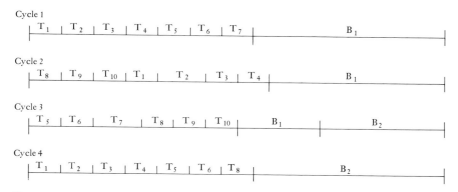

Figure 11.8 CPU allocation in time sharing.

2. Most of the terminal jobs are assumed to be doing very small tasks such as entering a statement or editing a statement. But T_2 in the second cycle and T_7 in the third are doing longer tasks, perhaps compilation or a debugging execution run. These longer tasks serve to prevent some terminal users from getting a chance during each cycle. If a terminal user attempted a really long compilation or execution, then other terminal users might be prevented from executing for several cycles.

3. The case of a terminal user completing his task is shown in Cycle 4 where there is no T_7.

4. The background is normal multiprogramming operation. B_2 may go into execution because B_1 is completed or because of some other interrupt on B_1, such as a request for input or output.

5. The figure ignores the operating system overhead, that is, the time the operating system itself is executing from the end of one program to the beginning of the next. The success of some time-sharing systems has been badly marred by the magnitude of this overhead.

This example surely raises at least as many questions as it answers. One, which we shall treat very briefly now, is how can a computer installation afford to provide enough main memory to keep many users' programs resident, particularly, for example, if many of them need a P-O language compiler to compile a source program? A partial, by no means complete, answer to this serious problem is the use of *reentrant* compilers. Normally, as with most programs, a compiler must initialize itself before it starts compiling a new source program. This involves setting certain constants and counters within itself. Thus, it can be operating on only one source program at a time. A reentrant compiler (or any reentrant program) is written, however, in such a way that no initialization or resetting is required or, to put it another way, no part of the compiler code itself ever changes. Thus many users' source programs can be compiled by *one copy of the compiler in memory* such that at a given instant each source program is at a different stage of compilation using this one copy.

Example 11.1 indicates at least one problem which our discussion of time sharing thus far cannot solve. This is, how can we guarantee a good response time to each terminal user who is doing a sufficiently small task, up to the limit of the number of terminals allowed on the computer? The solution to this problem constitutes our other meaning of time sharing.

11.3.4   Time Slicing and Paging

To some computer scientists time slicing and time sharing are synonymous. However, if, as here, we take time sharing to mean that the CPU will be shared

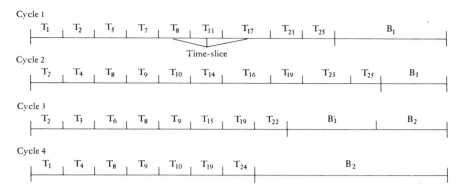

Figure 11.9   CPU allocation for time-sliced time sharing.

between many users, then time slicing refers to the idea that each cycle time, as defined in a previous section, should be subdivided into a number of quanta or *time slices,* a time slice being the *maximum* time any remote interactive terminal should be allowed to use the CPU during one cycle. The interval timer is set so that, if a terminal user's program executes as long as one time slice, an interrupt is generated and execution of that job is terminated until the next cycle. With a cycle time of 3 seconds, the time slice might be set at something between 50 and 100 milliseconds, thus enabling 25 or so users each to get a time slice during each cycle and still have some left for the background jobs. (Remember that many users will require much less than the full quantum; for example, on very fast computers the syntax checking of a single statement might require under 5 milliseconds; also, see 1. below). Figure 11.9 indicates CPU allocation for time-sliced time sharing (cf. Figure 11.8):

1. This figure assumes no priority system for the terminal users and, indeed, none is necessary since each terminal user is assured of his time slice each cycle. Note that, typically, users will not want a time slice each cycle since the typing time and thinking time at the terminal between statements usually takes at least a few cycles. In the example in Figure 11.9 some terminal users (e.g., T_{13}, T_{20}) required no time during the four cycles shown.

2. The split of time between terminal and batch users will vary because once all terminal users have had a chance to execute the rest of the cycle is given to batch users. Alternatively, the time given to batch users can be kept constant and the cycle time varied. Some systems try to time-slice the batch users also to give each some execution during each time slice.

3. Jobs like T_2 and T_8, which require their time slice in two or more consecutive cycles, may be assumed to be compiling or executing. It is reasonable that such users should have a slower response time (i.e., the time until the user gets a message at his terminal) than those entering or editing programs.

In the above we have slurred over the scheduling and software overhead problems associated with time sharing. Both are beyond our scope here. But, to conclude this discussion, we shall consider briefly the memory allocation problem, which becomes particularly serious for time-sliced time sharing.

In our discussion of multiprogramming in Section 11.1.2 we considered the problem of memory allocation (cf. Figure 11.3). Our discussion there assumed that when the main memory became *fragmented,* that is, when the available memory space was in bits and pieces scattered through the memory, the operating system would consolidate the programs still executing, thereby creating a single block of available memory. Now, if the total number of programs which can be in main memory at any one time is quite small, this may be a reasonable way to proceed. But, if this number is large, as it may well be for the time-sharing systems we have been describing in this chapter, such a method would seriously increase the software overhead. Therefore, it is worth considering another solution.

That solution in most common use today is called *paging* and is illustrated in Figure 11.10. This works as follows. Main memory is divided up into equal parts called (physical) *pages* which normally contain 500 to 1000 words. Each program and data are similarly broken up into *logical pages* as it is stored on some external storage medium (e.g., disk). When a program is to be brought into main memory to be executed, its pages are brought into main memory pages but *contiguous logical pages in the program need not be brought into contiguous physical pages in main memory* (see Figure 11.10). Thus, as long as there are enough available pages in main memory to accomodate the program, no matter how they are scattered, the program may be brought into memory. Or, in some systems, only those pages of a program needed right away are brought in and the rest only as needed. Therefore, only a few pages of main memory need be available to accommodate a new program.

Now the above is clearly easier said than done. Among the questions it raises, let us first discuss the most serious. Programs as we have been discussing them have always consisted of contiguous instructions, always in the same position in memory *relative* to each other. It is a comparatively simple matter to compile a program whose initial location is unspecified, but all of whose other addresses are specified relative to this initial location. When the program is brought into memory, it is then not difficult to locate it with respect to any initial address. But, if the program is going to be fragmented in main memory, the instructions in main memory will have different relative locations than in the contiguous compiled program. How can this be handled? The most usual answer to this is by providing a *page table,* which resides in main memory and contains the actual location of each page in memory. The location of the page table for the program in execution at any given time is contained in a special register called the *page*

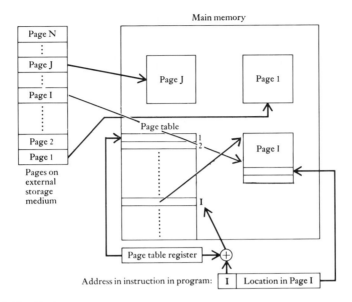

Figure 11.10 Paging.

table register (see Figure 11.10). Each instruction in the program has an address consisting of two parts, the page number and the location within the page. When reference is made in an instruction to any location in the program, the address in that instruction is not the *physical address,* but rather a *logical address* consisting of these two parts, the page number and the location within the page. The page number is used to enter the page table to determine where in physical main memory the page is located; then the location-within-the-page part of the address is used to find the actual physical word in memory. Since the need to refer to the page table in main memory on every instruction reference would markedly increase the software overhead, some computers provide a very high speed *associative memory* in which those page table entries referred to often are stored.

The page concept causes problems when the instructions being executed or a block of data runs off a page boundary, but paged time-sharing operating systems can handle this problem. Similarly, the operating system must have some mechanism for determining whether or not a new page that is referred to is in memory. One additional less than obvious advantage of the paging idea, including that part of it which does not require the whole program to be in main memory, is the ability to write programs which address a memory larger than the main memory of the computer, knowing that the page table association will take care of assigning the proper *physical addresses* to the *logical addresses* of the program. The ability to write programs as if you are dealing with a *virtual memory* much larger than the actual memory can be very convenient.

One alternative to the paging solution for the memory fragmentation problem with time-shared systems, which should be mentioned, is the use of very fast *swapping*. Computers which use this technique usually have in addition to their main magnetic core memory another core memory with larger capacity than the main memory. This *extended-core storage* or *large-core memory* (see Section 10.1.2.3) cannot normally be used to execute instructions—this is reserved for the main memory—but it can transfer data to and from main memory at very high speeds. Therefore, when the main memory in a time-shared system becomes so fragmented that no new programs can be brought in, all of main memory can be *swapped* with extended core which will bring in a whole new set of programs to main memory. While the *swapped-in* programs are executing in main memory, it will be possible to consolidate on the external storage medium the programs which have been *swapped out* preparatory to later swapping in. The price paid here is the swapping time, but this can be very small, perhaps only five or six milliseconds for a large memory. The cost may well be less than the software overhead of a paged system. Thus, while the swapping idea is surely less elegant than paging, it may prove more effective. Conclusive evidence on this is not yet in.

The discussion above has been, at best, a very quick and superficial description of the paging and swapping concepts and some of their implications. The reader who is really interested in how such systems work should refer to some of the references given in the bibliography in which he will find not only more complete discussions than we have given here but also discussions of related topics (such as *segmentation*) which we have not touched at all.

BIBLIOGRAPHIC NOTES

A valuable overview of operating systems placed in an historical context can be found in Rosin (1969). Books with useful material in this area are Fisher and Swindle (1964), Hassitt (1967), and Rosen (1967). Although remote computing and interactive computing are relatively recent developments, there is already considerable literature in these areas. Much of the pioneer work in this area was done at Project MAC (for Multiple Access System or Machine-Aided Cognition) at M.I.T. The article by Fano and Corbató (1966) presents a description, albeit a layman's, of early developments in time sharing with emphasis on the work at

Project MAC. (The entire issue of the Scientific American containing the Fano-Corbato' article is devoted to computers and is well worth the attention of students in a first course in computer science.) Popell (1966) contains a useful, although elementary discussion of time sharing with particular emphasis on business applications. A deeper, more thorough discussion may be found in Watson (1970).

Bibliography

Fano, R. M., and F. J. Corbato' (September 1966): Time-Sharing on Computers, *Scientific American,* pp. 129-140.

Fisher, F. P., and G. F. Swindle (1964): *Computer Programming Systems,* Holt, Rinehart & Winston, New York.

Hassitt, A. (1967): *Computer Programming and Computer Systems,* Academic Press, New York.

Popell, S. D. (1966): *Computer Time-Sharing,* Prentice-Hall, Inc., Englewood Cliffs, New Jersey.

Rosen, S. (1967): *Programming Systems and Languages,* McGraw-Hill Book Company, Inc., New York.

Rosin, F.F. (1969): Supervisory and Monitor Systems, *Computing Surveys,* vol. 1, pp. 37-54.

Watson, R. W. (1970): *Introduction to Time-Sharing Concepts,* McGraw-Hill Book Company, Inc., New York.

appendix A

a potpourri of computer problems

In many courses with contents similar to this book, an attempt is made to give the students problems of a "practical" nature from physics or engineering or numerical methods for computer solution. When I first started teaching such a course, many of the problems I assigned were from the area of numerical methods, reflecting my background as a numerical analyst. More recently I have assigned very few such problems and almost no problems which could be termed "practical" in any sense. There are two reasons for this.

First, it makes no more sense to assign such problems in an introductory computer science course than it did to assign the work, pressure, etc. problems which are now disappearing from basic calculus courses. I do not wish to ignore entirely the motivational advantage of problems related to the real world—it does exist—but it is easily exaggerated. Computer science, like calculus, can stand by itself. It provides its own motivation without any crutch from outside. The place to learn to apply computers (like calculus) is in courses whose subject matter deals with these applications.

Second, applications from the physical world or numerical analysis which are accessible to the lower division undergraduate tend not only to be trivial or oversimplified physically, but also to lead to logically simple and uninteresting computer programs. On the other hand, some quite elementary "impractical" problems, for example, from the area of game playing, can be quite complicated logically while requiring relatively few statements in a P-O language; therefore, they make almost ideal problems for an introductory course.

The problems are divided into three categories. In each category, the number of statements is what might be expected from an expert programmer:

> Elementary—which require no more than about 25 P-O language statements.
>
> Intermediate—about 50 statements.
>
> Advanced—75 or more statements.

Note that in most cases below the statement of the problem is not sufficient to be turned directly into a computer project for students because details of such things as input and output formats are missing. Rather, these statements are intended to delineate the problem in such a way that its translation to a computer project is straightforward.

ELEMENTARY PROBLEMS

1. Linear interpolation is the process by which values of a function f(x) at points other than the tabulated values, $x_1, x_2, \ldots, x_n$ are approximated by using the straight line joining two adjacent functional values (see Figure P1). Write a program to accept as input n pairs of numbers, each pair consisting of an argument followed by a value at that argument, and a value X at which an interpolated value is desired. The output should consist of X and the interpolated value.

2. Write a program which, given the number of pins knocked down by each ball in each frame in bowling, calculates the score for the game.

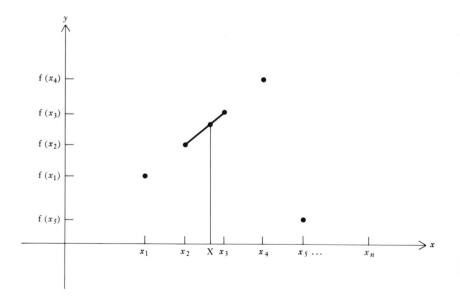

Figure P1   Linear interpolation.

3. Consider Boolean theorems stated in the form of a left-hand expression set equal to a right-hand expression and which involve no more than n variables. Write a main program to prove or disprove the theorem using truth table techniques. The program should call two subprograms to evaluate the left and right sides of the theorem.

4. The *bisection method* of finding solutions of the equation $f(x) = 0$ involves:

    i) searching for two values of x at which $f(x)$ has opposite signs, and
    ii) searching between these two values by successively halving an interval in which the function is known to change sign, finally resulting in as good an approximation as desired (see Figure P2).

Write a program which

    i) accepts as input two values of x, x_1, and x_2, between which a solution of $f(x)$ is desired, a search mesh size M, and an accuracy tolerance ϵ,

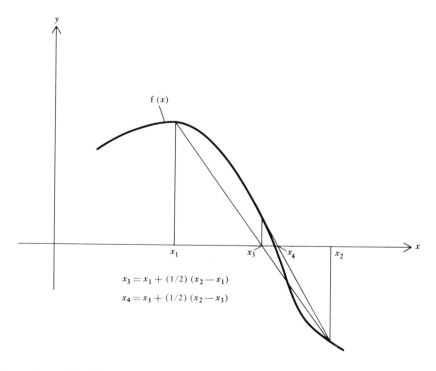

Figure P2   Bisection.

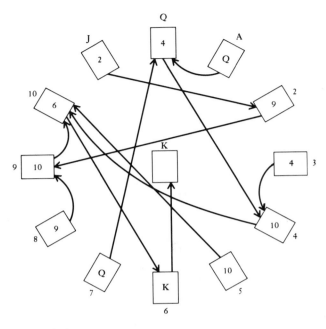

Figure P3   Clock solitaire.

ii) searches from x_1 to x_2 in steps of size M to find two values of x at which $f(x)$ has opposite signs; if there are none, stop and print out an appropriate message, and

iii) uses bisection to find a solution of $f(x) = 0$ which differs from the true solution by no more than ϵ.

5. Given the coordinates of two triangles as integers, each with a horizontal base, determine if the triangles are similar.

6. In the game of clock solitaire the 52 cards are placed in 12 piles of four cards each, one at each clock position and 1 pile of 4 cards in the center. Starting from the center pile, a card is removed from the top of the pile, placed face-up under the pile at the corresponding clock position (J at 11, Q at 12, K in center), a card is removed from the top of the pile under which the card was placed, etc. The game is won if all cards are face-up when the fourth king is placed face-up.

Now consider the 12 bottom cards of the 12 outer piles at the start of the game. Draw a line from each of these 12 cards to the pile at the corresponding place in the clock or to the center pile if the bottom card is a king (i.e., from a bottom 10 draw a line to the pile at 10 o'clock; see Figure P3). Now take the resulting graph (i.e., set of lines) and redraw it to show its structure (see Figure

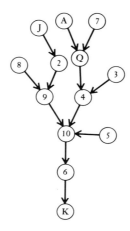

Figure P4   Redrawn graph for clock solitaire.

P4). It can be shown that, if and only if the resulting graph is a *tree* (i.e., all points connected and no closed paths), then the clock solitaire game will be won.

Given the 12 bottom cards, write a program to determine if the game will be won. The resulting program should be elementary (i.e., short), but will be logically quite complex.

INTERMEDIATE PROBLEMS

1. Given a checkerboard position and some suitable coding of the squares (unoccupied, white's man or king, black's man or king), write a program to determine the total possible number of checker moves by which white can capture at least one of black's pieces. (Count multiple jumps as one capture.)

2. Repeat Problem 5 under Elementary Problems without the assumption of integer coordinates or horizontal base. The test for similarity will then have to depend on a roundoff error tolerance. (Why?)

3. Given the thirteen cards of a bridge hand suitably coded into numerical form, determine

   i) if these cards form a legal bridge hand (i.e., no repeated cards), and
   ii) the number of cards in each suit, and
   iii) the point count of the hand (J = 1, Q = 2, K = 3, A = 4).

4. Consider Boolean expressions of the form

$$(((A \; op \; B) \; op \; C) \; op \; D) \ldots \ldots \qquad (op-\text{operator})$$

where each operator is AND or OR or one of these followed by NOT. Devise a coding for such expressions for input into a computer (without parentheses) which distinguishes between variable names (which may be repeated in the expression) and operators. With the coded expression as input, write a program to produce the truth table for the expression, with suitable headings, as output.

5. Write a program to determine which of two poker hands is the winning hand. Ignore suits so that the possible hands are four of a kind, a full house, three of a kind, two pairs, one pair, no pair.

6. Write a main program and subprograms to accept as input

    i) an integer N followed by
    ii) the N elements of a floating-point one-dimensional array
    iii) a mode tolerance (see below)

and compute the mean, mode, median, and standard deviation of the data in the array where

    i) The mean of A is the sum of all the elements divided by N.

    ii) The mode of A is the value of any datum whose value appears at least as many times in A as any other value. Two data items will be considered to have the same value if the magnitude of their difference is less than the mode tolerance. Assume the tolerance will be such that each datum will be in at most one set of values.

    iii) The median of A is a value in A such that half the remaining values of A are greater than or equal to the median value. If there is no such value, then the median is the mean of those two values of A such that half the remaining values are greater than or equal to the greater of the two, and half are less than or equal to the lesser of the two.

    iv) The standard deviation is the square root of the average value of the square of the difference between the values of A and the mean:

$$\text{St. dev.} = \sqrt{(1/N) \sum_{i=1}^{N} (A_i - \text{mean})^2}$$

7. Given the 52 cards in a deck divided into four bridge hands and a 53rd datum representing the trump suit, calculate the number of tricks won by North-South and East-West under the following assumptions:

i) The applicable rules of bridge concerning following suit, trumping, discarding, and leading to the next trick hold, and

ii) North leads to the first trick and a player *must* play the *first* legal card in his hand (assuming some ordering of the 13 cards) at each trick.

ADVANCED PROBLEMS

1. A professor got lost while walking in the woods one day. When he realized his predicament he sat down by the nearest tree and decided upon the following algorithm for finding his way to one of the two roads which traversed the woods:

> i) He would walk in straight lines from tree to tree until he found one of the roads. The woods were so dense that he would be able to see the road only when he was very close to it.
>
> ii) He had a piece of chalk in his pocket—naturally! He would place a chalk mark on each tree he reached so as not to walk in a circle. The chalk mark could be seen from any direction.
>
> iii) Starting from the tree where he was sitting, and at each tree he reached, he would put a chalk mark on the tree and then look around and decide which unmarked tree was closest to his position. Then he would walk in a straight line to this latter tree. If, however, a road was closer to him than any unmarked tree, he would walk directly to the road at its nearest point.

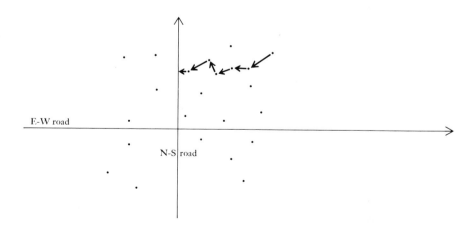

Figure P5   The lost-professor problem.

1973

JANUARY

S	M	T	W	T	F	S
	1	2	3	4	5	6
7	8	9	10	11	12	13
14	15	16	17	18	19	20
21	22	23	24	25	26	27
28	29	30	31			

FEBRUARY

.
.
.
.

DECEMBER

S	M	T	W	T	F	S
						1
2	3	4	5	6	7	8
9	10	11	12	13	14	15
16	17	18	19	20	21	22
23	24	25	26	27	28	29
30	31					

Figure P6   Calendar problem.

We shall assume our professor was lost in a forest of ideal trees with perfectly straight and infinitely slender trunks, all perfectly perpendicular to the ground. He too was ideal, with negligible dimensions. We shall further assume that, if two or more trees are at any time equidistant from the professor, he would choose the one whose direction from him was most nearly North, and if two were equally nearly North then he would choose the one of these to the East.

Let the two roads in the forest be an E-W one (the x-axis) and a N-S one (the y-axis). Then an example of a path he might follow is seen in Figure P5.

Write a program which, given the number of trees, the coordinates of each, and the tree at which the professor starts, produces as output the path followed by the professor and the distance traveled.

2. Using the material in Chapters 2 and 7, write a program which, given the initial position of the knight, will produce as output a knight's tour.

3. Do Problem 5 under Intermediate Problems, but now taking suits into account.

4. In the millennium starting with the year 1000, a leap year is any year divisible by 4, except those years divisible by 100 but not by 400. Write a program which accepts as input a single integer in the range 1000-1999 and produces a calendar in the format of Figure P6.

Acknowledgments and Bibliography

Some of the problems above have long histories. As most immediate sources for some of them, let me acknowledge Gilbert Berglass (Elementary Problem 2), A.J. Perlis and R.T. Braden (Advanced Problems 1 and 4), D. Knuth (Elementary Problem 6 in his book *The Art of Computer Programming*, vol. 1: *Fundamental Algorithms*, Addison-Wesley (1968), p. 377), and Martin Gardner (Elementary Problem 6 in his article in *Scientific American*, February 1968).

Sources of good lists of computer projects:

Perlis, A.J., and R.T. Braden (1965): *An Introductory Course in Computer Programming*, Monograph No. 7, Carnegie-Mellon University, Pittsburgh.
Gruenberger, F., and C. Jaffray (1965): *Problems for Computer Solution*, John Wiley & Sons, New York.

hints and answers to problems

CHAPTER 2

1. Each string has an even number of characters with the second half the mirror image of the first half; the first half can be an arbitrary string of a's and b's.

2. All nonnegative real numbers (with integral and fractional parts consisting of at least 0).

3. a)

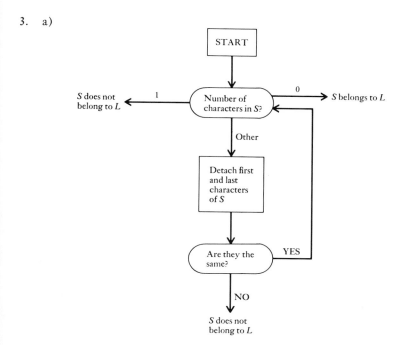

b)

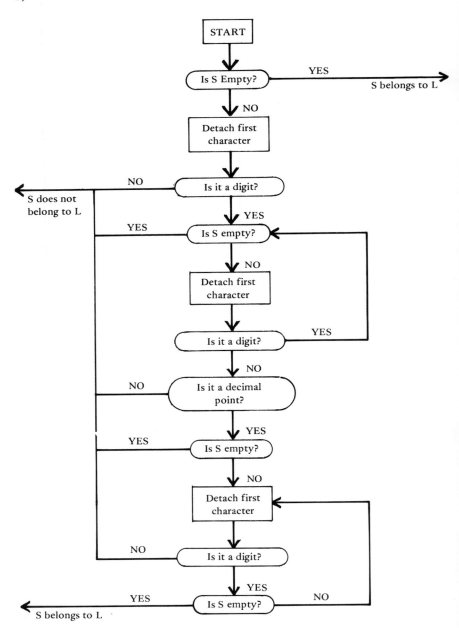

4.   a)

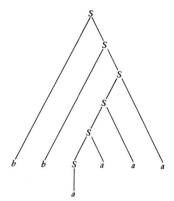

b)

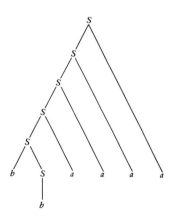

5.   a) An *a* followed by one or more *b*'s.

b)

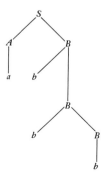

The number of parses is equal to the number of *b*'s; each parse puts a different number of *b*'s in *A*.

6. <FOUR LETTER WORD> ::= <LETTER> <LETTER> <TWO LETTER
                                              WORD> |
                                      <LETTER> <TWO LETTER WORD>
                                              <LETTER> |
                                      <TWO LETTER WORD> <LETTER>
                                              <LETTER> |
                                      <TWO LETTER WORD> <TWO LETTER
                                              WORD>

7. 4, 5, .4, .5, ..4, ..5, ...4, ...5

8. a) <S> ::= a | b | <S> a | b <S>
    b) 1. <S> ::= $a\,a$ | $b\,b$ | a <S> a | b <S> b
        2. <S> ::= <A> . <A>
           <A> ::= <α> | <A> <α>
           <α> ::= 0 | 1 | 2 | 3 | 4 | 5 | 6 | 7 | 8 | 9
        5. <S> ::= <A> <B>
           <A> ::= a | <A> <B>
           <B> ::= b | b <B>

9.   <S> ::= <D> <A> <L>
                  [3]
             <A> ::= <D> | <L> | <A> <D> | <A> <L>
             <D> ::= 0 | 1 | ... | 8 | 9
             <L> ::= A | B | C | ... | X | Y | Z

12. a) No. This would be a *loop* from which the program would never exit.
    b) Yes.
    c) Yes.

13.

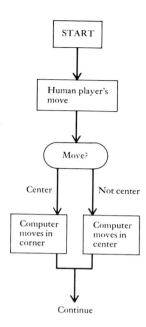

14. a) At the end of the first pass through the list, the last item is the last one in alphabetical order; at the end of the second pass, the next to last is in order; therefore, the flow should not go to the end of list at each successive pass.

b) Maximum occurs if the list is initially in reverse alphabetical order; in this case the number of interchanges for list of length N is

$$(N - 1) + (N - 2) + (N - 3) + \ldots + 3 + 2 + 1 = N(N - 1)/2$$

15. After START box, insert decision box "Is $a = 0$"; if yes, compute one root $-c/b$ and, if no, continue in flow chart as it is now.

16.

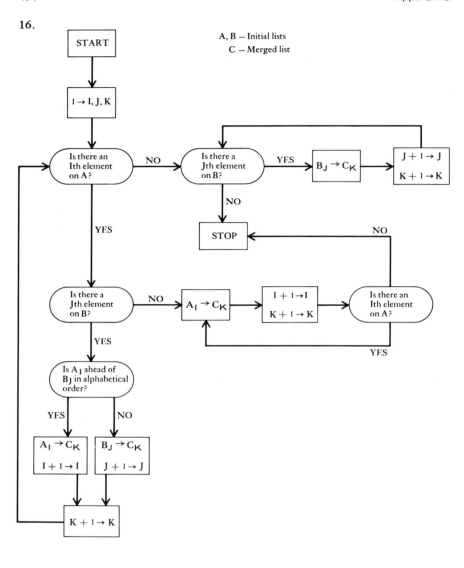

A, B — Initial lists
C — Merged list

17.

AB
.

D
/
C

or

A
\
B

CD
.

18. Let the coordinates of A, B, C, D be, respectively (a_1, a_2), (b_1, b_2), (c_1, c_2), (d_1, d_2). Then AB is given by

$$y = [(a_2 - b_2) x + a_1 b_2 - a_2 b_1] / (a_1 - b_1)$$

and CD is given by

$$y = [(c_2 - d_2) x + c_1 d_2 - c_2 d_1] / (c_1 - d_1).$$

19. Start : (6,7); 2: (8,8); 3: (7,6); 4: (6,8); 5: (8.7); 6: (6,6); 7: (4,5).

20. See Figure 7.2 of Chapter 7.

22. a) Legal in all four languages.
    b) Illegal in Cobol because no spaces are allowed in variables names.
    c) Legal only in Cobol because of hyphen.
    d) Legal only in Cobol because of initial digit.
    e) Illegal in many Fortran systems because of seven characters in name.

23. \<CHAR\> ::= \<LETTER\> | \<DIGIT\>
    \<FORTRAN NAME\> ::= \<LETTER\> | \<LETTER\> \<CHAR\> | ...
                    ... |\<LETTER\> \<CHAR\> \<CHAR\> \<CHAR\>
                        \<CHAR\> \<CHAR\>

24. \<END CHAR\> ::= \<LETTER\> | \<DIGIT\>
    \<CHAR\> ::= \<END CHAR\> | -
                    [28]
    \<CHAR STRING\> ::= \<CHAR\> | \<CHAR STRING\> \<CHAR\>
    \<COBOL NAME\> ::= \<END CHAR\> | \<END CHAR\> \<END CHAR\> |
                    \<END CHAR\> \<CHAR STRING\> \<END CHAR\>

with the added stipulation that at least one character is alphabetic.

CHAPTER 3

1.

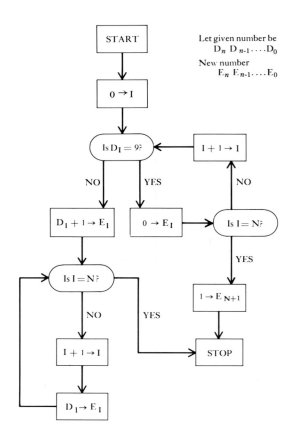

START

Let given number be
$D_n \; D_{n-1} \ldots D_0$

New number
$E_n \; E_{n-1} \ldots E_0$

$0 \rightarrow I$

Is $D_I = 9$?

$I + 1 \rightarrow I$

NO   YES   NO

$D_I + 1 \rightarrow E_I$

$0 \rightarrow E_I$

Is $I = N$?

Is $I = N$?

YES

$1 \rightarrow E_{N+1}$

NO   YES

$I + 1 \rightarrow I$

STOP

$D_I \rightarrow E_I$

2. a) 100011; b) 1011; c) 1001000111; d) 10010, remainder of 1; e) 1000110;
f) 1011, remainder of 10000; g) −1.00111

3. a) 001, 010, 011, 100, 101; b) 001; c) 1 from piles 1, 3, or 5; d) any move
will change logical sum in lowest order position affected in pile changed; e) since
winner will make logical sum 00...0 at end, at every move make move which presents opponent with logical sum of zero; he must give you nonzero sum after
which you can always give him zero sum again.

4. Continue as above until exactly one pile has more than 1 at your turn (this will always happen); then remove all or all except one object from this pile so as to leave odd number of piles with one object.

5. a) 32230; b) 326173366224; c) 135, remainder of 176; d) 402, remainder of 5.212

7. a)

+	0	1	2	3	4
0	0	1	2	3	4
1	1	2	3	4	10
2	2	3	4	10	11
3	3	4	10	11	12
4	4	10	11	12	13

x	0	1	2	3	4
0	0	0	0	0	0
1	0	1	2	3	4
2	0	2	4	11	13
3	0	3	11	14	22
4	0	4	13	22	31

   b) 1334; 10403432; 14, remainder of 2204

8. a) $b_3 2^3 + b_2 2^2 + b_1 2^1 + b_0 = b$ where the b_i's are binary digits and b is a hexadecimal digit
   b) Group binary digits in fours to convert to hexadecimal.

   c) $(101001000110.1011)_2 = (5106.54)_8$
      $(110111100010011.101000001)_2 = (6F13.A08)_{16}$
      $(3321.6614)_8 = (6D1.D8C)_{16}$

9. a) $(11111001.010011)_2 = (371.23 \ldots)_8$
   b) $(33.270)_8 = (27.359375)_{10}$
   c) $(110100010111011.001101110010100)_2 = (26811.215 \ldots)_{10}$
   d) $(301.43320 \ldots)_5 = (64.B44B \ldots)_{12}$
   e) $(223111.114 \ldots)_5 = (46AA.34 \ldots)_{12}$

10. $1/5^n = (2/10)^n$ which is a finite decimal; the converse is not true—consider quinary expansion of .1.

11. a) 0000, 0001, 0010, 0011 or 0100, 0101, 0110, 0111, 1000, 1001, 1010;
    b) 0000, 1001, 0111, 0010, 1011, 0100, 1101, 1000, 0110, 1111

12. a) 1101; b) 1001; c) 0100, 1001; d) 0111

13. A change of one bit will always result in an even number of 1s.

14. A hardware error will often result in having all memory elements set to zero; with even parity this is a possible configuration, with odd parity it is not.

15. First 2 bits: 11 for letters, digits, 01 for special characters; second 2 bits: 11 if no second punch, 00 for 12 punch or blank, 01 for 11 punch, 10 for 0 punch; last 4 bits: BCD equivalent of single punch or sum of double punches.

16. a) 2 digits, because on one digit the number could not indicate both the end of the number and a minus sign.

  b) 284, 76, −390, 110, 42, 06, 89

17. a) 010010, 011001, 100101, 010001, 101001, 111000
  b) SZNIRH

18. b), because C has only 1 decimal place; and e), because A x B has 4 decimal places, and D has 3 decimal places.

19. $2^{70} - 2^{35}$

20. 0246500000, 0304650000, 0400465000, 0500046500, 0600004650, 0700000465

21. No; for positive exponents it is same as excess−128, but for negative exponents it is different (e.g., −6 is 01111010 in excess−128, but 00000110 with the first bit as a minus sign).

22. a) 1.4×10^{38}; b) $.18 \times 10^{-38}$

23. Addition and subtraction: Express B as 0209300000 and then add or subtract mantissas; multiplication: no normalization necessary in this case; division: no normalization necessary since $.465 \div .93 = .5$.

24. All except (d).

26. 11011 → 10100, 11010 → 10101, 11001 → 10110, 10110 → 11001

27. 11011 → 10101, 11010 → 10110, 11001 → 10111, 10110 → 11010

28. a) Suppose B in A + B is negative and let numbers be 4 bits plus sign; call true absolute value of B, $\bar{B}$; then $B = 2^4 - \bar{B}$; $A + B = A - \bar{B} + 2^4$, but 2^4 is carry out of sign position so the result is correctly $A - \bar{B}$; the same reasoning applies if A or both are negative.

   b) Now $B = 2^4 - \bar{B} - 1$, so $A + B = A + \bar{B} + 2^4 - 1$, so that 1 must be added.

29. Let A be number, A_1 be ones complement, A_2 be twos complement; $A_1 + A = 2^n - 1$, $A_2 = 2^n - A$; thus $A_1 = 2^n - A - 1$ and $A_2 = A_1 + 1$.

30. In octal:

   a) 206562436561
   b) 203572702137
   c) 204757044672

31. Using three extra binary places: $7 \cdot 2^{-27}$

33. .2 and .3 both convert to 010, and .7 and .8 both convert to 110.

34. a) In octal: first half: 204 466314631, second half: 157 463146315
   b) maximum: $1.4 \times 10^{+38}$, minimum $.3 \times 10^{-30}$

CHAPTER 4

1. a) 0 ... 01001111101
   b) 100 ... 0110001
   c) 0 ... 011010100
   d) 0 ... 010110

2. i) The integer and fractional parts might be stored in two consecutive words.
   ii) The number might be stored as an integer in one word with the position of the decimal point in a second word.
   iii) The number might be stored in floating-point form.

3. a) <DECIMAL PART> ::= <DIGIT> | <DECIMAL PART> <DIGIT>;
      <NUMERIC LITERAL> ::= .<DECIMAL PART> |

             <DECIMAL PART> . <DECIMAL PART> | + <NUMERIC LITERAL> |
             − <NUMERICAL LITERAL>

b) <BINARY FIXED POINT CONSTANT> ::= 0B | 1B |
    0 <BINARY FIXED POINT CONSTANT> | 1 <BINARY FIXED
    POINT CONSTANT>

4.   Normalized in octal:

    a) 202500000000
    b) 577500000000
    c) 221550000000

5.   Nine, since a 27-bit mantissa allows the equivalent of just over eight decimal digits of accuracy.

6. $n = 5$ is the largest possible, for with any larger, no number with magnitude smaller than 1 could be stored; even with $n = 5$, the smallest possible exponent on the first word would be -20.

7.   Since any ′ after a first one at the beginning of a constant delimits the end of the constant, no ′ can be allowed or, if it is, as in PL/I, only in a special context (i.e., two ′ in a row).

8.   7000: 000001 000110 000100 000011 000001;
     360:   1111 0001 1111 0110 1111 0100 1111 0011 1111 0001

9.   In octal:

    a) 623143437060, 256721444743, 25 ...
    b) 040220543474
    c) 241446456324, 144645632414, 464563241446, 4563 ...

10. In hexadecimal:

    a) E2C9D3D3E840C5D7C1D4D7D3C5
    b) F4F24E5C5D4D
    c) C47DD6D5E3C47DD6D5E3C47DD6D5E3C47DD6D5E3

11. Briefly, because it is possible on the 360 to do arithmetic in either pure binary or in decimal using binary-coded decimal characters and, of course, in fixed- or floating-point.

12. a) A,B41 REAL by default
    b) J14 FIXED BINARY by default
    c) D10,E FLOAT DECIMAL by default

13. When the compiler is translating arithmetic expressions into machine language, it must know whether to compile fixed- or floating-point arithmetic instructions for arithmetic involving the values of a particular variable name; therefore, it must know which type of value the memory location assigned to the variable name will hold.

14. The Fortran and PL/I idea is more convenient, but the Algol method makes it harder to make errors.

15. <FORTRAN SUBSCRIPT> ::= <INTEGER VARIABLE> |
    <INTEGER VARIABLE> <ADD OP> <INTEGER CONSTANT> |
    <INTEGER CONSTANT> | <INTEGER CONSTANT> *
    <INTEGER VARIABLE> <ADD OP> <INTEGER CONSTANT>

16. a) 7.3 is illegal—no real constants
    c) semicolon is an illegal separator
    d) 9 + LL—variable must precede constant
    e) no commas are allowed in integer constants

17. a) fourth column—a_{14}, a_{24} ...
    b) sixth row—a_{61}, a_{62} ...

18. a) In many mathematical applications zero and negative values arise naturally; for example, the constant or leading term in a polynomial usually has a zero subscript.

    b) Quite useful when the expressions are integer expressions as in Fortran, but only rarely would floating-point expressions be useful.

19. a) 188; b) 4364; c) 1050

20. a) (i) 6485, 6458; (ii) 6483, 6525
    b) 6570-71, 6516-17

21. EQUIVALENCE (A(1,6),C),(B(1,26),D)

22. a) N = ID (J − 1) + I − 1
    b) JD · ID (K − 1) + ID (J − 1) + I − 1
    c) JD (I − 1) + J − 1; KD · JD (I − 1) + KD (J − 1) + K − 1

23. EQUIVALENCE (A(1,J + 1),B)

24. a)   Given position

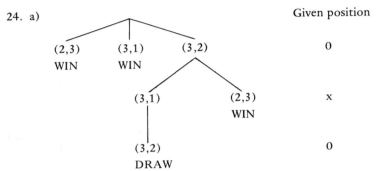

    b) PL/I: DECLARE 1 TICK, 2 R2C3, 2 R3C1, 2 R3C2, 3 R3C1, 4 R3C2,
              3 R2C3

25. Same as Figure 4.5, except C(1,1) ... C(2,2) is replaced by C(1), C(2), C(3),
C(4).

26. PL/I: DECLARE 1 STU REC, 2 SSNUM, 2 PAR NAME (2), 3 PAR AD-
           DRESS, 3 PAR BIRTHPLACE, 2 ADDRESS, 2 BIRTHPLACE, 2 MAJOR,
           2 GPA

27. a) FCD (2,3,2)
    b) E14F (1,4)
    c) D (2,1)
    d) H (2)

28. i) As a one-dimensional array in which the structure of the tree would be
lost.
    ii) As a two-dimensional array in which the elements would be so arranged
to retain some of the structure.

29. a) In 7468: 487, 3647; in 6295: change 3647 to 7468.
    b) In 3647: change 4235 to 0.

30. Hint: Every multiple branch must be organized as a sublist; thus, from the
head element A, there are four sublists for B, E (1), E (2), E (3).

31. 6, 8 — 23417 becomes 000110 111011 001000 000 101101101111001

CHAPTER 5

1. a) $a = 10^{40}$, $b = 10^{-60}$, $c = 10^{-60}$, $a \cdot (b \cdot c) = 0$, $(a \cdot b) \cdot c = 7\bar{9}$ 10000000;
    $a = 10^{40}$, $b = .71 \times 10^{-99}$, $c = -.71 \times 10^{-99}$; $a \cdot (b + c) = 0$, $a \cdot b + a \cdot c$
    $= 6\bar{0}$ 10000000
    b) $a = .9 \times 10^{99}$, $b = .9 \times 10^{99}$, $c = -.999 \times 10^{99}$, $(a + b) + c = 96$ 99999000,
    $a + (b + c) = 97$ 10000000

2. They involve only two operands.

3. Suppose true values of two numbers are 17.6863715 and 17.6841365; then the true difference is .002235; thus, the calculated result is wrong by 1 part in 2234, or more than 1 in 10000.

4. If $L + E < (I - 1) M - M$, then use logarithm, exponential; otherwise, use multiplication; this result is a slight oversimplification of the truth but essentially gives the right idea.

5. Note from Table 5.1 that double-precision and complex quantities cannot be mixed in the same expression.

6. a) -4; b) -9; c) 4; d) .1

7. If $I - (I/J) * J$ is zero, J is a divisor of I; otherwise, it is not.

8. a) i)   A ** B * C ** D * E ** F;
       ii) (A * B) ** (C ** D)
       iii) A * B ** C / (D ** E * F)
       iv) A ** B / C ** D / (E * F ** G)
    b) ii) could be replaced by (A * B) ** C ** D

9. SUBSCRIPTED, ARITHMETIC EXPRESSION, EXP OP, MULT OP, ADD OP, SIGNED TERM; <ADD OP><TERM>

10. Parenthesis rule in definition of primary—since arithmetic expression can be any combination of operands and operators; hierarchy is embodied in successive definitions of factor, term, signed term, and simple arithmetic expression.

11. Hint: Start of constant or variable is indicated by decimal point or digit or sign for the former and letter for the latter; then pick up all characters until one is reached which is not alphameric or a decimal point.

12. Hint: Start from the end of the expression and search backward for spaces; each time one is found move all characters after it forward one character.

13. a) ABC + / D *
    b) / + * AXB − * CXD
    c) A * B * C in PSN is either AB * C * or ABC **

14. a) ((A + (B / C) * D) / (F − (G * H))) * I
    b) A + B − (C * D) − ((E / F) * (G * (H / I)))

15. a) Hint: Consider either the left-to-right or right-to-left reconstruction of the arithmetic expression from the string; show that either precisely defines the expression corresponding to the Polish string.

    b) Without a special representation of the unary minus either reconstruction would lead to ambiguous situations with combinations of unary and binary minuses.

17. A B ~ C − *

18. For the first string the operand stack is A, AB, ABC, A ⌊B/C⌋, A ⌊B/C⌋ E,
A ⌊(B/C) * E⌋, ⌊A + (B/C) * E⌋, ⌊A + (B/C) * E⌋ F, ⌊A + (B/C) * E⌋ FG,
⌊A + (B/C) + E⌋ FGH, ⌊A + (B/C) * E⌋ F ⌊G * H⌋, ⌊A + B/C) * E⌋⌊F − (G * H)⌋,
⌊(A + (B/C) * E) / (F − G * H) ⌋, ⌊(A + (B/C) * E) / (F − (G * H))⌋I,
⌊((A + (B/C) * E) / (F − (G * H))) * I⌋.

19. In Figure 5.3, between Boxes 7 and 9 add a box which asks the question "Was symbol put on PSN string an operator?"; if the answer is "No," go to Box 9, but if it is "Yes," go to a new box which is the same as Box 2 of Figure 5.4, except that generated instructions stay in PSN string; then go to Box 9.

20. Because multiple assignment statements (i.e., A = B = C) are not allowed.

21. M = N + 1; N = M

22. Double-precision to complex prohibited because this would require making the double-precision part single-precision for the real part of the complex number and then inserting zero for the imaginary part; many of the other conversions are possible but equally unwieldy. But some, like complex to double-precision, would be hard to make even plausible.

23. No, because it requires more than one operator and, in addition, it contains exponentiation.

24. The free format of Algol and PL/I with the character : between label and statement allows labels to be inserted freely on cards before statements, while in Fortran they must be punched in columns 1 through 5.

25. a) Yes; nothing in syntax prevents a label from being repeated; anytime I could take on six values, but only three possible branches existed, a statement like this could be used.

   b) Algol: **switch** LABEL := L1,L2,L3,L1,L2,L3; **go to** LABEL (I);

26. a) If the expression in the logical IF involves only relational operators, the statement is true; for example,

   IF (A.LT.B) *st*

can be replaced by

   IF (A − B) 10,20,20
   10 *st*
   20

But, if the expression in the logical IF contains logical operators (see Chapter 9), then it cannot be replaced by an arithmetic IF.

   b) Arithmetic IF: IF expression <0 THEN GO TO label 1 ELSE IF expression = 0 THEN GO TO label 2 ELSE GO TO label 3; Logical IF: IF expression is true THEN statement ELSE CONTINUE.

27. a)

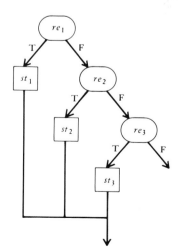

   b) A tree

28. Fortran:

```
            ---
            ---
            ---
        I = 10
    20  TEMP = A (I)
        A (I) = A (I – 9)
        A (I – 9) = TEMP
        IF (I.EQ.6) GO TO 10
        I = I – 1
        GO TO 20
    10  ---
```

CHAPTER 6

1.   No, because if the character is a left parenthesis, this could either indicate an arithmetic or logical IF or an assignment statement with a dimensioned variable IF.

2.   a)

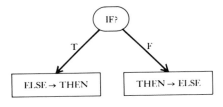

b)

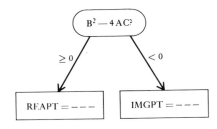

3.   a) A **real array** declaration is needed for A, B, C (three places); label not allowed in declaration; **begin** is missing before block with label L2; A is not dimen-

sioned in interior block so that $A[-5]$ is not allowed; in block with $C(4,4) := A$ statement, A is dimensioned; subscript 7 out of bounds in $C[7,3]$;

b) A (dimensioned)—Program —L2 block; C (first occurrence)—Program —L2 and L3 blocks.

4. a) The only savings possible over assigning a different location for each variable are to assign the same locations to F and G in block L3 and to two of the variables of block L4.

b) The 10 locations for C in block L2 could be used for part of the 25 needed for C in L3, and A and D in L2 could be used by B or C in L3. (Note: It is not necessarily true that a given Algol compiler will assign storage as efficiently as indicated above.)

5. Since PL/I allows more than one block at the highest level in a program, it is possible to structure programs so that independent parts may be executed in parallel if the computing system is a multiprocessor system.

6. Compress the given string into one in which blanks (except in string constants) are removed (see Problem 12 in Chapter 5).

7. a) Main missing feature is ability to get alphabetic characters printed for labeling purposes on output; price for achieving this is substantial complication of input and output statements (see Section 10.3).

b) Free format simpler to use but NAMELIST labeling facilities provide a much more readable and useful output format.

8. $N = 5$, A $(1,1) = 6.3$, A $(1,2) = 7.2$, A $(2,1) = 1.0E7$, A $(2,2) = 3.92E - 04$, A $(3,1) = 4.61$; A $(3,2) = -3.72$, B $(1) = 8.517$, B $(2) = 2.1$, B $(3) = -7.4E03$, B $(4) = 1.7$, B $(5) = 4.2E3$, B $(6) = 17.7$, B (7) not assigned a value.

9.
```
    DIMENSION A(3,2) B(7)
    NAMELIST/X1/N,A/X2/Y1, Y2
    READ, X1
    I = 1
  2 READ, X2
    B (I) = Y1
    B (I + 1) = Y2
    I = I + 2
    IF (I.LE.N + 2) GO TO 2
```

Card 1: $X1 N = 5, A = 6.3, 7.2, 1.0E7, 3.92E − 04,
Card 2: 4.61, −3.72,
Card 3: $END
Card 4: $X2 Y1 = 8.517, Y2 = −2.1,
Card 5: $END
Card 6: $X2 Y1 = −7.4E03, Y2 = 1.7,
Card 7: $END
Card 8: $X2 Y1 = 4.2E3, Y2 = 17.7,
Card 9: $END

10. Examples in Fortran: i) Omitting a statement label on any statement corresponding to a label in an arithmetic IF, and ii) Subscripting a variable which has not appeared in a DIMENSION statement.

11. i) An attempt to divide by zero or do any calculation which results in overflow or underflow.

ii) Use of a subscript outside the range specified (detected by some P-O systems and not by others); undetectable errors are ones which cause *a* possible computation or symbol manipulation to be performed but not *the* one intended by the programmer.

12. a) Missing operator between J and (or incorrect subscripting of variable J or incorrect character in variable name [J (I] ; a good compiler would print a MISSING OPERATOR message if J is not a dimensioned variable but should probably print out INCORRECT SUBSCRIPT FORM if J is dimensioned.

b) Most probable is failure to parenthesize −D so that INCORRECT OPERATOR SEQUENCE is a likely error message; another possible syntactic error is punching of − instead of an alphabetic character.

13. Possible for arithmetic IF because next statement must be labeled, if flow of program is ever to reach it, but a logical IF should never give rise to this message because the next statement is always reached if relational expression is false.

14. For Example 2.8: data for each of the five cases of Figure 2.12, plus the case where A and B or C and D are the same point; for Example 2.7: $a = 1, b = −3, c = 2$ for a test for real roots and $a = 1, b = 2, c = 2$ for a test for complex roots.

15. Figure 2.11: Needs test for case $a = 0$ and error exit when $a = b = 0$; Figure 2.13: No error exits needed since flow chart takes care of all possible cases.

CHAPTER 7

1.   a) .707 $(= \sqrt{2}/2)$
     b) 4.

2.   a) Entier

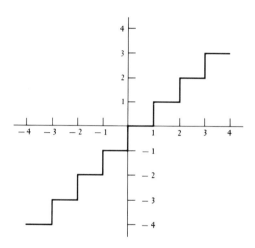

     b)

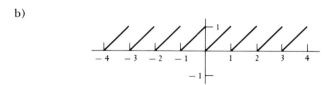

3.   a) 12, but note that 2.5 x 2.0 might, because of roundoff, result in something slightly less than 5, so that IFIX of this could in fact be 4, which would make the final value of N equal to 10 (or, perhaps, 9 (Why?)).
     b) FRACT = ABS (A) — FLOAT (IFIX(ABS(A)))

4.   a) EXP, LOG, SIN, SQRT, ATAN, ERF, and ERFC since all trigono- metric functions may be calculated from any one with the square root, all

logarithms may be calculated from any one, and all hyperbolic functions may be calculated from the exponential.

b) TRUNC, MOD, and FIXED can be expressed in terms of FLOOR; all others are needed.

5. a) Statement is true; suppose FUNCTION name is FCN; precede assignment statement with subroutine call with FCN an output argument; in assignment statement replace function call with FCN; replace FUNCTION statement with SUBROUTINE statement with same arguments plus FCN.

b) True, if CALL statement in main program replaced by dummy assignment statement which evaluates function for dummy argument.

6. a) A *dummy* argument is just the name of something; if subscripted variables were allowed, the subscripts would also have to be arguments.

b) In the calling statement a correspondence with the dummy argument is created; this correspondence must allow any type of scalar variable to be put in correspondence with a scalar dummy variable.

7. a) Divide absolute value by 2π and take remainder; if this is greater than π, subtract 2π.

b) Fortran:

```
FUNCTION SIN (X)
PI = 3.14159265
Y = AMOD (ABS(X), PI)
IF ((Y — PI) .GE.0) Y = Y — 2. * PI
SIN = Y — Y ** 3/6. + Y ** 5/120. — Y ** 7/5040. + Y ** 9/362880.
RETURN
END
```

c) Since $\sin x = \cos (\pi/2 - x)$, entry would first take argument and subtract it from $\pi/2$; ENTRY statement in Fortran, and other mechanisms in other languages allow this.

8. If the dummy argument is an array variable, because array expressions are not allowed in Fortran.

9. a) Would not be possible because there would have to be memory space allocated *in the subroutine* memory for all arrays.

b) Would be possible as long as sufficient memory space was allocated in the subprogram (and the programmer knew what he was doing!).

c) Would be possible.

10. Because, if this argument is called by name, the effect will be to change the value of an input argument in the *main* program.

11. b) For three-dimensional array: $L(A) + (K - 1) + N3(J - 1) + (N3)(N2)(I-1)$;

c) The first dimension, since it appears in none of the formulas for the location of an element.

12. J in main block: main block less first inner block; N in first inner block: this block less block near end in which N is declared again.

13. a)
```
        FUNCTION AMAX1 (X,N)
        DIMENSION X (N)
        AMAX1 = X (1)
        I = 2
     2  IF (X(I).GT.AMAX1)  AMAX1 = X (I)
        IF (I.EQ.N) RETURN
        I = I + 1
        GO TO 2
        END
```
b)
```
        FUNCTION SIGN (X)
        IF (X) 2,4,6
     2  SIGN = −1
        GO TO 8
     4  SIGN = 0
        GO TO 8
     6  SIGN = 1
     8  RETURN
        END
```

14. a)
```
    TRUNC: PROCEDURE (X);
            DECLARE (X,Y) FLOAT;
            IF X < 0 THEN GO TO L1; ELSE
            Y = FLOOR (X); GO TO L2;
        L1: Y = − FLOOR (ABS (X));
```

```
        L2: RETURN (Y);
            END TRUNC;

   b)  FLOOR: PROCEDURE (X);
            DECLARE (X,Y) FLOAT;
            IF X <0 THEN GO TO L1; ELSE
            Y = TRUNC (X); GO TO L2;
        L1: Y = TRUNC (X) −1;
        L2: RETURN (Y);
            END FLOOR;
```

15.   SUBROUTINE COORD (ROW,COL,MOVROW,MOVCOL)
        DIMENSION MOVROW (8), MOVCOL (8)
        I = 1
      2 MOVROW (I) =   ROW + 1
        MOVROW (I + 2) = ROW + 2
        MOVROW (I + 4) = ROW −1
        MOVROW (I + 6) = ROW −2
        I = I + 1
        IF (I.EQ.2) GO TO 2
        I = 1
      4 MOVCOL (I) =   COL + 2
        MOVCOL (I + 1) = COL −2
        MOVCOL (I + 2) = COL + 1
        MOVCOL (I + 3) = COL −1
        I = I + 4
        IF (I.EQ.5) GO TO 4
        RETURN
        END

16. A: L1 − L4

17. Both enable a subprogram to "know" where the value of a variable is stored without the name of this variable being communicated to the subprogram.

18. Mainly because they are defined in the body of the main program as procedures are in Algol and PL/I blocks.

19. ABS (X) = X.* FLOAT (SIGN(X))

20. If b or c is zero the triangle is degenerate; if $b^2 + c^2 = a^2$, COSANG = 0 and the calculation of ANGLE causes an arithmetic overflow; to guard against this latter, COSANG should be tested for zero and, if it is, ANGLE should be set equal to $\pi/2$.

CHAPTER 8

1. A counter could be inserted as follows: In initialization box set I = 1; in "NO" branch insert first a box to test I against some number, say 100; if I = 100, print an error message and stop; if I $\neq$ 100, increase I by 1 and go to update box.

2. a) First box—initialization; next two—computation; oval box—test; box at left—update.

b) Put I + 1 $\rightarrow$ I box before test; in test box ask question "Is I $>$ N?"

3. a) 1, 3, 1, 3, 1, 3, 1, 3, 1, 2

b) Iterative $f(Q(i)) = (i + 1)\, Q\,(i)$; Recursive: $g(N) = N$

4. Let coefficients $a_0, \dots, a_n$ be stored in array A as A (1), ..., A (N + 1); ignoring input and output:

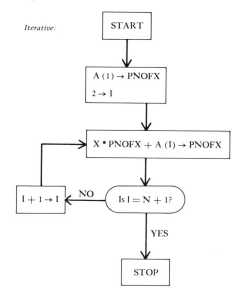

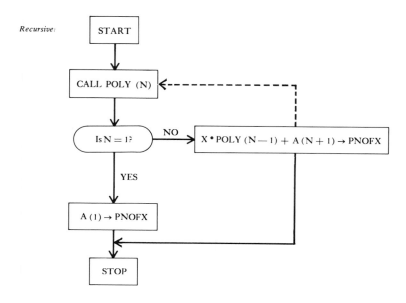

Recursive:

5. a) Major advantage is that the block following the **for** statement in Algol or DO statement in PL/I automatically defines the range of the iteration; moreover, the block structure guarantees that no two ranges can overlap.

b) When the last statement of the range is executed, the program, since it has no way of determining where the transfer came from, must make a standard assumption about this and proceed accordingly; the natural (Why?) assumption is that the transfer came from the inner loop, after which the inner loop variable is updated and tested; if the transfer came from an outer loop, obvious troubles can result.

6. As things are, a possible program fragment is

```
        K = N — 1
        DO 2 I = M, K
        J = K + M — 1
      2 A (J + 1) = A (J)
        A (M) = 0
```

since we must proceed from the top down. If negative increments were possible, the following could be done:

```
    K = N − 1
    DO 2 I = K, M, −1
  2  A (I + 1) = A (I)
    A (M) = 0
```

7.   Fortran: None, if prohibition against modifying variables in increment part is enforced.

Algol: Possible if **step** part does not take variable in direction of **until** part or if *re* after **while** remains true.

PL/I: Similar to Algol.

Cobol: Possible if *re* remains true.

8.   a) (i) and (ii) are null, (iii) may not be because of roundoff, (iv) besides giving values to I and J will also give value to K in DO-loop.

b) I cannot.

9.   a) Fortran: DO 10 I = J, K, L replaced by I = J before range and at end of range, I = J + L; IF (I.LE.K) GO TO beginning of range.

10. Ignoring input and output, in Fortran we have:

```
C      INITIALIZATION
       J = 1
   10  I = J + 1
       K = J
       ALARGE = A (J)
C      FIND LARGEST NUMBER IN REMAINDER OF LIST
    6  IF (A(I).LE.ALARGE) GO TO 2
       ALARGE = A (I)
       K = I
    2  IF (I.EQ.N) GO TO 4
       I = I + 1
       GO TO 6
C      SET UP TO DO REMAINDER OF LIST
       A (K) = A (J)
       A (J) = ALARGE
       IF (J.EQ.N − 1) GO TO 8
       J = J + 1
       GO TO 10
    8  STOP
```

11. For Fortran program: In second statement, change second 1 to 4; at statement labeled 4, put NFACT = 1, GO TO 1.

13.
```
      I = 1
   7  J = I * I
      K = J
   5  L = I + K * I
      M = L
   3  N (I,K,M) = I * L − K ** I
      IF (M.EQ.200) GO TO 2
      M = M + 1
      GO TO 3
   2  IF (K.EQ.30) GO TO 4
      K = K + 1
      GO TO 5
   4  IF (I.EQ.5) GO TO 6
      I = I + 1
      GO TO 7
   6  ---
```

14. In procedure, replace **if** statement by
```
begin    POLY : = A [0] ;
for  I : = 1 step 1 until N do
      POLY : = X * POLY + A [I] ;
end
```

15. a) Fortran:
```
      DIMENSION A (50,50)
      READ, N
      PRINT, N
      CALL PASCAL (A,N)
      M = N + 1
      DO 2 I = 1, M
      DO 2 J = 1, I
   2  PRINT, A (I,J)
      STOP
      END

      SUBROUTINE PASCAL (A,N)
      DIMENSION A (50,50)
      M = N + 1
```

```
      A (1,1) = 1
      DO 4 K = 2, M
      A (1,K) = 1
      A (K,K) = 1
      IF (K.EQ.2) GO TO 4
      L = K − 1
      DO 2 J = 2, L
    2 A (J,K) = A (J − 1, K − 1) + A (J, K − 1)
    4 CONTINUE
      RETURN
      END
```

16. a) $A(3,1) = A(2,A(3,0))$; $A(3,0) = A(2,1)$; $A(2,1) = A(1,A(2,0))$; $A(2,0) =$
$A(1,1)$; $A(1,1) = A(0,A(1,0))$; $A(1,0) = A(0,1) = 2$; $A(1,1) = A(0,2) = 3$; $A(2,1) =$
$A(1,3) = A(0,A(1,2))$; $A(1,2) = A(0,A(1,1)) = A(0,3) = 4$; $A(2,1) = A(0,4) = 5$;
$A(3,1) = A(2,5) = A(1,A(2,4))$; $A(2,4) = A(1,A(2,3))$; $A(2,3) = A(1,A(2,2))$;
$A(2,2) = A(1,A(2,1)) = A(1,5) = A(0,A(1,4))$; $A(1,4) = A(0,A(1,3)) = A(0,5) = 6$;
$A(2,2) = A(0,6) = 7$; $A(2,3) = A(1,7) = A(0,A(1,6))$; $A(1,6) = A(0,A(1,5)) =$
$A(0,7) = 8$; $A(2,3) = 9$; $A(2,4) = A(1,9)$; $A(1,9) = A(0,A(1,8))$; $A(1,8) =$
$A(0,A(1,7)) = A(0,9) = 10$; $A(2,4) = A(0,10) = 11$; $A(2,5) = A(1,11) =$
$A(0,A(1,10))$; $A(1,10) = A(0,A(1,9)) = A(0,11) = 12$; $A(3,1) = A(2,5) =$
$A(0,12) = 13$

b) $A(4,1) = 2^{2^{2^2}} - 3 = 2^{2^4} - 3 = 2^{16} - 3 = 65533$

CHAPTER 9

1. *Associative Law for Addition*

A	B	C	A + B	B + C	(A + B) + C	A + (B + C)
0	0	0	0	0	0	0
0	0	1	0	1	1	1
0	1	0	1	1	1	1
0	1	1	1	1	1	1
1	0	0	1	0	1	1
1	0	1	1	1	1	1
1	1	0	1	1	1	1
1	1	1	1	1	1	1

2. a)

A	A · A
0	0
1	1

b) $\underline{A}$ $\underline{A \cdot 1}$

      0   0
      1   1

c) By induction: theorem is true for $n = 2$; suppose it is true for $n - 1$; then

$$A \cdot (B_1 + B_2 + \ldots + B_n) = A \cdot (B_1 + \ldots + B_{n-1} + B_n) =$$
$$A \cdot (B_1 + \ldots + B_{n-1}) + A \cdot B_n = A \cdot B_1 + A \cdot B_2 + \ldots + A \cdot B_{n-1} + A \cdot B_n$$

3. a) i) $(A + B) \cdot (\overline{A} + \overline{B}) = (A + B) \overline{A} + (A + B) \overline{B} = A\overline{A} + B\overline{A} + A\overline{B} + B\overline{B} = A\overline{B} + \overline{A}B$

    ii) $\underline{A}$ $\underline{B}$ $\underline{\overline{A} + \overline{B}}$ $\underline{\overline{AB}}$

          0   0   1   1
          0   1   1   1
          1   0   1   1
          1   1   0   0

b) $\overline{A}BC + A\overline{B}C + AB = (A + B)(\overline{A} + \overline{B}) C + AB = (A + B) \overline{(AB)} C + AB$
    $= (A + B) \overline{(AB)} C + AB (1 + (A + B) C) = AB + (A + B) C (AB + \overline{AB})$
    $= AB + (A + B) C = AB + AC + BC$

4. $\underline{A}$ $\underline{B}$ $\underline{\overline{A + B}}$ $\underline{\overline{A}\overline{B}}$

      0   0   1   1
      0   1   0   0
      1   0   0   0
      1   1   0   0

5. If $A = 0$, $A + B = A + C$ implies $B = C$ and if $A = 1$, $AB = AC$ implies $B = C$

6. a) $\underline{A}$ $\underline{B}$ $\underline{A \mid A}$ $\underline{B \mid B}$ $\underline{(A \mid A) \mid (B \mid B)}$ $\underline{A + B}$

          0   0   1   1   0   0
          0   1   1   0   1   1
          1   0   0   1   1   1
          1   1   0   0   1   1

    b) $\underline{A}$ $\underline{B}$ $\underline{A \mid B}$ $\underline{(A \mid B) \mid (A \mid B)}$ $\underline{AB}$

          0   0   1   0   0
          0   1   1   0   0
          1   0   1   0   0
          1   1   0   1   1

    c) $\overline{A} = A \mid A$

7.   0000, 0001, 0010, 0011, 0100, 1011, 1100, 1101, 1110, 1111; weights are
2, 4, 2, 1.

8.   a) $(T_2 + T_4)(\overline{T}_2 + \overline{T}_4) = (T_2 + T_4)(\overline{T_2\,T_4}) = (\overline{\overline{T}_2\,\overline{T}_4})(\overline{T_2\,T_4}); \overline{T_2 + T_4 + T_8} =$
$\overline{T_2\,T_4 + T_8} = \overline{T}_2\,\overline{T}_4\,\overline{T}_8$
     b) $(T_2 + T_4)(\overline{T}_2 + \overline{T}_4) = T_2\,\overline{T}_2 + T_4\,\overline{T}_2 + T_2\,\overline{T}_4 + T_4\,\overline{T}_4 = T_4\,\overline{T}_2 + T_2\,\overline{T}_4$

9.   a) C_8: $\overline{T}_1\,\overline{T}_2\,\overline{T}_4\,\overline{T}_8 + T_1\,\overline{T}_2\,\overline{T}_4\,\overline{T}_8 = \overline{T}_2\,\overline{T}_4\,\overline{T}_8$
       C_4: $\overline{T}_1\,T_2\,\overline{T}_4\,\overline{T}_8 + T_1\,T_2\,\overline{T}_4\,\overline{T}_8 + \overline{T}_1\,\overline{T}_2\,T_4\,\overline{T}_8 + T_1\,\overline{T}_2\,T_4\,\overline{T}_8$
           $= T_2\,\overline{T}_4\,\overline{T}_8 + \overline{T}_2\,T_4\,\overline{T}_8 = (T_2\,\overline{T}_4 + T_2\,\overline{T}_4)\,\overline{T}_8$

No further simplification by this technique is possible here; note that $\overline{T}_8 = 1$
whenever C_4 is 1.

10. a) Consider adding 111 ... 111 + 00 ... 01; carry is produced $n-1$ times.

    b) On the average, augend and addend will start with eighteen 1-bits; on the
average, this will produce 9 carries at first time interval; at next time interval use
same augend with eighteen 1-bits and addend consisting of 9 carries from first
stage; average carries at second interval is 4, at third interval 2, at fourth interval 1.

11. $t + t_d$

12.   LOGICAL FUNCTION AND (A,B)
          LOGICAL A,B
          AND = (A.SS.B).SS.(A.SS.B)
          RETURN
          END

          LOGICAL FUNCTION OR (A,B)
          LOGICAL A,B
          OR = (A.SS.A).SS.(B.SS.B)
          RETURN
          END

          LOGICAL FUNCTION NOT (A)
          LOGICAL A
          NOT = A.SS.A
          RETURN
          END

13.   LOGICAL FUNCTION SS (A,B)

```
    LOGICAL A,B
    IF (A.AND.B) GO TO 2
    SS = .TRUE.
    RETURN
  2 SS = .FALSE.
    RETURN
    END
```

14. One possible one is:

$$((A \wedge B) \vee C) \wedge (((\neg D) \supset C) \vee (E \equiv A \wedge F))$$

15.
```
    LOGICAL FUNCTION IMPLIC (A,B)
    LOGICAL A,B
    IF (A.AND..NOT.B) GO TO 2
    IMPLIC = .TRUE.
    RETURN
  2 IMPLIC = .FALSE.
    RETURN
    END
```

16. Since PL/I has a right-to-left rule for these three operators, it is reasonable to put all three at the same level at the top of the hierarchy so that the initial right-to-left scan associates each of these operators (particularly the unary ones) naturally with its operands (or right operand).

17. LOGICAL EXPRESSION, CONSTANT, NOT, AND, OR

CHAPTER 10

1.   a) 2880
     b) Magnetic tape input is always faster than direct card input.

2.   a) Assuming 120 six-character words per minute—12 characters per second.
     b) 15 char/sec = 900 char/min; 1000 lpm x 132 char/line = 132,000 char/min; the printer is about 140 times faster.

3.   a) 42KC, 60KC, 120KC
     b) 112.5 inches per second

4.   a) 100 char/sec; b) 30KC; c) 54KC

5.   a) 525 seconds; b) 75 seconds; c) 30 seconds

6.   a) 240 milliseconds

b) 87 milliseconds; average arm movement is 66 2/3 ms, the determination
of which requires a little calculus.

7.   a) .024 seconds; b) .012 seconds

8.   a) 250; b) 1; c) .45

9.   Writing in pure binary requires only a direct transfer of what is in main memory to tape and vice versa, but if BCD is used the data must first be converted to
BCD on output and converted from BCD to binary on input.

10. a)   DO 2 I = 1, 10
            2 READ, A(I), B(I)

            DO 2 J = 1, 10
            DO 2 I = 1, 11, 2
            2 READ, C(I,J)

b) Implied DO-loops allow greater flexibility because there is no requirement with them that a new card be read by each READ statement.

11. Fortran:

            PRINT 100, B, D
            PRINT 100, A
            PRINT 101, N
        100 FORMAT (4E16.8)
        101 FORMAT (I3)

index